Soviet International Behavior and U.S. Policy Options

Soviet International Behavior and U.S. Policy Options

Edited by
Dan Caldwell
Pepperdine University

A Study of the Center for
Foreign Policy Development

Lexington Books
D.C. Heath and Company/Lexington, Massachusetts/Toronto

Library of Congress Cataloging in Publication Data
Main entry under title:

Soviet international behavior and U.S. policy options.

Includes index.
1. United States—Foreign relations—Soviet Union—Addresses, essays, lectures. 2. Soviet Union—Foreign relations—United States—Addresses, essays, lectures. 3. Soviet Union—Foreign relations—1975- —Addresses, essays, lectures. 4. United States—Foreign relations—1981- —Addresses, essays, lectures. I. Caldwell, Dan. II. Title: Soviet international behavior and US policy options.
E183.8.S65S58 1985 327.47 84-48047
ISBN 0-669-09125-1 (alk. paper)
ISBN 0-669-09124-3 (pbk.: alk. paper)

Published simultaneously in Canada
Printed in the United States of America on acid-free paper
Casebound International Standard Book Number: 0-669-09125-1
Paperbound International Standard Book Number: 0-669-09124-3
Library of Congress Catalog Card Number: 84-48047

To Beth, Ellen, and John
with love and devotion

Contents

Glossary of Acronyms

ALCM	Air-launched cruise missile
BAM	Baikal–Amur Mainline (railroad)
CMEA	Council for Mutual Economic Assistance (COMECON)
CoCom	Consultative Group Coordinating Committee
COMECON	Council for Mutual Economic Assistance (CMEA)
CPE	Centrally planned economy
CPSU	Communist Party of the Soviet Union
CSCE	Conference on Security and Cooperation in Europe
EAA	Export Administration Act
FBIS	Foreign Broadcast Information Service
FRG	Federal Republic of Germany
GATT	General Agreement on Tariffs and Trade
GDR	German Democratic Republic
GNP	Gross national product
ICBM	Intercontinental ballistic missile
IMEMO	Institute of World Economy and International Relations
IMF	International Monetary Fund
INF	Intermediate nuclear forces
IRP	Islamic Republican Party
KGB	Committee on State Security
MBFR	Mutual Balanced Force Reduction negotiations
MFN	Most favored nation
NATO	North Atlantic Treaty Organization
NEM	New economic mechanism
MNF	Multi-National Force (Lebanon)
OECD	Organization for Economic Cooperation and Development
OPEC	Organization of Petroleum Exporting Countries
PDRY	People's Democratic Republic of Yemen
PLO	Palestine Liberation Organization
PRC	People's Republic of China
RDF	Rapid Deployment Force
SALT	Strategic Arms Limitation Talks

SLBM	Submarine-launched ballistic missile
SLCM	Sea-launched cruise missile
START	Strategic Arms Reduction Talks
WTO	Warsaw Treaty Organization
YAR	Yemen Arab Republic

Acknowledgments

This book grew out of a project on Soviet international behavior sponsored by the Center for Foreign Policy Development at Brown University. The Center promotes research and discussion on U.S. policy for dealing with the Soviet Union. It brings together scholars from various disciplines and present or former practitioners in the executive and legislative branches of government. Their thinking is leavened when possible by engaging interested persons from public interest organizations, journalism, and politics and by taking account of public opinion. The objective is to develop policy ideas for the future which are well-founded in scholarship and experience and are at the same time easily accessible to citizens and politicians. The Center was founded in 1981 and incorporated in 1982 as a nonpartisan, nonprofit research institution. Logistics are provided by Brown University, where it is located. It is funded by grants from private individuals and foundations.

The director of the Center, Mark Garrison, originally conceived of this project and played a central role in the direction of it. Indeed, his influence on the material in this book was substantial, and I deeply appreciate his comments and criticisms on drafts of the chapters as well as his support of the production of this book.

Thomas J. Watson, Jr., chairman of the Center's Board of Advisers and former U.S. Ambassador to the Soviet Union, and Howard Swearer, president of Brown University, provided support and helpful advice on the project, and I would like to express my thanks to them.

Jack Snyder served as a consultant during the formative stage of the project and his advice was helpful and much appreciated. A number of others commented on the project, including Alexander Dallin, Robert Legvold, Marshall Shulman, John Stremlau, and Adam Ulam. Although not all of the recommendations that these, as well as other scholars and government officials, gave were accepted, they were carefully considered and much appreciated.

Most of the chapters in this book were presented as papers at seminars at the Center for Foreign Policy Development during 1983. Betty Garrison made the arrangements for these meetings with efficiency and grace, and all who participated in the project appreciated her work. Steve Gillon served as rapporteur for the seminars, and his summaries of the discussions were helpful in recounting the substance of the seminar discussions.

At each seminar, there was at least one and often two commentators for each of the papers. Those who served as commentators were Madeleine Albright, William Brown, Thompson R. Buchanan, Craig Dunkerley, Herbert Ellison, Abbott Gleason, Marshall I. Goldman, Selig Harrison, Jiri Hochman, Dennis Ross, Alvin Rubinstein, Thomas Simons, Newell Stulz, and Donald Zagoria. In addition, Larry Napper and Jeanne Christie led a discussion on Soviet policy in southern Africa. The chapters in this book were improved by the suggestions and criticisms of the commentators and both the authors of papers, and I thank them for their suggestions.

There were others who participated in the project whose contributions I would also like to acknowledge. A number of Brown University faculty members attended one or more of the seminars, and their comments and questions enlivened the meetings. William Beeman, Elliot Goodman, Whitney Perkins, and Newell Stultz were particularly helpful and their participation in the seminars was much appreciated. In addition, several postgraduate students and faculty members from the Naval War College, including Captain Clarence Armstrong, USN, Commander Michael Corgan, USN, Colonel Theodore Gatchel, USMC, and Commander Kenneth R. McGruther, USN, attended several of the seminars and provided their valuable perspective as career military officers.

I would like to thank Steve Gillon and Joyce Mullen who helped with the preparation of the bibliography and Phyllis Allsworth who typed several drafts of the manuscript with accuracy and, just as importantly, good cheer.

Finally, I would like to thank the contributors to this book who have written chapters I have found to be stimulating and thought provoking. I hope that readers of this book learn as much from the contributors as I have. It has been a pleasure to work with and to learn from them.

1
Introduction

Dan Caldwell

Since the end of World War II, the relationship between the United States and the Soviet Union has been the single most important bilateral relationship in international relations. And, for better or for worse, this will continue to be the case at least for the rest of this century. Given this fact, there are few subjects as important as the focus of this book: Soviet foreign policy and U.S. options for dealing with the USSR.

A prerequisite for effectively dealing with the Soviet Union is to understand what factors motivate Soviet international behavior. In the past, scholars have presented numerous explanations ranging from ideology to realpolitik, and at present there is no consensus on either the most significant determinants of Soviet foreign policy or the relative importance of these factors. In order to clarify this situation, in 1983 the Center for Foreign Policy Development at Brown University sponsored a research project with the following objectives: (1) to identify what constraints, stimuli, and values affect Soviet behavior toward particular countries, regions, and issue areas; (2) to determine, by means of a "consequences of options" approach, what factors are most likely to motivate Soviet policy in particular cases; and (3) to assess to what extent and how the United States can influence the direction and substance of Soviet international behavior.

In the language of social science research, the dependent variable of this study of Soviet foreign policy behavior and the independent variables include a large number of factors. In the past, some analysts have concluded that a single factor, such as Marxist–Leninist ideology, explains Soviet international behavior in all cases. This monocausal, universalistic approach is rejected in this study in favor of a multivariate, differentiated approach.

In order to fulfill the research objectives of this project, we asked a number of Soviet affairs experts from academia and government to analyze what factors motivated Soviet policy in their particular area of specialization. These experts were specifically chosen because of their dual expertise in Soviet foreign policy and the particular geographic or issue area under examination. We were fortunate in attracting a very able group of analysts of Soviet affairs to participate in the project.

The contributors to this book were asked to posit likely Soviet responses to several hypothetical U.S. policies ranging from militant to accommodating approaches. For example, in her study of Soviet policy toward Eastern Europe, Sarah Terry analyzes the likely Soviet reaction to five U.S. policy options: active U.S. support of opposition elements in Eastern Europe, the use of sanctions against Eastern Europe, a selective policy of balanced leverage, a resumption of liberal trade and credit policies, and acceptance of Soviet hegemony over Eastern Europe as legitimate.

After asking contributors to indicate the likely Soviet reactions to possible U.S. policies, we asked the authors to indicate which factors were the most important in influencing Soviet responses to particular U.S. policies. The explanation of the evidence and reasoning behind the contributor's choice of factors in a given case is, we believe, an interesting and innovative way of analyzing the determinants of Soviet international behavior. We call this methodology the consequences of options approach.

In order to facilitate comparison among the cases examined, we asked contributors to address the following questions:

> What are the present roles of the United States and the Soviet Union in the area under examination?
>
> What developments are likely over the next several years, and, given these developments, what are the range of options open to the United States?
>
> How would the Soviet Union be likely to respond to different U.S. options, and what are the most important factors that influence the Soviet reaction?

In the past, some analysts of Soviet international behavior have attempted to generalize on the basis of several (or even a single) case studies. It is clear, however, that Soviet leaders place very different priorities and values on different geographic regions. For example, Soviet leaders are clearly much more committed to the defense of Eastern Europe than Marxist states in Africa for a number of reasons. In the selection of cases to be examined in this project, two criteria were paramount: the importance of the case to the USSR, and the availability of analysts with dual expertise to complete the study. In addition, we wanted a wide range of cases in order to broaden the scope of our analysis of Soviet international behavior.

The cases in this volume focus on Soviet policy toward Eastern Europe, China, Japan, the Middle East, the Persian Gulf region, economic relations, and nuclear weapons and arms control. Thus, five cases focus on geographic regions and two on functional issue areas. We believe that this mix of cases constitutes a good foundation for the analysis of Soviet international behavior. We also recognize that the scope of this study is not comprehensive. There are no analyses of Soviet policy toward Western Europe, Latin America, Southeast Asia, South Asia, Africa, or toward science and technology. Researchers in the future could apply the consequences of options approach developed and applied in this volume to these, as well as other, cases.

A note on the sources employed by the contributors to this volume is needed. Some of the contributors, such as Hiroshi Kimura, have relied extensively on original Soviet sources in their analyses, while others have not. Each of the contributors, however, has had long training and/or experience in the field of Soviet studies and is very familiar with the contours of Soviet foreign policy.

The leaders of the Soviet Union, at least since the end of World War II, have viewed the protection of the Eastern European states from internal or external subversion as a vital Soviet interest. Indeed, with very few (if any) exceptions, analysts of Soviet foreign policy view the USSR's interest in Eastern Europe as second only to the protection of the Soviet homeland. In chapter 2, Terry contends that the USSR's policy toward Eastern Europe is motivated by three principal interests: geostrategic, economic, and political. Geostrategically, the Soviets view Eastern Europe as a vital military and cultural buffer between the West and the USSR. In addition, maintaining the division of Germany has been an extremely important Soviet foreign policy goal since 1945. Economically, the Soviet Union traditionally supported the Eastern European countries with aid, and credit, and more recently, energy resources. However, as both Eastern Europe and the Soviet Union face increasingly difficult economic challenges, such support, at least at past levels, is unlikely to continue. Even though Soviet economic support is likely to decline relative to the past, this does not mean that the Soviet leadership views Eastern Europe as any less important than in the past. On the contrary, given the political, historical, and ideological ties between Moscow and the Eastern European governments, there is little hope for the United States to move them out of the orbit of Soviet control in the foreseeable future. Only through a policy of "balanced leverage," Terry contends, can the United States hope to increase its influence in Eastern Europe.

Western analysts sometimes underemphasize the fact that the Soviet Union borders on Asia as well as Europe. By reason of geographical position alone, therefore, the USSR has a strong interest in Asia. The fundamental interest that the Soviet Union, like any other state, has is the protection of its homeland; and, rightly or wrongly, Soviet leaders perceive a significant enough threat to that vital interest from the People's Republic of China that they have stationed approximately fifty divisions in the Far Eastern theater.

In considering the hierarchy of Soviet interests in Asia, clearly the most important to Soviet leaders is their policy toward China. In talking with Soviet government officials, common people, or even dissidents about China, one can sense hostility and fear.[1] This is undoubtedly due to a number of factors, including a history of conflict between the two countries, Soviet fear of encirclement, a feeling among Soviets that the Chinese are ingrates, and racial differences and tensions. This sense of fear among Soviets is curious since China has nowhere near the economic, technological, and military resources possessed by the USSR. Why, then should the Soviets fear China?

In chapter 3, B. Thomas Trout analyzes the U.S.–USSR–PRC triangle. Trout contends that the "Soviet Union seeks to achieve and maintain independently guaranteed security both as an end to ensure preservation of the Soviet domestic regime and as an instrument to advance and protect the finite policy interests of the Soviet state." Given this view, China presents a threefold threat to the USSR: geostrategic, ideological, and regional.

Despite the fact that China's nuclear arsenal is but a small percentage of the Soviet Union's, it nevertheless poses a very real and significant threat given the awesome power of nuclear weapons. So much so, in fact, that during the SALT negotiation the Soviet Union proposed that if either the United States or USSR learned of "provocative actions" by a "third country" (clearly referring to China), then the two countries would take joint action to punish the "guilty party."[2]

In addition to the nuclear threat, China poses a substantial conventional military threat to the Soviet Union. Indeed, the PRC has the world's largest population (over 1 billion compared to the USSR's 270 million) and, therefore, the largest potential manpower pool from which to draft soldiers. This is a fact that clearly concerns Soviet leaders and may be one reason that the USSR has the most men under arms in the world (over 5 million for the USSR compared to a 4.1 million for the PRC).[3] Also of great concern to Soviet leaders in the early 1980s has been the possibility that the United States and/or Japan would assist with the modernization of the Chinese military. Such action would significantly raise the threat to the most basic Soviet interest: the protection of the Soviet homeland.

The People's Republic of China poses another more subtle threat to the USSR as a competitor for the leadership of Marxist–Leninist governments and groups in the world. Although most scholars who study the Soviet Union generally agree that the role of ideology as a determinant of Soviet foreign policy has declined in importance, ideological leadership remains a significant goal for Soviet leaders because it is a key element in their sense of the legitimacy—both of their regime and of the Soviet state as it exists today.[4]

That the Soviet Union has long been interested in Asia is evidenced by its support for the People's Republic of China (until the late 1950s), North Korea, and North Vietnam. Undoubtedly, part of the reason for this interest is geographic; Asia is the Soviet Union's southern flank. Since the late 1960s, the USSR has sought to construct a series of alliances around its perimeter in Asia.[5] Although the Soviets have successfully maintained close relations with Vietnam (and now operate naval units out of Danang and Cam Ranh), they have failed to develop their "Asian collective security system." In fact, the United States has come much closer to establishing such a system with its security arrangements with Japan and South Korea and its declared mutuality of security concerns with the PRC. Soviet leaders are concerned about the possible creation of a Sino–American security alliance. The USSR's major objective in Asia during the last half of the 1980s will be to prevent the completion of an anti-Soviet coalition including China, and to counterpose adequate military force against that contingency.[6]

In addition to the USSR's geostrategic, ideological, and regional interests in Asia, the Soviet Union also has a substantial economic interest. In many respects, Japan and the Soviet Union are ideal trading partners since Japan now has one of the world's most advanced industrial plants and yet lacks natural resources, of which the USSR has an abundance. As Kimura points out in chapter 4, Soviet policy toward Japan, at least on the surface, makes little sense in light of the economic realities.

The major obstacle blocking the improvement of Japanese–Soviet relations is the "Northern Territories" issue. These four small islands north of Hokkaido were ceded to the Soviet Union after World War II. Despite the great symbolic importance of these islands to

Japan, the USSR has refused to return them to Japan. Considering the fact that Japan currently has the eighth largest defense budget in the world[7] and considering the tremendous potential for the growth of Japanese–Soviet trade, Soviet intransigence on the Northern Territories is hard to fathom. The most logical explanation for Soviet policy is that the Soviets place a very high value on the islands for geostrategic reasons.

In keeping with the consequences of option framework employed throughout this book, Kimura analyzes six options for Japanese foreign policy: (1) continuation of its present policies including the maintenance of the U.S.–Japan Security Treaty; (2) a significant increase in Japanese defense spending; (3) reduced defense cooperation with the United States; (4) abrogation of the U.S.–Japan Security Treaty and the conclusion of a security treaty with the USSR; (5) alliance with the PRC; and (6) the pursuit of an independent path in foreign policy. Kimura analyzes likely Soviet reactions to each of these policy options and concludes that Soviet policy toward Japan is primarily motivated by geostrategic, economic, decision-making, psychological, and, to a lesser extent, ideological factors.

Most experts believe that a crisis in the Middle East and the Persian Gulf region is the most likely catalyst for a Soviet–U.S. confrontation in the future. There are several reasons for this judgment, including: both the United States and the USSR have close allies in the region; this area is relatively close to Soviet borders; oil from the region is vital to Western Europe and Japan; and this has been an area over which the United States and Soviet Union have competed with one another for influence for a long time. In their contributions to this volume, George Breslauer and Dennis Ross focus on this important area of the world.

In Breslauer's view, the Soviets believe that they have four roles to play in the world: superpower, continental power, global power, and leader of the world communist movement. Soviet leaders view the superpower role as the most important of these, and because the United States is the only other superpower in the world, Soviet leaders are first and foremost concerned about avoiding U.S.–Soviet confrontations. As a continental power, the USSR is concerned about the maintenance of its control over Eastern Europe. In addition, Soviet leaders are concerned about the protection of their borders, as the Soviet shooting down of the civilian Korean Air Lines jetliner in September 1983 clearly demonstrated. This concern leads to a Soviet concern over relations with bordering states, including China, Afghanistan, Iraq, and Turkey.

Since the 1950s, the Soviet Union has clearly emerged as a global power on the international scene. Breslauer contends that Soviet leaders are more concerned about the Middle East than any other Third World region, including South Asia, Southeast Asia, Africa, and Latin America.

According to Breslauer, within the overall context of avoiding direct confrontation with the United States, the Soviets' primary interest in the Middle East and Persian Gulf region is to consolidate and expand their influence with key regimes in the area. That is more difficult to accomplish than another Soviet objective: obstructing or denying the goals in the region of the United States and its allies. Given the respective interests and commitments of the United States and USSR in the area, it is not surprising that several crises have developed as a result of local conflicts. In these cases, the Soviets have demonstrated a general tendency to withdraw when faced with the likelihood of a direct U.S.–Soviet confrontation. However, in several instances the Soviets have shown a willingness to confront the United States. Breslauer analyzes the conditions under which the USSR has opted for such a strategy, and examines the Soviet response to the war in Lebanon during the summer of 1982 as a test case of his generalizations.

In his analysis of Soviet policy toward the Persian Gulf, Ross contends that "the Soviets remain determined to pursue their regional goals and are generally satisfied with their strategy." In contrast to other analysts, notably Karen Dawisha, Ross believes that the Soviets are not on the eclipse in the Gulf but are there to stay.[8] In particular, according to Ross, the Soviets would like to achieve arbiter status in the region and would also like to gain greater access to Persian Gulf oil, given the growing petroleum requirements of Eastern Europe and the USSR itself.[9]

In analyzing the Soviet propensity to take risks in the Persian Gulf area, Ross concludes that the Soviets have been anxious not to threaten the United States directly. As does Breslauer, he believes they place the highest priority on avoiding confrontation with the United States. But within that constraint, their objective is to reduce U.S. influence and involvement in the area. According to Ross, the Soviets are relatively satisfied with their strategy and believe that it has resulted in the erosion of the U.S. position in the region. In responding to the Soviet strategy, Ross believes the United States should develop its military presence in the Persian Gulf area, bolster the capabilities of local states to deal with local threats, and work with local states for both economic development and an amelioration of regional conflicts.

In their analyses of the Middle East and Persian Gulf, Breslauer and Ross agree that it has become a key area of Soviet interest and will likely continue to be in the foreseeable future.

In chapter 7, John Hardt and Donna Gold analyze Soviet commercial behavior with Western industrial nations including the United States. Hardt and Gold note that Soviet leaders in past decisions have emphasized political considerations of national security, sovereignty, and systemic continuity over the economic consideration of comparative advantage. The Soviet emphasis on political factors in various regions of the world often conflicts with the economic benefits that could be had by the USSR were it to emphasize economic over political factors. For example, Hardt and Gold note that Soviet insistence on retaining the Northern Territories has severely retarded the growth of trade between Japan and the Soviet Union, countries that, given their respective resources and industries, should be natural trading partners.

Hardt and Gold describe several alternative scenarios for the USSR and the West for future trade and conclude that the growth or further shrinkage of East–West trade is dependent on the course of economic development—autarky or interdependence—that Soviet leaders choose and the degree to which Soviet leaders perceive a threatening international environment. If they perceive hostile threats aimed at the USSR, then they will opt for an autarkic strategy of increased control over the economy. In an environment in which tensions are perceived as lessening, trade is more likely to develop.

Hardt and Gold also analyze alternative Soviet balance of payments projections and Soviet policies for stimulating or restricting trade. They conclude that East–West trade during the next decade is likely to follow a very different pattern than that of the 1974–1984 period with a sharp compartmentalization: agricultural trade for the United States and industrial trade for the OECD states. Divergence over trade policy could lead to West–West differences as well as East–West problems.

In chapter 8, Lawrence Caldwell describes the current history and future prospects for U.S.–Soviet arms control negotiations. In particular, he focuses on the INF and START negotiations since November 1983. He analyzes the breakdown of these talks and assesses the prospects for the resumption of them.

These chapters provide a penetrating view of Soviet international behavior and U.S. policy options for dealing with the USSR concerning some of the most important geographical regions and issue areas of today.

Notes

1. Seweryn Bialer, *Stalin's Successors: Leadership, Stability, and Change in the Soviet Union* (New York: Cambridge University Press, 1980), 157.

2. John Newhouse, *Cold Dawn: The Story of SALT* (New York: Holt, Rinehart and Winston, 1973), 189.

3. *The Military Balance 1983–1984* (London: The International Institute for Strategic Studies, 1983).

4. For a description and analysis of "policy legitimation," see B. Thomas Trout, "Rhetoric Revisited: Political Legitimation and the Cold War," *International Studies Quarterly*, vol. 19, no. 3 (September 1975), 251–284.

5. Arnold L. Horelick, "The Soviet Union's Asian Collective Security Proposal: A Club in Search of Members," *Pacific Affairs* (Spring 1974).

6. Donald S. Zagoria, "The Strategic Environment in Asia," in Donald S. Zagoria, ed., *Soviet Policy in East Asia* (New Haven: Yale University Press, 1982), 13.

7. Ibid., 8.

8. Karen Dawisha, "The U.S.S.R. in the Middle East: Superpower in Eclipse?" *Foreign Affairs*, vol. 61, no. 2 (Winter 1982–1983): 438–452.

9. Marshall I. Goldman, *The Enigma of Soviet Petroleum: Half Empty or Half Full?* (Boston: George Allen and Unwin, 1980).

2
The Soviet Union and Eastern Europe: Implications for U.S. Policy

Sarah Meiklejohn Terry

Defining Soviet Interests in Eastern Europe

The most important single point to remember about Soviet interests in Eastern Europe[1] is the region's centrality to Moscow's policy concerns, both domestic and international. Although other regions of the world are important to the USSR because of their strategic importance, economic resources, and/or political affinities (real or potential), none is so intimately linked to all three dimensions of Soviet interests—so much so that it is useful to regard Eastern Europe as falling somewhere between an internal and external determinant of Soviet policy.[2] That is, while these countries are not integral parts of the Soviet Union, and while Moscow benefits from the existence of a group of nominally independent states that supports its positions in international forums and enhances its great-power status, neither are they fully sovereign states with which Moscow conducts its relations according to standard diplomatic practices. Rather, they are perceived in many respects as extensions of the USSR's domestic political and economic system which—whether as the quasi-fiefdoms of the Stalinist era or as the junior partners in the post-Stalin "socialist commonwealth"—are expected to conform substantially to Soviet-defined policies and goals.

This perception on Moscow's part of its relations with Eastern Europe as more than an internal but less than an external matter has its roots in both historical precedent and ideological perspectives. Tsarist Russia long coveted parts of Eastern Europe, whether as a means of securing themselves from invasion (primarily Poland and

---

The author wishes to express her appreciation to Mark Garrison, Dan Caldwell, Madeleine Albright, and Jiri Hochman for their comments on an earlier draft of this chapter.

the north European plain), of creating a general political sphere of influence (Pan-Slavism), of undermining the Ukrainian nationalist movement (areas of mixed Ukrainian population from Eastern Poland to Bessarabia), or of securing ice-free ports on the Baltic (Estonia, Latvia, and Lithuania) and guaranteed access to the Mediterranean (the Balkans). If, moreover, Tsar Nicholas II could demand in September 1914 that the entente powers recognize Russia's right to "solve" the Polish problem as an internal affair, it is small wonder that Stalin expected to be accorded the same prerogative after World War II.[3]

At the same time, Moscow's tendency to regard the region as part of its internal domain is also an instinctive Leninist reflex dating back to the second Comintern Congress in 1920, when norms of Bolshevik party organization were extended to the international Communist movement as a whole. This is reflected today in the fact that relations with Eastern Europe, as well as with communist-ruled states, are coordinated more through the apparatus of the Communist Party of the Soviet Union (CPSU)—specifically the Central Committee's Department for Liaison with Ruling Communist Parties—than through the formal diplomatic channels of the Ministry of Foreign Affairs.[4]

With these general observations in mind, let us turn to the three key variables that have shaped Soviet interests in Eastern Europe since 1945: the geostrategic, the economic, and the political–ideological. In so doing, we should keep in mind that each of these dimensions has, at least potentially, both defensive and offensive aspects; that the relative importance attached to one or another has shifted over time, as has the balance between their defensive and assertive thrusts; and that they interact in ways that, while sometimes mutually reinforcing, are often contradictory.

The Geostrategic Variable

One need only glance at a map to comprehend the geographic and strategic importance of Eastern Europe to Russia or the Soviet Union. Although the Caucasus, Central Asia, and Siberia are in no sense peripheral or dispensable parts of the empire in Moscow's view, it is the European republics fronting on Eastern Europe that comprise the population and economic centers of gravity of the USSR, just as it is Eastern Europe that has served as the conduit for military or political penetration of these western regions of Russia, whether Tsarist or Soviet. Thus, the traditional interpretation of Soviet motives in extending its control over Eastern Europe after World War

II placed greatest emphasis on the region's role as a defensive glacis along the USSR's vital western rim; at least by implication, the potentially offensive attributes of East European geography as well as economic and ideological motives were viewed as secondary.

While security considerations clearly were and remain important to Moscow, there are several grounds for questioning not only whether this interpretation continues to be valid for the nuclear age, but also whether it was wholly accurate even for the immediate postwar period. There is ample evidence that, already in the early years of the war, Stalin's opposition to the reconstruction of a genuinely independent Eastern Europe—either in its prewar form as separate states or as some sort of federation—was conditioned less by strictly defensive or security considerations than by a desire to acquire forward positions for (or at the very least neutralize Eastern Europe as an obstacle to) the expansion of Soviet influence in Central Europe and the Mediterranean. More recently, the advent of intermediate and intercontinental-range nuclear weapons, with which each side can directly attack or retaliate against the other, has substantially diminished (although by no means eliminated) Eastern Europe's value as a strategic buffer zone. At the same time, the Soviets' attainment of nuclear parity with the United States, combined with the Warsaw Pact's buildup of its conventional forces during the 1970s, has enhanced the region's role as a forward base from which to exert pressure whether military or political, on NATO.[5]

Throughout the postwar period, the primary target of Soviet ambitions and anxieties in Europe has remained Germany. Moscow's longstanding objective of keeping that country divided, neutral, under Soviet control (or some combination of the three) has been aimed not only at preventing the reemergence of a united and potentially hostile adversary but, increasingly in the last two decades, at using Germany as an instrument of divisive diplomacy in Western Europe with the ultimate goal of weakening the U.S. position on the continent. These dual concerns are reflected in the priority attached by Moscow to its control over the "Northern Tier" states, that is, to the GDR both as the base for the bulk of Soviet troops stationed in Eastern Europe and as a key source of leverage over the Federal Republic; to Poland—and to a lesser extent Czechoslovakia—as essential elements of the control of the GDR.

Within the past decade, the increasingly global nature of the USSR's power, goals, and entanglements has added yet another dimension to Moscow's strategic interest in Eastern Europe unrelated to geographic location. While the progressive globalization of Soviet policy might have been expected to reduce the centrality of the region in Kremlin thinking, the Soviets have instead begun to alter their expectations of the East Europeans, coming to view them as junior partners in a common enterprise. Although unsuccessful in the late 1960s in securing even token Warsaw Pact support along the Sino–Soviet border, or later in expanding the Pact's jurisdiction to such non-European Communist states as Mongolia or Vietnam, Moscow has been more successful since the mid-1970s in inducing the East Europeans (no doubt in part through use of oil leverage in the aftermath of spiraling world energy prices) to act as proxies or otherwise contribute to the expansion of Soviet influence in the Third World. Again the most prominent role has been played by the East Germans, whose military advisers and administrators play key roles in Ethiopia, South Yemen, and Afghanistan. But most of the other countries have also participated directly or indirectly by providing training and technical services or military equipment (a subject to be explored further in this chapter).[6]

The Economic Variable

The USSR's economic interests in Eastern Europe, while less central than its strategic or political stakes, are similarly multifaceted and have evolved over time to reflect the shift in Soviet policy from a more or less defensive toward an increasingly assertive posture. In the early postwar period, Stalin pursued a two-pronged policy: first, blatant exploitation in which—in the guise of war booty, reparations, concessionary trade agreements, and so-called joint-stock companies—an estimated $14 billion in assets, resources, and current production was extracted from Eastern Europe for reconstruction of the Soviet economy; and, second, reorientation of the East European economies to serve Soviet development priorities and to render them dependent on Soviet raw material exports. By the end of the 1940s, balanced growth plans throughout the region had been scrapped in favor of ambitious industrialization and collectivization programs in the Stalinist mold, regardless of their appropriateness to the local resource base. Moreover, for several of these countries—most notably at this stage, Poland and Czechoslovakia—Soviet military requirements imposed an additional burden on industry. The establishment of the Council for Mutual Economic Assistance (CMEA) in 1949 marked less the beginning of genuine multilateral cooperation and integration within the bloc than the institutionalization of Soviet bilateral control over each member.[7]

Since the mid-1950s, when outright exploitation ceased, Soviet economic interests in the region have been less sharply defined, reflecting the trade-offs and ambiguities involved in achieving a balance among several competing priorities. Among the most important of these priorities have been: (1) the economic viability of the East European regimes as a prerequisite to their political stability; (2) economic integration through CMEA as a vehicle for maintaining the political cohesion of the bloc;[8] and (3) extraction of the maximum feasible East European contribution to Soviet economic goals, whether through exports of manufactures (often incorporating Western technology inputs), investment in Soviet resource development or economic assistance to Soviet Third World clients.

During the 1960s, at a time when Moscow had limited access to Western markets, Eastern Europe served as a growing and more or less captive market for Soviet energy and raw material exports in exchange for industrial and consumer manufactures. The advent of detente in the early 1970s brought with it the opening of most of the CMEA economies to large-scale credit-financed imports of Western technology intended to improve the quality and efficiency of production. The simultaneous effort to preempt the centrifugal forces that might be set in motion by increased East–West contacts through a stepped-up program of integration and specialization under the 1971 Comprehensive Program remained largely on paper until the mid-1970s, when the energy price spiral set off by the OPEC embargo of 1973–74 greatly increased Soviet leverage over its East European allies.[9]

It was the sharp run-up of world energy prices, initially in 1973–1974 and again in 1979–1980, that gave rise to the view that Eastern Europe in the last decade has become a net economic liability for the Soviet Union—a liability that it has continued to bear, however grudgingly, because of the region's overriding strategic and political importance. The essence of this argument is that between 1960 and 1980 the USSR provided its East European partners with implicit subsidies amounting to $87.2 billion (calculated in 1980 dollars), of which nearly $60 billion is attributable to the 1973–1980 period—that is, since the explosive rise in energy and raw materials prices on world markets. The subsidies are said to have arisen from two sources: from the underpricing of Soviet oil and other raw material exports to CMEA (on the basis of a formula that averages world market prices for the preceding five years); and, more controversial, from the overpricing of East European manufactures delivered to the Soviet Union in return.[10]

While it is true that Moscow has been reluctant to take full advantage of its increased leverage, no doubt for fear of the destabilizing effects, it nonetheless appears to have used its implicit energy subsidies to induce the East Europeans to increase their contributions to Soviet policy priorities, both domestic and foreign. Most important was the adoption in 1974 of a package of joint-investment projects, almost exclusively for the development of Soviet natural resources but also promising long-term access for the East Europeans.[11] Moreover, the deterioration of the region's terms of trade with the USSR as OPEC price increases were factored into the intra-CMEA price formula compelled these countries to supply the Soviet Union with rising quantities of "hard" goods (that is, goods salable on world markets or incorporating significant amounts of Western technology) for stable or declining deliveries of oil and other raw materials, often at the expense of their own domestic needs or exports to hard-currency markets.[12]

In addition, there are two other areas in which the East Europeans seem to bear a substantial economic burden primarily in the service of Moscow's policy goals: economic aid to Third World countries (including the less developed members of CMEA), and military production both for the Warsaw Pact and for sale to Soviet clients in the Third World. While this burden is largely hidden and difficult to quantify, the fragmentary data available suggest that it may be more onerous than is generally assumed. With respect to economic aid, the Soviets have been more successful than in WTO in expanding the purview of CMEA to include a number of Third World dependencies and clients as full or associate members, or merely as "observers," a status that still gives them access to low-interest credits and concessionary prices from the "developed" socialist states.[13] The economic burden of military production is even more elusive, but would appear to be especially heavy for the more industrialized of the East European countries—namely, Czechoslovakia, Poland, and the GDR. Although some of these sales—for example, to Libya, Iraq, or India—may bring in badly needed hard currency, the weight of recent evidence strongly suggests that military production both for WTO and external sales is heavily subsidized and, on balance, drains limited resources away from pressing domestic needs.[14]

The Political–Ideological Variable

Moscow's principal political stake in Eastern Europe over the last four decades has been the establishment and perpetuation of socialist regimes in its own image, thus enhancing both the domestic and international legitimacy of the Soviet system, as well as its ability to secure its strategic and economic interests. The existence of a loyal band of countries that call themselves socialist, organize themselves roughly along Soviet lines, belong to a Soviet-led alliance, and generally defer to Moscow on matters which Moscow deems important serves to fortify the Soviet Union's superpower status as well as its claim to represent a universal model of socialism. Similarly, maintenance of the basic structure of Soviet-style centrally planned economies (CPEs), together with the coordinating mechanisms of CMEA, facilitates Moscow's ability to coopt East European resources for Soviet-defined goals.

To be sure, practical considerations have compelled successive Soviet leaderships to settle for less than total systemic or foreign policy conformity. Hence, the unique position of private agriculture and the Catholic Church in Poland since 1956; the Gierek regime's relative tolerance of the domestic opposition in the 1970s; the continuing existence of subsidiary political parties and the somewhat more active role that representative institutions play in several of these countries; the "new economic mechanism" and Kadar's quasi-populist style of leadership in Hungary; Romanian leader Ceausescu's neo-Stalinist strategy of national integration and unorthodox foreign policy; and the GDR's special relationship with the Federal Republic—to mention only the most obvious examples of systemic and policy nonconformity.

The resulting diversity has been cited by some Western observers as evidence of the "benign neglect" with which Moscow treated its East European allies, especially in the 1970s, and, therefore, as an indication of the latters' relative autonomy in running their own affairs. Nor can there be much doubt that the Soviets derive certain advantages from this diversity, whether by design or simply by turning necessity into virtue. Allowing the regional parties to make concessions to local conditions and national tradition tends to mask the nature of Soviet control and bolster domestic stability, while a kind of division of labor has emerged at the international level. Thus, the more conservative regimes such as the Bulgarian or Czechoslovak have proved useful as ardent defenders of Soviet orthodoxy (as in polemics with the "Euro-communist" parties or by propagating Moscow's definition of "developed socialism"), while the more "liberal" regimes such as the Hungarian or, until 1980, the Polish have served as valuable links to the West from which the Soviets derived both political and economic benefits. Similarly, the special GDR–FRG relationship has given Moscow an added measure of leverage over Bonn and provided at least indirect access to West German technology.[15]

Yet, the ongoing crisis in Poland demonstrates clearly—as did the earlier invasions of Hungary and Czechslovakia—that there are finite limits to Moscow's tolerance and that it continues to regard its ideological stake in Eastern Europe as being fully as important to its security as its strategic interests. Short of such clearcut confrontations, of course, it is difficult to say with any certainty precisely where those limits lie, or how much autonomy the East Europeans may enjoy in altering secondary aspects of their systems. How free are the other parties, for instance, to adopt Hungarian-style economic reforms or to emulate Romania's maverick foreign policy? Are such changes facilitated or impeded primarily by internal factors—by, for example, the character of the leadership, especially its cohesiveness and control over the domestic situation, or its skill in manipulating Moscow's multiple and often conflicting concerns? Or do the Soviets themselves play a decisive (if sometimes discreet) role in determining the degree of regional diversity?

There are no easy or automatic answers to these questions. The evidence of Soviet control is largely circumstantial, while the mechanisms of such control—whether through CMEA or WTO, energy deliveries, interparty contacts of the special role of the Soviet ambassador—remain for the most part hidden behind a rhetorical barrage of "socialist equality." Nonetheless, such evidence as exists suggests the following conclusions: first, Moscow is not about to loosen its grip on Eastern Europe to the extent that its basic objectives there—in particular, its leverage over Germany, its status as leader of the socialist world, or perpetuation of the essential features of its model of socialism—might be threatened. On the other hand, the Soviets will tolerate, perhaps even encourage, diversity so long as it complements or at least does not impinge on those overriding priorities. Within these limits, they appear to differentiate among the countries on the basis of such factors as strategic location, economic importance, or reliability of the leadership. Thus, the critical Northern Tier may have less flexibility than the others, while Hungary may be allowed more latitude because of its peripheral position as well as Moscow's demonstrated confidence in Kadar. Similarly, Romania's deviance may be tolerated because it is strategically less sensitive and almost entirely surrounded by other bloc members.

The Brezhnev Strategy

At the most basic level, Moscow no doubt expected the three dimensions of its interests in Eastern Europe to be mutually reinforcing—with political and ideological conformity both facilitating and being facilitated by economic controls, and each enhancing the security interests of the USSR—and it expected that its position in

Eastern Europe would be compatible with its domestic and broader international goals. In practice, it has proven more difficult to square the circle: Soviet insistence on systemic conformity has often run counter to the requirements of economic viability and political stability in Eastern Europe, while the periodic reimposition of orthodoxy on wayward members of the bloc tends to weaken the Warsaw Pact as an instrument of the USSR's broader strategic goals.

Soviet policy toward Eastern Europe in the wake of the 1968 invasion of Czechoslovakia can be understood largely in the context of the need to resolve this tension between viability and cohesion. On the one hand, the challenge of the Prague Spring forced Moscow to redefine its strategy of alliance management in a way that would permit the East Europeans to address their mounting internal problems, but without the unacceptable political risks of the Czech reforms. At the same time, the Soviets' approach to the bloc was also shaped by evolving perceptions of their own needs and interests, reflecting both the USSR's enhanced global capabilities and ambitions and a desire to tap the resources of their CMEA partners in the pursuit of 'common' goals. Hence, Brezhnev's three-pronged strategy for the 1970s: (1) East–West detente with attendant increases in credit-financed trade and technology transfer to both Eastern Europe and the USSR; (2) a reassertion of Soviet ideological initiative, less in order to impose rigid conformity than to place limits on systemic diversity;[16] and (3) as noted above, renewed emphasis on economic integration within CMEA, soon expanded to include a growing number of Moscow's Third World clients.

The first half of the decade augured well for the new policy: escalating levels of East–West trade and credits sustained growth rates and boosted living standards throughout the bloc, and without the need for destabilizing reforms; even global economic developments, in particular the quadrupling of oil prices in 1973–1974, initially seemed to favor Moscow's hand, providing it with a flexible but effective form of leverage over those East Europeans who might be tempted to stray too far from the fold or to neglect their obligations to "international socialism."[17] Yet, by the end of the decade, Brezhnev's strategy lay in shambles—a failure of which the Polish crisis provided the most dramatic but by no means the only example. Across the board, with the partial exceptions only of Hungary and the GDR, failure to carry out basic reforms left the East bloc regimes unable to take advantage of the imported technology; growth rates had fallen markedly from the levels of a decade earlier; living standards were stagnant or declining; food shortages and debt burdens rising. In brief, most of the political and economic tensions that

Brezhnev hoped he was laying to rest after Czechoslovakia were threatening to reemerge in even more acute form—and at a time when the international and domestic climates alike offered fewer options for dealing with them.

The Challenge of the 1980s

Eastern Europe's new "time of troubles" could hardly have come at a less opportune moment. The death of Leonid Brezhnev in November 1982, although not unanticipated, set in motion what in all probability will be a lengthy succession process. Combined with the Soviet Union's own multiple economic ills, this process will heighten the risks and narrow the options available to Moscow for maintaining stability in the region. Soviet succession politics have typically had a destabilizing effect on Eastern Europe. While only those parties that are already experiencing domestic dislocations and turmoil are likely to be seriously destabilized, neither the record of past succession periods nor the present situation in Eastern Europe can provide much comfort to Brezhnev's heirs.

The Soviet invasion of Hungary occurred three years and eight months after Stalin's death in March 1953, the Warsaw Pact invasion of Czechoslovakia three years and ten months after Khrushchev's removal in October 1964. In neither case does the timing appear to have been coincidental. In the first instance, the rapid-fire shifts in Soviet policy in the three years following Stalin's death—the Moscow-initiated New Course, Malenkov's defeat in the "second industrialization debate," followed by the beginnings of de-Stalinization with Khrushchev's secret speech to the Twentieth Party Congress—had a whipsaw effect on the more vulnerable East European regimes. In Hungary, in particular, Malenkov's defeat left the hapless Nagy at the none-too-tender mercies of the unreconstructed Stalinist, Rakosi. By the time the Kremlin leadership had recognized its mistake, the frustrated aspirations of Nagy's countrymen for a more humane form of socialism had boiled over into unacceptable demands and open revolt. Similarly, the vaguely "liberal" or reformist signals emanating from Moscow during the late Khrushchev period and the early stages of the 1965 economic reform, together with the apparent quiescence of the re-Stalinizers in the immediate post-Khrushchev period, ultimately contributed to the excesses of the Prague Spring.[18]

The present Kremlin leadership is assuredly aware of this past pattern of misperception and miscalculation. Inasmuch as Brezhnev's strategy toward Eastern Europe throughout the 1970s was in large measure aimed at averting a repetition of the miscalculations that led to the Czechoslovak crisis (and with Poland as a blunt and continuing reminder of the potential for instability in the region), his former colleagues and immediate heirs are likely to be highly sensitive to the problem. Nonetheless, there are several reasons why, despite whatever precautions the post-Brezhnev (and now post-Andropov) leadership may take, the "succession factor" will again have an unsettling effect on Soviet–East European relations.

First, while a succession period in the Soviet Union is necessarily characterized by a greater preoccupation with internal issues, its destabilizing effects on Eastern Europe are due less to such inattention on Moscow's part than to the dynamics of the process itself: the inevitable jockeying for position among competing factions in the absence of institutionalized mechanisms for the transfer of power, the equally inevitable policy shifts as one group edges out its rivals, plus the pervasive opaqueness of Soviet political discourse which temporarily masks or distorts those shifts. It is these features of the process, rather than any disagreements within Soviet elites over Moscow's fundamental interests in the region, that tend to have ripple effects on the East European regimes, disorienting their leaderships or shifting the balance of power among factions within their parties.

Second, the remarkable stability of the Brezhnev leadership between 1964 and 1982 has now become an element of instability in the post-Brezhnev period; moreover, the high rate of natural attrition that will affect several layers of Soviet power during the remainder of the decade will be complicated by parallel successions in several of the East European countries. Third, the acute nature of the economic problems afflicting both the Soviet Union and most of its East European allies will accentuate the competition for available resources, and, therefore, for political power, both within the individual countries and on a blocwide basis. These last two factors—the multistage and multidimensional nature of the ongoing succession process, and the acuteness of the blocwide economic crisis—merit more extended comment.

The Multistage, Multidimensional Succession

Long before Brezhnev's death, it was conventional wisdom that the penalty for the stability of his eighteen-year reign would be a protracted two-stage succession. Stage one, it was assumed, would involve the emergence of an interim "caretaker" government made up largely of Brezhnev's aging colleagues and committed essentially to a policy of "Brezhnevism without Brezhnev," but unlikely to last more than five-to-six years. By contrast, the wholesale generational turnover, affecting not only top party and governmental posts but reaching down into the second and third layers of the Soviet power structure, would come in stage two and would bring to the fore groups whose political attitudes were largely unknown and untested and whose exposure to the outside world (including Eastern Europe) was minimal.

Initially, the selection of Yuriy Andropov as Soviet party leader for the first or caretaker stage seemed to promise something more than "Brezhnevism without Brezhnev," with the prospect of a less wrenching transition to stage two. The fact that he was "only" sixty-eight years of age at the time he assumed the general secretaryship, together with his reputation not only as a tough and shrewd chief of the KGB but as one of the more pragmatic and efficiency-minded members of the Brezhnev collegium, raised expectations both in the Soviet Union and in Eastern Europe that he would move quickly and decisively to attack the accumulated economic problems of the Brezhnev era and to begin rejuvenating the leadership.

Moreover, insofar as Soviet–East European relations were concerned, Andropov's appointment brought to power the only remaining member of the Brezhnev team (after Suslov) with lengthy exposure to the problems of the region. While most Western observers tended, at least initially, to focus on his role as the Soviet ambassador to Hungary during the 1956 invasion or as head of the KGB for fifteen years, it is also relevant that Andropov was the Central Committee secretary responsible for supervising relations with the East European parties between 1957 and 1967, a decade that witnessed a gradual relaxation of Soviet policy toward the region and an unprecedented degree of experimentation in several of the countries. Among East European moderates in particular, Andropov's prior associations with the region, especially in the 1960s, were seen as boding well for a better understanding of their problems and a more permissive attitude toward reforms, at least of the economic variety.[19]

Such expectations were not entirely unfounded. The first months under the new leadership witnessed a vigorous campaign against corruption and inefficiency at all levels, the replacement of a number of key officials and a resurgence of reformist thinking reminiscent of the Malenkov and Kosygin phases of the last two successions. Andropov himself repeatedly and sharply criticized the half-measures and foot-dragging characteristic of past reform attempts and hinted at the need for a major overhaul of the economic management system, in the process admonishing Soviet planners to study the experiences of the more innovative East European economies. In addition, by the end of 1983, an inner core of younger associates of the general secretary mostly in their late fifties and early sixties, had begun taking shape in the Politburo and Central Committee Secretariat.[20]

Yet, at the time of Andropov's death in February 1984, a mere fifteen months after his appointment, his regime could claim no concrete policy changes to its credit. Moreover, despite the favorable references to the need to study the applicability of East European experience to the Soviet economy, this interest was not translated into a green light for further systemic reforms in these countries. Rather, the emphasis in Moscow's approach to the region continued to be on caution and conformity, the "dovetailing of economic and social decisions" and "joint appraisal of collective experience," which will help "to bring the structures of economic mechanisms closer together." Now Andropov's death and his replacement by an even older member of the Brezhnev collegium, Konstantin Chernenko, implies a prolongation of the transition period, in which Eastern Europe's pressing problems will be relegated to a back burner while contending factions and generations in the Kremlin sort themselves out.[21]

Adding to the potential for instability in Soviet–East European relations will be the parallel succession processes that we can expect to see by the mid-to-late 1980s in several of Moscow's regional dependencies. Four of the party leaders in question are seventy years of age or older (Zhivkov in Bulgaria, Kadar in Hungary, Husak in Czechoslovakia, and Honecker in the GDR), the first two of whom have held their positions for more than a quarter of a century; only in Hungary has there been a concerted attempt to bring a new generation of leaders into positions of genuine responsibility. In Poland and Romania, the other two full members of the bloc, the leaderships are somewhat younger but, for different reasons, are also vulnerable to rapid change: in Poland because of the ongoing political and economic turmoil in the wake of the crushing of Solidarity; in Romania because of the dismal economic performance and political oppressiveness of the Ceausescu regime. Thus, the legacy of leadership continuity that has characterized both the East European and Soviet scenes over the last decade or so will in all probability be rapid leadership turnover in the next decade, with unpredictable consequences for the political stability of the bloc.

The Economic Dimension

Regardless of who is CPSU general secretary, or for how long it can be predicted that the Soviet–East European relationship will loom large on his agenda of problems for the remainder of the 1980s and that economics—both the precarious state of the East European economies and the declining ability or willingness of the Soviet Union to prop them up in time of crisis—will be a major constraint on the management of those relations.

Over the last fifteen years, economic growth across the region has fallen sharply, from an aggregate annual increase for the six countries of 7.3 percent of the 1971–1975 plan period, to 4.0 percent in 1976–1980 and, according to an early Western estimate, to 1.4 percent for 1981–1985. Even excluding the data for Poland, where national income was expected to drop by an average of 3.3 percent over the five years (ranging from a low of −13.0 percent in 1981 to a modest recovery level of +2.0 percent in 1985), growth rates in the remaining countries, including the stronger performers such as Bulgaria and the GDR would show a marked deterioration from the levels of a decade earlier.[22]

Three years into the current plan period, this sober estimate appeared somewhat too pessimistic. The recession of the early 1980s seemed to have bottomed out in 1982, while preliminary results for the East European six in 1983 showed a growth rate of 3.3 percent.[23] Nonetheless, whatever the outcome of the 1981–1985 plans, all of the East European economies without exception face major structural adjustments as the support mechanisms that sustained growth rates in the 1960s and 1970s—cheap and abundant Soviet energy and raw materials, followed by the massive influx of Western credits—have run their course and become the liabilities of the 1980s. In particular, the failure on the part of these countries (with the partial exception of Hungary) to take advantage of credit-financed imports of Western technology in order to adapt their industrial structures and economic mechanisms to the demands of the post-OPEC embargo environment has left them with what might best be called "deferred tasks" of modernization, which will prove far more difficult to solve in today's climate of economic austerity and credit stringency than had they been addressed in the 1970s.

Most commonly recognized is the failure to modernize industrial plants to achieve competitive levels of labor productivity and resource efficiency. Instead, Western credits were used to expand capacity (using mostly older energy-intensive technologies) and to boost consumption levels well beyond what could be justified by increases in productivity. In addition, the changes in planning and management mechanisms and incentive structures also necessary to achieve improved efficiency and product quality were not introduced. A second area of deferred or incomplete modernization is agriculture where years of overcentralization and underinvestment, followed by more years of inappropriate policies—insufficient adaptation of inputs to specific crops, overutilization of the land to maximize short-term results, persistent discrimination against the private sector, and artificially low prices—have led to declines in growth rates for agricultural output (in some cases even depressing output in absolute or per capita terms). No less serious, although less often mentioned, has been the neglect of essential infrastructure investments—the development and maintenance of rail transport and other distribution networks, housing, health care and social services, and (a problem that is assuming urgent proportions) pollution control—all of which have taken a back seat to "productive" investments.

As the East European regimes attempt to cope with these deferred tasks, they are finding that the external economic climate only complicates their domestic dilemmas. In relations with the West, both the high level of outstanding hard-currency indebtedness and the reluctance of Western banks and governments to extend new loans is forcing them to maximize exports at the expense of domestic consumption. At the same time, the difficulty of selling their uncompetitive manufactures on world markets has caused them to slash imports, in turn depriving themselves of technology and other inputs necessary to improve product quality or to begin solving their problems of energy conservation and pollution abatement, for which technology available within CMEA is generally inferior. In the East, the sharp deterioration in Eastern Europe's terms of trade with the Soviet Union, as the latter raises energy and raw material prices to world levels and demands higher quality manufactures in return, further aggravates the drain on resources available for domestic use.

In view of the importance attached in recent years to a gradual improvement of living standards as the major underpinning of system legitimacy, such trends have serious implications for political stability in the region. The combination of competing domestic priorities, pressures to export more and better goods to both West and East, and the curtailment of imports of Western goods and technology means that even a return to the more favorable growth rates of the 1970s (however unlikely for most of the region), or the cautious return of Western banks to East European markets, would in themselves be insufficient to overcome the downward pressures on consumption or the negative consequences for stability. It would obviously be rash to predict any repetition of the Solidarity movement elsewhere in the bloc; still, we should not forget that it was similar strains on domestic resources and consumption levels that brought about the growing paralysis of the Polish economy after 1977. And while none of the other countries shares the particular mix of cultural-historical characteristics and postwar experiences that led to the emergence of a broad-based and coherent opposition movement in Poland, most are showing increasing signs of social malaise as economic performance declines. Whether in the form of mere consumer dissatisfaction, more deep-seated alienation and dissent, or, increasingly in several countries, social exhaustion and withdrawal, the implications for Soviet policy are both serious and complex.[24]

In the past, Moscow's management of crises in its East European dependencies has been facilitated by two key factors: first, that at any one time the crisis has been limited to a single country (even in 1956 the climax of the Polish events had passed before the Hungarian situation got out of control); and second, that despite the shortcomings of its own economy, Soviet resources have always been sufficient to tide over the faltering regime, and by so doing to avert unwanted political change. In the foreseeable future, neither of these conditions seems likely to hold. On the one hand, the pervasiveness of the region's economic malaise increases the probability either that crises may erupt spontaneously and more or less simultaneously in two or more countries, or that the ripple effects of a crisis in one of these economies may be enough to tip the balance in others.

On the other hand, Moscow's capacity (not to mention willingness) to mediate future political crises with timely infusions of economic largesse, either as a supplement to or substitute for the use of military force, is open to serious question on several grounds. Like its East European counterparts, the Soviet economy is experiencing a long-term secular slowdown.[25] With annual growth rates for 1981–1985 not expected to exceed the 2.5 percent level and with numerous choke-points similar to those afflicting the East European economies—especially in such critical sectors as agriculture, transportation, metallurgy, energy and resource development, and technological innovation—any future Soviet leadership will be hard pressed to find the resources necessary to rescue future Polands, especially in view of the spiraling cost of such rescue efforts.[26] Indeed, as we have already seen, the Soviet economy which long acted as a buffer between Eastern Europe and the harsh realities of the world market is rapidly becoming a contributing factor in the region's problems.

Implications for Soviet Policy

What, then, are the options available to the post-Brezhnev, now post-Andropov, leaders for protecting Soviet interests in Eastern Europe—above all, for ensuring the stability of the region? Simple logic would seem to suggest that they will finally have to choose. After all, hasn't the Brezhnev-era expectation that they could have their cake and eat it too—that they could demand of their regional clients both economic viability and systemic orthodoxy, as well as tangible support for Soviet interests abroad—proved illusory and now dangerously destabilizing? Yet, the choice is one that several Soviet leaderships have successfully evaded in the past. Moreover, the alternatives all involve compromises—whether of ideological principle, economic interest, or raison d'etat—that Moscow will find both distasteful and costly and that may prove especially difficult in a transition period. Recognizing that each country poses a somewhat different set of problems, making regionwide generalizations superficial, a brief summary of the basic options and trade-offs will nonetheless serve to point up the core dilemmas facing the new Kremlin leaders.

If only because of the hopes aroused by Andropov's brief tenure, the possibility that the Soviets may now be forced to acknowledge the need for fundamental economic reforms merits consideration. Even if they are not ready to contemplate such reforms at home, it is at least conceivable that they will prove willing to tolerate, perhaps even encourage, systemic experimentation in the smaller East European economies, where limited resource bases and heavy dependence on foreign trade compound the deficiencies of the Soviet-style CPE. Already Hungary has been permitted to resume and extend the economic reforms initiated in the 1960s, while Bulgaria has begun to move in a similar direction. From Moscow's viewpoint, the main appeal of this option would be the prospect of easing the resource burden on the Soviet economy and eventually of generating a greater East European contribution to Soviet-defined goals. Yet therein lies the rub; for, the real benefits of reform would lie well in the future, in long-term economic capabilities and political stability, while near-to-medium-term costs (and potential political risks) would be high.

Even under the most favorable circumstances, meaningful economic reform in Eastern Europe is not a quick fix, but a complex process that can easily be derailed—whether by shifts in the domestic balance of power, by policy and/or leadership changes in Moscow, by the absence of slack in the economy to ease the dislocations of transition, or (most commonly) by a combination of the above. The lesson of the Hungarian experience of the 1960s (itself far from problem-free) is that the restoration of economic equilibrium, in particular the reorientation of economic priorities toward domestic (and primarily consumer) needs, the weeding out of reform opponents from sensitive positions throughout the bureaucratic structure, as well as consistent Soviet support (in this case extending over nearly a decade) were all essential to the implementation of the NEM.[27] Yet, in the mid-1980s, none of the East European regimes (including potentially a post-Kadar regime in Hungary) enjoys this constellation of favorable domestic and external conditions. Not only are their economies strained and seriously unbalanced, but in most the leaderships are either divided or dominated by antireform factions.

Moreover, on the assumption that Western credits to Eastern Europe in the foreseeable future will do little more than refinance existing debt (if that), the Soviet Union remains the only source of the financial resources essential for the successful introduction of reforms. While Moscow is clearly determined to phase out subsidies on its energy exports, a continuing net flow of Soviet resources into the region could take other forms: a continuation or expansion of trade credits; elimination or severe curtailment of East European aid to Soviet Third World clients; or a similar curtailment of CMEA's "long-term target programs" which are primarily oriented toward meeting Soviet development needs, often at the expense of balanced development of the East European economies.[28] In one sense, of course, this would merely represent a return to a long-standing policy of subsidizing the region; at the same time, the fundamental shift in the rationale for such a policy should not be overlooked. Until now, Soviet economic assistance (and leverage) has been used almost exclusively as a counterweight to reform. By contrast, Moscow would now have to use its assistance to facilitate reform; moreover, it would have to do so at the expense of competing domestic and global priorities—and, potentially, of the political cohesion of the bloc. A policy shift of this magnitude would demand foresight and decisiveness uncharacteristic of an established leadership, much less one in the process of consolidating its hold on power.

A second possibility is that Moscow will swing back toward a kind of neo-Stalinist orthodoxy, on grounds that the dangers of political erosion within the bloc from the more open policy of recent years far outweigh the putative economic benefits, which in any event proved all too shortlived. Such a policy is less improbable than the first, at least in the sense that it reflects the traditional biases of the system. Not only would it have obvious appeal for the present conservative leadership in the Kremlin (and presumably for many East European apparatchiki fearful for the implications of reform for their personal fortunes); the rising generation of supposedly more pragmatic leaders could also find it tempting as they are faced with the necessity of proving their ideological credentials in the protracted power struggle to come. Yet this option, too, offers no panacea for

Soviet dilemmas in Eastern Europe. Pursued with any consistency, it implies a continued willingness to buy political allegiance with economic bandaids—minimizing the risk of instability in the short term at the expense of continuing economic stagnation and potentially even greater political instability in the longer term. Practical considerations also militate against this choice. The need for food imports alone makes any notion of Stalinist-style autarky for the bloc as a whole unthinkable, while the selective isolation of the East European economies (improbable in light of their external debts) would merely increase the burden they represent for the USSR without addressing the underlying causes of their instability.

Finally, there is the possibility, even the probability, that Moscow will simply fail to make a clearcut choice. Certainly the message of the first year-and-a-half after Brezhnev's death has been that, whether out of indecisiveness or the illusion that they can go on indefinitely imposing conflicting demands on their East European allies, the Soviets will continue to "muddle through" as long as they can. Thus, what we are most likely to see is a continued willingness to tolerate limited diversity on an ad hoc basis where it seems desirable to ease localized tensions or where Moscow sees some economic or diplomatic benefit (for example, Hungary's membership in the IMF or the intra-German relationship). At the same time, the post-Brezhnev leaderships, Chernenko's even more firmly and dogmatically than Andropov's, seem determined to demand both absolute loyalty to the central principles of the system and continued East European contributions to broader Soviet goals.[29]

Defining U.S. Interests in Eastern Europe

The asymmetries between Soviet and U.S. interests and influence in Eastern Europe could hardly be more striking. Where proximity and history have given the Soviet Union a vital and comprehensive stake in the region, distance and the low intensity of U.S. relations with Eastern Europe (especially in comparison to relations with Western Europe) have contributed to a perception that we have no immediate or tangible interests of either an economic or strategic nature in these countries. Leaving aside for the moment the question of whether this perception is justified, it has given rise to a fundamental duality in the U.S. approach to these countries which dates back at least to World War I.

At the rhetorical level, distance has permitted us to indulge our moral commitment to democratic ideals with little concern for the practical obstacles to their realization. Thus we have repeatedly presented ourselves as champions of the independence and right to self-determination of the East European peoples—witness, Woodrow Wilson's "Fourteen Points" in 1917, Franklin D. Roosevelt's "Atlantic Charter" and "Declaration on a Liberated Europe" during World War II, or John Foster Dulles's calls for "rollback" and "liberation" in the 1950s. Such postures have been dictated as much or more by domestic political considerations—by the need to generate public support whether for a hot war with Germany or for a cold war with the Soviet Union, or by partisan competition for ethnic votes—than by a realistic appraisal of our ability to influence the situation in Eastern Europe.[30] But the impact on the self-image of the United States as a staunch defender of East European rights has been no less durable for that.

On the other hand, at the practical level, U.S. policy toward the region has generally been defined by the larger great-power balance, in effect acknowledging our limited stake and leverage there but, more often than not, also failing to use the leverage we did possess to promote our stated goals. During the interwar years, this meant that together with the West European powers, Great Britain in particular, Washington shared the view of Eastern Europe as a *cordon sanitaire* whose primary purpose was to isolate the Bolshevik menace from the rest of the continent. At the same time, we were no more willing than the European powers to provide the economic assistance without which none of these newly created or re-created states could hope to become a viable political entity. Thus, despite U.S. withdrawal from active involvement in European affairs in this period, Washington implicitly shared responsibility for allowing Eastern Europe to fall increasingly under the control and influence of Nazi Germany.[31]

With the second world war, U.S. interests in Eastern Europe came to be defined largely in terms of the emerging superpower relationship with the USSR. While the state of Soviet–American relations is only one of many factors (and by no means the decisive one) shaping Soviet policy toward Eastern Europe, it plays an overriding role in U.S. policy toward these countries. During rare and brief periods of relatively cordial U.S.–Soviet relations, for instance, Washington has appeared to accept a Soviet sphere of influence in Eastern Europe as more or less legitimate, or at least as something we could or should do nothing about. Thus, at the height of the Grand Alliance, despite the president's personal attachment to universalistic solutions and abhorence of "spheres of influence," the Roosevelt administration showed a distinct reluctance to consider any proposal for the postwar reconstruction of the region that did not have Stalin's explicit approval—a posture that effectively conceded to the latter the right to determine what would or would not be regarded as "anti-Soviet."[32] Similarly, during the first blush of detente in the late 1960s and early 1970s, the Soviet invasion of Czechoslovakia caused only a brief delay in President Johnson's push for the opening of strategic arms talks with Moscow, while his successor, Richard Nixon, explicitly admitted Washington's disinterest in altering the East European status quo.[33]

At the other extreme, in periods of high tension—despite our rejection of Soviet domination or reiteration of our commitment to liberation—we have treated the East European countries largely as extensions of the Soviet Union and as instruments of its interests, applying to them essentially the same economic and political restrictions as we applied to Moscow. Hence the drastic restrictions on U.S. and, through the so-called Coordinating Committee (CoCom), Western trade with all CMEA countries beginning in 1950—restrictions that were only gradually eased with the thawing of cold war tensions in the 1960s.[34] Most recently, the Reagan administration responded to the imposition of martial law in Poland in December 1981 by slapping even more severe sanctions on Warsaw than on Moscow, on the assumption that the worse the economic situation in Poland the greater the pinch on the USSR and that in any event, as Secretary of Defense Weinberger so ineptly put it, martial law leader General Wojciech Jaruzelski was merely a Soviet general in Polish uniform.[35]

Between the two extremes, in the periods of "competitive coexistence" that have dominated the post-Stalin era, Washington has sought to encourage both domestic liberalization within the various East European countries and greater foreign policy independence from Moscow through a policy of "differentiation." Whether in the separate guises of "peaceful engagement" under President Kennedy or "bridge-building" under Johnson, differentiation from the second Eisenhower administration through Reagan's has taken the form of rewarding East European countries—with most-favored-nation (MFN) status, preferential credit treatment, expanded cultural ties, or other political and economic concessions—according to the degree of their assertiveness vis-à-vis Moscow. Thus, after 1956, Poland was the first Soviet bloc country to be granted credits and low-interest loans and, in 1960, MFN status; in the mid-1960s, some restrictions on trade with Romania were eased as that country regained a modicum of autonomy from Moscow, while in the 1970s both Romania and Hungary joined Poland in enjoying favorable tariff treatment.[36]

Rather than eliminating the underlying duality of U.S. policy, however, differentiation has merely incorporated the conflicting elements into a single approach. On the one hand, every administration since the mid-1950s has tacitly acknowledged a Soviet sphere of interest in Eastern Europe and has been unwilling to risk a confrontation over developments in the region. On the other hand, the implied logic of differentiation could only be regarded by the Soviets as a direct challenge to their interests as they perceived them. As proposed early in the Kennedy administration, a policy of "peaceful engagement" (as it was then called) should:

> (1) aim at stimulating further diversity in the Communist bloc; (2) thus increasing the likelihood that the East European states can achieve a greater measure of political independence from Soviet domination; (3) thereby ultimately leading to the creation of a neutral belt of states which, like the Finnish, would enjoy genuine popular freedom of choice in internal policy while not being hostile to the Soviet Union and not belonging to Western military alliances. . . .[37]

While most U.S. administrations have avoided such exaggerated hopes of democratic evolution, the common denominator of all differentiated approaches to these countries has been the goal of weakening Soviet control and influence, and has been so understood by Moscow.

In light of this inherent conflict, it is hardly surprising that the policy of differentiation, in practice if not in intent, should be seen as essentially reactive, rather than as evidence of Washington's leverage; that is, preferential treatment of one or another regime has been granted after the fact, as a reward for demonstrated deviance, rather than as an inducement to alter its behavior. This is not to say that the policy has been wholly ineffective. No doubt the threat, whether implied or explicit, of a cutoff in credits or suspension of MFN status has been served to moderate certain policies in one or two of these countries.[38] But such influence has at best been limited to peripheral areas of policy. In no case have we been able to influence the fundamentals of the system—or, as shown by recent events in Poland, to prevent a reversal of liberalization in progress. The lesson, especially of the last decade and a half, has been that the sources of domestic and foreign policy behavior in Eastern Europe, including the extent of conformity with or divergence from Soviet norms, remain overwhelmingly internal and subject to the limits of Moscow's tolerance. Moreover, even where differentiation has yielded marginal gains, it has not been free of moral dilemmas—as in Romania, where Ceausescu's limited defiance of Moscow must be weighed against its neo-Stalinist domestic policies.

In brief, by shaping our policy toward Eastern Europe in terms either of fluctuating goals vis-à-vis the USSR or of our moral commitment to democratic ideals, we have failed to define a policy toward the region itself which is consistent with our limited influence there or with reasonable expectations of Moscow's response. At the same time, we are entering a period when, given a careful and measured definition of our interests, our potential leverage may be greater than it has been in four decades.

U.S. Policy Options and Soviet Responses

Given the scope and depth of the problems that will afflict Eastern Europe through the rest of this decade, the range of possible scenarios in Soviet–East European relations—therefore, also the range of choices facing U.S. policymakers—will be both broad and complex. The following discussion of U.S. options in its relations with Eastern Europe will be based on three basic assumptions flowing from the preceding analysis.

First, while a repetition of a movement with the organizational and programmatic scope of Solidarity is unlikely in the wake of the combined object lessons of martial law and Poland's continuing economic malaise, the potential for social tension and political turmoil in Eastern Europe will be high through the remainder of the decade; this is because strains on consumer satisfaction will undermine the main source of stability, and overlapping succession struggles in the USSR and Eastern Europe will give rise to factional maneuvering.

Second, because the Soviets under most contingencies seek to shield problems in their inner family from full public view and to disguise the extent of their own involvement, the choices for U.S. policymakers will tend to be poorly defined–clouded by uncertainty over the true state of affairs or where responsibility lies. (The controversy over the extent of Moscow's complicity in the imposition of martial law in Poland in December 1981, as well as the ambiguous manner in which it was lifted in July 1983, with the incorporation of many of the emergency powers associated with martial law into the constitution and civil codes, are graphic examples of the problems of interpretation and the moral dilemmas that the United States is likely to face in the future.)

The third assumption is that, rhetoric aside, Washington will continue to accord Eastern Europe low priority, with the result that U.S. policy will continue to be primarily reactive and that we will be unwilling to risk a major confrontation over the region. That is, while U.S. policy will continue to be primarily reactive and that we will be unwilling to risk a major confrontation over the region. That is, while U.S. policy will continue to respond to events in these countries, as well as to the overall state of U.S.–Soviet relations and perhaps increasingly to pressures from our Western European allies, we are unlikely to undertake genuine policy initiatives in this area.

On the basis of these assumptions, I have identified five hypothetical policy options, ranging from "hard" to "soft," as follows:

1. Active support of opposition elements in Eastern Europe in order to destabilize the existing regimes, either to promote democratic change in the region or to curb Soviet activism elsewhere;
2. Use of sanctions against Eastern Europe as a way of influencing Soviet behavior, whether in the region or elsewhere (leverage defined as the "stick" almost to the exclusion of the "carrot")';
3. A selective policy of balanced leverage (conditionality) for the purpose of broadening the options open to East Europeans and encouraging economic stabilization, but without challenging Soviet hegemony in the region;
4. A resumption of the liberal trade and credit policies of the 1970s (the carrot without the stick), on the assumption that expanding East–West contacts will eventually lead to liberalization in Eastern Europe; and
5. Acceptance of Soviet hegemony in the region, either as legitimate or as something we can or should do nothing to change.

In posing these options in such basic terms, I recognize that each encompasses a range of possible motives and specific policy alternatives and that the dividing lines among them are not always sharply defined. In addition, U.S. policy toward Eastern Europe at any given time may contain elements from more than one category. These nuances will emerge as we consider each of the options, beginning with the two ends of the spectrum and working toward the middle.

Option 1. Destabilization/Democratization

This option involves active encouragement and support of opposition elements within one or more of the East European countries in order to destabilize the existing regime(s) either to promote democratic change, thereby undermining Soviet hegemony in the region, or to curb Soviet activism elsewhere.

Before considering the pros and cons of this option, I should emphasize that it is not a policy that Washington has actively pursued in the past—rumors of a U.S. role in abetting the Hungarian revolutionaries in 1956 and Polish and Soviet allegations of C.I.A. complicity in the emergence of Solidarity in 1980 notwithstanding.

Nor, in view of its incompatibility under most contingencies with my third assumption above, is it a policy that I believe we are likely to pursue in the future. At the same time, it is an option about which several U.S. administrations have entertained illusions—most notably in the form of the "liberation" and "rollback" slogans of the 1950s and, more recently, in President Reagan's calls for "democratization" in the East European and other communist countries.[39] And, while both the Carter and Reagan administrations wisely avoided overt intervention in the recent Polish crisis, the language of the latter was not always so restrained. Thus, if only because democratization or destabilization at the expense of Soviet interests remains part of our rhetorical agenda—and in light of the opportunities (and temptations) that continuing regional instability will afford—the implications of this option are an essential part of any review of U.S. relations with and influence in Eastern Europe.

Regardless of the precise form that destabilization might take, any such deliberate policy on our part would necessarily be based on one of the following premises: first, that the Soviet bloc is so fragile—economically, politically, and militarily—that the Kremlin can be forced to make unpalatable concessions concerning one or more of its Warsaw Pact allies, and ultimately even to relinquish its control; alternatively, that by destabilizing one or more of these countries, we can increase the economic and military burden that they impose on the Soviet Union, thereby compelling the latter to devote more of its resources of its immediate backyard and to curtail its commitments elsewhere; or, in a variant of the second, that weakness and instability in Eastern Europe will at the very least make these regimes less reliable as partners in pursuit of Soviet objectives—whether those objectives are defined in terms of participation in joint-resource development in the USSR itself or support for Moscow's foreign policy goals (for example, toward Western Europe, the Mediterranean and the Middle East, or Third World countries).

Even on cursory analysis, these positions are mutually inconsistent in terms of anticipated outcomes; moreover, they are based on quite different appraisals of the intensity of Soviet interests in Eastern Europe. In the first instance, the primary U.S. objective would be promotion of internal liberalization or democratization within the region, presumably coupled with increased autonomy from Moscow, on the assumption that the Soviet stake there is negotiable. On the other hand, the second and third alternatives, while based on a more realistic understanding of the centrality (or non-negotiability) of Eastern Europe's status, would give priority to a weakening of overall Soviet capabilities at the expense of regional liberalization and/or autonomy. In fact, on closer examination it seems likely that all of the above rationales would prove counterproductive, limiting rather than enhancing U.S. influence and reinforcing Moscow's determination to maintain close control over the region.

Historical experience strongly suggests that destabilization (whatever the source) does not lead to democratization, or even liberalization, but to renewed repression—either as a result of direct Soviet intervention, or as in Poland, invasion by proxy—and to an even closer identification of the threatened regime with Moscow. The only successful examples of an East European country regaining its independence wholly (Yugoslavia and Albania) or partially (Romania), or achieving a degree of domestic liberalization within the bloc (Hungary), have occurred not as a result of internal instability or weakness, but under the auspices of a cohesive communist regime in full control of its domestic situation. Moreover, in no case has such a challenge to Soviet interests been the result of a Western initiative; on the contrary, all of the regimes involved have specifically rejected such influence and have sought to legitimize their departures from Soviet orthodoxy in Marxist–Leninist terms. What is true is that in Yugoslavia, Romania, and, to a lesser extent, Hungary, Western support after the fact has been a factor in maintaining the autonomy achieved. But in each case that support has been for the existing regime, not its opponents, while instability is generally seen, in East and West, as an opening for Moscow to reassert its control.

The alternative rationales—that we can reduce the USSR's capabilities outside its immediate sphere either by compelling it to divert resources to Eastern Europe or by reducing the utility of its WTO and CMEA allies—are more plausible at least in a superficial sense. On the assumption that the Soviets' hold on Eastern Europe is non-negotiable, we may indeed be able to force them to prop up a crisis-ridden ally. As noted earlier, however, such episodes have so far done little to moderate their underlying goals in the region or their behavior elsewhere. Indeed, instability in Eastern Eruope has, if anything, prompted Moscow to adopt a more confrontational posture in relations with the West, while a restoration of Soviet control has tended to pave the way for a relaxation of East–West tensions.[40]

Option 5. Disinterest/Disengagement

This option involves the acceptance of Soviet hegemony in Eastern Europe either as legitimate or as a fact of life that the United States cannot or should not attempt to change.

Lying at the opposite end of the spectrum from the first, this option has also been a fringe influence on U.S. policy toward Eastern Europe. Were Washington to adopt such a stance today, it would presumably be based on one of the following assumptions: first, that the United States has no intrinsic interests in Eastern Europe, or at least that the superpower relationship is of such overriding importance that we should not complicate it by seeking marginal advantage in Moscow's backyard; or, second, that the Soviets are more likely to permit change in the region if they perceive no external challenge to their stake there, and, therefore, that a "hands-off" approach as part of a more general relaxation in U.S.–Soviet relations is the best way to encourage liberalization in Eastern Europe. While option 1 (destabilization) has long been part of our rhetoric but never a policy that we have actively pursued, this option is one we have occasionally approximated in fact but which we cannot openly admit to.

Historically, as noted earlier, Washington came closest to such a policy during a brief period in World War II, when Roosevelt accepted in his own mind that the ideal of self-determination for Eastern Europe would have to be sacrificed to the cause of allied unity. As he confided to Archbishop Francis Spellman in September 1943, "There would be no point in opposing Stalin's territorial demands because the Russian leader had the power to take these areas, regardless of what Britain and the United States did"; the East Europeans "would simply have to get used to Russian domination." Even then U.S. policymakers had only a dim awareness of Soviet intentions in the region and, at least in some quarters, entertained naive notions concerning the possibilities of a "democratic evolution" of the USSR.[41] Three decades later, despite Nixon's stated disinterest in altering the status quo and the much misunderstood and maligned "Sonnenfeldt doctrine," the detente of the 1970s saw no U.S. disengagement from Eastern Europe.[42] At other times, we have selectively shown minimal interest in one or another East European country, not because we viewed Soviet domination as in any sense legitimate but because the chances of exercising any influence seemed so unpromising. (A good example would be Hungary in the early 1960s, after the shock of the Soviet invasion had passed but before the reforms of the second half of the decade had caught our attention and begun to alter our image of the Kadar regime.)

The sparseness of the historical record, together with the fact that much of the existing record is clouded by a mixture of motives and policy indicators, makes the implications of this option particularly difficult to assess. Nonetheless, it deserves at least brief consideration if only because it helps to clarify certain aspects of Soviet behavior.

Two basic questions need to be addressed here. First, does the United States in fact have intrinsic interests in Eastern Europe—not simply in the sense of whether we would like to see political change there, but whether events in these countries can have a significant impact on our fundamental security interests? Second, are we more likely to have a beneficial influence by explicitly disengaging ourselves from the region? Or, a somewhat different way of asking the same question, do the Soviets attach sufficient importance to a cooperative relationship with the United States that they would be willing to make meaningful concessions in the degree of their control over Eastern Europe in order to establish and maintain that relationship, so long as their basic security interests were assured? If the answer to the first question is no, then the second loses much of its relevance. On the other hand, if the answer to the first is yes, then the option of disengagement becomes a realistic policy choice only if the answer to the second is also affirmative.

There are several grounds for arguing that the United States does have vital interests in Eastern Europe, although we have never consistently defined or articulated them. In the most obvious and immediate sense, the region's massive hard-currency debt gives us an interest in seeing the viability of these economies restored, not simply because of the financial losses we (and especially our West European allies) would incur there in the event of a default (whether by Poland alone or followed by one or more of its neighbors), but because of the domino effect that default might have on the international monetary system.[43] Apart from the debt question, however, and regardless of what we may think of the political system there, we also have a more basic interest in the long-term stability of the region. In this century alone, two world wars have broken out in Eastern Europe, not because of the actions of the East Europeans themselves but because of competing great power ambitions in a region of chronic economic weakness and political instability. Even today, only the Middle East can compete with Eastern Europe in its potential for spawning superpower conflict.

The implications for this option are not immediately clear. On the one hand, the mere existence of such a large debt would seem to make a policy of disengagement impractical in the near term; in addition, as earlier sections of this chapter strongly suggest, long-term stability can no longer be assured by a perpetuation of the existing political system or structure of Soviet–East European relations. On the other hand, if it could be shown that the most likely way to promote essential changes is to declare our disinterest in exploiting Moscow's difficulties in the region—and that by doing so we could both foster economic stabilization (whether through systemic change or a reduction in the burden of military spending) and even encourage gradual political liberalization—then disengagement would be a viable policy option consistent with a realistic, though modest, interpretation of our influence and interests.

The major flaw in this argument—and in the disengagement option itself—is that, while correctly recognizing the centrality of Soviet interests in Eastern Europe, it focuses exclusively on the defensive side of Soviet policy, ignoring the implications of the assertive, expansionist side. If Eastern Europe were important to the Soviet leaders primarily as a defensive buffer zone, then disengagement might indeed foster a loosening of controls since they would have less reason to fear that we would attempt to use these countries as a *cordon sanitaire* to threaten or isolate them. On the other hand, if, as I have already argued, Eastern Europe represents an integral and indispensable increment in the USSR's superpower status—enhancing its domestic and international legitimacy as well as increasingly its foreign policy capabilities—then disengagement is unlikely to have a significant positive impact on Moscow's behavior or expectations, although the historical evidence on this point is mixed.

During World War II, Roosevelt's optimism that he could "keep Stalin from going too far by stressing the unfavorable world reaction this would provoke," and by "making the Russians feel more secure" through dismemberment of Germany and postwar economic aid,[44] proved totally unrealistic. Instead Stalin merely exploited Western disinterest first to pressure the East European exile governments to seek accommodation with Moscow on the latter's terms, and then to consolidate his hold over the region.[45] By contrast, the detente of the 1970s had a somewhat contradictory effect in which the Soviets tolerated limited diversity in domestic policies and in contacts with the West, but only with the expectation that these would ultimately contribute to "common," largely Soviet-defined goals. One instance in which disengagement may have had a beneficial effect was in the selective (and so far unique) case of Hungary in the 1960s, where a Western policy of "benign neglect" likely contributed to Khrushchev's and then Brezhnev's confidence that Kadar's experiments were containable. In brief, the record suggests that disengagement can at best have a marginal effect on Moscow's perceptions but cannot alter the basic direction of Soviet policy in the region, which will continue to be determined by the internal dynamics of the bloc and broader Soviet ambitions not amenable to Western influence.

Between the extremes of destabilization and disengagement, the remaining three options all involve the use of political and/or economic leverage as a means of influencing the situation in Eastern Europe, and all fall short of an outright challenge to the Soviet position there. However, they differ markedly according to underlying assumptions concerning the nature and purposes of the leverage to be applied, as well as expectations concerning the Soviet response. We will look first at the two forms of unbalanced leverage—defined first primarily as "the stick without the carrot" (option 2) and second as "the carrot without the stick" (option 4)—and will conclude with option 3, or "balanced leverage."

Option 2. Economic and Political Sanctions

This option involves the imposition of economic and political sanctions against one or more East European country or countries for the purpose either of promoting domestic change or of influencing Soviet behavior, whether in the region or elsewhere.

The basic motivations and premises underlying this option do not differ materially from those in option 1. What is different are the instrumentalities, namely, the use of political and economic sanctions against an offending East European regime, rather than destabilization through support of opposition elements—but for essentially the same purpose of extracting unpalatable concessions both from Moscow and its East European client. Thus, the question that needs to be addressed here is whether sanctions have proven, or are likely to prove, a more effective vehicle either for influencing developments within the region or for altering Soviet behavior.

Washington's reaction to the imposition of martial law in Poland in December 1981 provides the most clear-cut example of such a policy. With the benefits of hindsight, it also provides the most graphic illustration of the limitations of this option.

On 23 December 1981, ten days after General Jaruzelski suspended the Solidarity trade union and imposed martial law on this country, the Reagan administration announced a package of sanctions. These included: suspension of all government-sponsored shipments of agricultural and dairy products; halting of the planned renewal of Poland's line of export credit insurance through the Export–Import Bank (including $100 million for poultry feed already agreed upon); suspension of landing privileges for the Polish airline "Lot"; and withdrawal of Poland's fishing rights in U.S. waters. Although not announced at the time, it soon became apparent that Washington would also refuse to open negotiations on a rescheduling of Poland's $12 billion debt to Western governments, effectively stalling all such negotiations; nor would it consider Poland's application for membership in the International Monetary Fund. A final punitive action, taken in response to the formal dissolution of Solidarity (until then only suspended), was withdrawal of MFN status in October 1982. For some administration officials, even these measures were not enough; among the harsher actions proposed, especially by Defense Secretary Weinberger and United Nations Ambassador Jeane Kirkpatrick, was to declare Poland in default of its huge debt.[46]

Washington's conditions for lifting the sanctions were threefold: release of political detainees, the lifting of martial law, and a restoration of "the internationally recognized rights of the Polish people to free speech and association." If these conditions were met, Reagan stated, "we in America will gladly do our share to help the shattered Polish economy." Although it was not spelled out in so many words at the time, the U.S. position was widely interpreted to mean that full restoration of the legal status of Solidarity—a demand that was clearly unacceptable both to Warsaw and Moscow—was a precondition for removal of the sanctions. This impression was confirmed by the statement accompanying the suspension of Poland's MFN status nine months later, in which the president now explicitly reiterated U.S. support for the union: "By outlawing Solidarity,. . . . [the Polish authorities] have made it clear that they never had any intention of restoring one of the most elemental human rights—the right to belong to a free trade union."[47]

Even here U.S. policy was not free of ambiguities. While the stated goal was to influence the martial law regime in Poland, a second motive was to alter Soviet behavior, and not only in Poland. As Frederick Kempe of the *Wall Street Journal* wrote concerning the continuing argument over default: "Proponents of declaring a Polish default argue that it would put the financial burden of the Polish economy where it belongs, on the Soviet Union's shoulders. This in turn would so drain the Soviets of capital that they would reduce military spending and be less capable of foreign adventurism. The secondary purpose would be to punish the Polish martial-law government." Although the threat to declare default remained only that, the confusion over motives—whether our goal was to influence or punish and whether the primary target was Poland or the Soviet Union—was never resolved.[48]

How well have the sanctions served any of these goals? Two and a half years after the imposition of martial law, the conclusion has to be that they have not only been unsuccessful but largely counterproductive. By promising aid in the future at the price of concessions that struck at the core of Soviet political interests in Poland, the Reagan administration grossly overestimated its leverage. As a result, the sanctions have cost Washington much of its influence in that country while contributing to the increasing truculence of Soviet policy in Europe and elsewhere.

In Poland itself, the lesson to be drawn is that sanctions are likely to be effective only if the target can be isolated. In Eastern Europe, however, we cannot isolate Poland or any other country; we can only drive them into greater dependence on Moscow. This is not to suggest that the sanctions have not hurt—they have, although Polish claims on this score are wildly exaggerated.[49] But to the extent that they have further weakened the economy, they have left the Polish regime more vulnerable to Soviet pressures—as witnessed by the agreement signed during General Jaruzelski's May 1984 visit to Moscow, which will bind the Polish economy more closely than ever to the Soviets.[50] Both factors—the economic weakness and increased vulnerability to Moscow—diminish the prospects for domestic liberalization; not only does continuing economic disequilibrium undermine attempts at meaningful reform, but even modest moves toward political reconciliation are made more difficult by the need to avoid any suggestion that they represent concessions to Western (especially U.S.) pressures.

Under the circumstances, pledges to "help the shattered Polish economy" on condition that Poland comply with demands that Moscow has made plain it finds wholly unacceptable are seen as hypocritical, especially in view of Washington's inability or unwillingness to impose effective sanctions on the Soviet Union itself. This has only compounded the confusion over U.S. motives and reinforced the impression that the Reagan administration valued Poland primarily as an instrument of its confrontational posture vis-à-vis the Soviet Union, in turn arousing deep resentment among those Poles most closely associated with the country's Western-oriented economic policies and further damaging prospects for reform.[51]

The Polish crisis has also demonstrated the limits of our ability to influence Soviet behavior or to have a significant impact on its foreign policy capabilities. If anything, the sanctions facilitated Moscow's task not only in bringing the Jaruzelski regime to heel, but in turning the Polish crisis into an object lesson for the rest of the bloc. Not only did the United States provide a convenient scapegoat on which to blame all of Poland's economic woes; more importantly, the unavailability of further Western assistance, except under unacceptable conditions, brought home to the others the dangers of becoming excessively dependent on a fickle capitalist West. In addition, the ineffectiveness of the Reagan administration policy to respond to Poland—in particular, the abortive attempt to place curbs on Western technology for the Soviet gas pipeline—served only to enhance Moscow's ability to play on divisions within the Western alliance.

Option 4. Resumption of Liberal Trade and Credit Policies

This option consists of a resumption of the liberal trade and credit policies of the 1970s on the assumption that expanding East–West contacts will eventually lead to liberalization in Eastern Europe as well as the Soviet Union.

The policy pursued through most of the 1970s represents the opposite side of the leverage coin from the preceding option. Although the contrasts between them—in terms of instruments, assumptions, and goals—are not as starkly drawn as between the extremes of destabilization and disengagement, they are clear enough. The second option was based on a rather heavy-handed application of the stick (sanctions) with only a hint of the carrot (indefinite promises of economic assistance or other benefits at the cost of core political concessions) whereas this option is based on generous servings of carrots (especially in the form of readily available credits on liberal terms) almost to the exclusion of the stick (conditionality or linkage of the benefits, current or future, to the meeting of specified conditions).

Of course, U.S. policy toward Eastern Europe in the 1970s cannot be defined solely in these terms. At least three caveats should be mentioned here. First, Washington continued to follow a policy of differentiation, favoring those countries that demonstrated greatest domestic or foreign policy autonomy from Moscow. Second, there are several specific attempts, either by the United States alone or by the Western allies jointly, to attach political conditions to commercial or other concessions. The most important of these were: (1) the Jackson–Vanik amendment to the Trade Reform Act of 1974, requiring liberalized emigration policies in exchange for MFN status from the United States; and (2) the Helsinki Agreement of 1975, where the Western powers insisted on the inclusion of Basket III on humanitarian rights and expanded cultural contacts, in addition to Baskets I and II on security and economic cooperation. Third, the United States continued to apply restrictions on technology transfer through CoCom—although these restrictions were significantly eased after the late 1960s, while differences within NATO made even more technology available to the East than Washington felt prudent.[52]

Nonetheless, the fact remains that, with the exception of MFN status under the Jackson–Vanik amendment, the very extensive liberalization of economic policies (availability of credits and technology) was never explicitly linked to specific concessions by the other side, while expansion of other ties (for example, cultural, educational, or scientific agreements) were linked at most to limited, often technical issues (settlement of prewar commercial claims or cooperation in international drug trafficking) rather than to core political or economic issues. Even the MFN exception was only a partial one, as the provisions of Jackson–Vanik—provisions rejected outright by Moscow—were clearly bent to allow Romania and Hungary to qualify for that favored tariff status. Rather, the expanded scope of relations was viewed by Washington as an incentive to the East Europeans to modify their behavior.[53]

The behavior of Western creditors in the 1970s was motivated in large part by factors unrelated to East–West relations—in particular, by the flood of OPEC deposits in Western banks that needed to be recycled and by the competitive search for new markets as the embargo-spawned stagflation slowed Western economic growth; but their eagerness also involved assumptions about the likely Soviet and East European response to expanded East–West contacts. In contrast to option 1 and 2—which aim at compelling Moscow and its regional clients under external pressure to make unpalatable concessions on issues related to essential aspects of their domestic systems or foreign policy interests—this option seeks to encourage more gradual and limited change from within the system. In this case, the underlying assumption (hope?) was that rising levels of material prosperity and technological efficiency would both undercut the acute sense of inferiority and suspiciousness so characteristic of the Soviets and create a constituency for a progressive expansion of East–West cooperation. This in turn would lead to a "web of entanglements" (as Secretary of State Kissinger called it) that would gradually moderate the more assertive aspects of Soviet foreign policy behavior, while fostering a climate conducive to liberalization and reform both in the USSR and Eastern Europe. In brief, this policy shared with option 5 a primary (although by no means as one-sided) emphasis on the defensive dimensions of Soviet policy, but differed in that it saw positive (in the sense of nonintrusive and nonthreatening) engagement rather than disengagement as the best way to promote change.[54]

By the end of the decade, it was clear that these assumptions and hopes were unfounded. An argument which may have some validity for other areas of the world is that it was the unresolved contradiction between the Soviet and U.S. conceptions of detente, together with Moscow's perception that it was receiving too meager economic benefits at the cost of hostile intrusions in its internal affairs (in the form of Washington's preoccupation with human rights), that led to the increasing assertiveness of Soviet behavior in the second half of the 1970s. In Eastern Europe, however, the evidence strongly suggests that Brezhnev never had any intention of allowing detente or a larger Western economic presence in the region to weaken the Soviet hold there. On the contrary, his purpose from the outset was to use the infusion of Western credits and technology as a substitute for systemic change, as a way of restoring the stability of the region while enhancing its economic capabilities and maximizing its contributions to Soviet goals elsewhere. This strategy, far from being the product of Moscow's disappointment with detente, was already visible in its main outlines by 1971–1972.[55]

There is also a practical reason why this option is not viable for the 1980s. If, as argued above, Eastern Europe's accumulated debt makes disengagement impractical, it also makes a resumption of the liberal and largely unconditional credit policies of the 1970s moot in that an essential ingredient—excess capital in search of attractive markets—is no longer there. To the extent that any new Western money flows into the region, it will be limited mostly to refinancing existing debts in the hope that they might eventually be repaid. Moreover, there is no reason to believe that most of the East European leaderships would be much more inclined now than they were ten years ago to use unconditioned assistance as an opportunity to repair their systemic ills rather than simply to buy a little more time. Nor is there much reason to think that the present leadership in the Kremlin would be inclined to let them—or that Moscow would welcome another wholesale infusion of Western capital which, while it brought undoubted if temporary benefits, is now (as debts) a major factor in the region's instability.

At the same time, that instability poses serious dilemmas for the Soviets which, as we have already seen, their economy is in no condition to resolve. Thus, however anxious they may be about the disruptive influence of a continuing Western presence on popular aspirations or the centrifugal impact on CMEA, the consequences for themselves of cutting Eastern Europe off from the West—in terms of the cost either of propping these countries up or of restoring order in the wake of yet another crisis—are equally distasteful. This perhaps opens the way for a more discriminating and selective form of engagement, one that might contribute to Eastern Europe's long-term stability and yet remain within the bounds not only of the West's limited influence there but of the limited resources that are likely to be available.

Option 3. Balanced Leverage

Option 3 involves a selective policy of balanced leverage (conditionality) for the purpose of broadening the options open to the East Europeans and encouraging economic stabilization, but without challenging Soviet hegemony in the region.

This option is based on three key assumptions, the first two of which are by now sufficiently familiar that they can be summarized briefly: (1) that we have a fundamental and long-term interest in the stability and economic viability of the East European societies (if not in their present political systems); and (2) that the intensity of the Soviet stake in the region severely limits our leverage there and, therefore, that we should not squander it on unrealistic political demands that will only be provocative and result in a reduction rather than an increase in our influence. The third assumption is that, in the Eastern Europe of the 1980s, the quest for stability will require these regimes to focus their resources increasingly on domestic issues to meet the pressing social needs of their populations as well as essential and long deferred tasks of modernization. As noted earlier, the most urgent of these problem areas include the energy- and material-intensiveness of their economies, low labor productivity, rampant environmental pollution, inefficient agriculture, and, in several countries, serious declines in health care and other social services.

A policy based on these assumptions would differ from the preceding option, as well as from all previous attempts at "differentiation," in two important respects. First, it would insist on strict conditionality for credits or other benefits on grounds that, while sanctions to punish "undesirable" behavior have proved counterproductive, policies providing incentives for "desirable" behavior are neither politically effective nor any longer economically prudent. Second, conditionality should not be based on such vague and loaded criteria as liberalization or autonomy from Moscow, but on economic performance in specific sectors keyed to the areas of cooperation. For instance, assistance to agriculture—whether in the form of technical cooperation, mechanization, or credit-financed imports of feed-grains and other supplies—could be placed on a step-by-step basis, with each step dependent on the effectiveness with which earlier aid was used. Similarly, credits for importation of pollution control technology could be tied to commitments to comply with international standards and adoption of appropriate public health measures and so forth. In other words, our sights should be set on selective, carefully-defined and (insofar as possible) apolitical goals related to overall socio-economic stabilization, rather than on producing some ill-defined "deviation" from Soviet orthodoxy.

Such programs could be further depoliticized by channeling the funds and other assistance through more neutral international or multinational institutions, from which it might be easier to accept strict conditionality than from Washington directly. The most obvious candidate is, of course, the IMF to which Romania and Hungary already belong.[56] (It could be argued that the most damaging of the Reagan administration's sanctions against Poland, from the point of view of both their and our long-term interests, was the refusal to consider that country's application to the IMF; had they been allowed to join, it would have provided a relatively neutral lever for encouraging or compelling the Poles to take a number of measures that many recognize as necessary but that have so far proved politically unattainable.) The possibility of other innovative arrangements, tailored to specific situations, is suggested by the Catholic Church's proposal to establish a foundation to aid private agriculture in Poland. The idea, first raised during a visit of a delegation from the West German Episcopate to Poland in June 1982, is to raise money from Western governments, Church, and other private organizations to buy agricultural equipment and supplies, which would then be resold to Polish farmers in local currency; the accumulated funds in zloty would then be used for public projects in Poland.[57]

Clearly there are several possible objections to this approach. First, it might be argued that the United States should not be helping regimes that it regards as illegitimate and repressive to overcome problems that are largely the result of their own misguided policies. Moreover, an explicit rejection of political conditionality might be interpreted as abandonment of the United States' moral commitment to the basic human rights of the East European peoples. To this I would answer that the U.S. would only be abandoning demands that it has been unable to effect in the past in exchange for the opportunity to have a positive influence on the quality of their lives. Meaningful improvements in performance in most of these economies will require greater responsiveness to popular needs and aspirations, a significant reallocation of resources away from Soviet-defined priorities, as well as changes in planning and management procedures. This in turn may give rise to a second objection, namely that a focus on performance and stabilization, as opposed to liberalization, is little more than a distinction without a difference. In a sense, of course, this is true. What it does, however, is to shift the onus away from U.S. (or Western) demands and place it on the East European regime to demonstrate its willingness to cooperate in the solution of long-standing problems.

What are the prospects that this approach might be more successful than other attempts to influence Eastern Europe? In particular, how are the Soviets likely to react to what in essence would be an attempt to take advantage of the stresses and ambiguities in their situation to expand the options available to their East European allies? Here the potential pitfalls and obstacles are as numerous as they are familiar. Moscow may not accept the distinction between stabilization and liberalization; even if it does, it may be unwilling to agree to the necessary reallocation of resources. For instance, it could try to take advantage of new Western assistance to an East European country by hiking Soviet demands for high-technology exports (much as some credit-financed imports of Western technology in the 1970s were passed through to the USSR), or by otherwise adjusting relative burdens within the bloc (for example, by extracting additional contributions to CMEA's less developed members).[58] On the other hand, the Soviets too have an overriding interest in stability in Eastern Europe (although their understanding of what constitutes stability may differ in important respects from the West's or even Eastern Europe's). Given their own narrowed options—and if we avoid treading directly on their core political and security interests—they may be willing to tolerate a degree of Western intrusion in the economic realm. Thus, despite "muted disapproval," they allowed Hungary to join the IMF,[59] although this does not necessarily mean that others, in particular the more important industrial countries, would be allowed to follow suit.

Even where Moscow does not exercise its veto, the results of this option are bound to be limited, giving the West a small margin of influence in return for some difficult choices and compromises. A case in point is the Church-sponsored fund for Polish agriculture, where two years after it was first proposed negotiations were still hung up on the question of who was to control the distribution of the funds, with the Polish government demanding strict supervision by its agencies and the Church insisting on the right to ensure that the funds are used for the intended purposes—that is, to help the private farm sector, long discriminated against by the Polish regime in favor of the much smaller and less efficient state and cooperative sectors. In the end, the Church may be faced with a choice between abandoning the project altogether and accepting the diversion of some (perhaps most) of the funds from the intended beneficiaries.[60] Even IMF involvement is no guarantee that Western assistance will be used effectively or fairly, or that it will contribute to stability. In Romania, more than ten years of IMF membership have yielded no meaningful changes in the essentially Stalinist economy, while the Ceausescu regime has imposed a draconian austerity program on the population that may well turn the country into a powder keg. By contrast, the Hungarians have been more sensitive in introducing essential austerity measures, while pushing ahead with reforms aimed at making their economy more competitive.[61] Obviously much depends not only on the nature of the conditions (generally kept confidential) that the IMF imposes for its loans, but also the policies of the leadership and its political style.

Last but hardly the least of the potential pitfalls is the nature of the U.S. policy process itself: in particular, frequent changes in leadership with consequent policy inconsistencies and demands for quick results, and the politicization of issues for domestic political gain, leading to a preference for policies that will "play well in Peoria" (regardless of how dissonant they may sound in Moscow, Prague, or Warsaw). An additional but critical problem is the all too frequent disunity within the Western alliance. Without making light of the very real difficulties of policy coordination in democratic societies with market economies, where competition within and among countries tends to obscure common interests—and, in Eastern Europe, to play into Moscow's hand—we must accept that our ability to moderate Soviet behavior in these countries is marginal.

This does not mean that we should ignore, much less condone, violations of basic human rights. On the contrary, we should continue to press for the freeing of political prisoners and the cancellation of pending trials of Solidarity activists in Poland, and condemn the harrassment and maltreatment of dissidents in Romania, Czechoslovakia, or wherever else they may occur. But it does mean that we must avoid posing demands that constitute a frontal challenge to what the Soviets perceive as their most vital interests in the region. Thus, to link demands for political concessions explicitly to trade and economic relations only makes such change more difficult.[62] At the same time, it is possible that the more circumspect approach outlined above could give us a small margin of leverage over political issues by making it clear to a given East European regime (and indirectly to Moscow) that, while we recognize our inability to alter the basic features of their system, we regard political repression and privation as incompatible with long-term stability.

In brief, we should be guided by British philosopher Edmund Burke's maxim that "most political decisions are a choice between the disagreeable and the intolerable." In the past, we have too often tended to exaggerate our influence and pose demands that Moscow viewed as more intolerable than the obviously disagreeable burden of propping up its economically fragile (and sometimes politically unstable) allies. Our goal should be to reverse the equation: to so define our policy toward Eastern Europe that the Soviets will come to see stability there—even with significant U.S. and Western involvement and even at the cost of some measure of Soviet control—as merely the disagreeable alternative when compared with the costs of continued instability and stagnation.

Notes

1. For the purpose of this chapter, Eastern Europe is defined as the six full members of the Soviet bloc: Bulgaria, Czechoslovakia, the German Democratic Republic (GDR), Hungary, Poland, and Romania.

2. For a discussion of Eastern Europe as a not quite internal but less than fully external determinant of Soviet policy, see Andrzej Korbonski, "Eastern Europe," in Robert F. Byrnes, ed., *After Brezhnev: Sources of Soviet Conduct in the 1980s* (Bloomington: Indiana University Press, 1983), 290–344. My own thinking concerns the nature and evolution of Soviet interests in the region was influenced by work done as a member of the Working Group on Eastern Europe for this project, which was sponsored by the Center for Strategic and International Studies, Georgetown University.

3. See, for example, Sarah Meiklejohn Terry, *Poland's Place in Europe: General Sikorski and the Origin of the Oder-Neisse Line, 1939–1943* (Princeton: Princeton University Press, 1983), 172–74.

4. In addition to the Department for Liaison with Ruling Communist Parties, the central role of the CPSU Central Committee apparatus in supervising relations with Eastern Europe is evident from the frequent exchanges of visits and conferences among other key officials of the several communist parties. Soviet ambassadors to the East European countries also tend to be people of some political importance in the USSR (as opposed to professional diplomats) and may play an active role in the domestic politics of the East European country. For instance, in Bulgaria in the 1960s, the Soviet ambassador was popularly known as "the Governor" and regularly traveled around the country with Bulgarian leaders; Paul Lendvai, *Eagles in Cobwebs: Nationalism and Communism in the Balkans* (London: Macdonald and Company, 1970), 206. Concerning the active role that the Soviet ambassador to the GDR reputedly plays even today in Politburo decisions, see Angela E. Stent, "Soviet Policy toward the German Democratic Republic," in Sarah Meiklejohn Terry, ed., *Soviet Policy in Eastern Europe* (New Haven: Yale University Press, 1984), 43; and Ronald D. Asmus, "Abrassi-

mov Removed as Soviet Ambassador to the GDR," *Radio Free Europe Research* [*RFER*], RAD Background Report/136 (14 June 1983).

5. See, for example, David D. Finley, "Some Aspects of Conventional Military Capability in Soviet Foreign Relations," ACIS Working Paper No. 20 (Los Angeles: UCLA Center for International and Strategic Affairs, (1980).

6. Ernst Kux, "Growing Tensions in Eastern Europe," *Problems of Communism,* vol. 29, no. 2 (March/April 1980), 34–35; and Melvin Croan, "A New Afrika Korps?" *Washington Quarterly* (Winter 1980), 21–37. According to a recent report, three East European countries—Bulgaria, Czechoslovakia, and the GDR (along with Cuba and Vietnam)—also have combat troops in Afghanistan; *New York Times,* 20 December 1982. In addition, the Soviets are reportedly making increased use of East European intelligence services to conduct their military and technological espionage in NATO countries, with the East Germans, Bulgarians, and Czechs again playing the most prominent roles; *New York Times,* 24 July 1983.

7. Paul Marer, "The Political Economy of Soviet Relations with Eastern Europe," in Terry, ed., *Soviet Policy in Eastern Europe;* and Michael Checinski, "Poland's Military Burden," *Problems of Communism,* vol. 32, no. 3 (May/June 1983) especially 31–36.

8. The "viability versus cohesion" theme was first elaborated by J.F. Brown in "Detente and Soviet Policy in Eastern Europe," *Survey,* vol. 20, no. 2/3 (Spring/Summer 1974), 46–58. For a longer exposition, see Brown's *Relations Between the Soviet Union and Its East European Allies: A Survey* Report R-1742-PR (Santa Monica: The Rand Corporation, 1975).

9. Marer, "Political Economy of Soviet Relations with Eastern Europe," and John P. Hardt, "Soviet Energy Policy in Eastern Europe," both in Terry, ed., *Soviet Policy in Eastern Europe.*

10. The most detailed articulation of this argument is to be found in the works of economists Michael Marrese and Jan Vanous, especially their *Implicit Subsidies and Non-Market Benefits in Soviet Trade with Eastern Europe* (Berkeley: Institute of International Studies, 1983). For a critique of the Marrese–Vanous view, especially of their calculation of the subsidies arising from East European manufactures exports, see Marer, "Political Economy of Soviet Relations with Eastern Europe." With the recent downturn in world oil prices, and assuming relative price stability over the next several years, the subsidies deriving from Soviet energy exports to Eastern Europe—which remained very high through 1981–1982 because of the 1979–1980 OPEC increases—will be phased out by 1984 or 1985. Should world oil prices continue to slip, the East Europeans could actually end up paying more than world market prices for Soviet oil.

11. See Marer, "Political Economy of Soviet Relations with Eastern Europe"; and John Hannigan and Carl McMillan, "Investment in Resource Development: Sectoral Approaches to Socialist Integration," in John P. Hardt, ed., *East European Economic Assessment,* Part II: *Regional Assessments* (A compendium of papers submitted to the Joint Economic Committee, Congress of the United States) (Washington: U.S. Government Printing Office, 1981), 259–295.

12. After a decline of nearly 25 percent from 1970 to 1980, Eastern Europe's terms of trade with the USSR dropped an additional 6 percent in

1981 and an estimated 6–8 percent in 1982. Jan Vanous, "East European Economic Slowdown," *Problems of Communism*, vol. 31, no. 4 (July/August 1982), 5 and 8; and Wharton Econometric Forecasting Associates [WEFA], "Recent Developments in Intra-CMEA Trade," *Centrally Planned Economies Current Analysis*, vol. 3, no. 37 (20 May 1983), 5.

13. Full members of CMEA now include Mongolia, Cuba, and Vietnam; North Korea and Yugoslavia are associate members; Laos, South Yemen, Ethiopia, Iraq, and Angola have "observer" status; Kux, "Growing Tensions in Eastern Europe," 34. While it is impossible to calculate the burden that aid to the less developed members of CMEA and other Soviet Third World clients imposes on Eastern Europe, a partial survey of the Polish experience in the late 1970s is instructive. Between 1977 and 1980, Poland's trade with four Soviet client states (Cuba, Vietnam, Syria, and Angola) showed both substantial increases in total trade turnover (especially in 1979 and 1980) and, more importantly, dramatic increases in Poland's trade surpluses with each of them. Since none of these countries was likely to be able to cover its deficit in hard currency, Poland's surplus exports amounted to subsidies. Moreover, given the precipitous deterioration of their own economy in this period, it is inconceivable that the Poles would have begun shipping Cuba in 1978 or 1979 such items in short supply at home as pharmaceuticals, powdered milk, meat products, textiles and knit goods, as well as a wide variety of metallurgical and electrical machine products. Exports to the other countries as well included a wide range of industrial goods, again including some deficit items. In return, the Poles imported goods of marginal to moderate importance—or important goods (for example, phosphorous) but in such small quantities that they could not possibly justify the trade surpluses. While the stated amounts involved were relatively small—Poland's combined trade surplus with the four countries in 1980 amounted to just short of 500 million devisa zloty (about 1 percent of total exports in that year and something more than 7 percent of Poland's overall trade deficit)—it was still a significant sum for a country in such dire economic straits. Moreover, to the extent that the Poles (and other East Europeans) must give the less developed countries favorable trade terms similar to those granted by Moscow, the economic burden on them is understated. See *Rocznik Statystyczny Handlu Zagranicznego* (Warsaw: Glowny Urzad Statystyczny) for the years 1976 through 1980, and the *Maly Rocznik Statystyczny 1981* (Warsaw: GUS, 1982); and Lawrence H. Theriot, "Cuba Faces the Economic Realities of the 1980s," in *East–West Trade: The Prospects to 1985* (Studies prepared for the use of the Joint Economic Committee, Congress of the United States) (Washington: U.S. Government Printing Office, 1982), 104–135. See also note 29 below.

14. Most estimates of the burden of military expenditures on the East European economies are based largely on the official defense budgets of these countries, which include primarily manpower costs but exclude most research and development and procurement costs. See, for example, Thad P. Alton, Gregor Lazarcik, Elizabeth M. Bass, and Wassyl Znayenko, "East European Defense Expenditures, 1965–78," *East European Economic Assessment*, Part II, 409–433. Moreover, while sales of military equipment might at first blush appear economically beneficial—especially those to

countries outside the Warsaw Pact, which often bring in badly needed hard currency—there is evidence to suggest that military production in general is heavily subsidized, and military sales to Third World countries even more so. While evidence concerning the latter relates mostly to the USSR, it is likely that the East Europeans end up sharing the burden. See, Checinski, "Poland's Military Burden"; Thomas A. Wolfe and Edward A. Hewett, "A Puzzle in Soviet Foreign Trade Statistics and Possible Implications for Estimates of Soviet Arms Exports to Developing Countries," in John P. Hardt, ed., *Soviet Economy in the 1980s: Problems and Prospects* (Selected papers submitted to the Joint Economic Committee, Congress of the United States), part 2 (Washington: U.S. Government Printing Office, 1982), 575–581; and June Kronholz, "Is India's Romance with Russia Losing Its Thrill?" *Wall Street Journal,* 14 June 1982. The last mentioned cites a 1980 agreement between the USSR and India with a face value of $1.8 billion, but which is reputed to have a market value of $7–8 billion.

15. See Stent, "Soviet Policy toward the GDR"; Andrzej Korbonski, "Soviet Policy toward Poland"; and Sarah M. Terry, "Theories of Socialist Development in Soviet–East European Relations"; all in Terry, ed., *Soviet Policy in Eastern Europe.*

16. For more extended treatment, see Terry, "Theories of Socialist Development."

17. Circumstantial evidence of the way in which Soviet "oil leverage" was used against Poland after 1973 is summarized in Korbonski, "Soviet Policy toward Poland," 69–71.

18. See, for example, Francois Fejto, *A History of the People's Democracies: Eastern Europe Since Stalin* (New York: Praeger, 1971), chapters 1–5; and Michel Tatu, *Power in the Kremlin: From Khrushchev to Kosygin* (New York: Viking Press, 1970), especially 429–493 and 538–539. See also Terry, "Theories of Socialist Development."

19. See, for example, R.W. Apple, Jr., "Some Insights Into Andropov Gleaned From Budapest Role," and John F. Burns, "Andropov's Changes: Early Pace Bogs Down," *New York Times,* 28 December 1982, and 5 May 1983; also Allen Kroncher, "Waiting for the Economic Reform," *Radio Liberty Research* [*RLR*], RL 133/83 (16 June 1983).

20. For a review of Andropov's tenure as general secretary, see Jerry F. Hough, "Andropov's First Year," *Problems of Communism,* vol. 32, no. 6 (November/December 1983), 49–64.

21. See, for example, O. Bogomolov, "Obshchee dostoyanie: obmen opytom sotsialisticheskogo stroiltel'stva," *Pravda,* 14 March 1983; also the interview with Bogolomov on Radio Prague, 6 April 1983, as reported in *RFER,* Czechoslovak Situation Report 7 (19 April 1983); and Robert L. Hutchings, "Andropov and Eastern Europe," *RFER,* RAD BR 26 (24 February 1984).

22. Vanous, "East European Economic Slowdown," 13–14.

23. Jan Vanous, "Macroeconomic Adjustment in Eastern Europe in 1981–83" (in 3 parts), Wharton Econometric Forecasting Associates, *Centrally Planned Economies Current Analysis,* vol. 3, nos. 24–25, 26–27, and 28–29 (13, 18, and 23 April 1984), especially part II.

24. For more details concerning these structural problems and their

implications for political stability in Eastern Europe, see Sarah M. Terry, "The Implications of Economic Stringency and Political Succession for Stability in Eastern Europe in the Eighties," in John P. Hardt, ed., *East European Economic Stringencies* [tentative title] (Selected papers submitted to the Joint Economic Committee, Congress of the United States), part 1, (Washington: U.S. Government Printing Office, 1984).

25. See, for example, Abram Bergson, "Soviet Economic Slowdown and the 1981–85 Plan," *Problems of Communism,* vol. 30, no. 3 (May/June 1981), 24–36; and Robert W. Campbell, "The Economy," in Byrnes, ed., *After Brezhnev,* 69.

26. The example of Poland's three most recent crises is instructive. After the December 1970 Baltic Coast strikes, a Soviet hard-currency loan of $100 million was apparently sufficient to overcome the immediate crisis (in part because it was soon augmented by the influx of Western credits). In the wake of the June 1976 food price riots, Soviet aid was reportedly on the order of $1.3 billion in ruble and hard-currency loans; by then $100 million would have been enough to cover a mere two months' interest on Poland's Western debt. For the most detailed attempt to reconstruct Soviet aid to Poland in 1980 and 1981, see Elizabeth Ann Goldstein, "Soviet Economic Assistance to Poland, 1980—81," in Hardt, ed., *Soviet Economy in the 1980s,* part 2, 556–574. The author gives a total of $10.4 billion (including $470 in loans from CMEA banks) for the two years, but this figure includes $7.5 billion in implicit trade subsidies which are determined by the standard CMEA price formula and are thus unrelated to the crisis—and which are, in any event, subject to the reservations noted above (note 10). Subtracting the $7.5 billion leaves a Soviet aid figure for 1980–81 of $2.9 billion; it is likely that additional loans and trade credits (as opposed to implicit subsidies based on price formula) raised the total to at least $4.5 billion by the end of 1982.

27. For accounts of this period in Hungary, see Fejto, *History of the People's Democracies,* 112–115; and Benett Kovrig, *Communism in Hungary: From Kun to Kadar* (Stanford: Hoover Institution Press, 1979), 338–365.

28. In view of persistent East European dissatisfaction with the terms of participation in the CMEA joint investment program in the 1970s (see note 11 above), no new multilateral investment projects of this nature have been announced for the 1980s. Instead, the new direction in CMEA specialization and cooperation is the development of so-called long-term target programs in five key sectors–energy and raw materials, machine building, industrial consumer goods, agriculture and food processing, and transportation—of which the first two have so far been given priority. The emphasis in these target programs will be on bilateral agreements (primarily between the Soviet Union and the individual East European countries) for coordination of research, investment and production.

29. In January 1984, a U.S. State Department source reported that Moscow is compelling the East Europeans to increase their trade subsidies to Cuba (no doubt to help that country meet its pressing debt-service obligations) despite their own economic and debt problems. In 1982, such subsidies apparently amounted to more than $400 million, most of which came

from Romania, Czechoslovakia, and Poland; the latter two together with Hungary have recently signed new trade protocols with Cuba, substantially increasing the level of bilateral trade (and presumably trade subsidies). *RLR*, RL 35/84 (18 January 1984). East European resistance to growing Soviet pressure for bloc cohesion, and by implication the subordination of their own national needs to Soviet-defined goals, has recently surfaced in several interesting ways. The first concerns the CMEA summit first proposed by Brezhnev at the Twenty-Sixth CPSU Congress in February 1981. After more than three years of preparations and several postponements, due largely to the fact that each of the East European countries has been pressing for consideration of its special needs, the summit was rescheduled for June 1984; *Wall Street Journal*, 16 April 1984. Equally interesting is the ongoing dispute within the bloc over the proper place of national interests as opposed to "the principles of Socialist internationalism" in determining the policies of individual socialist states. For a review of the dispute, especially of an authoritative Soviet rejection of the notion (initiated by a Central Committee secretary of the Hungarian party and reprinted by the East German party daily, that national interests should take precedence over international interests except in extraordinary circumstances), see *RLR*, RL 173/84 (30 April 1984).

30. For the most detailed study of U.S. policy toward Eastern Europe from World War II through 1970, see Bennett Kovrig, *The Myth of Liberation: East–Central Europe in U.S. Diplomacy and Politics since 1941* (Baltimore: Johns Hopkins University Press, 1973).

31. Concerning West European policy toward Eastern Europe in the interwar period, and especially the equanimity with which some British officials viewed the expansion of German influence in the region, see Terry, *Poland's Place in Europe*, 27 and note 26. See also David E. Kaiser, *Economic Diplomacy and the Origins of the Second World War: Germany, Britain, France and Eastern Europe, 1930–1939* (Princeton: Princeton University Press, 1981).

32. Terry, *Poland's Place in Europe*, 324–325 (especially note 32), 331–333; also Robert Dallek, *Franklin D. Roosevelt and American Foreign Policy, 1932–1945* (New York: Oxford University Press, 1979), especially 297–298.

33. Kovrig, *The Myth of Liberation*, 281–282, 292–293.

34. Ibid., 93; and Robert V. Roosa et al., *East–West Trade at a Crossroads: Economic Relations with the Soviet Union and Eastern Europe* (A Task Force Report to the Trilateral Commission) (New York: New York University Press, 1982), 79–89.

35. For details, see the relevant section of this chapter.

36. Jerry F. Hough, *The Polish Crisis: American Policy Options* (Washington: The Brookings Institution, 1982), 9–10; and Kovrig, *The Myth of Liberation*, 233–236.

37. Zbigniew Brzezinski and William E. Griffith, "Peaceful Engagement in Eastern Europe," *Foreign Affairs*, vol. 39, no. 4 (1961), 642. Reprinted with permission. Copyright Council on Foreign Relations, 1961.

38. The most recent example was the Reagan administration's threat to withdraw MFN status from Romania over the proposed application of

an "education tax" (to be paid in hard currency) on Romanians wishing to emigrate. See, for example, *RFER*, Romanian Situation Report 5 (17 March 1983).

39. This policy was first enunciated by President Reagan in London before the British Parliament, 8 June 1982; the text of the speech was published by the State Department's Bureau of Public Affairs in *Current Policy*, no. 399. The speech itself was followed up by a conference on "Democratization in Communist Countries," sponsored by the State Department in October of that year. For a negative Soviet response to this initiative, see Y. Kornikov, "Poland Rebuffs the Latter-Day 'Crusaders,'" *International Affairs*, Moscow, no. 11 (November 1983), 121–133.

40. Thus, Moscow's positive response to West German Chancellor Willy Brandt's second *Ostpolitik* initiative in 1969 (in sharp contrast to the outright rejection of the first initiative in 1966–1967 by the Kiesinger–Brandt coalition) is generally thought to have been facilitated by the 1968 Warsaw Pact invasion by Czechoslovakia, which demonstrated to East and West alike the USSR's determination to maintain its position in Eastern Europe.

41. John Lewis Gaddis, *The United States and the Origins of the Cold War, 1941–1947* (New York: Columbia University Press, 1972), 90 and 136; see also note 32 above. Gaddis goes on to suggest that, at least by the time of the Teheran Conference in November 1943, there was "no real ambiguity about Stalin's objectives in Eastern Europe" within the Roosevelt administration (p. 137). While this was true with respect to Stalin's boundary demands and a general desire to establish a Soviet sphere of influence in the region, this should not be understood to mean that U.S. policymakers grasped at this point the extent and nature of the control Stalin would establish. That realization came only later, after the Yalta Conference.

42. See note 33 above. Concerning the so-called Sonnenfeldt doctrine, named after Helmut Sonnenfeldt, then counselor of the Department of State, whose confidential presentation on U.S. policy toward the Soviet bloc to a conference of U.S. ambassadors in early 1976 caused something of a sensation when leaked to the press in distorted form, see Raymond L. Garthoff, "East Europe in the Context of U.S.–Soviet Relations," in Terry, ed., *Soviet Policy in Eastern Europe*, 315 and 323.

43. See, for example, Frederick Kempe's dispatch in *Wall Street Journal*, 26 February 1982.

44. Gaddis, *The United States and the Origins of the Cold War*, 136.

45. The argument, often put forward by revisionist historians, that the final Stalinization of the East European regimes beginning in 1948 was primarily a defensive reaction to hostile U.S. actions (Truman Doctrine, Marshall Plan, response to the Berlin Blockade, et cetera) is also not substantiated by the evidence. Rather, the real reason was Stalin's intolerance of the incipient diversity within the international communist movement. See, for example, Joseph R. Starobin, "Origins of the Cold War," *Foreign Affairs*, vol. 47, no. 4 (July 1969), 681–696.

46. Concerning the initial set of sanctions, see *New York Times*, 24

December 1981; on Poland's IMF application, *Wall Street Journal,* 8 December 1981, and 10 January 1983; on the suspension of MFN status, *New York Times,* 10 October 1982; on pressure for harsher measures, *Washington Post,* 15 January 1982.

47. *New York Times,* 24 December 1981, and 10 October 1982.

48. *Wall Street Journal,* 26 February 1982. Reprinted by permission of *The Wall Street Journal.* Copyright Dow Jones and Company, Inc., 1982. All rights reserved. The most extreme suggestion for using Poland as a tool for punishing the Soviet Union was made by news commentator and sometime advisor to the Reagan administration George Will on ABC's "This Week with David Brinkley" (4 September 1983); he suggested that the West should now declare Poland in default as a way of punishing the Soviet Union for shooting down the Korean Air Line's 747 three days earlier. The idea was that a Polish default would have a ripple effect, bringing all of Eastern Europe to the brink of bankruptcy and placing the entire burden on the Soviet economy.

49. See Timothy Garton Ash, "Judging Polish Moves," *New York Times,* 12 July 1983. According to Ash, Polish officials claimed that in the two-and-a-half years following their imposition, Western (primarily U.S.) sanctions had cost Poland some $12 billion, but were able to detail less than $300 million of that amount. (Presumably much of the rest was a more than generous Polish estimate of the new loans they might have received in the absence of sanctions.) In addition, as Ash and others point out, the refusal of Western governments "to negotiate rescheduling of official debt was in practice a short-term benefit to Poland, which simply paid no interest in 1982."

50. *New York Times,* 5 May 1984.

51. As one Polish economist confided to a U.S. visitor: The West's actions against Poland are all the more injurious because the Poles were the most Western-oriented of the East Europeans. If we have encouraged this only to make them vulnerable then a revival of economic relations with the West will not be in Poland's interest.

52. Garthoff, "Eastern Europe in the Context of U.S.–Soviet Relations," 320–335; and John P. Hardt and Kate S. Tomlinson, "Soviet Economic Policies in Western Europe," in Herbert J. Ellison, ed., *Soviet Policy toward Western Europe: Implications for the Western Alliance* (Seattle: University of Washington Press, 1983), 194–199.

53. Garthoff, loc. cit. It should be noted that the West Europeans were even less inclined to use political or economic conditionality than the United States.

54. For a cogent and sophisticated presentation of this kind of positive engagement, see, Marshall D. Shulman, "Toward a Western Philosophy of Coexistence," *Foreign Affairs,* vol. 52, no. 1 (October 1973), 35–58. It should be noted that Shulman took a balanced view of Soviet interests in Eastern Europe here; nonetheless, he concluded that "over time the Soviets may come to appreciate their own interests in a more resilient relationship which

permits the states of Eastern Europe to participate actively in the functional forms of association which are developing across Europe."

55. Concerning Brezhnev's strategy of alliance management articulated in the wake of the 1968 invasion of Czechoslovakia, see the section above. Concerning the differing Soviet and U.S. interpretations of detente, see Alexander L. George, "The Basic Principles Agreement of 1972: Origins and Expectations," and Coit D. Blacker, "The Kremlin and Detente," in Alexander L. George et al., *Managing U.S.–Soviet Rivalry: Problems of Crisis Prevention* (Boulder: Westview Press, 1983), 107–117 and 119–137.

56. Poland and Czechoslovakia were among the founding members of the IMF in 1947 but were both forced to withdraw in the early 1950s. Romania was the first East European country to rejoin in 1972. Hungary applied in November 1981, at the same time as Poland; but, unlike the Polish application which is still pending, Hungary's was accepted in May 1982. *Wall Street Journal,* 8 December 1981; and *New York Times,* 17 October 1982.

57. *RFER,* Polish Situation Report 10 (5 July 1983); and Sarah M. Terry, "Pursuing the Impossible in Poland: U.S. Should Reappraise Its Limits in Influencing Policies There," *Los Angeles Times,* 6 July 1983.

58. See note 29 above concerning recent Soviet pressure for increased East European subsidies to Cuba; see also note 61 below.

59. *Wall Street Journal,* 8 December 1981. According to the same article, Romania's membership, in addition to being "an expression of [its] maverick policies," was also "an economic experiment to be monitored closely by the Soviets."

60. In April 1984, the Polish Sejm adopted a new law on private foundations, clearly aimed at circumscribing the autonomy of this agricultural fund; see *RFER,* Polish Situation Report 8 (27 April 1984). The Church's response was not yet evident. By July 1984, the government appeared to have acceded to Church control over dispersal of funds.

61. Concerning Romania, see Terry, "Economic Stringency," section V; concerning Hungary, see *Wall Street Journal,* 7 February and 23 March 1983. In connection with the suggestion made above that Moscow might take advantage of Western assistance to impose additional bloc burdens on a recipient country, it is interesting to note that shortly after the Hungarians were admitted to the IMF they were instructed to make about $350 million in credits available to Poland.

62. Thus, U.S. sanctions have apparently made it more difficult for the Jaruzelski regime to drop charges against key Solidarity activists and advisers, a move that many within the leadership themselves regard as essential to restoring a modicum of political stability, because it would appear to be a concession to imperialist demands. *New York Times,* 14 May 1984. The amnesty announced on July 21, 1984, does not negate this observation. Although the desire for new Western credits was unquestionably a factor

in the timing of the amnesty, the primary pressures for this move were domestic; in addition, Western sanctions in all probability delayed the amnesty, while contributing to the isolation and further deterioration of the Polish economy.

3
Soviet Policy toward China: Implications for U.S. Policy

B. Thomas Trout

Because of its potential, strategic position, and political posture, China is an obvious and abiding concern of Soviet foreign and security policy. With the Sino–Soviet split of the 1960s and the rapprochement between the United States and the People's Republic of China in the 1970s, that concern was also connected to U.S.–Soviet relations, giving rise to what is now commonly characterized as the U.S.–USSR–PRC triangle. This characterization is meant to convey the notion that any one of these nations, in its relations with any one of the others, must take account of its relationship with the third. And each must be concerned with the state of relations between both of the others. Indeed, all three nations have suggested such a dynamic in their conduct toward one another.

In addressing the real issues and events of this triangle, this dynamic has introduced a further important condition. Only the Soviet Union must contend with the threat—whether credible or not—of direct and simultaneous conflict along its immediate security perimeter with both other nations. Thus the triangle has meant something more than a mere depiction of a set of relationships. Concentrated on the role of China, the balance of these relationships was seen to provide an instrument of policy—the "China card"—which the United States would be able to use to influence Soviet international conduct. The evidence suggests, however, that that image may be neither a valid nor reliable characterization of the structure of these relationships, at least from the perspective of Soviet interests. At a time when the Chinese position has become increasingly dynamic and U.S.–Soviet relations increasingly strained, it is important to examine the factors which motivate Soviet policy toward China and to explore the implications for United States foreign policy.

China and U.S.–Soviet Relations

China became an issue in U.S.–Soviet relations as a consequence of changes in the political landscape of Asia and realignments in the structure of the international order during the development of U.S.–Soviet detente. Initially, the People's Republic of China appeared simply as an adjunct to Soviet–American cold war confrontations. The Chinese Communist Revolution, coming at the height of bipolarity and followed by Chinese entry into the Korean War, pushed the PRC ("Red China") firmly into the framework of U.S. containment policy. China was perceived to be an integral component of the Soviet bloc, perhaps as much by the Soviet Union as by the United States. This perception sustained an atmosphere of hostility with the United States and dictated a pattern of Chinese interaction with the Soviet Union based on weakness and dependence. However, divisions in the communist world in the 1950s following the death of Stalin began a process of change in which the PRC played an increasingly active part. China seized upon the turmoil of that period not only to redefine its relationship with the Soviet Union—recasting the role of both nations in the communist world—but also to shift its overall international posture. In the process, past grievances between the Soviet Union and China began to deepen and significant differences in their contemporary political expectations and requirements began to emerge.

At the same time, the Soviet Union and the United States had also begun to realign their foreign policies to adjust to the increasingly multidimensional world of the 1960s. Together with reconfigured relations within the communist world, producing a more fragmented pattern of Soviet influence, that change was marked by Soviet pursuit and achievement of nuclear parity and the identification of the Third World as a serious area of competitive concern for both the United States and the Soviet Union. By the end of the decade, these adjustments had laid the groundwork for expanded contacts between the U.S. and USSR. Under the direction of Richard Nixon and Henry Kissinger, these contacts eventually formed the structure of U.S.–Soviet detente, a relaxation of tension through negotiation on a wide variety of issues, but concentrated on the strategic nuclear balance. Detente in turn formed part of a larger U.S. vision of the international order–the "grand design"—which had as its central purpose the long-standing U.S. goal of moderating and directing Soviet international conduct.

In the midst of this realignment, the smoldering differences of the Sino–Soviet split flared into open conflict in 1969 along the

Ussuri/Amur River. These events and the intense Soviet reaction to them sensitized Nixon and Kissinger—who were already predisposed toward rapprochement with China—to the possibilities for using contacts with the PRC as part of the foreign policy structure designed to moderate Soviet behavior.[1] There were also more immediate factors which conditioned United States policy, including the changing situation in Asia—occasioned in part by the impending U.S. withdrawal from Vietnam and expressed in the Nixon Doctrine—and an overall U.S. posture of retrenchment. In the course of 1970 and 1971, the United States developed an approach to China which culminated in the historic visit of President Nixon in February 1972 and a formal accord setting the conditions for U.S.–Chinese relations (the Shanghai Communiqué). Similar awareness of U.S. withdrawal and retrenchment, coupled with growing Soviet strength, animated Chinese interest in this approach. The United States and the PRC then entered a lengthy and involved process of negotiations which ended in December 1978 during the Carter administration with the announcement of formal "normalization" of relations between the two nations.

Nixon and Kissinger's use of rapprochement with China to moderate Soviet conduct and to increase Soviet involvement in the system of international contacts, judging from the Soviet response, seemed at first to be successful.[2] The initiative was sustained by common Chinese and U.S. concern for the growth of Soviet power, encoded in references to hegemony, which found its way into the wording of the Shanghai Communiqué of 1972 and the normalization agreement of 1978, as well as appearing in a number of other related statements, both formal and informal (including the Sino–Japanese Treaty of Peace and Friendship in August 1978). Nonetheless, the substance of contacts between the United States and the PRC concentrated on diplomatic questions—especially the difficult problem of United States commitments and relations with Taiwan—and on the expansion of scientific, cultural, and economic contacts. While the Ford administration authorized sales of items with military utility (jet engines and computers, which were not authorized for sale to the USSR), no material expression of the agreed-upon resistance to Soviet hegemony emerged from the relationship.

Conditions surrounding the U.S.–PRC relationship remained fluid and, within a relatively short period of time, began to change. Soon both the potential influence of China as an instrument of U.S. policy and the overall structure of U.S.–Soviet detente had begun to erode. By the time of the 1976 election in the United States, with no evident change in either Chinese domestic or foreign policy after Mao's death and with no success in eliciting U.S. interest in turning detente against the PRC, the Soviet leadership's concern for China had increased and their willingness to make concessions to the pressures of U.S.–Sino accord had lapsed. These shifts tended to leave China as a more isolated issue, apart from the larger structure of detente, which had in any case also largely deteriorated. In that capacity, the PRC itself acquired a more influential status in the set of emerging relationships. And, with China as a more discrete issue, the implicit and heretofore muted security aspects of the now apparent U.S.–USSR–PRC triangle began to take on greater substance.[3]

Security issues had, of course, been implicit from the beginning in the actions of all three principals. The Chinese were initially receptive to rapprochement in order to use the U.S. relationship as a counterweight to increasing Soviet presence in Asia. The United States had approached China as one prospective element in a framework that was expected to impel the Soviet Union toward a more responsible and moderate international role. And the Soviet Union, having repeatedly expressed its concern with growing Chinese strength (including the slow but steady development of Chinese strategic nuclear forces), had consistently acted in military terms. After the Sino–Soviet split, there was a buildup of Soviet ground forces along the Chinese border, which increased after the Ussuri/Amur River clashes, and an expansion of Soviet naval forces in the Pacific. All that was lacking in this triangle was a catalyst to precipitate more open consideration of the inherent security components.

Even before such an event was to occur, however, the groundwork for the U.S. response had begun to develop. A domestic political dispute over increased Soviet military strength which surfaced during the 1976 presidential campaign sharply criticized detente and effectively ended its future for U.S. policy. The growth of Soviet power and influence then persisted as a central issue in policy debates thereafter. Accordingly, as negotiations for normalization of relations with China proceeded through 1977 and 1978, despite a public posture of "evenhandedness," the Carter administration focused on the utility of establishing a security relationship with the PRC—including the transfer of military-related technology—as an instrument in U.S.–Soviet relations; and U.S. policy began to associate itself increasingly publicly with Chinese concerns.[4] Between March 1978 and August 1979, prior to the Soviet invasion of Afghanistan, leaders of the United States expressed U.S. interest in a "strong and secure" China and publicly reaffirmed the antihegemony orientation of U.S. ties with the PRC.[5] In November 1978, Secretary of State Vance announced that the United States would not object to arms sales from NATO allies to China, and China in turn showed great interest in such weapons.[6]

Further suggestions of security considerations also came from the PRC. During his visit to the United States to mark the beginning of formal relations, Chinese Vice Premier Deng Xiaoping took every opportunity in both official and unofficial gatherings to issue a widely publicized commentary condemning "Soviet hegemony." Deng made similar comments in Japan, the major security client of the United States in Asia, on his way home to China, at which point the PRC launched its "punitive invasion" of Vietnam, the major Asian security client of the Soviet Union. In the wake of these events, Vice-President Mondale, visiting China in August 1979, stated that "any nation which seeks to weaken or isolate China in world affairs assumes a stance counter to American interests" and compared the emerging relationship between the two countries favorably to that between the United States and Europe.[7]

The Soviet Union displayed a predictable sensitivity to these events. While the normalization talks were under way, the Soviet leader, Brezhnev, referred specifically to the China card as "a short-sighted and dangerous policy" which its authors would "have cause to regret."[8] And, after formal announcement of normalization, Soviet commentary focused directly on the arms potential in the relationship, indicating that observers should be "wary" of the implications.[9] Following an exchange of letters between President Carter and Brezhnev on the U.S.–PRC normalization (which were not published), Soviet sources carefully rejected a favorable interpretation Carter had placed on the Soviet posture, stressing that Brezhnev had only stated that diplomatic relations between states were "natural." Shortly afterward, Brezhnev himself granted an interview to *Time* magazine and warned the United States that the delivery of weapons to China would be "playing with fire" and that using the U.S.–PRC relationship as "an instrument of pressure on the world of socialism" was "presumptuous naivete."[10] The Soviet press later suggested U.S. complicity in China's invasion of Vietnam and called for repudiation of the Chinese action. At the June 1979 Vienna Summit between Carter and Brezhnev, the latter introduced the subject of China and noted emphatically that "it would be a serious mistake . . . to use Peking's anti-Soviet attitudes to the detriment of the Soviet Union."[11]

It was in this atmosphere, in December 1979, that the Soviet Union invaded Afghanistan, the catalyst needed to bring security considerations to the surface of the U.S.–USSR–PRC triangle. Though not directly connected, that invasion was nonetheless related to Soviet concerns over the status of China. Afghanistan was both an integral part of the broad Soviet view of international security directed at extending Soviet global influence and a key link along the Soviet security perimeter between the European and Asian theaters. In particular, Soviet presence in Afghanistan was responsive to the South Asian political balance, involving its support of India and U.S. support for Pakistan, and to the relative levels of U.S. and Chinese interest in the region. Over time, the Soviet position in Afghanistan had, in fact, assumed a status almost equivalent to that of an Eastern European regime. Afghanistan was about to fall from Soviet influence in a vital and increasingly unstable region where there were extensive Soviet political interests (the Khomeini revolution was under way in Iran—adjacent to the large Islamic population of Soviet Central Asia). In such circumstances, when feasible employment of either direct or indirect political controls had failed, the Soviet Union had resorted to the use of military force. Those controls failed in Afghanistan and the Soviet Union invaded.

More than any other, that event drew attention to the security aspects of the U.S.–China relationship. In a visit to the PRC immediately following the Soviet invasion of Afghanistan (which had been scheduled previously to discuss arms control), Secretary of Defense Harold Brown emphasized that explicit security ties linking the European and Asian theaters were essential to both U.S. and Chinese security.[12] Brown announced that the United States was prepared to move "from passive to more active forms of security cooperation" and made specific public reference not only to Soviet forces in Afghanistan but also Soviet support for Vietnamese forces in Kampuchea as a common U.S.–Chinese concern. In a return visit in May, Chinese Vice Premier Geng Biao spoke publicly about the favorable conditions for military trade with the United States (though with an emphasis on defensive arms).[13] A subsequent two-week visit in September by the U.S. undersecretary of defense for development, research, and engineering was used to announce approval of sales of "nonlethal" U.S. military equipment to China, emphasizing technical support.[14] This visit also resulted in the establishing of two U.S. intelligence collection sites in China to monitor Soviet missile testing. These were not publicly revealed until later, although the Soviet press had identified and condemned them at the time of the visit.[15] Even without public disclosure of those sites, however, the security focus of the visit was clear. Shortly afterward, as if to emphasize the point, a Defense Department study was leaked to the *New York Times* indicating that U.S. officials viewed China as a potential ally in any U.S.–Soviet conflict.[16]

The Reagan administration sustained these initiatives in its own framework of "linkage" politics designed to influence Soviet conduct. The concept of linkage was a remnant of the Nixon–Kissinger era of Soviet–American detente, intended to link the U.S. response to Soviet behavior (or misbehavior) in order to make negotiation a more attractive alternative. It was now applied in a direct and instrumental way to link China to U.S.–Soviet relations. The question of arms sales to China raised by the Carter administration was thus reintroduced in response to Soviet pressure on Poland during the Solidarity crisis early in 1981. On a tour of NATO countries, Secretary of Defense Weinberger "hinted" to reporters that the United States might sell weapons to China if there were a Soviet intervention in Poland. Although stating, "there's no linkage yet," Weinberger emphasized the word, "yet."[17] The Reagan administration also indicated, on the eve of a visit to China by Secretary of State Haig in June 1981, that China's trade status would be reclassified so that it could receive lethal as well as nonlethal weapons and that the United States would be responsive to specific Chinese requests.[18] On departure, Haig reported that his discussions would focus on the "convergence of strategic views . . . common concerns about Soviet expansionism and the activities of Soviet proxies."[19] At the end of the visit, both sides emphasized the threat of "hegemonism" to the area. Haig also formalized the anticipated authorization of arms sales to China on a case-by-case basis and announced that a Chinese delegation, led by their defense minister, would visit the United States to discuss details. At the same time, newspaper reports revealed the establishment of the U.S. intelligence collection stations to monitor Soviet missile tests.

After the Haig visit to China, however, a renewed proposal for sales of "defensive armament" to Taiwan raised a significant obstacle to any further development of the U.S. security relationship with the PRC. Taiwan had been a lingering problem, despite its reduction to "unofficial" status in U.S. policy and the termination of American–Taiwan defense agreements following normalization. For domestic more than foreign policy reasons, President Reagan had been vocally critical of this downgrading and had suggested on assuming office that he would seek to alter the unofficial status of U.S.–Taiwan contacts.[20] Under pressure, he retreated from that stance but persisted in his intent to provide military support. With the prospect of renewed arms sales to Taiwan, the Chinese postponed indefinitely a return visit to explore their own arms sales prospects which had been cleared by the Haig trip. The Reagan administration then appeared to concentrate on an effort to negotiate an agreement in which arms sales to Taiwan would be continued as a concession for some level of arms sales to the PRC. The PRC, however, remained firm in its opposition and the issue became increasingly contentious. It was only partially resolved by a communiqué in August 1982 which incorporated the unofficial status of Taiwan and specified a gradual reduction in for arms sales within a specified time limit.[21] The Chinese cooled the relationship and continued to express their displeasure but did not break off serious contacts with the United States.

Throughout 1982 and 1983, while this issue obscured the question of a security relationship between the United States and the PRC, a resumption of direct contact between the Soviet Union and China seemed to diminish its prospects even further. In the face of worsening U.S.–Soviet relations, the Soviet Union had renewed its efforts toward normalizing its own strained relationship with China. Brezhnev made several public references during 1982 to the Soviet desire to re-establish formal negotiations with the Chinese over the differences between them. These efforts led to the reopening of formal Sino–Soviet talks focusing directly on security issues, including the presence of Soviet troops on the Chinese border, Soviet forces in Afghanistan and continuing Soviet support for Kampuchea. After Brezhnev's death, his successor, Yuriy Andropov, reiterated Soviet interest in normalization and met with the Chinese foreign minister in Moscow at Brezhnev's funeral. Despite lack of progress on the specific issues and some evident hardening of tone on both sides, the formal talks were also sustained after Andropov's brief tenure by his successor, Konstantin Chernenko.

In the meantime, the United States began a slow process of repairing its relationship with China, highlighted by a series of official state visits: Secretary of State Shultz in February 1983, Secretary of Commerce Baldridge in May 1983, Secretary of Defense Weinberger in September 1983, Secretary of the Treasury Regan in March 1984, and, finally, following a visit to Washington by Chinese Premier Zhao Ziyang, President Reagan in April 1984. The emphasis in these visits was on the resolution of the Taiwan issue and the promotion of trade in support of China's overall modernization. The United States appeared to compromise on Taiwan and the tenor of the U.S.–PRC relationship improved markedly. Although the American leaders consistently referred to the threat of Soviet power and the common interests of the United States and China in resisting its expansion, these references were generally lower key than in past meetings. Still, even though subdued, the concentration on an appropriate response to Soviet expansionism remained central to the issue and both Shultz and Weinberger met with Chinese Defense Minister Zhang Aiping and discussed U.S. military sales to the PRC.

In June 1984, Zhang came to the United States to establish the foundation for arms sales to China, focusing again on defensive weapons such as short range air defense and antitank missiles.[22]

China as a Strategic Resource for U.S. Policy

Throughout these developments, while approaching China on the basis of common resistance to Soviet hegemony, the United States repeatedly expressed its position in terms of strategic interests. During the 1980 campaign, Reagan addressed U.S.–Chinese relations as a "globally strategic" partnership, echoing a reference to shared "strategic concerns" already introduced by Vice-President Mondale in 1979.[23] In his pronouncements on the issue, Haig had consistently referred to the relationship with the PRC as a "strategic imperative" and had spoken directly of "strategic benefits" to be gained because "U.S. and Chinese security policies are basically compatible."[24] In an exchange of letters with the Chinese leadership in April and May 1982, President Reagan referred pointedly to the "common threat of expanding Soviet power and hegemonism" and again linked it to "bilateral and strategic" concerns shared by the two nations.[25] And, although deleted from public broadcast by the Chinese, Reagan spoke in China during his visit of the Soviet strategic threat.[26]

The reference to strategic interests in these statements represents a loose application of the concept. None of the references seems in a literal sense to be operationally linked to the Soviet–American strategic balance. Nor has there been any indication that the U.S.–Chinese security relationship has addressed the nuclear strategic setting. There does, however, appear to be a direct connection to theater issues. There are broad implications to U.S. statements which may be interpreted as a transformation of the "stable structure" of detente into a recrudescent structure of containment, linking Western Europe and Japan to China in an anti-Soviet coalition through the instrument of a U.S.–PRC security relationship. The earlier Mondale and Brown statements linking Europe and Asia with United States and Chinese security suggest the prospects for such a connection. So do encouragement of arms sales from Western Europe to China and the Sino–Japanese contacts opposing Soviet hegemony in Asia.

One of the more common characterizations of the security import of the U.S.–PRC relationship, both inside and outside of government, has been the assertion that the Chinese "hold down" Soviet divisions along its borders which might otherwise be deployed to

Europe. Recent estimates indicate that one-fourth of Soviet ground forces and one-third of their air defense forces are deployed in the Far Eastern region.[27] The association between these deployments and the European theater appeared in the Department of Defense study leaked to the press in 1979 which indicated that the United States has considered the impact of China in the event of European conflict (and vice versa) and argued that China's "pivotal role" in the global balance made it beneficial to the United States "to encourage Chinese actions that would heighten Soviet security concerns."[28] A more recent statement indicates again that the Reagan administration "plans to strengthen military ties with China" as part of a reformulated approach to Asian security.[29] The inference to be drawn from such statements certainly includes at least the prospect for an anti-Soviet coalition ringing Soviet territory.

The Chinese have reinforced this position in public statements which encourage a strong NATO and an increase in Japanese defense capabilities and responsibilities. The Chinese received the Japanese prime ministers Suzuki and Nakasone in state visits (during which they reiterated the common concern for "hegemonism").[30] In this regard, it should be noted that, although some Chinese analysts have in fact expressed a view of the need for an anti-Soviet coalition, it has been generally in terms of Asian issues.[31] The two issues, other than the direct presence of Soviet forces on the Chinese border, which have provided substance to references to Soviet hegemony have consistently been Afghanistan and Kampuchea. In such specific regional issues, the security aspects of the U.S.–Chinese relationship have tended to be most direct. The U.S. concern for Soviet presence in Afghanistan focused on the strengthening of Pakistan as a bulwark against further Soviet expansion, with suggestions of providing military support to China for assistance should the need arise. China on the other hand judged the level of U.S. assistance to Pakistan as insufficient and focused its attention on the Soviet military presence in Vietnam and its use against Kampuchea, a matter of less concern to the United States.[32] The Soviet Union in the meantime remains highly sensitive to all such regional security issues which have, after all, been an integral part of their Asian military presence.

In all of these developments, any connection between the U.S.–PRC security relationship and U.S.–Soviet arms competition has remained implicit rather than explicit. Even in the more assertive statements by Haig, an effort was made to disavow such an overt connection.[33] In his visit to China in February 1983, Secretary Shultz was expressly cautious, indicating that he was "prepared to discuss" arms sales "in the framework of earlier discussions" which he noted "essentially emphasized defensive problems."[34] At the same time, before his departure, a meeting with the Chinese defense minister was added to Shultz's schedule producing agreement to set up a bilateral committee to discuss military cooperation. A Chinese Ministry of Defense delegation subsequently visited the United States in February–March 1984.[35] In a similar vein, prior to President Reagan's visit, Shultz would only say that, given PRC and U.S. interests, it would "make sense" to discuss arms sales.[36] That was followed by the June visit of the Chinese defense minister to the United States which, although it elicited public references to the imbalance of Chinese and Soviet forces on the Sino–Soviet border, formally spoke only of "the possibility of agreements being reached in the future."[37] The tone of the U.S. approach was thus tempered as the issues grew more complex, but, implicit or not, the security focus of the relationship remained evident.

Despite periodic disavowals, the United States persists in approaching these relationships as part of the larger objective of restraining the Soviet Union, based on the long-standing premise that Soviet international conduct can be moderated and controlled through the manipulation of external tension. The moderation of Soviet international conduct is perceived as a global requirement for U.S. policy under the Reagan administration and it is evident that this goal is to be achieved by developing military capability at all levels to counteract or actively confront Soviet power. As a part of that effort, the approach to China seems to anticipate a kind of regional maintenance of the balance of power in order to serve the broader interests of restraining the Soviet Union globally. At the level of the regional balance, however, while the security relationship appears simpler and more direct in terms of the Soviet presence and the Soviet threat, it is more complex in terms of Asian relationships, particularly with the Soviet predilection for using proxy forces and political controls. As is evident, it is much more difficult operationally to keep the regional security issues toward Soviet power (upon which U.S. policy seems to be based) within the global perspective.

More broadly, the U.S. approach has been linked both rhetorically and substantively with the overall military balance. In emphasizing military strength as a critical component of its overall policies, the Reagan administration has suggested that an active arms competition would compel the Soviet Union to negotiate favorably toward arms limitations and, more important, arms reduction. The United States has signaled, in other words, that it will compete actively with the Soviet Union so that no possible relative advantage will come from any increase in Soviet military strength. Reagan on several occasions has suggested that this might take the form of forcing unacceptable economic burdens on the USSR which would in turn make arms negotiations the only reasonable course for Soviet policy.[38] When applied in the framework of the Soviet security outlook, however, the outcome of that approach may be tenuous. And it may be particularly so if the instrument for manipulating Soviet conduct is China.

Soviet Policy and Asia

While events and interests clearly change the shape and direction of policy applications, Soviet conduct over the years has consistently focused on several broad concerns: a preoccupation with territorial security requiring a continuing assessment of the political as well as the military environment surrounding the USSR, an effort to manage levels of risk generated by the strength and capabilities of principal adversaries, and the integration into policy of both the perceptual and legitimative considerations of Marxist–Leninist ideology. Within these concerns, the framework of Soviet foreign policy has remained virtually the same since consolidation of the Stalinist system. The Soviet Union seeks to achieve and maintain independently guaranteed security both as an end to ensure preservation of the Soviet domestic regime, and as an instrument to advance and protect the finite policy interests of the Soviet state.

Ideologically, Soviet policy has concentrated on the growing advantage in the "correlation of forces" between the socialist and capitalist worlds. This theme, used since World War II to account for significant shifts in Soviet influence, was especially prominent in the account of major Soviet foreign policy achievements given by Brezhnev at the Twenty-Fifth Party Congress in 1976. In a wide-ranging report representing both a summary and prospectus for contemporary Soviet policy, Brezhnev noted: "The transition from cold war and the explosive confrontation of two worlds to the easing of tension was connected above all with changes in the correlation of forces in the world arena."[39] This triumphant statement conveyed the essence of detente from the Soviet perspective. Socialism, under progressive Soviet leadership, had gained, and capitalism, before that inexorable force, was in retreat. The favorable movement of the correlation of forces expresses the Soviet view that a realignment of the international order necessitated change in U.S. policies. Detente was seen as a measure of growing Soviet strength, which in turn makes pursuit of negotiation with the capitalist powers ("peaceful coexistence") consonant with continuing commitment to revolutionary movements ("national liberation"). Indeed, detente was construed by Brezhnev to create the preconditions for the continued advance of socialism.[40] Brezhnev's successors to some extent sustained that theme, arguing that detente is a desirable condition, despite the apparent disintegration and rejection of it in U.S. policy. The worsening of U.S.–Soviet relations has produced a greater focus on concrete security issues and less emphasis on the general notion of detente.[41] It has not, however, lessened Soviet commitment to detente as the proper form for the U.S.–Soviet relationship.

Pragmatically, Soviet efforts to achieve security have operated in two policy areas. One has concentrated on the military and economic strength of the Soviet Union as measured against the perceived strength of the capitalist world. From its introduction by Stalin in the Soviet industrialization drive ("to overtake and surpass the developed capitalist countries"), the first priority in this effort has remained with the armed forces—strengthening the defense establishment and expanding defense-related industry. Since 1945, that effort has concentrated necessarily on the relative military balance with the United States. Sometime in the late 1960s, as a result of its military development, the Soviet Union finally achieved sufficient strength to profess superpower status. Not surprisingly, the Soviet leadership considers such status—current Soviet international authority and an assertive Soviet global presence—to be linked to continued possession of disposable military power at a level commensurate with that of potential adversaries. Soviet possession of that power is seen as a further manifestation of favorable alteration in the "correlation of forces."

The second active area of Soviet policy concentrates on territorial security. Despite gains in relative military strength, the Soviet Union suffers from a lingering sense of vulnerability focused on securing its periphery, a concern which occasionally surfaces dramatically, as in the case of the downing of a South Korean airliner in September 1983. The Soviet Union has maintained its security priorities principally through the exercise of political controls. When these have failed, however, military threats and military force have been employed. Eastern Europe, because of proximity and historical experience, has been at the forefront of this pattern. But Soviet leaders have also consistently identified their concern not only with overt military conditions, but also with the political configuration of the states on the Soviet periphery. In recent years, they have had to do so in the face of the additional vulnerabilities perceived to have been brought by the nuclear strategic setting and by the emergence of the

People's Republic of China as an independent international political actor.

As a consequence, Soviet policy has endeavored to build a structure of secure and advantageous relationships along its perimeter. In the 1950s, this effort aimed at counteracting the U.S. presence there. Since the emergence of the Sino–Soviet schism in the mid-1960s, it has also aimed at counteracting enhanced Chinese influence. This structure has taken the form of treaty relationships ranging from friendship and assistance pacts—military and economic—to a variety of forms of trade. Soviet willingness to make such commitments appears to revolve around combined perceptions of instability along its security perimeter and regional or global changes which affect that perimeter. The preeminent concern for the presence of a hostile or potentially hostile China is then a major contributing factor to the wide range of Soviet policy relationships extending throughout the area and to the Soviet military presence along that perimeter, from Afghanistan and the Indian Ocean to Vietnam and Laos.

The security of the Soviet–Asian periphery is a significant part of Soviet policy concerns. The Soviet Union has approached Asia as part of a continuous perimeter extending from Europe through the Middle East, South Asia, and Southeast Asia. From a strategic perspective, Asia represents the southern flank of the USSR. Soviet spokesmen have suggested this perspective in a variety of statements, including continuing references to creation of an "Asian collective security system," a concept first introduced by Brezhnev in 1969.[42] This concept seems to envision a series of interrelated bilateral agreements patterned after the Soviet European system, though without the integrated military component. Such a system would then link together states within the immediate or extended sphere of Soviet security.[43]

With the quantitative and geographical growth of Soviet military capability and the expansion of its global political involvement during the 1970s in pursuit of these objectives, Soviet policymakers have nonetheless been careful in the use of such power. They have tended to be indirect and restrained even when faced with incidents on the Soviet Union's own borders (such as the Ussuri/Amur River clashes with China in 1969, or the Solidarity crisis in Poland in 1980–1981), or with threats to client states (as in the case of Vietnam, both during the United States involvement there and, more recently, the Chinese invasion). Soviet policy has preferred instead to rely on political processes supported by the presence of military force, including diplomatic bargaining and negotiations, the use of surrogate forces, or, more extensively but less successfully, utilization of military and economic assistance programs. When these have failed, as in Afghanistan, force is used. Overall, however, Soviet military presence has tended most often to provide a backdrop to Soviet policy, active but uncommitted.

China as a Restraint on Soviet Policy

The Soviet Union has acquired an evident and self-conscious awareness of its superpower status and that awareness has a bearing on Soviet responsiveness to external pressure whether applied in arms competition or negotiation. As a product of detente, the negotiating environment has clearly become an important Soviet policy consideration with value outside of the substance of negotiation as well as within. For example, lagging productivity and slower growth have made the choice between defense needs, on the one hand, and domestic economic needs, on the other, a serious Soviet problem. These conditions argue for constructive arms negotiation with the United States to reduce defense costs and a sensitivity to pressures applied to security concerns. But that Soviet policy also considers the prospect for negotiation to be a function of the "correlation of forces." In the Soviet view, as a reflection of the advance in Soviet power and international authority, the framework for negotiation is favorable to the Soviet Union. That condition argues for preservation of the Soviet position of acquired, visible strength and high sensitivity to the image of relative influence conveyed by the atmosphere of negotiation with the United States.

Hence, the external environment, domestic choices and the attractiveness of negotiation are linked. While there is some evidence from Soviet statements that they are responsive to the economic implications for them in trying to match a determined U.S. defense buildup the Soviet Union has consistently indicated that it must account in its strategic doctrine and force levels for the presence of the Chinese threat.[44] Any characterization of a strategic association between the United States and Chinese interests is, therefore, inextricably bound with Soviet strategic concerns. The revelation during Haig's visit to China that U.S. intelligence collection was being conducted on Chinese soil by Chinese technicians of Soviet strategic missile tests may or may not have been intended to correlate with the notion of China as a "strategic imperative" for the United States, but for the Soviet Union—sensitive to historical concern for a two-front confrontation—it could not have been reassuring.

More generally, Soviet conduct suggests that, in order to sustain its international power and authority, the Soviet Union will bear a sustained level of arms competition at the sacrifice of domestic needs. That choice seems particularly true if necessitated by a direct challenge from the United States or by increased levels of international tension, especially along its periphery. That is the clear message conveyed in a number of recent developments in the Soviet Union. In March 1982, Chief of the Soviet General Staff Nikolai Ogarkov, in a book published by the Ministry of Defense, urged emphatically that the Soviet leadership not shirk from the requirement to maintain strategic and conventional military strength.[45] In October 1982, apparently at the initiative of the defense minister, Brezhnev (in what became his final address) met with the Soviet military leadership and in a brief address assured them of the Party's commitment to defense.[46] This occasion was noteworthy not only because of its public reporting and its relationship to Ogarkov's earlier admonition, but also because Brezhnev chose it to reiterate Soviet overtures toward China. Brezhnev's successors, Andropov and Chernenko, were both present at the meeting and both began their tenures with similar assurances and similar overtures.[47] Since then, the military has become a more visible presence in the Soviet Union. For example, Ogarkov appeared in a news conference to discuss the downing of the South Korean airliner and in a national press conference to discuss the Soviet position on arms negotiations.

The question at issue for the United States is then whether the regional security balance in which China is principally interested can be used as an effective instrument in the global objectives which define U.S.–Soviet relations. In the case of China, the Soviet Union has repeatedly and unequivocally stated that it would not be receptive to any expanded or formal U.S.–Chinese security ties, especially in the area of arms or military technology.[48] After Deng's visit to the United States and the subsequent PRC invasion of Vietnam, a Soviet journalist commented: "Anything you do for China is bad for us; . . . it will probably stiffen us rather than soften us."[49] According to President Carter, when he indicated at Vienna that the relationship with China was good for the United States, Brezhnev "shouted, pleasantly enough, 'certainly not good for the Soviet Union'."[50] In every case in which security ties with China have been advanced, authoritative Soviet warnings have been issued, including direct statements to NATO as well as to the United States, indicating the seriousness of the Chinese threat from the Soviet perspective.[51]

Recall that the U.S. policy initiatives calling for a "strong and secure" China in 1978 and 1979 preceded the Soviet invasion of

Afghanistan. Soviet decision-making in that instance may have taken the evolving U.S.–Chinese relationship into consideration before deciding to commit its forces, but it is more likely that the decision was based on the Soviet leadership's assessment of the political circumstances and significant security objectives involved and the level of acceptable risk measured against those priorities. It is doubtful, in other words, that the China factor had any bearing at all. Similarly, there is no evidence that the Soviet relationship with Vietnam, supporting the Kampuchean invasion, was moderated or redirected by suggestions of prospects of a U.S.–Chinese security relationship. Indeed, if anything, the more persuasive interpretation is that the Soviet presence in Vietnam has been reinforced by the U.S. rapprochement with China rather than constrained by it. In each instance, the Soviet Union appears to have been stiffened not softened.

Soviet concern for military strength relative to preceived adversaries has been an essential component of Soviet policy. The Soviet Union has justified the size and composition of its armed forces, both externally and internally, in part by emphasizing the duality of its threat environment. Given both domestic and strategic considerations, Soviet preparedness must include the threat from China as well as the threat from Europe. Although all informed assessments indicate that the Chinese military is not sufficiently modern to represent a significant independent threat (one might note that the readiness factor for Soviet troops in Asia is appreciably less than in Europe), there is some evidence that the Soviet Union exercises its forces in scenarios which include Chinese action in the event of a European conflict. Such deployment suggests that Soviet forces in Asia are less "held down" than might seem to be the case. The presence of Soviet troops along the Chinese border does not necessarily mean fewer Soviet forces in Europe, only more overall. The pressure of a U.S.–Chinese security relationship (especially if the United States provided the PRC with arms and technology) may compel an increase in Soviet military force to compensate for a perceived increase in the level of threat. Perhaps one way of demonstrating this point is to note the dual deployment of the Soviet SS-20 intermediate-range missiles in both Europe and Asia and the proportionate balance between them—about half the number in the Soviet Far East region as in Europe.

However, the Soviet policy framework is not so elementary. Soviet concern for territorial security also focuses on the political configuration of nations along its periphery, including China. The Soviet tendency to favor political to military solutions has consistently impelled them toward diplomacy and negotiation. In the case of

China, this impulse has made rapprochement a recurring theme of Soviet policy, part of a consistent pattern of diplomatic efforts with which the Soviet Union has addressed its continuing concern for a two front confrontation. Those efforts are once again prominent in Soviet policy with the resumption of Sino–Soviet normalization talks.

Beginning in October 1982, alternating between Beijing and Moscow, the Chinese and Soviet delegations have met regularly each March and October. The Chinese insist that these are "consultations" not negotiations. These meetings represent the continuation of a series of efforts in the past four years on the part of the Soviet Union to regularize its relations with China, beginning with the Chinese announcement in 1978 that the 1950 Treaty of Friendship with the Soviet Union would not be renewed. The Soviet Union then expressed an interest in establishing principles to govern Sino–Soviet relations similar to those developed in the detente period with the United States.[52] These efforts intensified as U.S.–Chinese normalization talks proceeded but were interrupted by the Chinese attack on Vietnam and the Soviet invasion of Afghanistan.[53] It was then nearly three years before the slow process of establishing conditions for discussion began again, leading to the present sequence of talks.[54]

While the meetings have continued, there has been little change in the representation of issues by the two sides. Chinese conditions for normalization not only include resolution of border issues (actually separate negotiations), but also address Soviet withdrawal from Afghanistan, reduction of Soviet military strength in Mongolia and on the Chinese border and an end to Soviet support for Vietnam.[55] As the talks were to begin, Chinese party leader, Hu Yaobang, stated that normalization was contingent upon the Soviet leadership taking "practical steps to lift their threat to the security of our country."[56] Chinese spokesmen continue periodically to decry Soviet "hegemonism" and "social imperialism" in a variety of public forums and to refer to the Soviet threat, including the statement during Secretary Weinberger's visit by the Chinese defense minister that: "We all know from where the threat to world peace comes."[57] The Chinese have also begun to express growing concern over the presence of Soviet SS-20s deployed to the Asian theater.[58]

The Soviet approach has remained somewhat more reserved, though no less critical. Public efforts toward accommodation have regularly referred to the status of domestic policies in China and have attributed the lack of constructive relationship to the persistent anti-Soviet stance of the Chinese leadership. While indicating that normalization was of "no small importance," Brezhnev still lamented in his address to the Soviet military that "no radical changes in the foreign policy of the People's Republic of China are to be seen so far."[59] Soviet statements have also regularly rejected the conditions expressed by the Chinese as an acceptable basis for negotiation.[60] In his 1984 Supreme Soviet election speech, while reiterating that the Soviet leaders are "consistent proponents of this normalization," Chernenko stated this rejection explicitly, indicating that the Soviet Union would not accept "any agreements to the prejudice of the interests of third countries," a clear reference to the issues of Afghanistan, Kampuchea, and Mongolia.[61] Despite such statements and periodic attacks in their respective presses, both sides have tended to maintain guarded public postures toward one another. Following Reagan's visit to China, for example, the Soviet Union postponed the scheduled visit of a Soviet vice premier, the highest ranking Soviet official to have visited China since 1969. Still, while there is little to suggest easy or imminent rapprochement between China and the Soviet Union, there is clear evidence of continuing Soviet interest.

An additional factor deserves mention when considering the prospects for Soviet–Chinese normalization, although it is difficult to assess and even more difficult to demonstrate. That is the evident presence of Soviet racism against the Chinese (one is reminded of the reference to "margarine communists" attributed to Molotov in contemplating the likelihood of a Chinese communist revolution). Reports of encounters with racist attitudes in the Soviet Union directed against the Chinese (and Central Asians as well) are commonplace. However, the impact of these attitudes on policy is not easy to assess. The presence of racist attitudes is simply not demonstrable in Soviet policy statements. At the same time the prevalence of such attitudes means that they cannot be totally dismissed. In the same way that U.S.–Soviet detente was domestically constrained by the underlying sense that the Russians could not be trusted, making all negotiated instruments therefore suspect, normalization of relations between the PRC and the Soviet Union is constrained by the level of reliance on negotiation that the Soviet leadership can manifest in policy. That constraint will in turn affect the structure of the relationship. Neither side has so far abandoned references to the adversary tendencies of the other, even though the tone has changed markedly. Hence, while "man-in-the-street" racism may be present in the Soviet Union, the driving force for normalization appears to be predicated more on matters of mutual interest and lingering differences, than on prevailing racial attitudes.

Soviet Security and U.S. China Policy

The pattern of the U.S.–USSR–PRC triangle is not symmetrical. Both before and after the Sino–Soviet split, the United States has approached the People's Republic of China from the perspective of U.S.–Soviet relations. In effect, the PRC has approached the United States and the Soviet Union from that perspective as well. Since the Sino–Soviet split (which was in part engendered by Soviet refusal to underwrite Chinese foreign policy militarily) and the end of the war in Vietnam, the United States and the PRC have each considered the other as a counterweight to the Soviet threat. That evident fact has left the Soviet Union with just three options: to accommodate both the PRC and the United States, to accommodate one of them, or to accommodate neither of them. Soviet policy has attempted all three, sometimes simultaneously, but has shown a preference to deal principally with one country or the other.

However, the foundation for Soviet policy objectives remains independently guaranteed security. In its approach to the United States during containment as well as the negotiations of detente, the Soviet Union has been consistently tough and uncompromising on security issues. While making concessions at low-cost or in high-interest areas, no concessions have been made which would affect or be perceived to affect materially Soviet domestic integrity, the established Soviet security sphere, or the overall military balance. It is unlikely that the Soviet Union will yield the status it has acquired through increased military power either through default in active arms competition, through negotiation, or through subjugation to pressure in the regional balance of power. And that observation seems equally true of Soviet policy in Asia as it does in Europe. With an inflexible preoccupation with territorial security, the Soviet Union measures requisite levels of military capability against the capabilities of potential adversaries (and their allies). The Asian theater is an integral part of Soviet security, linked strategically and geographically with the entire perimeter of the USSR. Accordingly, the Soviet Union has historically acted to avoid the risk of a two-front confrontation whether manifested in military or political terms.

In dealing with the Soviet Union, United States policy has focused particularly on the growth of Soviet power in both military strength and political influence. The Reagan administration has set out to counteract that buildup militarily and to find avenues for arms reductions (which are perceived as equitable and domestically defensible). Given the Soviet orientation, it is unlikely that these ends will be realized by increasing the threat environment in which the Soviet leadership acts. Intensifying the concern for the military composition of hostile forces in the Asian theater is counterproductive to efforts to restrain defense spending in the USSR. Past patterns suggest that overt challenges tend to affect the internal institutional balance within the Soviet Union and to reinforce those whose interest is in sustaining the arms buildup. Once again one might note the deployment of the SS-20 in the Soviet Far East region was at least coincident with the improvement of U.S.–Chinese relations leading to normalization.

Similarly, insofar as the United States seeks to reduce strategic (and eventually conventional) arms through negotiation, it is counterproductive to provide legitimacy for the Soviet requirement to account in their force structure for potential conflict on two fronts. In neither case is there reason to assume either from past Soviet conduct or from professed Soviet security interests that the Soviet Union will be persuaded to moderate its preoccupation with security by means of U.S.–Chinese security ties. With a record of seeking to manage risk through strength and through negotiation, an inability to resolve larger security issues will more likely impel the Soviet Union in Asia toward an increased Soviet military presence and toward intensified regional diplomatic efforts. Viewed then in terms of U.S.–Soviet relations, the security relationship with China may prove a questionable form of restraint. The Chinese are principally concerned with Soviet hegemony in Asia. The Soviet Union is concerned with the Chinese threat in Asia and has responded largely through Asian-based actions. It is the United States which tends to configure these concerns as "globally strategic." But pressure applied in one area is not likely to produce Soviet restraint in other areas or on other issues. It is much more likely to elicit a Soviet response directed at the specific point of pressure.

Hence, although for the time being it appears to be a moot point, arms competition elsewhere will probably not be affected by U.S. pressure through the Chinese security relationship. Given past Soviet conduct, a more probable response will be that which appears in fact to be developing: an increase in Soviet force levels to compensate for the altered threat environment; an intensification of diplomatic effots in order to manage levels of risk perceived in that environment; and a continuing concentration on building responsive political influence. There are additional factors to be taken into account. In terms of regional politics, the other Asian powers have voiced strong reservations regarding a "strong and secure" China underwritten by United States security ties.[62] Chinese interests in Asia, except for the issue of Soviet "hegemonism," are not necessarily congruent with U.S. interests. The conflict between China and Vietnam over Kampuchea should raise questions about the level of military commitment that the United States wishes to make in order to deal with Soviet expansionism.

Soviet Policy and U.S. Options

There are a variety of options which lie before the United States in approaching China as a factor in dealing with the Soviet Union. One option, of course, would be to establish formal security ties with the PRC. This approach assumes Chinese receptivity which, for the present at least is unwarranted, and United States interest which is regularly disavowed. It is difficult, therefore, to envision actual conditions in which either side would be willing to seek a formal alliance against the Soviet Union. Those conditions would most likely be dictated by a material shift in the Soviet posture, both diplomatically and militarily which, of course, would already have so altered the landscape to have made an alliance a necessity rather than an option. The purpose of a formal U.S.–PRC alliance would be to present the Soviet Union with a situation of high risk in an area of high priority. Should such an alliance become a prospect before the fact—that is, without some substantial Soviet change (which is unlikely)—then it would undoubtedly provoke the conditions it would presumably be designed to counteract. The Soviet Union would have to intensity its concern for territorial security, increase its level of preparedness (usually, though not necessarily, measured in volume) and expand overall military capabilities commensurate with the increased threat. A formal alliance would be likely to make them less rather than more tractable with regard to overall policy objectives and would, in particular, complicate the prospects for arms reduction under the framework of equality that the United States has advanced in its negotiating positions.

A second more realistic option for United States policy is what may be described as entente with the PRC, manifested in a formal U.S.–Chinese accord. Such an accord would have two distinctive characteristics. First, it would be exclusive, purposefully setting the Soviet Union apart from the interests of the two principals and, at least formally, deactivating the triangle. Second, it would be comprehensive and not simply the sum of parts comprising separate agreements on discrete issues. Entente would thus extend the U.S.–Chinese relationship beyond both normalization and the pursuit of economic or commercial ties. It may or may not contain formal defense arrangements, but would in any case fall short of an alliance. Realistically it would require the United States to adopt an unequivocal one-China policy. Such an approach (which now appears domestically feasible in the United States though still problematical) would in all probability increase pressure on the Soviet Union. Not only would the Soviet Union have to consider itself the object of accord by default and act accordingly, it would also have to anticipate further development. Entente would generate the same fears that would be generated by a formal alliance, unless it contained specific "confidence building" provisions clearly demarcating its military limits and expressly reassuring Soviet security interests which the Soviet Union has already sought to develop in its talks with the Chinese.[63] Even then, formal U.S.–Chinese entente would make the Soviet Union anxious and, therefore, probably animate diplomatic and political pursuits similar to but perhaps more intense than those that are now under way. Though less likely to elicit direct military response, depending on the level of closeness between the United States and China and the state of the situation in the Asian region in general, such a relationship would still require Soviet attentiveness to long-term security aspects inherent in the problem and, therefore, continue to be a restraining factor in calculating formulas for U.S.–Soviet arms reduction negotiations.

A third option is that of detente with China, the fluctuating pattern that exists today, in which both U.S. and Chinese leaders have endeavored to keep the relationship flexible. This option provides the widest range of choices and gradations, including some form of security ties. The United States has in effect identified its policy goals in this way, stating a desire to have "an enduring defense relationship which will move in measured steps" which "mirror the slow but steady growth of the U.S.–China political and economic relationship."[64] While the United States attempted to include a "one-and-a-half" China policy as part of this option by preserving the relationship with Taiwan at some level, the PRC made it clear that such a policy would retard any further development, and the United States retreated. As the tension of the Taiwan issue illustrates, U.S.–Chinese detente reduces the level of risk for the Soviet Union, by opening its own options in the area. Unlike entente, detente comprises a set of separate and distinct agreements that can be addressed, and countered, on an issue-by-issue basis. Detente preserves the counterbalancing elements of the triangle, making the Soviet Union the subject as well as the object of the relationship. All three would be able to pursue several objectives simultaneously. That condition would again probably enhance the atmosphere of diplomatic and political option for the Soviet Union to achieve its interests in the Asian region. And it would make Soviet China policy somewhat more autonomous of other areas as indeed it is now. At the same time, insofar as either implicit or explicit security considerations are part of U.S.–Chinese detente, they will continue to generate a higher level of sensitivity by the Soviet Union to its own security problem. This seems certain to be the case as the slow movement toward the sale of U.S. defensive weapons systems to the PRC takes on substance.

Finally, one can mention what is perhaps the least plausible option in the contemporary setting: resumption of a U.S.–PRC cold war. The conditions for a renewed level of hostility between the United States and China would include either an independent source of international power for China, or some close, anti-U.S. coalition with the Soviet Union. Neither of those conditions seems likely. Were they to occur, however, the United States would actively oppose Chinese policy interests; and, depending on the circumstances, it would either put the Soviet Union in a low-risk situation, giving them maximum freedom of manuever in Asia, or become the object (as it was in 1969) of Soviet efforts to form an anti-Chinese coalition. By the same token, were such an option to be pursued, there would probably be less stability in that region unless China and the Soviet Union were able to work out some acceptable line of demarcation for their respective interests. Given the range of important differences in both outlook and foreign policy objectives between these two nations, such agreement whether implicit or explicit seems as unlikely as the cold war option itself.

This is, in fact, a complex and dynamic moment in the network of relationships that define the triangle of U.S.–USSR–PRC relations. The war in Afghanistan has not gone easily for the Soviet Union and there are recurring reports of peace feelers. India and Pakistan, major actors in the region, are in the process of establishing at least a modus vivendi. The PRC itself, although seeking closer commercial ties with the United States, seems to be interested in shifting back to a "three worlds" view, condemning hegemonism on the part of either the United States or the Soviet Union and identifying itself with Third World interests. The USSR seems to be acting within a set of constraints in all areas. All of these factors present the United States with the necessity of pursuing a policy that is synchronous and flexible toward the Soviet Union and China alike. The military threat in Asia must be dealt with as just that and not forcibly linked to political or military terms with larger issues of the strategic nuclear balance or the resolution of security in Europe. The Asian regional balance is itself a key factor which demands careful U.S. attention. And in these circumstances, it seems especially important to be sensitive to the many dimensions of the U.S.–PRC relationship that are outside of the framework of U.S.–Soviet relations. Manipulation of tension in the region, whether through pursuit of a U.S.–PRC security relationship or through some other form of regional pressure is an uncertain policy with an even less certain impact upon Soviet international conduct.

Notes

1. Henry Kissinger, *White House Years* (Boston: Little, Brown, 1979), ch. VI.

2. See Harry Gelman, *The Politburo's Management of Its America Problem* (Santa Monica: The Rand Corporation, April 1981), 22.

3. Richard Solomon notes that the security aspect was already a factor in 1971 when Kissinger suggested assisting Pakistan through China in the Indo–Pakistani War. Richard H. Solomon, "American Defense Planning and Asian Security: Policy Choices for a Time of Transition," in Richard H. Solomon, ed., *Asian Security in the 1980's: Problems and Policies for a Time of Transition* (Santa Monica: The Rand Corporation, 1979).

4. Harry Harding, "Managing U.S.–China Relations," in Colonel Franklin D. Margiotta, ed., *Evolving Strategic Realities: Implications for U.S. Policymakers* (Washington: National Defense University Press, 1980), 39. Differences within the Carter administration were specifically directed at the impact of the U.S.–Chinese relationship on U.S.–Soviet relations with Secretary of State Vance adopting a more conciliatory posture and National Security Adviser Brzezinski a more hard-line posture (see *New York Times,* 16 January 1979). Continuation of this debate was revealed in the leaking of a Pentagon study recommending military aid to China (see note 16).

5. *New York Times,* 14 May 1978, 28 August 1979, and 30 January 1979.

6. Harding, "Managing U.S.–China Relations," in Margiotta, ed., 46.

7. *New York Times,* 28 August 1979.

8. Reported in broadcast commentary, "West Faces 'Serious Risk of Miscalculation' in Arming PRC," *Foreign Broadcast Information Service, Soviet Union* 78-243, C-1, C-2 (hereafter cited as *FBIS, SOV*).

9. *Pravda,* 19 December 1978.

10. *Time,* 22 January 1979.

11. *Boston Globe,* 18 October 1982. Soviet Foreign Minister Gromyko had alluded to this exchange at a press conference on 25 June 1979 *FBIS, SOV* 79-141, AA-14.

12. *New York Times,* 6 January 1980.

13. *New York Times,* 28 May 1980. At this time, Brown reiterated the view that "a strong NATO and a stable Northeast Asia are essential to the security of the United States and China."

14. *New York Times,* 9 September 1980; *Asian Wall Street Journal,* 15 September 1980.

15. I. Lebedev, "Po Povodu Odnogo Vizita," *Pravda,* 23 September 1980.

16. Richard Burt, "Study Urges U.S. Aid to Chinese Military," *New York Times,* 4 October 1979.

17. *Washington Post,* 5 April 1981. At the same time a State Department spokesman stated that it was not accurate to say that a strongly worded letter from Reagan to Brezhnev on Poland had "no China angle to it." *New York Times,* 6 April 1981.

18. *New York Times,* 5 June 1981; 6 June 1981.

19. *New York Times,* 19 June 1981.

20. Ronald Reagan, "Decency for Taiwan," *New York Times,* 28 January 1979.

21. *Department of State Bulletin* 82 (August 1982), 45.

22. *New York Times,* 14 June 1984.

23. *Washington Post,* 26 August 1981.

24. Walter J. Stoessel, Jr., "Developing Lasting U.S.–China Relations," Address given on behalf of Secretary Haig before the National Council on U.S.–China Trade, 1 June 1982, *Department of State Bulletin,* 82 (July 1982), 51.

25. *Department of State Bulletin,* 82 (August 1982), 45.

26. *Christian Science Monitor,* 27 April 1984.

27. *Aviation Week and Space Technology,* 11 June 1984, 22–23.

28. See Burt, note 16. Another Pentagon study had been revealed in January 1980, which, while acknowledging that Chinese military action would have a key role if there were war in Europe, was more critical of China's military capability (Drew Middleton, "Pentagon Studies Prospects of Military Links with China," *New York Times,* 4 January 1980). This article appeared on the eve of Defense Secretary Brown's visit to the PRC.

29. *New York Times,* 7 June 1982.

30. *New York Times,* 28 September 1982; *Christian Science Monitor,* 26 October 1982; *Christian Science Monitor,* 26 April 1984.

31. Henry Kamm, "China's Aim in Asia: To 'Contain Soviet,' " *New York Times,* 12 April 1981.

32. *Christian Science Monitor,* 2 April 1982. This account quotes Deng Xiaoping from an interview with the Japanese newspaper *Yomiuri Shimbun:*

> The very fact that the United States offered Pakistan so small an amount of aid shows that American policy toward South Asia is a wavering one. As for China, it has cooperated with Pakistan to the limit of its ability, but Chinese equipment is backward.

After Afghanistan, will the Soviet Union strike Pakistan first, or Iran? We need to pay careful attention. Again, China's own strength is insufficient to deal with this problem.

33. "Interview for *Great Decisions*," 16 March 1981, *Department of State Bulletin*, 81 (June 1981), 26.

34. *Christian Science Monitor*, 3 February 1983.

35. *Christian Science Monitor*, 19 April 1984.

36. Ibid.

37. *New York Times*, 14 June 1984.

38. *Washington Post*, 12 June 1980.

39. *Pravda*, 25 February 1976.

40. Ibid.

> . . . detente and peaceful coexistence refer to the relations between states. . . . Detente does not in the least abolish nor can it abolish or alter the laws of class struggle. . . . We make no secret of the fact that we see detente as a way to create more favorable conditions for peaceful socialist and communist construction.

41. *New York Times*, 23 November 1982; 18 February 1984.

42. Howard M. Hensel, "Asian Collective Security: The Soviet View," *Orbis* (Winter 1976), 1564–1580; Arnold L. Horelick, "The Soviet Union's Asian Collective Security Proposal: A Club in Search of Members," *Pacific Affairs* (Spring 1974), 269–285.

43. For a persuasive examination of the concept of such a Soviet security system, see: Avigdor Haselkorn, *The Evolution of Soviet Security Strategy: 1965–1975*, (New York: Crane, Russak, 1978).

45. N.V. Ogarkov, *Vsegda v gotovnosti k zashchite otechestva* (Moscow, 1982).

46. *New York Times*, 28 October 1982.

47. *New York Times*, 13 November 1982; *New York Times*, 23 November 1982; 18 February 1984.

48. See, for example Fedor Burlatskiy, "New Alliance's Shadow over Asia," *Literaturnaia Gazeta*, reprinted in *FBIS-SOV-81-164*, B-1–B-5.

49. David K. Shipler, "China Has People, US Has Machines, Russia Has Fear," *New York Times*, 28 January 1979.

50. *Boston Globe*, 18 October 1982.

51. Steven I. Levine, "The Soviet Perspective," in John Bryan Starr, *The Future of U.S.–China Relations* (New York: New York University Press, 1981), 83–85. See also: I. Aleksandrov, "Ehskalatsiia Bezrassudstva: Po Povodu Vizita A. Heiga v Pekin," *Pravda*, 27 June 1981; Iu. Zhukov, "Riskovannaia Stavka," *Pravda*, 6 July 1981; *Krasnaia zvezda*, 9 June 1981; *Pravda*, 5 May 1984.

52. I. Aleksandrov, "Naperekor Istoricheskoi Pravde," *Pravda*, 8 December 1979.

53. Thomas W. Robinson, "Choice and Consequence in Sino–American Relations," *Orbis*, 25 (Spring 1981), 42; Kenneth G. Lieberthal, "Sino–Soviet Conflict in the 1970's: Its Evolution and Implications for the Strategic

Triangle," R-2342-NA (Santa Monica: The Rand Corporation, 1978), 183–184, 189–191.

54. The current talks began with overtures in February from Soviet Premier Tikhonov, *New York Times,* 16 February 1982. In March, a group of Chinese economists visited the USSR. In May, the leading Soviet Sinologist, Mikhail Kapitsa, visited Beijing, *New York Times,* 22 May 1982. Then there were speeches delivered by Brezhnev during 1982 (Tashkent, 24 March 1982; Baku, 26 September 1982; and in Moscow before the Soviet military leadership, 27 October 1982).

55. *Christian Science Monitor,* 11 November 1979; 26 October 1982. In the latter case, an interview between Deng Xiaoping and a Japanese politician, Soviet action in Afghanistan and support for Vietnam in Kampuchea were also mentioned with regard to current negotiations.

56. *Christian Science Monitor,* 28 September 1982.

57. *Christian Science Monitor,* 27 September 1982.

58. *New York Times,* 18 September 1983; 7 October 1983.

59. *New York Times,* 28 September 1982.

60. I. Aleksandrov, "O Sovetsko-kitaiskiie Otnosheniia," *Pravda,* 19 May 1982.

61. *Pravda,* 2 March 1984.

62. *New York Times,* 16 February 1982.

63. *Christian Science Monitor,* 28 March 1984.

64. *Aviation Week and Space Technology,* 11 June 1984.

4
Soviet Policy toward Japan

Hiroshi Kimura

The making of foreign policy in the Soviet Union, as elsewhere, is not simply an exercise in rational choice. Rather, it is a complex process influenced by a large number of diverse factors. Soviet policy toward Japan is particularly hard to understand because Soviet policy has often appeared to be self-defeating. This appearance is perhaps the result of an attempt to achieve incompatible objectives that the USSR hopes to accomplish vis-à-vis Japan. What is even more puzzling is that Soviet leaders seem to be aware of these contradictions but have been unwilling to change their policy toward Japan. The principal objective of this chapter is to examine the factors that motivate what appears to outsiders to be the confusing Soviet policy toward Japan. I will do this by: (1) briefly reviewing post–World War II Japanese foreign policy; (2) presenting various options for Japanese foreign policy and the likely Soviet response to each of these alternatives; and (3) examining the major determinants of Soviet foreign policy.

Post-1945 Japanese Foreign Policy

Since the end of World War II, Japanese foreign policy has gone through several phases. In the first ten years following the war, Prime Minister Shigeru Yoshida sought to achieve Japanese foreign policy objectives through a diplomatic and military alliance with the United States. Given the costs of the war to Japan and the willingness of the United States both to assist Japan with rebuilding and to provide

---

An abridged version of this chapter was published in *The Washington Quarterly*, Summer 1984. The author would like to thank the Center for Foreign Policy Development at Brown University and the Center for International Security and Arms Control at Stanford University for supporting the writing of this chapter. He would also like to thank Dan Caldwell, Herbert Ellison, and Mark Garrison for their comments on an earlier draft.

military protection for Japan, this policy made a great deal of sense and for most of the post–World War II period relations between the United States and Japan have been close and friendly. However, when President Nixon's visit to China was announced without informing Japan ahead of time and when the Organization of Petroleum Exporting Countries embargoed oil shipments to Western countries in 1973–1974, the power and the reliability of the United States as an ally were questioned.

As U.S. power appeared to be decreasing, Soviet power appeared to be on the rise. These developments presented Japan with a choice, and following the Soviet invasion of Afghanistan, Prime Minister Masayoshi Ohira announced that Japan would become more active and would undertake sacrifices to support the Western community. To support this position, Japan implemented sanctions against the Soviet Union called for by President Carter, proposed the Pacific Ocean Basin Concept, and allowed the Japanese Self-Defense Forces to participate for the first time in joint naval exercises with the navies of the United States, Canada, Australia, and New Zealand. These measures resulted in a marked deterioration of Japanese–Soviet relations, particularly in trade and economic matters; since 1980, Japan has dropped from second to fifth place in the ranking of Soviet–Western trade partners. Ohira's diplomacy, born out of Japan's increased awareness of its responsibilities within the Western community, was decidedly pro-Western.

Mr. Ohira's successor, Zenko Suzuki, went one step further toward what can be called the "globalization" of Japanese security interests. In a communiqué issued jointly with President Reagan on 8 May 1981, the Japanese prime minister recognized that "the alliance between Japan and the United States is built upon their shared values of democracy and liberty." Acknowledging the "desirability of an appropriate division of roles" between the two countries, Suzuki further clarified his position by promising that Japan would take steps to bolster its defense capabilities to extend to several hundred miles off its shores and 1,000 miles of its sea lanes.[1]

Yasuhiro Nakasone, Japan's current prime minister and perhaps the most articulate, charismatic political leader of postwar Japan, maintains two views, internationalist and nationalist. On the one hand, he has been trying harder than any of his predecessors to accelerate the process of Japan's globalization. Based on his general recognition that "Japan is today at a major turning point in its postwar history," Nakasone stated in his major program speech to the

Diet for the year 1983 that "in the age of international mutual interdependency when Japan's destiny is [almost] automatically linked with that of the world," it is necessary for Japan to "live together with the people of the world," without indulging in "self-righteousness or egocentrism," and to "play her role in the world," the role conceived "not from Japan's own position but from the much larger world perspective."[2] Nakasone repeated this basic foreign policy orientation, during his visit to the United States in January 1983: "I would exert my leadership on our nation so that our people will make more effort [for Japan] to become a harmonious member of the international community."[3] What Mr. Nakasone meant by "international community," is inter alia the "Western community" (in Ohira and Suzuki's terms) in which the United States occupies the dominant position. To make this position clear, the new Japanese premier repeatedly stated that "the fundamental principle of Japanese diplomacy lies in making efforts" to promote solidarity with the Western countries, particularly with the United States,"[4] and "to fulfill her obligations as a member of the West."[5] The sensation caused by the labeling of U.S.–Japan relations as an "alliance" by the previous premier, Suzuki, was due to the term's strong connotation of military alliance. The furor did not prevent the much bolder Premier Nakasone from going beyond confirming relations between Japan and the United States as none other than a military alliance to take the further step to describe those relations as "unmei kyodotai"—that is literally translated as "a community bound together with a common destiny."[6]

However, the foregoing must not be taken to mean that what Nakasone has been trying to do is simply a continuation at a faster pace of the policy of his predecessors such as Ohira and Suzuki, who awakened the Japanese to the responsibilities of membership in the Western community and promoted the globalization of Japan's foreign policy. Nakasone appears to have another view, one that makes his political, diplomatic, and security posture quite unique, and even unprecedented in postwar Japanese history. For instance, Nakasone has not kept it a secret that he advocates *jishu* diplomacy and defense of Japan. The meaning of *jishu* is autonomous and independent; what Nakasone means by *jishu* diplomacy and *jishu* defense is that the Japanese diplomacy ought to be decided and carried out by the Japanese themselves and the defense of Japan must be provided primarily by the Japanese themselves.[7] In Nakasone's words, "only when it [the effort to defend Japan] is insufficient, can it be supplemented, but never replaced by arrangements with others."[8] Neither *jishu* diplomacy nor *jishu* defense are new, and yet, given Japan's excessive dependence on U.S. security arrangements in the past, they sound somewhat nationalistic, due to the de-emphasis on depending on others, particularly the United States.

Nakasone has been surprisingly consistent in this regard for quite some time, despite his notorious nickname "political weather vane." Nakasone justifed this political opportunism as necessary to increase his influence and climb up the ladder of faction-ridden Japanese politics. At any rate, it is almost astonishing to realize that as early as 1956, only five years after the signing of both the San Francisco Peace Treaty and the Japan–U.S. Security Treaty, Nakasone had already suggested that "the current unhealthy, abnormal relations between the protector [the United States] and the protected [Japan] be corrected as soon as possible through Japan's shifting of its position to self-defense so that Japan can cooperate with the U.S. more as a genuinely equal, independent, friendly nation."[9] What the future Japanese prime minister of twenty-six years later was proposing at that time to Richard Nixon, then vice-president, was that the then prevailing Japan–U.S. Security Treaty be amended into a treaty of alliance of security on an equal footing and that U.S. military forces be gradually withdrawn from Japan in proportion to the increase of the Japanese self-defense forces. It would be, therefore, less surprising a quarter of a century later to note that Nakasone claims that the proposals he has been making constantly with regard to *jishu* diplomacy and defense were "eminently reasonable."[10] Repeating his own long-standing conviction that "complete independence would only come when Japan was capable of administering and depending upon itself," Mr. Nakasone has put forward exactly the same two proposals as those he made to Nixon in 1956. In *My Life in Politics* (1982), an unusual document prepared in English for U.S. high officials and intellectuals upon his nomination as prime minister, Nakasone wrote: "To attain Japanese independence in national defense, (1) the security treaty with the United States should be revised to put equal responsibility on both parties, and (2) U.S. military forces should be gradually removed from Japan."[11]

What Premier Nakasone intends to do in the field of security can be summarized as a twofold effort: to exert more positive effort toward military cooperation with the United States and to place more emphasis now than at any preceding time upon "self-reliant efforts." These two complementary efforts are designed to achieve the same objective: assuring Japan protection from its major potential adversary, the USSR. In fact, Nakasone himself has summarized his security efforts in one phrase, "the establishment of an autonomous [*jishu*] defense capability linked with the United States."[12] And yet the chances still are that at least in theory both these efforts may not always coincide with each other, as is clearly the case in relations between the United States and France. Some astute observers have reported that they sense the development of a Gaullist–type of nationalism in Nakasone's foreign policy statements.[13] For example, Nakasone has said, "I will do my utmost to increase military spending of Japan, not because of what America says, but because it constitutes a primary obligation for Japan as an independent nation."[14] How Nakasone will manage to coordinate these two efforts remains to be seen. Similarly, what also remains to be seen is Nakasone's policy toward the Soviet Union. So far the policy of the Japanese prime minister toward this potential adversary has been nothing but a faithful continuation of his predecessors. However, it cannot be completely ruled out, at least hypothetically, that Nakasone will be tempted to make some accommodations with the Soviet Union, not in spite of but precisely because of the fact that it is the main source of threat to the national security of Japan. Because of his ambition to succeed where former Japanese leaders have failed in making a breakthrough in the long diplomatic stalemate with the USSR, Nakasone may well initiate a new Japanese foreign policy.

Japanese Foreign Policy Options

In this section, I will describe the foreign policy options available to Japan concerning its relations with the United States and the Soviet Union. These options consist of both those that are now feasible and those that are hypothetical. I will then predict likely Soviet responses to each of these options.

The first and most obvious policy option is simply to continue the present policy. It appears likely that Japan will make a steady effort to increase its defense spending, but not to a dramatic extent. Despite high expectations among many Americans for strong, new leadership under Nakasone and the continued and increasing pressure exerted by the Reagan administration, even Nakasone may be unable to do much, given the so-called "consensus-first" political climate of Japan, plus heavy domestic restraints. Nakasone may end up as a leader who will have done slightly more than others and yet nothing spectacular. More concretely, the defense-related expenditures of Japan will exceed the equivalent of 1 percent of the Japanese GNP for the fiscal year and the so-called "Midtern Defense Program

Estimate for Fiscal Year 1983–1987" will also be realized. The transfer of defense-related technology from Japan to the United States could be conducted smoothly.[15] Even if all of these actions are taken by Japan, the United States will still not be satisfied with Japan's effort. Soviet leaders would rhetorically complain about the militarization of Japan, but would probably be relieved that Japan was not contributing more to the Western defense effort.

The second option is that Japan would increase her defense capabilities dramatically but within the larger framework of the U.S.–Japan military alliance, or more broadly, within the framework of U.S. global strategy. The difference between the first and the second options would be a matter of degree. Under this second option, Japan would carry out much more purposefully and at faster speed what U.S. administrations have been persistently pressing Japan to do: undertaking annual increases of defense spending to the NATO level of 3 percent, the 1,000 nautical-mile sea lane defense, the transfer to the United States of not only defense-related technology but also military weaponry itself, admission of U.S. nuclear weapons into Japanese territory, and so on. As a result, the U.S.–Japan Treaty for Mutual Cooperation and Security would be amended to reflect Japan's greater defense effort. Undoubtedly this move would be welcomed most by the United States and least by the USSR.

The third alternative to Japan is to move in the direction of more "omnidirectional" or "equidistant" diplomacy. Japan might lessen the degree of cooperation with the United States by closing down U.S. bases on military facilities in Japan which as of 1984, number 128. Instead, Japan might make some accommodation with the Soviet Union by concluding a peace treaty, with or without the reversion of two of the Northern Islands—Habomai and Shikotan, in exchange for better cooperation from the Japanese on the development of Siberia and the Far Eastern part of the USSR. This option would be welcomed by Moscow but certainly not by Washington.

The fourth and most drastic alternative is for Japan to reverse its post-World War II alliance with the United States to the Soviet Union. Tokyo would abrogate the U.S.–Japanese Security Treaty which would result in the dismantling of all U.S. military bases and facilties in Japan. This is certainly the worst possible option for the United States since it would lose one of its most important allies, what Secretary of Defense Caspar Weinberger has called "a pillar of our whole forward defense strategy in the Asia–Pacific region."[16] If this option was implemented, Japan might conclude a treaty of nonaggression with the USSR. Clearly, the Soviet Union would gain the most from this alternative.

A fifth option would be for Japan to abrogate the U.S.–Japanese Security Treaty and to establish an alliance with the People's Republic of China. While the United States would hardly welcome such a development, the Soviet Union would actively oppose it.

A sixth alternative would be for Japan to build a strong military of its own so that it would become a genuinely independent state in terms of defense. In order to enjoy that status, Tokyo might abrogate the security treaty with Washington without concluding any military arrangement either with Moscow or with Beijing. Japan might revise some portions of its "peace consititution," particularly Article 9, the clause renouncing war potential.[17] If Japan were to follow the logic of this option, it would develop its own nuclear weapons, just as France did.[18] Few countries, if any, would welcome the development of a Japan rearmed far beyond the requirements of the situation.

How would the Soviet Union react to the six alternative Japanese foreign policy options described above? Rather than dealing individually with each alternative, I will identify and analyze the most likely general Soviet reactions and the reasons for these reactions.

Separation of Tokyo from Washington

It can be safely said that Moscow will continue to attempt to separate Tokyo from Washington; Lenin taught that "the more powerful enemy can be conquered by . . . the most thorough, careful, attentive, skillful and obligatory use of even the smallest rifts between the enemies."[19] Besides this Bolshevik tradition, there is another, perhaps more important, reason why Soviet leaders, whoever they may be, will continue to apply this policy toward Japan. Soviet leaders do not perceive Japan by itself to be a significant power in military terms; however, when Japan commits its resources to the support of U.S. foreign policy, it becomes a formidable power in the Kremlin's eyes. Dmitrii V. Petrov, the head of the Japan Section of the Soviet Academy of Sciences' Far Eastern Institute, still considers in 1981, as he did almost ten years ago in 1973, that "Today and in the near future Japan will be unable independently to solve strategic tasks and conduct offensive large-scale operations."[20] Having said this, however, Petrov hastened to add that "the militarization of Japan has been indissolutely linked with U.S. military-strategic doctrine and the American foreign policy, which assigns a major role to the military alliance with Japan in achieving its regional and global ends."[21]

Whatever the reason behind its policy of divide and rule, the

Soviet Union will attempt to do its utmost in order to drive a wedge between Japan and the United States by resorting to persuasion, bluffs, encouragement, entreaties, and all other means available to it. One kind of Soviet effort is persuasion. Moscow will try to explain to the Japanese what the new U.S. global strategy is and how dangerous the role Japan is expected to play in that U.S. scheme is. In the Soviet perception, the U.S. ultimate goal of world domination will never undergo any change in the future. What will change is the method. Due to increasing U.S. awareness of its relative decline of power and also its realization of the fact that Japan and other allies have grown enough to be able to undertake more burdens than before, Washington will, in the Soviet view, pressure its allies to assume more diffuse responsibilities. Moscow warns, that Japan's role as a partner or "accomplice," particularly in the Asia–Pacific region, will be increasing significantly.[22] Washington is, in the Soviet prediction, going to convert the present U.S.–Japan security treaty arrangement of a rather unilateral nature into that of NATO-type, with a more equal, bilateral nature; in Soviet words, "NATOization" will take place, so that a "bridge" between these two military allied blocs can be created.[23] The Soviets also are greatly concerned about U.S.–Japan cooperation in the field of defense-related microelectronics, computers, lasers, and other advanced high technology necessary for the development of future weaponry.[24] Soviet leaders believe that such cooperation will definitely increase in the future.

As one of the best means of applying the tactics of divide and rule to Tokyo, Moscow most probably will keep pointing out the possible or actual contradictions between Japan and the United States. It is the basic Soviet perception that, although both U.S. and Japanese elites have so far found enough common interests to justify close relations across the Pacific, they will find their fundamental differences increasingly difficult to bridge. The gap between these two states will continue to grow as Japan challenges the United States not only in economics but in almost all other fields. Particularly serious contradictions are likely to come to the surface, according to Moscow's prediction, when "Tokyo starts to obtain more independence than it has had within the framework of its military alliance with the U.S.A."[25] With Nakasone's ascent to power, this process appears to have already started. Moscow also will encourage Tokyo to become less dependent on Washington. On the one hand, the Kremlin does not want to see Japan grow into an overly independent and militarily strong state in the future, but on the other hand, the USSR certainly would not welcome a Japan wholly dependent upon the United States. Unlike Western European allies of the United States which "have claimed more or less independence [from the United States] and freedom of action for the protection of their national interests," Japan, in the Soviet judgment, "has not even tried to do that."[26] Tokyo appears to the Soviets too content with the status of "an obedient junior partner," always "blindly copying the U.S. position" and "at the disposal of its overseas patron's instructions."[27] According to the Soviet judgment, Japan has been excessively exploited as a very convenient, most faithful "partner" or "ally" by the United States, in exchange for "an honorable membership card of the Western community."[28] No matter how U.S. politicians label Japan with such flattering terms as "equal partner," "a vital cornerstone," and so on, Japan is—the Soviets warm—simply used by the Pentagon as "a territory for accommodating [U.S.] air force and naval bases" and relied upon because of her "material and productive capability from the viewpoint of securing military actions in Asia."[29] The Soviets thus warn that in case of emergency The United States would not necessarily come to help Japan, which enjoys "less support among American citizens than does Western Europe."[30] Consequently, the Soviets will advise, as they have in the past, that the Japanese should abrogate the unreliable and unnecessary alliance with the United States.

With the purpose of alienating Japan from the United States and others, the Kremlin will also keep playing the role of benevolent judge. Soviet leaders will make the case, that it is not necessarily the innocent Japanese, but rather the U.S. imperialists (and Chinese expansionists) who are primarily responsible for pushing Japan onto the dangerous course of "remilitarization" and "anti-Sovietism." The Soviets thus will advise the Japanese not to succumb but rather to persistently resist "the pressures" and "demands" exerted on Tokyo from Washington (and Beijing).[31] It can be recalled at this juncture that, carefully avoiding the risk of directly opposing Japan, Leonid I. Brezhnev criticized instead the United States and the PRC; this is best illustrated in his speech at the Twenty-Sixth CPSU Congress, when he stated, "In Japan's foreign policy course, negative factors are becoming stronger—playing second fiddle to the dangerous plans of Washington and Beijing and a tendency towards militarization."[32] Having said this, the late general secretary was cautious enough to add, "However, we do not think that these are Tokyo's last words, so to speak, and we hope that foresight and understanding of the country's interests will prevail there. As before, the USSR favors lasting and genuine good-neighbor relations with Japan."[33] Under Konstantin U. Chernenko and his successors, there is no reason to believe that the USSR will stop wooing Japan by strongly criticizing the United States and China while muting criticism of Japan.

Prevention of Japan's "Globalization" and "Militarization"

Another important Soviet reaction will be criticism of and moves to prevent the globalization and the rearmament of Japan. Japan's trend to "globalization," as explained above, involves a growing awareness of its membership in the world or to be more exact, Western community and a readiness to accept responsibility for defense commitments commensurate with its economic capability. As the Soviets perceive it, Japan intends to become a world power with interests throughout the world. The transition of Tokyo's principles of foreign policy conduct from the "Yoshida doctrine," which concentrated on the economic welfare of the Japanese people, to the "globalism doctrine" is regarded by the Soviets as a "very substantial, qualitative change."[34] The Kremlin has good reason not to welcome such a transformation of Japan. Tokyo's transition to a position of global diplomacy is, according to Soviet judgment, dictated "not so much by Japan's individual national interests as its 'membership of the club' of imperalist states,"[35] thus taking "a course of confrontation with the Soviet Union."[36] With the hope that Japan will forever remain the state of the immediate postwar world whose concern was confined strictly to her own narrowly defined interests and particularly to the defense of her territories, Moscow will, as in the past, keep trying hard to persuade Tokyo not to get interested in the affairs of "third countries," such as Afghanistan and Poland; in the Soviet view these countries "do not have anything in common with the interests of Japanese people."[37] It is also unnecessary and even dangerous to the security of Japan, according to the Soviets, for Japan to participate in such joint naval exercises as the U.S.–Canada–Australia–New Zealand exercises conducted in the Pacific Ocean "thousands of miles away from the Japanese coast, far beyond the boundaries of the Far East."[38] What will be likewise intensified is the Soviet campaign against the Japanese plan to undertake the so-called "1,000 mile sea-lane defense." Referring to these exercises, D.V. Petrov has written: "This means an essential expansion of function of the Japanese 'Self-Defense Forces.' It would mean that Japan's

Navy is going to act thousands of miles away from the coast of its own country."[39]

One of the major reasons why the Kremlin has been, and will continue to be concerned about Japan's "globalization" tendency is that this process is in practice almost inevitably accompanied by what the Soviets refer to as the "remilitarization" of Japan. Except for the unlikely case in which Japan would move away from the United States and/or closer to the USSR, Moscow would not welcome what they term the "remilitarization" of Japan.

This proves to be the case, particularly since Japan's effort to increase its defense forces is targeted almost exclusively against the threat from the Soviet Union. As the Soviets see it, "anti-Sovietism and militarism [in Japan] are intertwined into a single mass."[40] On the other hand, the Soviets are also probably correct to observe that the United States does not like to see Japan overly strong militarily either. What the United States persistently wants to see is Japan remaining as its faithful, junior partner with a reasonable, but never exceedingly large, amount of armament and, more importantly, supporting the framework of the U.S. global strategy. However, it seems to Soviet observers an almost inevitable and irreversible trend that Japan will accelerate its rearmament drive in the future toward the development of independent military forces. Factors which drive Japan in that direction are, in the Soviet view, the "weakening of the American guarantee for the security of Japan and U.S. credibility as perceived" and "shifting the forces of American attention to Western Europe and the Middle East."[41] Whatever the reasons are, Petrov notes: "The [Japanese] proponents of militarization state that Japan should rely on her own forces and build up her 'defensive capabilities,' i.e., her military potential."[42]

A salient feature of the Soviet campaign against "remilitarization" of Japan is its preventive character. What Moscow is concerned about is clearly not the present level of the Japanese Self-Defense Forces—which is almost insignificant compared with the Soviet military forces in terms of budget, size, and kinds of weaponry—but the potential that they may, unless prevented, grow into a strong military power in the future. I. Ivkov, presumably the pen name of Ivan Kovalenko, the deputy chief in the International Department of the CPSU in charge of Japanese affairs, candidly admitted in 1978 that "the process of militarization of Japan has not yet become all-embracing."[43] Having said this, however, Ivkov, along with other Soviet Japan and security specialists, hastens to call attention to the fact that Japan commands "advanced, up-to-date, the newest technology,"[44] which in their judgment, could be "quickly and easily switched, converted, or re-equipped to serve military purposes."[45] In short, Japan has, in the Soviet view, "a powerful military-industrial potential [*potentsial* or *vozmozhnost*], which makes it possible for the Japanese ruling circles, whenever necessary, to build up a multimillion man army and equip it with advanced military technology."[46] While stressing the potential power of Japan, the Soviets do not place much trust in the intentions of the Japanese government to keep its potential within a reasonable, limited scale.[47] According to the Soviets, the existence of the political capabilities—are almost automatically identified as the threat itself. This perception is in a marked contrast to the Japanese who perceive threat only when actual, not potential, military capability is linked with the adversary's intention to use coercion against Japan. In any event, what worries the Soviets is the direction in which Tokyo is moving and the traditional rapid speed of transformation of Japan once she sets her course. Lest it becomes too late to counter such a transformation of Japan, the Soviets seem determined to nip the "resurgence of Japanese militarism" in the bud.

One clever way of discouraging Japan from moving in the direction of "globalization" and "remilitarization," is the Soviet contention that "the Japanese are forgetting the lessons of history."[48] This theme is characteristic of a campaign, initiated in the Brezhnev era, in which Moscow called attention to the fact that "Japanese ruling classes in 1930s and 1940s dragged the otherwise peaceful and innocent Japanese people into the dangerous path of militarism, which finally culminated in the disaster of World War Two." I. Ivkov reminded the Japanese of the devastating consequences of the war: "The World War took a toll of two million Japanese and another eight million Japanese received heavy injuries. About one-third of the country's national wealth was destroyed. Japan was the first country to experience atomic bombings which took away 300,000 lives."[49] Having perhaps sympathetically underlined the misery that the Japanese public suffered from World War II, the message which the Soviets really want to convey to the Japanese is the warning that it is foolish and potentially devastating for the Japanese to forget such a traumatic experience as this. Dmitrii F. Ustinov, Soviet minister of defense, for example, accuses: "[Yet] revanchist forces [in Japan] are trying to bury in oblivion the tragic lessons of the last War and to persuade their country's people to support the idea of reviving Japan as a 'mighty military power.' "[50]

What is interesting to observe in this campaign is that Moscow has been warning that "lessons of the past" must be remembered not only by the Japanese but also by the Soviets, the Americans and all other people in the world. While demonstrating that "the Soviet people remember well the lessons of the last war [of Japanese militarism],"[51] the Soviets warn Americans, who they also believe would not like to see a militarist Japan, that "the United States cannot ignore the experience of history of Japan's militarism in the 1930s and 1940s, which led to Pearl Harbor,"[52] There is no need for us to recall that the circumstances of Japan and the world in the 1980s are quite different from those in the 1930s and 1940s; it is no easy matter to determine to what extent the lessons of the past can be applied to the contemporary period. These comparisons and analogies will, no more than in the past, prevent the Soviets from warning against the revival of Japanese militarism. What they are trying to exploit is obvious: the human propensity, in Western social scientists terms, to "overlearn from traumatic events" or to "learn too much from what happens to themselves" and to apply the "lessons of the past to the changed context."[53]

Improvement of Soviet–Japanese Relations Through Bargaining

Another major reaction to Moscow will be to reinforce efforts to improve its relations with Tokyo. Japan's rise in the international community has led the Soviets to revise somewhat their previous inclination to underestimate Japan, an assessment caused by their proclivity to evaluate other states primarily in terms of military capability. For their attempts to improve their relations with Japan, what means will be available to the Kremlin? This question seems quite relevant, due to the fact that what the Soviets will be able to do with regard to Tokyo is greatly influenced by the instruments at their disposal. It is appropriate, therefore, to identify and examine Soviet policy options toward Japan in terms of resources accessible to them. Let us start by examining those instruments which can be used as a carrot, leaving the stick for later discussion.

Trade and Fishing. There are few powerful and effective instruments available to Moscow to improve relationships with Tokyo. One conceivable instrument is of the economic variety. Generally speaking, the Soviets do not hesitate to use economic tools for noneconomic, political purposes. In other words, they often link political and economic issues. There appear to be good reasons for the Soviets to believe this tactic of linkage will work particularly well vis-à-vis Japan, given Japan's dependence on foreign energy and raw materials resources. In practice, however, this tactic has serious limitations, largely due to recent Soviet international adventures and poor economic performance. Consequently, it is the USSR and not so much Japan that needs more active promotion of trade and economic relations between the two countries. For example, it is not Tokyo but Moscow that has persistently proposed the conclusion of a long-term economic agreement with the purpose of stabilizing long-term bilateral trade relations between USSR and Japan. A Soviet call for a meeting of the Joint Japanese–Soviet Economic Conference, which has been suspended by Japan since 1979, is another illustration. Furthermore, it is appropriate to recall at this juncture that Japan has frozen its economic relations with the USSR as a part of the sanctions against the Soviet invasion of Afghanistan and pressure on Poland. True, this policy caused some losses to Japanese businessmen as well. However, unlike West Germany, where relatively small enterprises are engaged in trade with the USSR and hence the problem of unemployment is more threatening, comparatively large corporations are dealing with the Soviet Union in Japan, which means Japan does not necessarily need extensive business relations with the Soviet Union. Undoubtedly the Soviet Union has been suffering more than Japan from the sanctions. Having made the unusually candid remark that "now the Soviet Union finds itself in an economically difficult situation, due to, among other things, the sanctions by the United States and its allies," Nikolai S. Patolichev, Soviet minister of foreign trade, was quoted by the February 1983 Japanese business delegation to Moscow as asking that Japan cooperate in promoting improved trade relations with the USSR.[54] Instead of pursuing tactics of linking politics with economics, Moscow is nowadays advocating to Tokyo a policy of separating politics from economics.

Another instrument which appears to serve as a carrot is fishing rights. Fishing issues were previously manipulated skillfully by the Kremlin with the aim of inducing diplomatic concessions from the Japanese government and influencing its positions in other fields in Soviet favor. With the advent of the so-called "200-nautical-mile fishing zone" around 1976–1977, however, they ceased to play such a role any longer. To begin with, the USSR was adversely affected (to a greater degree than Japan) by the implementation of 200-mile fishing zones. As a result, the Soviet Union has not taken a generous policy toward Japan regarding the question of fishing quotas in its coastal waters. Based on the so-called "principle of equal quota," what Moscow and Tokyo agreed, for instance, are total fishing quotas of 700,000 and 640,000 tons, respectively for Japanese and Russian fishermen within the other's 200-mile zone. Whereas the Japanese quota became about half of the previous one of 1,220,000 tons, the Soviet quota has remained the same or even increased above the former level of 500,000–600,000 tons. Furthermore, in an exchange of a 60,000 ton difference, the Japanese side has been paying the USSR a fee in foreign currency, which the Soviet Union badly needs. As these quotas have become almost a stable standard acceptable for both the USSR and Japan, the Japan-Soviet negotiations on fishing rights have recently become pro forma, almost ceremonial, lasting only about ten days.[55] Thus, the fishing issue has ceased to be a serious source of dispute or a resource for manipulation by the Soviets.

Northern Territories. The territorial issue is the most effective political instrument which can be exploited by the Kremlin. The Northern Territories, that is, the four islands just off Hokkaido, seized by the USSR at the end of World War II but claimed by the Japanese as their sovereign territory, constitute the primary stumbling block to any improvement in relations between the Soviet Union and Japan. In fact, the Japanese government regards the reversion of these islands to Japanese control as a sine qua non of any meaningful rapprochement and appears persistently determined to regain control of the islands. This provides Moscow with substantial bargaining leverage. And although the Soviet government has taken the official position that the territorial question is resolved once and for all, it is probable that the Soviet Union is simply waiting until it can utilize this bargaining card most effectively.

The Kremlin's ultimate goal with regard to Japan is to change Japan into a close and reliable ally in Asia, to such an extent that Moscow can manipulate Japan's domestic and foreign policy decisions and utilize fully her advanced technology and know-how to assist the Soviet economy. In exchange for such an alignment, what may be roughly labeled "Finlandization" of Japan, the Kremlin would be pleased to readily give the Northern Islands to Japan, an exchange of Japan's four big industrialized islands for the four tiny northern, barren islands. The next basic scenario the Kremlin hopes for is one in which Tokyo would move away from the United States and pursue equidistant diplomacy vis-à-vis Washington and Moscow. In order to encourage and even push Japan to move into such a diplomatically neutral or non-aligned direction, the Soviet government under Chernenko and his successors might also agree to the return of two, if not all the Northern Islands to Japan as an incentive. It may be useful to recall in this connection that in 1955 the Soviet government under

Khrushchev agreed to withdrawal of Soviet military forces from Austria on the condition among other things, that Austria would become a neutral state. To be sure, historical analogies must be drawn very carefully, as Ernest R. May warns in *"Lessons" of the Past,*[56] but this scenario should not be completely ruled out.

The third or minimum objective of the Soviet government with regard to Japan is to let Tokyo stop, or reduce the magnitude of, its anti-Soviet campaign and increasing military cooperation with the United States. In order to achieve this goal, Moscow would be glad to sign a peace treaty with Tokyo, giving to Japan only two islands, that is, the Habomai Islands and the Island of Shikotan, as stipulated in Article 9 of the Soviet–Japanese Joint Declaration. The Soviet government has officially denied the validity of Article 9 since Japan renewed its security treaty with the United States in 1961. The Soviet government was so displeased by this commitment to the Western camp that it took the position that the Japanese side could no longer expect the USSR to fulfill its pledge to transfer the two islands. However, chances are that Moscow will go back to this compromise formula again, because it will need a peace treaty and good relations with Tokyo far more than in the past.

Accommodation with China

In his *Politics Among Nations,* Hans J. Morgenthau suggests that nations have three choices in order to maintain their relative power positions: (1) they can withhold the power of other nations from the adversary; (2) they can add their own power to the power of other nations; and (3) they can increase their own power.[57] We have already discussed the Soviet's possible resort to the first method, that is, their increasing effort to separate Japan from the United States and other members of the Western community, but the Soviet Union will probably not succeed in its attempt to divide and rule. Consequently, it will be tempted to resort to the second and third choices suggested above by Morgenthau.

One objective which the Soviet Union considers desirable and feasible in its attempt to preserve Morgenthau's second alternative is to form an alliance with the People's Republic of China (PRC). Evidently Japan is another, and perhaps even better, candidate to become a Soviet ally. And, in fact, during his last years in office, Brezhnev made almost identical appeals to both China and Japan, apparently believing that either country's acceptance of the invitation would be a great achievement. These appeals were best illustrated by Brezhnev's overtures at the Twenty-Sixth CPSU Congress in February–March 1981[58] and at Tashkent in March 1982.[59] As could readily be predicted, however, Japan categorically turned down these overtures. In contrast, China has shown a much more positive reaction.[60] Encouraged by the far more receptive responses from Beijing, the Soviets seem to have decided to work first with China, leaving Japan until later, illustrated by Brezhnev's speech at Baku in September 1982.[61] The Soviet strategy appears to be one of making a breakthrough first with Beijing, and then to do the same with regard to Japan. Brezhnev's successors have also demonstrated that they will not only continue, but will also pursue with greater boldness and at a quicker pace than their predecessor this strategy of normalizing relations with the PRC with the aim of isolating Japan and the United States.[62]

The reconciliation of differences with Beijing would bring a number of benefits to Moscow. In addition to improving the position of the Soviet Union in the world and particularly in Asia, Sino–Soviet rapprochement would end the possible formation of a Washington–Tokyo–Beijing axis targeted against Moscow, thereby providing Moscow with a way out of its awkward isolation in Asia. Moreover, it would enable the Soviet Union to increase its bargaining power vis-à-vis Japan and the United States. In the military-strategic field, accommodation with Beijing would also provide Moscow great relief and help. If the presence of the whole or parts of "one million Soviet troops" (in the words of China's paramount leader, Deng Xiaoping) along the Sino–Soviet border ceased to be necessary and the number were reduced, it would help the USSR lessen its military burden as well as financial costs. The Kremlin could threaten the West, including Japan, since the troops and SS-20s formerly stationed on the Sino–Soviet border could be transferred elsewhere. It is possible that a Sino–Soviet detente would deprive Japan of economic profit and that the USSR could use this possibility as a threat. It is a well-known fact that the trade between the USSR and the PRC has been growing at rapid speed in the past several years. According to Vladimir N. Sushkov, a deputy minister of foreign trade, these two countries are expecting an increase in two-way trade in 1983 to about one billion dollars, a threefold increase over 1982.[63] Furthermore, if the Soviet Union were to invite a number of Chinese workers to Siberia and the Soviet Far East, one of the major bottlenecks for economic development in these regions—the shortage of labor—would be resolved. This development might reinforce Soviet leverage over Japan.[64]

At the same time, however, rapprochement between the PRC and the Soviet Union would not bring to Japan (or to the United

States) solely adverse effects. Rapprochement or normalization is a relative term, and the following three variants may be distinguished: a repair of state-to-state relations; further accommodation with some substantial breakthrough or compromise formula on disputed issues; genuine rapprochement with the resurrection or establishment of the Sino–Soviet alliance.[65] In each of these variants, the impact of improved Sino–Soviet relations upon Japan (and sometimes upon the United States) would not be so severe as one might first suspect. Let us consider each of these three alternatives in greater detail.

To begin with, a limited degree of relaxation of Sino–Soviet tensions which, according to some Western observers has already started, is a normal and even desirable development.[66] Since April 1980, a year after China publicly announced its intention to abrogate the 1950 Sino–Soviet treaty of alliance, the PRC and the USSR have no treaties or agreements to regulate their relations. This is a dangerous situation. It is, therefore, quite natural and understandable for these two powers to make efforts to achieve the normalization of state-to-state relations, with the aim of reducing tensions between them. Otherwise there is an ever-present possibility that frictions and clashes along the disputed frontiers might trigger an all-out Sino–Soviet war, from which no one could profit.[67] In this regard, a minimal level of Sino–Soviet reduction of tensions is beneficial to all nations in the world, not only the United States and Japan.

Even if Sino–Soviet relations went beyond rapprochement, such a development would still bring some benefits to Japan. Namely, if Moscow and Beijing stopped antagonizing each other to the extent that neither of them would criticize the other's conduct of foreign policy, Tokyo would be able to return to a policy of evenhandedness between Moscow and Beijing. Then, Japan would be able to assist with the construction of the Baikal–Amur Mainline (BAM) through financial and technical cooperation, which has to date been at least partially obstructed by the opposition of Beijing. Likewise, Tokyo would be able to extend more economic and technological assistance to the PRC, without worrying about reactions or interference from the Soviet side. Moreover, if the talks on the disputed borders between the USSR and the PRC should some way find a formula of "adjustments," it might help the Soviets become more flexible with regard to the Japanese request of negotiating on the Northern Islands, which the Soviets have adamantly refused.

It is well known that the Chinese side has repeatedly mentioned that three obstacles must be cleared before Beijing's relations with Moscow can be normalized. These obstacles are the presence of Soviet troops along the Sino–Soviet borders and in Mongolia, the Soviet intervention into Afghanistan, and Soviet help for Vietnamese troops occupying Kampuchea. Should a compromise formula be found for any one of these sensitive issues, the positive outcome would not only benefit the two countries concerned but undoubtedly would be shared widely by many other nations, including the United States and Japan. Removal of Soviet troops from Afghanistan, and Vietnamese withdrawal from Kampuchea, which the West has been unable to achieve despite its strenuous efforts, would be in the interest of the West and the countries concerned. Suggesting that a future Sino–Soviet detente could redound positively to the United States, Secretary of State George Shultz said in 1982, "If through their discussion, [Chinese leaders] can persuade the Soviet Union to get out of Afghanistan and, in effect, get out of Kampuchea, so much the better."[68] Reduction of Soviet forces facing China would be also helpful in reducing international tensions, providing they were not redeployed against Japan, Europe, or the Middle East.

The final point to be discussed is the implication of Sino–Soviet military alliance upon U.S.–Japan relations. Any step in the direction of such an alliance would certainly be met with deep and profound suspicion and fear by other countries. It could possibly restore a sense of Western unity and cause the United States to refocus its attention on the Asian region. Viewing itself as unable to control the possible formation of a Sino–Soviet alliance in Asia, the United States would press Japan harder to rearm substantially so that she could serve as an almost equal partner in the common defense against the Soviet Union and China.[69] As a result, Japan would become a very strong military power, which would be counterproductive to the Soviet Union, at least in part offsetting those benefits which accommodation with Beijing would bring to Moscow.

Military Buildup and Bluff

The final choice for the Kremlin is the third of Morgenthau's alternatives: to increase its own power capability, particularly its military potential. Almost without regard for the kind of foreign policy orientation Tokyo may take from now on, Moscow appears unlikely to stop its military buildup in the Far East and in the vicinity of Japan. It would be appropriate and useful to recall how Moscow responded to those major diplomatic actions which the Japanese government took in the late 1970s and early 1980s: signing of peace treaty with Beijing, reinforcement of the campaign for the return of the Northern Territories, and increased military cooperation with the United States. These steps were taken by the Japanese government as measures in its view necessary to protest and counter the unfriendly, uncooperative, and even aggressive attitude and behavior of the Soviet Union toward Japan. Of course, the Soviets do not accept such Japanese explanations or excuses. Regardless of which side has the more convincing rationale to justify its own account, what is interesting to observe is the fact that the Soviet Union reacted to each of these Japanese actions almost exclusively with further military buildup (redeployment of about one division of military forces on three of the Northern Islands, deployment of the *Minsk* and *Novorossivsk* and *Ivan Rogov* in their Pacific Fleet, deployment of Backfire bombers and SS-20 missiles, and so on).

Why, then, are the Soviets doing this? To begin with, the Soviets appear to be firmly convinced that there is a need for them to undertake military measures to cope with possible or actual formation of anti-Soviet military alliance by the United States, Japan, South Korea, and/or the PRC in Asia. It is also worth recalling that the Soviets are great believers in the political use of military might. Possibly based on their experiences in dealing with Japanese prisoners of war in Siberia, some Soviet party apparatchiki and high government officials in charge of Japanese affairs appear to still have the idea that the Japanese can be easily intimidated. It is debatable and doubtful that a bluff based on the buildup of military might is an appropriate means to apply to contemporary Japanese who tend to be impressed not so much by military achievement as by economic performance. However, since other effective instruments of influence are not available to Moscow for dealing with Japan, a strategy of bluffing ("waving the stick") will continue to be one of the major instruments of policy on which the Kremlin is likely to rely in the future.

The Kremlin's strategy for blackmailing Japan will be a combination of warning of the dangerous situation in which Japan would get involved, and "countermeasures" (*otvetnye mery*) the Soviet Union would take should its warning be ignored by Tokyo.[70] The Kremlin will continue to warn, in particular Tokyo, of the risk that would be inevitably brought about by Japan's increasing trend to militarism in alliance with the United States. Considering Japan as a country which is expected to play, in the U.S. strategy, the role of "a frontline base of the U.S. nuclear strategy," "arsenal of U.S. nuclear weapons," and "U.S. nuclear hostage," Moscow will keep threatening the Japanese with an admonition that "such a position will easily invite nuclear reprisal to Japan."[71] The remarks made by incumbent Japanese Prime Minister Nakasone during his trip to Washington on 17–20 January 1983, that Japan is "the unsinkable aircraft carrier" to check Soviet military buildup in the region brought a Soviet warning that Japan could be risking a Soviet attack with nuclear weapons.[72] The Soviet official news agency *Tass* on 19 January 1983, stated:

> The authors of such plans would make Japan a likely target for a response strike. And for such a densely populated, insular country as Japan, this could spell a national disaster more serious than the one that befell Japan thirty-seven years ago. This forces the Soviet Union, as has been stated repeatedly, to adopt appropriate measures [against Japan] to offset the emerging danger.[73]

Commenting again on this remark by Nakasone, Soviet Foreign Trade Minister N. Patolichev, even threatened the president of the Japanese Chamber of Commerce and head of the largest delegation of Japanese notables in the entire history of Soviet–Japanese trade, saying in February 1983: "The unsinkable aircraft carrier would sink in twenty minutes once the war occurred."[74]

What one must bear in mind is that the Soviet bluff is not simply an oral bluff but very frequently is accompanied by actual deeds. Take, for example, Moscow's warning in October 1982 of Soviet "appropriate measures" against Tokyo's decision to accept the U.S. plan to deploy in 1985 about 50 F-16 jet fighters at the Japanese base Misawa. As early as December 1982, the Soviets replaced its supersonic fighter-bombers (MIG-17s) with more sophisticated aircraft (MIG-21s) on Etorofu, one of the disputed Northern Islands, an action which was interpreted by U.S. analysts as one of these Soviet measures.[75] A clearer countermeasure was made public in January 1983, when General Secretary Yuriy V. Andropov and Foreign Minister Andrei A. Gromyko were reported as having said that the Soviet Union would "redeploy to the Soviet Far East some of the SS-20 medium range missiles which might exceed the agreed-upon quota for the European zone, in order to counter a military base at Misawa in Japan."[76] In addition to these events, the Soviet shoot-down of Korean Air Lines flight 007 with 269 passengers, including twenty-eight Japanese, served to clarify in the minds of the Japanese the realities of Soviet policy in Northeast Asia. In particular, the KAL incident underscored the extraordinary and deep-seated Soviet obsession with the security of their borders and the perceived military-strategic importance to the Soviets of the Sea of Okhotsk area. More broadly, this incident revealed that the Soviet Union is willing to use its military forces as a coercive physical means and not simply as an adjunct to its diplomatic-political instruments of statecraft.

Major Determinants of Soviet Policy toward Japan

The number of factors that influence Soviet foreign policymaking seems boundless.[77] Any factor that exerts influence in one way or another on the making of Soviet foreign policy decisions can be regarded as one of its determinants. According to one Soviet writer, the following variables are seen at work as determinants of foreign policy: historical traditions, standards of political behavior, geographical conditions, demographic characteristics, religious, cultural, and psychological factors.[78] If searching for the determinants of Soviet foreign policy can be likened to searching for the proverbial needle in the haystack, the problem in searching for the determinants of Soviet policy toward Japan is that there is no haystack in which to search.[79] And yet these difficulties do not excuse us from trying to do our best in our efforts to detect which independent factors and variables are more relevant than others. In this section of the paper, I will examine what I consider to be the principal determinants of Soviet foreign policy.

Ideology

"Ideology" remains an elusive term and may be interpreted in such a broad way as "a set of beliefs, values, traditions" and operational codes.[80] But, if we understand it in a much narrower sense to mean Marxism–Leninism, ideology is not likely to play a particularly significant role in Soviet future actions and reactions to Japan. One of the major goals of Marxism–Leninism is transformation of the world along socialist lines. But this ultimate goal has ceased to be a dominant determinant of Soviet foreign policy behavior. Among other things, the pragmatic post-Brezhnev leadership must be aware of the fact that a socialist Japan would not necessarily bring much profit to them. Japan under a socialist economy would be far less efficient, less productive, and hence, less useful. Under these conditions, a socialist Japan would be a greater burden to the USSR than a capitalist Japan. Politically, it might become a source of trouble to Moscow in terms of the international communist movement, as socialist China or the Eurocommunist countries have been. Rather, it will be more desirable for the Soviet Union to continue relations of peaceful coexistence and economic cooperation with capitalist Japan. Recognizing this, some Soviets have advocated the continuation of a policy of peaceful coexistence as the guiding principle of Soviet foreign policy toward Japan. For example, Timofey Guzhenko, Soviet minister of the maritime fleet and chairman of the Soviet–Japan Society, stressed at the third Soviet–Japan roundtable held in Tokyo on 20–22 April 1982: "Despite the difference in social systems, cool consideration of the objective necessity of peaceful coexistence between the USSR and Japan has helped these two countries achieve concensus on the isues of cooperation, including a series of difficult questions."[81] There is no reason to assume that the Kremlin will drastically change this policy of coexistence with Japan in the foreseeable future.

Thus Marxist–Leninist ideology per se appears unlikely to constitute an insurmountable obstacle for the Kremlin leaders in making a deal with Japan. If there is any obstacle in this field, it would not be Marxist–Leninist ideology in itself but rather the embodiment of the ideology, that is, the Soviet system. The Soviet political and socioeconomic system has had, and continues to have, adverse effects upon the USSR's relations with Japan. For instance, the totalitarian political regime of the USSR will continue to be threatening enough to deter Japan from seeking a closer relationship. The planned economy (still excessively centralized, despite some possible reform under Andropov and Chernenko) and completely state monopolized trade, coupled with bureaucratic inefficiency and secretiveness will also discourage Japanese businessmen and government officials from seeking closer trade and economic relations, unless they have no other choice in their efforts to diversify Japan's sources of raw materials and energy resources or are driven to desperation to find a way out of severe economic depression.

Geopolitical and Military-Strategic Factors

Recent dramatic developments in science, technology, transportation, and communication have been overcoming physical and geographical barriers and handicaps to a remarkable degree and at great speed.[82] Yet some geographic factors remain significant and will continue to play an important role in international politics for some time to come.

The history of Russia illustrates well that country's desire for warm-water seaports and access to the ocean. In this regard, geographically located at important exits to the Pacific, Japan occupies a vital position for the USSR. On 2 September 1945, the day Soviet forces seized Shikotan and the Habomai Islands, Josef Stalin proudly declared that "henceforth, the Kuril Islands shall not serve as a means to cut off the Soviet Union from the ocean or as a base for a Japanese attack on our Far East."[83] In practice, however, both Soviet navy and merchant vessels can go in and out of Pacific waters only by free passage through three straits, that is, Tsushima, Tsugaru, and Soya (La Perouse). This means that if these strategic straits should be closed for any reason (for example, antiship mines), Soviet ships would be confined to the Sea of Okhotsk or the Sea of Japan and passage into the Pacific would become difficult if not impossible. This is, of course, the worst scenario for the Soviet Union, and illustrates how crucial it is for the USSR to keep the route open and available. The geographic and strategic significance of Japan to Soviet ambitions and interests in East Asia and the Pacific region leads to two contradictory Soviet approaches toward Japan. On the one hand, if the Soviet leaders are to a substantial degree rational decision-makers, they would view it essential to attempt to build good and friendly relations with Tokyo in exchange for some concessions on their side, including the return of the Northern Islands. On the other hand, the Soviet leaders would be tempted to not only make firmer its possession of these islands but also even dare to seize Hokkaido so that free passage of the Soviet ships through the Soya straits could be guaranteed.

Geographic proximity quite frequently gives rise to conflict over various issues such as demarcation of borders, territorial waters, economic fishing zones, distribution of underwater resources, emigration, and military security. Japanese–Soviet relations are no exception to this rule, and, as previously noted, the problem of the Northern Territories question constitutes a stumbling block for improving bilateral relations between these two neighboring countries. The major reason why the Kremlin will not assent to the reversion of the territories to Japan can be assumed to lie in the geopolitical value the region holds in terms of Soviet military strategy vis-à-vis the United States and Japan. The islands are situated at the very points which control passage from the Pacific Ocean into the Sea of Okhotsk. On two occasions—1952 and 1964—Nikita Khrushchev unintentionally revealed the real Soviet interest in the area, saying: "It should be kept in mind that, for us, these Islands are of small economic importance but of great strategic, and defensive (*strategicheskoe, oboronnoe*) importance."[84] There are signs that the Chernenko government has built, and will continue to build, a huge military-industrial complex along the Sea of Okhotsk, spanning Siberia, Sakhalin, Kamchatka, and the Kurile Islands. Submarine-launched ballistic missiles (SLBMs) already based in the sea of Okhotsk region have a range that covers almost every part of the United States. On the other hand, however, the Soviet military buildup in the Sea of Okhotsk area has crucial strategic vulnerabilities as well. Owing to advanced anti-submarine warfare technology, the United States could track all SLBM-equipped Soviet submarines. In order to prevent such tracking, it is, therefore, vital to the Soviets that they turn the Sea of Okhotsk into an inland sea, open to themselves alone. Above all, it was with the aim of making the Sea of Okhotsk a sanctuary that the Soviet Union has stationed ground troops on three islands in the Northern Territories—Etorofu, Kunashiri, and Shikotan. It is precisely this geographical and military-strategic consideration that has been made, and continues to make, Soviet leaders hold on to the territories even at the expense of what might otherwise be gained.

Economics

Marxism–Leninism is an ideology based on the doctrine of material determinism with special emphasis upon economic stratification. Successive Kremlin foreign policymakers have attached particular weight to economic determinants of Soviet policy. For example, Lenin stated that "the very deepest roots of both the internal and foreign policy of our state are shaped by economic interests."[85] Brezhnev also stressed at the Twenty-Sixth Party Congress (1981) that "precisely in the field of economics lie the fundamentals of active foreign policy."[86] No need to be reminded, however, that official pronouncements are one thing and actual practice is quite another in Soviet politics. That is to say, what is really relevant to this analysis is the answer to the question: To what extent do economic factors in reality influence Soviet foreign policy toward Japan?

Among Western Sovietologists and even Soviet politicians there seems to be consensus that the Soviet Union will face a difficult economic situation in the 1980s, in practically all sectors, that is, capital, energy, labor, management, agriculture, and technology. In his last public speech, addressed to Soviet military leaders on 27 October 1982, Leonid I. Brezhnev frankly acknowledged: "There are difficulties and shortcomings. Metal, fuel and transport continue to be bottlenecks . . . The situation in capital construction is improving slowly . . . A great deal of work is being done in agriculture in order to eliminate in the future the need for grain purchases abroad."[87] How difficult the economic situation in the Soviet Union will be is a matter of conjecture. According to the worst-case scenario, it will be an economic crisis, and even according to more optimistic scenarios, the Soviet Union will face economic stagnation far more severe than in the 1970s.[88] It appears there are three options to prevent the Soviet economy from getting worse.[89] One is what can be termed "systemic" reform, requiring fundamental changes in the Soviet economic system. Should such reform be conducted, it would be advantageous for the Japanese economy, which can always use an additional large market and trade partner. However, it is difficult to speculate whether the Soviet government under Chernenko or his successors will dare to undertake such a bold, revolutionary reform as the systemic reform of its economy.

The second option is "within system" reform involving some organizational and institutional changes which fall far short of changing the Soviet socialist system. The post-Brezhnev governments have tried to implement the second option, as demonstrated by the steps already undertaken (for example, a campaign against corruption, tightening of labor discipline and morale, promises of more material incentives and more independent decision-making in enterprises and collective firms). When Yuriy Andropov delivered his first major policy speech before the CPSU Central Committee on 22 November 1982, he spoke of the need to "take account of the experience of fraternal countries" in revitalizing the Soviet economy.[90] He could have meant the Hungarian or other East European economies but certainly not the capitalist economies. It is debatable to what extent these within system reforms will exert a favorable impact upon the stagnated and declining Soviet economy. After discussing the Soviet economy's existing numerous deficiencies and intractable problems, Andropov himself candidly acknowledged in the same speech that he "does not have ready recipes for their solution."[91] Undoubtedly the USSR is a resource-rich country, but natural resources become economic assets only when they are successfully and efficiently extracted and utilized. The problem for the Soviet Union is that it alone cannot extract the natural resources in Siberia and the Far East cheaply and rapidly enough, a fact that has led Soviet leaders to consider a third option.

The third option is to drastically increase the Soviet economy's dependence upon foreign technology, capital, and labor resources beyond the magnitude which the Soviet Union under Brezhnev depended upon them. Under this option, the Soviet Union would become a resource-supplying country in exchange for advanced technology and products, a situation which would be psychologically humiliating but which would enable it to grow without changing its economic system. In any case, what is relevant to our context is that the importance of Japan, the second largest economic power in the world, will then loom large for the USSR. Recently Soviet leaders have revealed openly that they cannot afford to develop the European part of the country, Western Siberia, Eastern Siberia, and the Soviet Far East at the same time.[92] Faced with labor problems and an almost insurmountable shortage of technology and capital investment, the

Soviets have been forced to concentrate on redeveloping the first area, while relying on Western countries to help them develop the second area.[93] The point is that in both areas the Soviets badly need the advanced technology, such as oil well drilling technology, from the West.[94] Unless they are able to obtain such technology, they will be unable to redevelop the first area, not to mention developing the second. In the second area, the Soviets need the active participation of Japan more than that of other countries. The geographic proximity of the two countries naturally makes Japan the ideal economic partner to provide the capital, technology, and the market for the resources of the area. The problem of rising transportation costs generated by escalating oil prices makes Japan a particularly attractive trading partner. In addition, Japan is the best market for Sakhalin offshore oil and gas. And as far as the Baikal–Amur Mainline railroad goes, even when it is finally completed it will take many years to pay off the investment unless Japan contributes. As Professor Allen Whiting has written in his book *Siberian Development and East Asia: Threat or Promise:*

> Japan must weigh heavily in Moscow's decision on the development of East Asia Siberia. Japanese capital and technology are essential in attaining the desired goals of resources extraction and economic expansion. Japan also offers the only markets of significance for exports like timber, coal and gas. Without that market the production of East Asia Siberia have little chance of earning foreign exchange to serve the overall Soviet economy. Japan thus occupies a central position in Moscow's calculations, in inputs as well as outputs.[95]

Such a vital or essential role as Japanese economic and technological potentialities could play for the Soviet economy has often tempted some Western observers to draw rather sweeping conclusions. For example, Seweryn Bialer has gone so far as to make the bold prediction that the Soviets could court Japan by returning to the Japan–Soviet Joint Declaration of 1956 which would "allow the return of the southernmost Kurile Islands to Japan in return for new Japanese agreement to help develop Siberia."[96] However, what an otherwise very astute observer on Soviet conduct of foreign affairs is neglecting when it comes to Soviet behavior in the Far East is that the economy is not the sole determinant of Soviet foreign policy, precisely the point that Professor Bialer has made elsewhere.[97]

The Decision-making Structure

"Inept," "counterproductive," "very unimaginative, if not stupid," "almost a total disaster," or "diplomatic failure" are adjectives which have been frequently used to describe Soviet foreign policy toward Japan. If Moscow really appreciates the geographic, economic, and diplomatic importance of Japan to the Soviet Union, there are many ways by which it could do a much better job vis-à-vis Tokyo. Yet, Moscow has kept doing exactly what it is not supposed to do, and Soviet leaders have often ended up seeing precisely what it does not want to see take place. Tokyo's signing a peace treaty with Beijing, the reawakening of the Soviet threat and defense-consciousness among Japanese, revitalizing the movement for the return of the Northern Islands, increasing military cooperation with the United States—these are some examples of recent Japanese behavior which were, at least in the Japanese view, either directly caused or at least accelerated by Soviet attitudes or conduct toward Japan.

Part of the possible answer to the question of why Soviet Japan policy has been counterproductive or self-defeating seems to lie in the structure of Soviet foreign policymaking. As a result of private conversations with Soviet specialists on Japan, many Japanese and American foreign policy experts have concluded that some Soviet specialists are aware of the fact that Soviet actions toward Japan have not been intelligent and effective. Official denials notwithstanding, they know, for example, that there is a territorial problem in Japan's claim to the Northern Islands. Moreover, they recognize that the impasse on this issue serves Chinese and U.S. objectives insofar as it inhibits a Soviet–Japanese rapprochement.[98] The problem is, however, that Japan specialists in the USSR do not have much influence upon the Kremlin's policymakers toward Japan. They are researchers with such research institutes in the USSR's Academy of Sciences as the Institute of Oriental Studies, the Institute of Far Eastern Studies, the Institute of World Economy and International Relations (IMEMO), and the Institute for the Study of the U.S.A. and Canada. Referring to researchers in these institutes (*institutniki*) or to international relations analysts (*mezhudunarodniki*) at other Soviet Academy of Sciences research institutes, Dimitri K. Simes, formerly a researcher at IMEMO and now a senior associate with the Carnegie Endowment for International Peace in the U.S., provides an answer to the question of why their influence on policymaking will remain severely constrained in the future: "First, they are somewhat outside the institutional decision-making process. Most of their staffers are not cleared for classified work. . . . Second, while many key officials at the Institute have come from the Central Committee apparatus, the Foreign Ministry and the KGB, there are few instances of scholars moving to important party and government jobs."[99] Simes concludes that "those institute personnel . . . are . . . used as advisors rather than as policymakers. The bureaucratic distinction between consultants and apparatchiki is much more marked and important in the Soviet Union than in the American case."[100]

From her own experience as a specialist in Japanese affairs, Galina Orionova, another defector from the Institute for the Study of the U.S.A. and Canada, provides an intriguing espisode in 1978 which helps understand how the party disregards information from academic sources. She explained that scholars from various institutions met to consider the Sino–Japanese rapprochement. All agreed that it was mistaken policy to "treat the Japanese as inferior," that "they were not militarist" and had a right "to deal with China on their own terms." However, the party ignored the scholars' advice. Orionova thought it unlikely that more than 2 percent of the material was read by anyone of importance. Through one of her colleagues married to a man who worked for the Party Central Committee, Orionova learned that documents from academic institutions go straight into the wastebasket.[101]

Ivan Kovalenko, deputy chief in the Party's International Department, currently occupies the highest position in the CPSU held by a Japanologist. He has been identified as the "commander-in-chief" of Soviet policymaking toward Japan. However, as Professor John Stephan of the University of Hawaii has written, there is no means of detecting to what extent Kovalenko influences the Soviet top leadership's policy decisions toward Japan.[102] Kovalenko's influence upon Soviet Japan policy seems to be smaller than that of Mikhail Kapitsa, a Sinologist and one of the Soviet deputy foreign ministers for Soviet China policy. Kovalenko was in charge of public relations and communist education of Japanese prisoners of war in Siberia and he appears to Japanese who have met him to hold the notion that the Japanese are easily intimidated. This is an out-of-date notion, because the Japanese have fully recovered from World War II and have regained a national sense of confidence. Many Japanese believe that as long as Kovalenko or someone who shares his outdated views occupies an important position in Soviet policymaking with respect to Japan, the possibility of improvement of bilateral relations will be slim.

The Soviet World View

The mind-set of individual decision-makers is an important variable that influences Soviet foreign policy behavior. It is an amorphous, elusive, amalgam of many elements: values, beliefs, images, and even psychological dispositions. Nobody knows exactly how or why Soviet leaders make decisions. In fact, Soviet decision-makers themselves probably do not know the complete answer to this question. The answer undoubtedly varies over time, depending upon issues and circumstances. Judging from what Soviet leaders have said and what they have done, however, it is not impossible to detect what kinds of things matter to Soviet decision-makers most.

There are many characteristics of the mind-set of Soviet political leaders which make them relatively distinct from their counterparts in other countries. In this chapter, however, there is only enough space to discuss the one that seems the most relevant subject matter: the Soviets' belief in power—particularly Soviet over-confidence in the convertability of military force into substantial political influence. One of the core principles of Soviet operational code appears to be the belief that life is a constant, ruthless struggle, in which the stronger wins over the weaker, a belief summarized in the Russian phrase *Kto kvo?*, which can be translated as "Who will destroy whom?"[103]

In explaining how people of the Soviet Union and of the United States differ so greatly in their attitudes toward power, Hedrick Smith quotes the following from the Soviet dissident, Pavel Litvinov: "You should understand that the leaders and the ordinary people [of the Soviet Union] have the same authoritarian frame of mind. Brezhnev and the simple person both think that might is right. That's all. It's not a question of ideology."[104] The Russians like the "*krepkii khoziain*" (strong master) such as Stalin and the strong country, such as the United States, and despise weak leaders, such as Khrushchev and the small countries.[105] As Dimitri Simes put it: "The Russians have a traditional respect for power."[106] Smith conveys his surprise, when hearing a Swedish diplomat talk about this Russian trait and vent his bitter frustration at the short shrift given Sweden and other small nations by Moscow: "The Russians respect power. They deal with you Americans with respect because you have power, because there is something behind your words. But they don't deal with us that way. We're not powerful. We're a 'little' country."[107]

The Soviets think of Japan as a small country without any raw materials. Dmitrii Petrov, a Soviet Japanologist, has observed: " . . . extraordinary poverty in natural resources makes the Japanese economy exclusively dependent upon foreign trade . . . Here lies one of the problems of Japan."[108] He also points out the military weakness of Japan: "Japan, in size of armed forces, quality of military techniques, size of military budget and all other indices, cannot be compared to the USA and countries of the 'Common Market.' Japan does not have her own atomic weapons nor independently decided strategic problems."[109] These observations and remarks were made in 1973. During the period since that time, Japan has undergone such a tremendous transformation that much of Petrov's assessment is out of date. Japan has overcome the 1973–1974 "oil shock," surpassed the Soviet economy in terms of industrialized output, and is considered to have the capacity to surpass even the United States in some areas of economic performance in the near future. Owing to such economic accomplishments by Japan, it appears, as the Soviets have recently come to realize, that a lack of natural resources is not necessarily a handicap for the Japanese. The Soviets are now even eager to learn from the Japanese economy and management to cure their inefficient, unproductive economy. When it comes to the military field, however, the Soviet assessment of Japan still remains low. The Soviets believe that without nuclear weapons of her own Japan is not yet a full-fledged independent military power. Petrov thus remarked in 1981: "Today and in the near future Japan will be unable independently to resolve strategic problems and conduct offensive large-scale operations."[110]

In the Soviet perception and in the Soviets' list of foreign policy priorities, the United States still occupies the most important position—so much so that Moscow does not seem to realize even the need to develop a policy oriented toward Japan alone. Underlining that Soviet Japan policy is nothing other than a function, or almost automatic extension, of Soviet global strategy, Basil Dmytryshyn, a professor at Portland State University, holds that the Soviets simply do not have a clear, distinct, positive policy toward Japan. Offers which they have made have been only "spinoffs of Soviet policy toward the United States and/or toward China."[111] Such an interpretation seems to be still valid, and receives endorsement even from Soviet spokesmen. Yuriy Bandura, former Tokyo correspondent and currently deputy director of the international department of *Izvestiia,* for example, writes in his article contributed to the Japanese periodical *Jiyu* (Freedom) as follows: "The title prepared for my article by the Japanese editor, i.e., 'What Does the Soviet Union Want from Japan,' is misleading and somewhat perplexes me, because there is nothing that can be specifically called a Soviet policy toward Japan which is aimed solely at Japan among Soviet foreign policy goals. . . . Even when concrete questions regarding Japan are being considered, they are based on the general line of foreign policy adapted for the party and government."[112]

The basic strategy of Soviet foreign policy seems to be "let us do business with the United States first, leaving a short while for the others at the later stages." In a list of Soviet foreign policy priorities, the global-scale confrontation with the United States occupies the primary and highest place. [113] Relations with Japan, in contrast, take a secondary place in that list, subordinated to the primary objective of struggle with the United States. The Soviets appear to believe that whether or not the USSR does good job vis-à-vis the United States on the global level more or less determines its interactions with other countries in other regions. More concretely, if the USSR happens to lose the battle with the major adversary, the United States, it would almost mean that there would no longer be any use for the Soviets to make much effort elsewhere. Conversely, if it could win the major battle with the United States, it would make its victory or success in other areas a lot easier, or even automatic. Only within such a framework of Soviet perception of current world situations—and concomitant strategy in international affairs—can we explain why the Soviet Union has maintained a counterproductive position toward Japan. Namely, they firmly believe in or expect final victory over their arch opponent, the United States, so the Soviet leaders do not care much in the meantime about their temporary losses or failures in diplomacy toward Japan.

However, Soviet strategy toward Japan is based on premises which are wrong, unrealistic, or increasingly out-of-date, including the belief that the role of military strength carries extraordinary weight in assessing the "correlation of forces" (*sootnosheniie sil*)[114] and the belief that the United States is the major and almost exclusive concern of Soviet diplomacy. It thus becomes necessary, if the Soviets are to be successful in their conduct of Soviet foreign policy toward Japan, that the Soviets undergo, above all, a kind of mental reprogramming—for instance, a transformation from obsession with military strength to a more nonmilitary (such as economic, scientific-technological, or psychological) oriented mentality. Having undergone such a mental transformation, the Soviet leaders could realize more than now the urgency of forming a distinct foreign policy toward Japan, a policy which is not simply an extension of their U.S. strategy but one independent enough to be distinguishable from it, taking full account of specific conditions of Japanese–Soviet relations. Such a transformation or modification of traditional perceptions, values and images is, of course, difficult to effect and cannot be done overnight.

The Interaction of the Determinants of Soviet Foreign Policy

In the preceding pages we have sought to identify those variables which the author regards as the principal factors that influence Soviet foreign policy toward Japan. What is the relationship among these variables? How and to what degree does each of these factors exert an influence on Soviet policy toward Japan and under what conditions and during which time period?[115] These are naturally the next and probably more important questions to be asked. Unfortunately, however, these are questions which can never be answered accurately and convincingly enough.[116] As Professor Alexander Dallin, who has written several seminal articles on the subject of the domestic determinants of Soviet foreign policy, has concluded, there is "no technique or methodology that permits us to assign weights to the ingredients in the mix."[117] The interrelationship between ingredients remains by definition in a state of constant flux, varying over time and contingent upon issues and circumstances.[118] Once realizing that there is no methodology for defining the interconnection among variables, probably the best we can do is speculate, that is to say, attempt to intuitively and impressionistically make some assessment and judgments (subject to revision) regarding Soviet future action.[119]

The major Soviet policy aims toward Japan seem to be as follows: (1) to prevent closer Japanese ties with the United States, Western Europe, and the PRC, and to keep the Sino–Japanese Peace Treaty from turning into a military pact, thereby forming a de facto anti-Soviet military alliance among the United States, Japan, and the PRC; (2) to thwart security consciousness or "resurgence of militarist tendencies" in Japan; (3) to encourage Japan to separate its political differences with the Soviets from their economic goals so as to gain Japan's participation in trade and joint economic development in Siberia and the Far East on a much larger scale and for longer periods of time; and (4) to contain what the Soviets have termed the "unjustified and unlawful" Japanese demands for the Northern Territories and keep them from hindering favorable Soviet–Japanese relations. As readily seen, these aims are incompatible with one another. For instance, the hard-line stance of the Soviets on the territorial question negates other objectives, namely the goals to draw Japan into closer political and economic cooperation with the USSR; to weaken Japanese relations with the United States; to prevent the mutual cooperation of Japan, the West, particularly the United States and China; and to prevent Japanese anti-Soviet defense consciousness from getting awakened and reinforced. Despite these obvious incongruities among the objectives, Moscow has arduously insisted on pursuing these four major objectives simultaneously. Moreover, the means employed by Moscow to achieve these goals, particularly the stress placed on military leverage, has proved to be self-defeating. Since the end of World War II the Japanese have been extraordinarily naive and insensitive to the problem of their national security and military threats from other countries. However, in observing the heavy-handed attitudes and coercive policies of the USSR, and in particular, their reliance on military force to achieve ends, the Japanese have gradually come to suspect Soviet motivations and to look for ways to maintain their own security.[120]

If the observation is accepted as an accurate picture of recent Soviet foreign policy toward Japan, it does seem to suggest that, among other things, Soviet foreign policy has not been made and conducted rationally, carefully calculating gains and losses.[121] What then does this mean to our present concern of assessing the relative weight of each of the variables? It means that first, economic variables do not weigh heavily in Moscow's foreign policymaking toward Tokyo; second, such intangible factors as the Japanese sentiment toward the lost Northern Territories and anti-Soviet feeling play far less significant roles; third, the weight of such intangible and nonrational elements as the Soviet inclination to view the power of a nation in military terms and hence to underestimate the power of Japan as a state and a nation, that is, the inertia of the Soviet decision-making process, weighs quite heavily.

However, the weight each variable is assigned to play in Soviet policy toward Japan is subject to change over time. To be sure, it will continue to be an error to equate the USSR's urgent economic necessity for the import of high technology and Siberian development with its willingness for diplomatic compromise in other areas (like the territorial dispute with Japan).[122] Yet it is reasonable to assume that in the long run the economic consideration will increase its weight in the foreign policy decision toward Japan. It is naive to expect that the Soviets will come to regard it more beneficial to return the Northern Islands to Japan in exchange for such an intangible factor as pro-Soviet feeling among the Japanese, as the United States did in the reversion of Okinawa. In the long run, however, the Soviets will gradually change their perceptions of and attitudes toward Japan so that the weight of such factors as economic and technological capabilities of the Japanese will gain relative weight in their foreign policy formation. The rationalization process of Soviet foreign policymaking may be frustratingly slow, but is bound to come.[123] The recent remark made by Vitalii Kobysh, chief of the U.S. section, International Department of the CPSU's Central Committee, may be interpreted to illustrate that this process has already started. In a report on his visit to Japan in December, Kobysh wrote in *Literaturnaia Gazeta:*

> Although Japan does not belong to the category of great power, her weight in the contemporary world is very significant and is constantly growing. . . . Toward the end of this century Japan's GNP will constitute 12 percent of that of the whole world. It is unrealistic not to take this into consideration when analyzing the correlation of forces in the whole arena. . . . As demonstrated by the experience of this country, today the influence of a state is not determined by its military potential.[124]

Of course, it is premature to emphasize this remark as indicating any significant change in the Soviet assessment of relative weight of variables, particularly because of the propagandistic function of the Soviet public pronouncements. Soviet statements obviously should not be taken literally. Yet, given the fact that Soviet official pronouncements play an important role as an educational and guiding function and as a means of esoteric communication to let the Soviet people know the official party line, it is worthwhile keeping in mind that a change in the relative weight of variables is slowly taking place. In place of the traditional assessment of Japan, derived from heavy dependence upon military factors, a new mix with more emphasis upon nonmilitary, above all economic and technological factors, may be gradually emerging.

In conclusion, study of Soviet foreign policy is a ceaseless work, which requires assessing the mix of determining variables at each moment according to the issues, making assumptions and constantly testing against them what the Soviets may do at the next moment. Even if one does such a job painstakingly, there is no guarantee that anyone analyzes the subject well enough to predict with certainty. Nevertheless, one must continue the work with the dim hope that perhaps a slightly better explanation of Soviet foreign policy formation might emerge. And sometimes such a slight margin means a lot.

Notes

1. *Sankei Shimbun, Yomiuri Shimbun,* and *Asahi Shimbun,* 9 May 1981.
2. *Yomiuri Shimbun* (evening edition), 24 January 1983.
3. *The Washington Post,* 19 January 1983.
4. *Yomiuri Shimbun,* 11 December 1982.
5. *Yomiuri Shimbun,* 10 December 1982.
6. For what alliance means to Nakasone, see *Yomiuri Shimbun,* 20

January 1983, and for what he meant by *"unmei kyodo tai,"* see *Yomiuri Shimbun,* 20 January 1983; *The Christian Science Monitor,* 31 January 1983.

7. John K. Emmerson and Leonard A. Humphreys, *Will Japan Rearm? A Study in Attitudes.* (Stanford: Hoover Institution on War, Revolution and Peace, 1973), 135.

8. Yasuhiro Jinbo, *Ningen Nakasone Yasuhiro* (*Yasuhiro Nakasone: A Person*) (Tokyo: Toyokoron-sha, 1978), 131; Prime Minister Nakasone also said in the new year's press interview that "Japan defends itself as much as it can, but asks to let the U.S. defend what Japan's effort is not sufficient to defend." See *Yomiuri Shimbun,* 1 January 1983. See also Makoto Momoi, "Basic Trends in Japanese Security Policies," in Robert A. Scalapino, ed., *The Foreign Policy of Modern Japan* (Berkeley: University of California Press, 1977), 361.

9. Yasuhiro Nakasone, *Nippon no Shucho* (*Japan Speaks*) (Tokyo: Keizai Orai-sha, 1954), 94.

10. Yasuhiro Nakasone, *My Life in Politics,* 1982, 14.

11. Ibid., 26.

12. Ibid., 23.

13. For a U.S. view that predicted even before the advent of Nakasone to power that "the 1980s and 1990s will see the Japanese version of Gaullism," see Isaac Shapiro, "The Rising Sun: Japanese Gaullism?" *Foreign Policy* no. 41 (Winter 1980–1981), 62–81.

14. For instance, *New York Times,* 27 December 1982.

15. For composing these six scenarios, I am grateful to three possible choices that were anticipated by David MacEachron, "The United States and Japan: The Bilateral Potential," *Foreign Affairs,* vol. 61, no. 2 (Winter 1982–1983), 406–407; see also Robert A. Scalapino, *Major and the Major Powers: Implications for the International Order* (Washington: American Enterprise Institute for Public Policy Research, 1972).

16. *United States Security Relations with Northeast Asia: An Address by Secretary of Defense Caspar Weinberger* (Stanford: Northeast Asia–United States Forum on International Policy, 1982), 3. His predecessor, Harold Brown, described Japan as "the keystone of our security position in the Far East." *Department of Defense: Annual Report Fiscal Year 1981* (Washington: U.S. Government Printing Office, 1981), 50.

17. Tetsuya Kataoka, *Waiting For A "Pearl Harbor": Japan Debates Defense* (Stanford: Hoover Institution Press, 1980), 6.

18. For the best article on the question as to whether or not Japan will go nuclear, see Herbert Passin, "Nuclear Arms and Japan," in William H. Overhold, ed., *Asia's Nuclear Future* (Boulder: Westview Press, 1977), 67–132.

19. V.I. Lenin, *Polnoe sobranie sochinenii,* 5th ed., vol. 41 (Moscow: Politizdat, 1963), 55.

20. D.V. Petrov, *Iaponiia v mirovoi politike* (Moscow: Mezhdunarod-

nye otnosheniia, 1973), 4–43; and D.V. Petrov, "Militarizatsiia Iaponii-ugroza miru v Asii," *Problemy dal'nego vostoka,* no. 1 (1981), 51.

21. Ibid., 57.

22. V.P. Lukin et al., red., *SShA i problemy tikhogo okeana* (Moscow: Mezhdunarodnye otnosheniia, 1979), 37, 122, 157, passim; *Izvestiia,* 7 August 1980; S. Modenov, "Tokio v farvatere politiki Vashingtona," *Mezhdunarodnaia zhizn',* no. 4 (1981), 60; and V. Golovnin, "Tikhookeanskie mirazhi tokiishikh politikov," *Aziia i afrika segodniia,* no. 7 (July 1980), 7.

23. N. Nikolaev, "Zigzagi politiki Tokio," *Mezhdunarodnaia zhizn',* no. 9 (1981), 40; *Pravda,* 16 May, 25 May, 26 August 1981 and 19 January 1982; D.V. Petrov, "Vozrozhdenie iaponskogo ekspansionizma," in S.N. Morozova, red., *Gegemonizm: c epokhoi v konflikte* (Moscow: Progress, 1982), 196–197.

24. *Pravda,* 20 August 1981; 14 and 19 November 1981 and 19 January 1982; *Krasnaia zvezda,* 18 December 1981; 10 August 1982; Iu. Kuznetsov, "Kuda tolkaiut Iaponiiu," *Kommunist,* no. 4 [1230] (March 1983), 101.

25. N.G. Feduloka, "Perestroika voenno-politicheskoi sistemy imperializma in Asii," in D.V. Petrov, red., *Mezhdunarodyne otnosheniia v aziatsko-tikhookeanskom regione* (Moscow: Nauka, 1979), 226.

26. V. Dal'nev, "Chto meshaet razvitiiu sovetsko-iaponskikh otnoshenii," *Mezhdunarodnaia zhizn',* no. 1 (1981), 53.

27. *Izvestiia,* 14 August 1982; D.V. Petrov, "Politika iaponii v Azii," in Petrov, red., *Mezhdunarodnye otnosheniia* . . . , 99; Modenov, op. cit., 61; *Pravda,* 28 July 1979; 8 September and 21 December 1980; *Izvestiia,* 22 January, 9 February, 4 May and 20 July 1980; 16 January 1981; *Krasnaia zvezda,* 13 June and 3 August 1979 and *Izvestiia,* 20 July 1980.

28. *Izvestiia,* 27 May 1980.

29. *Pravda,* 28 December 1979.

30. O.N. Bykov, "Vneshnepoliticheskaia strategiia SShA v aziatsko-tikhookeanskom regione," in Petrov, red., *Mezhdunarodnye otnosheniia* . . . , 48.

31. *XXVI s'ezd Kommunisticheskoi Partii Sovietskogo Soiuza (23 Febralia-3 marta 1981 goda): Stenograficheskii otchet,* vol. I (Moscow: Politizdat, 1981), 42; O.V. Vasil'ev, "Nekotorye problemy vneshnei politiki Iaponii v 1980 g.", *Iaponiia 1981: Ezhegodnik* (Moscow: Institut dal'nego vostoka, 1982), 44, 46, 54; L.P. Pinaev, *Evoliutsiia voennoi politiki Iaponii: 1959–1980 gg.* (Moscow: Nauka, 1982), 58; V.M. Mazurov, *SShA–Kitai–Iaponiia: perestroika mezhgosudarstvennykh otnoshenii (1969–1979)* (Moscow: Nauka, 1980), 154–156; *Pravda,* 28 May 1980; *Izvestiia,* 20 July 1980; *Krasnaia zvezda,* 22 December 1981.

32. *XXVI s'ezd* . . . , vol. I, 42.

33. Ibid., 43.

34. D.V. Petrov, "Vozrozhdenie iaponskogo ekspansionizma," 186; and Iu. Bandura in *Izvestiia,* 16 August 1980.

35. *Izvestiia,* 16 August 1980.

36. Petrov, "Vozrozhdenie iaponskogo ekspansionizma," 198.

37. D.V. Petrov, "Vneshniaia politika Iaponii na rebezhe 70–80-kh godov," *Iaponiia 1980: Ezhegodnik* (Moscow: Institut dal'nego vostoka, 1981), 71–72.

38. Petrov, "Vozrozhdenie iaponskogo ekspansionizma," 199; *Pravda,* 2 February 1982; Modenov, op. cit., 62; Petrov, "Militarizatsiia Iaponii," 61.

39. Petrov, "Militarizatiia Iaponii," 58; *Krasnaia zvezda,* 25 November 1979; *Pravda,* 21 July 1982.

40. *Pravda,* 5 May 1979.

41. Petrov, "Militarizatiia Iaponii," 52.

42. Ibid.

43. I.I. Ivkov, "Iaponskii militarizm podnimaet golovu, "*Problemy dal'nego vostoka,* no. 3 (1978), 46.

44. Ibid., 46; Petrov, "Vozrozhdenie iaponskogo ekspansionizma," 190.

45. Ivkov, op. cit., 46–47.

47. Ibid., 48; Modenov, op. cit. 60: *Krasnaia zvezda,* 25 October 1981; Petrov, "Militarizatiia Iaponii," 51, 52; Paul Langer, "Soviet Military Power in Asia," in Donald S. Zagoria, ed., *Soviet Policy in East Asia* (New Haven: Yale University Press, 1982), 260–261.

47. Ivkov, op. cit., 47.

48. Dal'nev, "Chto meshaet razvitiiu sovetsko–iaponskikh otnoshenii," 55; *Krasnaia zvezda,* 30 August 1980, 14 December 1981, and 27 August 1982; *Izvestiia,* 29 August 1980.

49. Ivkov, op. cit., 47.

50. *Pravda,* 2 September 1980.

51. Ibid.

52. *Krasnaia zvezda,* 6 October 1980.

53. Robert Jervis, *Perception and Misperception in International Politics* (Princeton: Princeton University Press, 1976), 218, 228, 232, 234, 240, 263, 275, and 276. See also Ernest R. May, *"Lessons" of the Past: The Use and Misuse of History in American Foreign Policy* (New York: Oxford University Press, 1973), ix–xiii; Klaus Knorr, "Introduction: On the Utility of History," in Klaus Knorr, ed., *Historical Dimensions of National Security Problems* (Lawrence: University of Kansas Press, 1976), 1–4.

54. *Asahi Shimbun* and *Hokkaido Shimbun,* 24 February 1982.

55. *Asahi Shimbun,* 5 December 1982; *Mainichi Shimbun,* 7 December 1982. Consequently, Nikolai Kudriavtsev, first deputy fisheries minister and head of the Soviet delegation, was quoted as proposing that "Let us complete all our negotiations in a short period of time," and in fact the fishing negotiation between Japan and the USSR has become very brief since 1979. *Foreign Broadcast Information Service* (Soviet Union), 22 November 1979.

56. May, op. cit., ix–xiii; Knorr, op. cit., 1–4.

57. Hans J. Morgenthau, *Politics Among Nations: The Struggle for Power and Peace* (New York: Knopf, 1961), 181.

58. *XXVI s'ezd . . .*, vol. I, 27–28, 46.

59. *Pravda*, 25 March 1982.

60. Mineo Nakajima, *Chuso–domei no shogeki: Nihon no Anzen to keizai wa donaru ka* (*Shock of Sino–Soviet Alliance: What Will Be the Security and Economy of Japan?*) (Tokyo: Kobunsha, 1982), 167.

61. *Pravda*, 27 September 1982.

62. Donald S. Zagoria, "Gauging the Sino–Soviet Thaw," *The New Leader*, (29 November 1982), 4; Vladimir Petrov, "China Goes It Alone," *Asian Survey*, vol. 23, no. 5 (May 1983).

63. *Yomiuri Shimbun* (evening edition), and 11 March 1983; *Yomiuri Shimbun*, 15 March 1983; *Asahi Shimbun*, 15 March 1983; *The Christian Science Monitor*, 18 and 28 March 1983; *New York Times*, 20 March, 1983.

64. Nakajima, op. cit., 246–247.

65. In developing these three variants, I am indebted to the suggestion by Professor Nakajima. Nakajima, op. cit., 54.

66. For example, see Nakajima, op. cit., 134–174.

67. Zagoria, op. cit., 5.

68. Quoted from *Far Eastern Economic Review*, (3 December 1982), 37.

69. Robinson, op cit., 7–8.

70. *Krasnaia zvezda*, 9 October 1982; *Pravda*, 11 November 1982.

71. *Krasnaia zvezda*, 29 April 1982 and 3 November 1982; *Izvestiia*, 29 May 1982; *Pravda*, 21 February 1982; *Yomiuri Shimbun* (evening edition), *Mainichi Shimbun* (evening edition), and *Hokkaido Shimbun* (evening edition), 20 January 1983.

72. *The Washington Post*, 19 January 1983. It turned out later what Nakasone actually said in Japanese is that Japan should be "a big aircraft carrier (*okina koku bokan*)" to block the Russian planes. *The Washington Post*, 20 March 1983.

73. *Mainichi Shimbun* (evening edition), *Yomiuri Shimbun* (evening edition), and *Hokkaido Shimbun* (evening edition), 20 February 1983; *Foreign Broadcast Information Service* (Soviet Union), 19 January 1983, c8.

74. *Yomiuri Shimbun*, *Asahi Shimbun*, and *Hokkaido Shimbun* (evening edition), 24 February 1983; *Nihon-keizai Shimbun*, 28 February 1983.

75. *New York Times*, 30 December 1982.

76. *Die Welt*, 17 January 1983; *Mainichi Shimbun* and Yomiuri Shimbun (evening edition), 18 January 1983; *Washington Post*, 18 and 19 January 1983; *The Times* (London), January 19, 1983; *Christian Science Monitor*, January 21, 1983; *New York Times*, 3 April 1983.

77. Christer Jönsson, "The Ideology of Foreign Policy," in Charles W. Kegley, Jr. and Pat McGowan, eds., *Foreign Policy: USA/USSR* (Beverly Hills: Sage Publications, 1983), 91.

78. *Politicheskie sistemy sovremennosti* (Moscow: Nauka, 1978), 14, 20 and 21.

79. Veron V. Aspaturian, "The Domestic Sources of Soviet Policy Toward China," in Douglas T. Stuart and William T. Tow, *China, the Soviet Union, and the West: Strategic and Political Dimensions in the 1980s* (Boulder: Westview Press, 1982), 39.

80. Jönsson, op. cit., 93.

81. Timofey Guzhenko, "Ajia no heiwa to anzen (Peace and Security of Asia)," *Jiyu*, no. 7 (July 1982), 33.

82. For an argument that distance has ceased to play a big role, see Albert Wohlstetter, "Illusion of Distance," *Foreign Affairs*, vol. 46, no. 2 (January 1968), 242–255.

83. John J. Stephan, "Soviet Approaches to Japan: Images Behind the Policies," *Asian Perspective*, vol. 6, no. 2 (Fall/Winter, 1982), 135.

84. I.V. Stalin, *Sochineniia*, vol. 2 (XV) (1941–1945), edited by Robert H. McNeal (Stanford: The Hoover Institution on War, Revolution, and Peace, 1967), 213–215.

85. Quoted by Sidney I. Ploss, "Studying the Domestic Determinants of Soviet Foreign Policy," in Erik P. Hoffmann and Frederic J. Fleron, Jr., eds., *The Conduct of Soviet Foreign Policy*, Second edition (New York: Aldine Publishing Company, 1980), 78–79.

86. *XXVI s'ezd . . .*, vol. I, 49.

87. *Pravda*, 27 October 1982. For a much bolder suggestion to learn from economic management in East European countries, see *Pravda*, 16 March 1983.

88. Seweryn Bialer, "The Harsh Decade: Soviet Policies in the 1980s," *Foreign Affairs*, vol. 59, no. 5 (Summer 1981), 1005.

89. Joseph S. Berliner, professor at Brandeis University, proposed four alternatives: the "conservative," the "reactionary," the "radical," and the "liberal" models. Joseph S. Berliner, "Managing the USSR Economy: Alternative Models," *Problems of Communism*, vol. 32, no. 1 (January/February 1983), 40.

90. *Pravda*, 23 November 1982.

91. Ibid.

92. John P. Hardt, Ronda A. Bresnick and David Levine, "Soviet Oil and Gas in the Global Perspective," *Project Interdependence: US and World Energy Outlook through 1990* (Washington: Congressional Research Services Library of Congress, November 1977), 798.

93. Marshall I. Goldman, "The Role of Communist Countries," in David A. Deese and Joseph S. Nye, eds., *Energy and Security* (Cambridge: Ballinger Publishing Company, 1981), 123.

94. Allen S. Whiting, *Siberian Development and East Asia: Threat or Promise?* (Stanford, California: Stanford University Press, 1981), 112; and Marshall I. Goldman, *The Enigma of Soviet Petroleum: Half-empty or Half-full?* (London: George Allen & Unwin, 1980), 126–128.

95. Whiting, op. cit., 112.

96. *Christian Science Monitor*, 8 November 1982. In an interview with *Newsweek* magazine, which asked "Do you think the Soviets would

be willing to consider giving the Kurile Islands back to Japan?", Dr. Bialer replied: "Yes. Japan is one of the natural partners of the Soviet Union in developing the richness of Siberian resources. Their policy with regard to Japan has been very unimaginative, if not stupid. Maybe a new leadership will have the flexibility to try to reach some compromise with Japan that will enable Japan to have better relations with the Soviet Union and to invest in Siberia." *Newsweek,* 11 October 1982, 60. Reprinted with permission.

97. Seweryn Bialer, ed., *The Domestic Context of Soviet Foreign Policy* (Boulder: Westview, 1981), particularly 409–441.

98. John J. Stephan, "Asia in the Soviet Conception," in Zagoria, ed., *Soviet Policy in East Asia,* 43.

99. Dimitri K. Simes, "National Security under Andropov," *Problems of Communism,* vol. 32, no. 1 (January/February 1983), 37.

100. Ibid. for the role and degree of the influence of area specialists and "*mezhdunarodniki*" (internationalists), see also Rose E. Gottemoeller and Paul F. Langer, *Foreign Area Studies in the USSR: Training and Employment of Specialists* (Santa Monica: Rand Corporation, 1983), 73–77; and Oded Eran, *Mezhdunarodniki: An Assessment of Professional Expertise in the Making of Soviet Foreign Policy* (Isreal: Turtledove Publishing, 1979), 331.

101. Nora Beloff, "Escape from Freedom: A Defector's Story," *Atlantic Monthly,* November 1980, 45.

102. Stephan, "Asia in the Soviet Conception," 31.

103. Alexander L. George, "The 'Operational Code': A Neglected Approach to the Study of Political Leaders and Decision-Making." *International Studies Quarterly,* vol. 13, no. 2 (June 1969), 202.

104. Hedrick Smith, *The Russians* (New York: Ballantine Books, 1976), 250.

105. Ibid., 249.

106. Statement by Dimitri Simes in U.S. Congress, Senate, Committee on Foreign Relations, United States Senate, *Perceptions on Relations Between the United States and thee Soviet Union* (Washington: U.S. Government Printing Office, 1979), 94.

107. Smith, op. cit., 264.

108. D.V. Petrov, *Iaponiia v mirovoi politike,* 39–40.

109. Ibid., 41.

110. Petrov, "Militarizatiia Iaponii," 51.

111. Basil Dmytryshyn, "Current Trends in Soviet Foreign Policy," Paper presented to the Japan–U.S. Society in Sapporo, February 1979, 12.

112. Yuriy Bandura, "Soren wa nihon ni nanio nozomuka? (What does the Soviet Union want from Japan)," *Jiyu* (January 1982), 158.

113. This is an old fashioned view of the world, but the Soviets still seem to consider U.S.–Soviet relations as the basic relations upon which, for example, quadrilateral relations among the United States, USSR, PRC, and Japan in Asia depend; see for example, Bykov, op. cit., 53.

114. Of course, the public pronouncements in the Soviet literature emphasize that "correlations of forces cannot and should not be reduced to the correlations of the military potential of states" and "it is the aggregate balance of the political, economic, military, social, and scientific-technological capabilities." Stephen Gibert et. al. *Soviet Images of America* (New York: Crane, Russak, 1977), 22–23; G. Shakhnazarov, "K problme sootnoshniia sil v mire," *Kommunist,* no. 3 (February 1974), 86; *Vzaimosviaz' i vzaimovliianie vnutrennei i vneshnei politiki* (Moscow: Izdatel' stvo Nauka, 1982); Dimitri K. Simes, *Detente and Conflict: Soviet Foreign Policy 1972–1977* (Beverly Hills: Sage Publications, 1977), 39; *Soviet Diplomacy and Negotiating Behavior: Emerging New Context for U.S. Diplomacy* (Washington: U.S. Government Printing Office, 1977), 522.

115. Hoffmann and Fleron, op. cit., 31.

116. David W. Paul of Princeton University writes that "Understanding the process of Soviet foreign policy-making can sometimes be a frustrating challenge," partly because "there is no simple approach which will immediately enlighten the policy-making process." David W. Paul, "Soviet Foreign Policy and the Invasion of Czechoslovakia: A Theory and a Case Study," *International Studies Quarterly,* vol. 15, no. 2 (June 1971), 159.

117. Alexander Dallin, "The Domestic Source of Soviet Foreign Policy," in Seweryn Bialer, ed., *The Domestic Context of Soviet Foreign Policy, op. cit., 380.*

118. Vernon V. Aspaturian, "Internal Politics and Foreign Policy in the Soviet System," in R. Barry Farrell, ed., *Approaches to Comparative and International Politics* (Evanston: Northwestern University Press, 1966), 286.

119. Dallin, op. cit., 380.

120. Paul F. Langer, "Changing Japanese Security Perspectives," in Richard H. Solomon, ed., *Asian Security in the 1980s: Problems and Politics for a Time of Transition* (Cambridge: Oelgeschlauger, Gunn & Hain, 1979), 79.

121. Marshall Shulman, "Trends in Soviet Foreign Policy," in Michael McCGwire et al., eds., *Soviet Naval Policy* (New York: Praeger 1975), 8–10.

122. Dallin, op. cit., 361.

123. Alexander Dallin, "All 'Orwellian Pigs'?" *Encounter,* vol. 42, no. 6 (June 1974), 84.

124. Vitalii Kobysh, "Est' vykhod iz tupika" (There is an exit from the impasse) *Literaturnaia Gazeta,* no. 51 (4909), 22 December 1982.

5
The Dynamics of Soviet Policy toward the Arab–Israeli Conflict: Lessons of the Brezhnev Era

George W. Breslauer

This chapter examines Soviet policy toward the Arab–Israeli conflict. It explores the ways in which the Soviets define their interests in that region of the Middle East, and the conditions under which they employ one means or another in order to advance those interests. Generalizations are based on the record of Soviet behavior patterns during the Brezhnev era. This chapter constitutes a reconceptualization and synthesis of existing literature on the subject, rather than reportage of new research findings. For that reason, it does not cite original Soviet sources.

Section I places the Middle East within the overall hierarchy of Soviet foreign policy priorities. Section II ranks Soviet goals and priorities within the Middle East. Section III discusses the means by which the Soviets have sought to attain their goals in the arena of the Arab–Israeli conflict. Section IV discusses the Soviet response to the Israeli invasion of Lebanon in June 1982, asking whether that response was inconsistent with the previous eighteen years of Soviet policy, and speculating on how the current Soviet leadership might respond to the further development of events on the Lebanese and Syrian fronts.

Sections I–III introduce conceptual distinctions that, for ease of reference, are summarized in Table 5–1.

For comments on earlier drafts of this chapter, the author would like to thank Vinod Aggarwal, Dan Caldwell, Mark Garrison, Alexander George, Ernst Haas, Martha Brill Olcott, Dennis Ross, and Yahya Sadowski.

Table 5–1
Soviet Roles, Goals, and Tactics

Soviet Roles in International System (Ranked)	*Soviet Goals in Middle East (Loosely Ranked)*	*Soviet Postures/Tactics (Unranked)*
Superpower	Avoid nuclear war	Confrontation
Continental power	Influence-consolidation/ expansion	Competition
Competitive global power	Acquire strategic assets	Collaboration
Leader of world communist movement	Denial of above to competitors	Avoidance
	Confrontation-avoidance	
	Economic self-aggrandizement	
	Support for local communist parties	

The Middle East in Soviet Foreign Policy Priorities

The Soviet state, like any other, seeks to survive as an entity and to ensure the immunity of the homeland against external attack. Beyond this universal first priority, however, Moscow's foreign policy priorities can be grouped under four world roles that the Soviets ascribe to themselves: superpower, continental power, global power, and the leader of the world communist movement. These terms, of course, are not Soviet in origin. But they express, in descending order of priority, the ways in which Soviet leaders under Brezhnev defined their roles in the international system.

As a superpower, the main Soviet goal is to keep pace with, and selectively outstrip, the United States in the strategic nuclear arms race. Having rejected the Khrushchevian doctrine of "minimum deterrence,"[1] the Soviets under Brezhnev came to define strategic parity as a necessary condition for avoiding strategic threats and humiliation by the other superpower. Thus, the affirmation of Soviet superpower status through the attainment and maintenance of strategic equality came to be defined as a precondition for adequately playing her other roles in the international system.

The role of continental power constitutes a second—albeit mightily important—level of priority. Within this category, some goals are more important than others. Maintenance of control over Eastern Europe is probably the number one priority, for the Soviets have thus far consistently defined such control as a prerequisite for protecting the homeland against attack—or the state against internal challenges. Competing for second place within this category are the China and NATO issues; the relative importance of each probably depends upon the circumstances of the moment. When the China front is threatening, it clearly becomes a matter of highest Soviet concern. When, however, the China issue is dormant, and the Western front is threatening, then NATO may be a higher Soviet priority in protecting her status as a continental power. The Soviets seek to play upon divisions within NATO in order to head off the further militarization, or the political–military reintegration, of that alliance. Here the issue of theater nuclear weapons is currently most important, but the general issue goes beyond military concerns. It encompasses the gamut of political, diplomatic, and military issues that reinforce the NATO–Warsaw Pact confrontation, and that strengthen the Atlantic dimension of the NATO alliance. Perhaps the lowest Soviet priority goal in playing the role of continental power is the southern rim of the USSR, on which Afghanistan, Iran, and Turkey border. Instability on Soviet borders is a matter of strategic concern to Soviet policy planners. Some borders (such as Europe and China) are more important than others (such as Afghanistan and Iran). But the less important borders, I would guess, are more important to the Soviets in periods of instability than are issues of Third World competition that are not contiguous to the borders of the USSR. In other words, to the Soviets, Afghanistan and Iran are not just another set of Third World countries.

The Soviets also define the USSR as a competitive global power, determined to compete with the United States and others for influence and allies throughout the Third World.[2] Other things being equal, performance of this role is of lower priority to the Soviets than securing their status as superpower and continental power. And within this role, the Soviets probably possess a hierarchy of priorities. I think the Middle East is one of the highest-priority Third World issues for the Soviets. Generally speaking, the Middle East does not rank high in Soviet foreign policy priorities, for it is superceded by all the priorities noted above under the first two roles. But within the third-order role of global competitor, the Middle East may well rank number one.

This is so for a number of reasons. First, the Middle East is unusually close to Soviet borders, and to the sea lanes in which U.S. naval vessels and Western oil tankers make their way. Second, Soviet diplomatic and military involvement as a patron of Middle East regimes is of long standing, representing perhaps the longest and deepest Third World commitment of the post–Stalin era. Third, the region has been one of continuing East–West confrontation, due to the periodic Arab–Israeli wars, as a result of which superpower commitments have been broadened and deepened, and superpower prestige put on the line. Fourth, many Arab countries have hard currency with which to pay for weapons.

South Asia, primarily because of India's size and her relationship to the China issue, probably vies with the Middle East for number one priority within this level. The relative priority of South Asia and the Middle East and Persian Gulf region (that is, the Middle East, broadly defined for the moment) probably varies with the circumstances of the moment (about which more below). The lower priorities within this level are distant from Soviet borders: Southeast Asia, Sub-Saharan Africa, and Latin America.

The fourth, and lowest, level of Soviet foreign policy concerns relates to their role as leader of the world communist movement. To be sure, the Soviets are determined to maintain and advance their status as the primary ideological and organizational referent for ruling and non-ruling communist parties. They would invest a good many foreign policy resources to avoid being supplanted in this role (that is, by the PRC). But, under normal circumstances the Soviets appear to place higher priority on securing and advancing their global, continental, and superpower status than on seizing opportunities to advance their status as leader of the world communist movement. Priorities within this level are also discernible. Soviet willingness to curry support from ruling communist regimes, such as Vietnam or Cuba, appears to outweigh Soviet willingness to take risks, or make painful trade-offs, on behalf of nonruling communist parties worldwide.

It is crucial to bear in mind that the Soviets do not define any of these roles as expendable. That is, pursuit of gains in a higher priority role will not take place at the expense of abandoning a lower-priority role completely. (This may have been a major mistake in the most optimistic scenarios for detente in the early 1970s: the claim that, in exchange for arms control and trade, the Soviets would essentially or eventually abandon their role as competitive global power.) Where the Soviets entertain trade-offs is with respect to goals within and across the roles.

This analytic separation of relative Soviet priorities by role should not be allowed to obscure the fact that, in practice, these roles are highly interconnected. For example, certain events or circumstances in the Middle East might have implications that engage Soviet self-conceptions or public image as a continental power. Thus, a major defeat for Soviet weaponry in that region might compromise the credibility of Warsaw Pact military strength. Similarly, some geographic concerns consistently engage multiple Soviet roles. The China issue, for example, challenges Soviet continental power status. But it also challenges Soviet global power status when it competes vigorously with Soviet alliance-building strategies in the Third World and challenges Soviet leadership of the world communist movement when it competes for ideological or organizational loyalty, or when it challenges Soviet reliability as a patron (for example, after the Chinese invasion of Vietnam in 1979). The specific circumstances surrounding the "China issue" at any point of conflict will determine which role or roles are invoked and, therefore, how high a priority the Soviets place on winning.

Nor do the circumstances per se always dictate which role will be invoked, for this is partly contingent on how the Soviets previously defined the issue. Take Nicaragua, for example. Would a U.S. invasion of that country challenge the Soviet world image? Perhaps not. For while the Soviets have expressed considerable rhetorical and material solidarity with the Sandinista regime, they have not signed on as a military protector of the regime in international relations. Nor have they embraced the regime as a bona fide member of the socialist community. Hence, the Soviets could attempt to avoid having a U.S. invasion of Nicaragua (in contrast to Cuba) defined as a challenge to their status as global power or leader of the world communist movement.

An issue left unclear by my geographic definition of roles is where to place such functional concerns as trade. Just as all states usually seek to survive as entities and to protect the homeland against attack, so do states seek to establish the kinds of economic relations with others that would contribute most to well-being (however defined by each government). Yet, in the case of economic relations, the question of the price to be paid for such benefits is paramount. In the Soviet Union under Brezhnev, trade, credits, subsidized imports, and the like came to be defined as high-priority items, for they serviced a number of important domestic and foreign policy goals: (1) maintenance of domestic order by alleviating the consumer situation; (2) maintenance of political peace within the Politburo by reducing budgetary strains and allowing the postponement of hard policy choices (defense versus consumption, economic reform versus maintenance of the command economy); (3) strengthening of the U.S. and West European stake in avoiding a return to policies of acrimony, confrontation, and containment; and (4) prospectively greatly strengthening the relative Soviet position in international markets (through Siberian development). The Soviets proved unwilling to abandon any of their world roles for the sake of these trade benefits but showed signs of willingness to make compromises on the issue of Jewish emigration and on low-priority Third World issues. Just how much they might have been willing to sacrifice is now impossible to say, for rare was the case when the prospect of large trade benefits was posed as a trade-off for specific foreign policy goals.

Another issue not fully addressed by my framework is the question of grand strategy. In playing their roles, are the Soviets primarily out to achieve a position of undisputed hegemony, or are they primarily concerned to consolidate their status as a global power, continental power, superpower, and leader of world communism? Given the highly competitive nature of the international system, it is likely that Soviet leaders never feel complacent that their status in these roles is secured or consolidated irreversibly. The arms race, the confrontations with NATO and the PRC, the competition for allies in the Third World—all have had a zigzag quality to them. And given that the Soviets have been playing catch-up for thirty years in their superpower and global power roles, they are likely to be very sensitive to signs that their gains are in danger of being lost. Then too, what we know of Soviet military and political doctrine leads us to believe that Soviet leaders base their thinking on premises that reinforce the natural push in the competitive relationship toward worst-case thinking and a blurring of the line between offensive and defensive behavior. Such beliefs include: (1) expect continuing conflict with your adversaries; (2) expect that there is nothing so sure as change in international relations; and (3) the best defense is a good offense—hence, maintain the initiative. Thus, Soviet leaders themselves do not even know whether they are ultimately oriented toward hegemony or consolidation of their status. In an ideal world, they are probably inclined toward hegemony. In the real world of dangers, constraints, obstacles, and trade-offs, the Soviets rarely, if ever, have the luxury of attempting to achieve sustainable hegemony on a consolidated base. And they know it.[3]

Soviet Goals and Priorities in the Middle East

I have already defined the Middle East as perhaps the highest Soviet priority-area in its self-conception as a global power. That circumstance accounts for the fact that specific goals associated with the role of global power rank highest in the list of Soviet priorities in the Middle East. Thus, the primary Soviet goal in the region is to consolidate and expand influence with key regimes in the area. A closely related (and almost as important) goal is to gain strategic assets for use in the on-going geostrategic rivalry with the United States.[4] Such strategic assets include: military bases astride the major sea lanes of the region; port facilities to service the Soviet fleets in the Mediterranean and Indian Oceans; and anti-Western allies on whom to rely to compete with pro-Western or anti-Soviet states.

Specialists on Soviet policy in the Middle East often disagree as to whether influence-building or strategic rivalry is the higher priority in the minds of Soviet foreign policymakers.[5] Yet I have not encountered a methodology for determining the relative importance of these two motivations. I list influence-consolidation as the primary goal, not because I believe (or can know) that Soviet policymakers consciously rank it as such, but for other reasons. Clearly, the Soviets seek both influence and strategic assets. However, their clients in the region are not satellites of the USSR. When Czechoslovakia wanted to leave the Warsaw Pact, it was invaded; when Egypt threw out Soviet military personnel, those personnel left. Given, then, that the Soviets do not typically claim or exercise the right of control over their clients' fundamental decisions, Soviet leaders know that influence-consolidation is a prerequisite for maintaining hard-won strategic assets—or for getting them in the first place. Thus, in my mind, the issue is not the relative ranking of these goals in the minds of Soviet leaders, so much as the interrelationship between the goals in practice.

There is a negative corollary of each of these goals. In addition to consolidating and expanding Soviet influence and acquiring assets of strategic importance, Soviet leaders also place a high priority on denying to the United States and the PRC (also, but more selectively, Western European countries) opportunities to do the same. The relative importance of these negative goals (vis-à-vis the positive goals) probably varies with circumstances. Were an anti-Soviet alliance (à la the Baghdad Pact) to be forming in the region, led by anti-Soviet great powers, the Soviets would be likely to place highest priority on undoing the threat—either through undermining the alliance or leap-frogging it. On the other hand, in more "normal" circumstances of the region since the early 1960s, the Soviets are faced with constantly shifting alliances, opportunities, and threats. Under these conditions, the Soviets seize opportunities to reduce U.S., PRC, or West European influence in the region as these come along, but they only do so when such reduction can be achieved at acceptable cost and risk, an issue to which I will return below.

How, then, are we to rank these negative goals relative to the positive ones? Surely the Soviets would ideally place higher priority on acquiring influence and assets for themselves than on simply denying these to others. The Soviets would like to be involved everywhere, to substantiate their claim to being a recognized global power. Given that urge, "acquisition" must be a higher goal than "denial." But in practice, the relative weight will depend on circumstances, more specifically, on the perception of opportunities. When the Soviets have relatively few opportunities for acquisition, they will place high priority on denial. Denial goals are often easier to attain at acceptable risk. On the other hand, when things are going well, the Soviets will feel less threatened by U.S. or PRC gains, and will place higher priorities on consolidating influence and acquiring strategic assets than on blocking marginal gains by competitors. In either case, though, it is important to bear in mind that both the positive and the negative goals are very important to Soviet leaders, given the competitive game into which they are locked, and given the strong tendency toward worst-case calculations and zero-sum thinking among actors locked into such games.

Still another very important goal for Soviet leaders is to avoid a dangerous confrontation with the United States that could get out of hand and escalate potentially to a nuclear war. In this case as well, it is easy to call this goal an important one, but more difficult to rank precisely its relative degree of priority. In its most extreme form—nuclear confrontation that gets out of hand—such confrontation-avoidance would have to rank as the highest Soviet goal in the Middle East.[6] But that does not tell us very much about variations in Soviet behavior over time, for most of the action takes place well below that threshold. And below that threshold, the Soviets have shown themselves to be willing to confront the United States directly, both in the form of threats and through military involvement, when they deemed it necessary to protect vital interests. I will discuss later the conditions under which the Soviets have been willing to confront. For the moment, I want to argue that confrontation-avoidance per se cannot rank as the highest Soviet goal, if only because the Soviets have been willing to confront in order to protect higher-priority values. On the other hand, the relative lack of frequency of Soviet confrontational behavior, and the caution and risk-aversion that characterized Soviet Middle East policy under Brezhnev, suggest that confrontation-avoidance ranks fairly high in the Soviet preference-ordering.

Another Soviet goal or interest in the region is economic. This interest is relatively recent in origin, and is not as deep as the U.S.,

West European, or Japanese economic stake in the region, but it has been growing steadily since the early- to mid-1970s.[7] I have in mind Soviet sales of conventional arms to countries in the region that can pay for the arms with Western hard currency. The Soviets increasingly need that hard currency to pay for imports of Western grain, meat, consumer goods, machinery, steel pipe, and the like. The Soviets do not have very much else to sell to these countries that is attractive relative to what is available in the Western markets. But arms they have in abundance, and they have usually been demanding petro-dollars on delivery. This Soviet economic interest is real and growing, but I see it as a reinforcing, not an independent, cause of major Soviet commitments in the region. I would rank it well below influence-consolidation, strategic assets, denial, and confrontation-avoidance in the Soviet goal structure.

Specialists on Soviet policy in the Middle East typically list another goal, interest, or motivation of Soviet policy—advancement of ideology—if only then to write off its importance. In a broader sense, I consider ideology to be an important drive behind the Soviet self-conception as a global power—as an advocate and, at times, defender of pro-Soviet, "anti-imperialist" forces. But in the present discussion, such is not the issue. Instead, those who depreciate ideology as a shaper of Soviet interests in the Middle East typically have in mind party-to-party relations. On this score, I would agree with them. The Soviets have almost always placed their relations with states and existing governments in the region at a higher level of importance than their relations with communist parties within those countries. When client-governments, in Iraq, Egypt, or elsewhere slaughtered or imprisoned communists en masse, the Soviets have expressed displeasure or even occasionally held up arms shipments briefly, but they have not broken ties or otherwise disavowed their status as military or political patron of the government involved. Thus, the Soviets have placed a much higher priority on influence consolidation, strategic assets, denial, confrontation-avoidance, and economic interests than they have on fidelity to party comrades in Arab states.

This ranking of Soviet priorities within the Middle East in turn reflects the relative importance the Soviets place on their world role. The global power role determines the three highest-ranking goals in the region. Confrontation-avoidance is not near the top of the list simply because the Soviets define being a global power in the region as nonnegotiable: they will confront to avoid being driven out of the area. The lowest priority accorded to party-to-party relations, in turn, reflects the low priority the Soviets place more generally on their role as leader of the world communist movement.

What is the source of the Soviet determination to play the role of global power? Here I would distinguish between primary sources and reinforcing factors. In contrast to those analysts who view Soviet behavior as primarily cultural in origin,[8] I see a real break in Russian history occurring in 1917 as regards the global power dimension. Whatever the continuities between Tsarist and Soviet foreign policy behavior (and there are many), this is not one of them. The Tsars viewed Russia as primarily a continental power; the Bolsheviks embraced an ideology that was global in perspective. To be sure, consolidation of Soviet power on the continent soon came to be of higher priority for the Bolsheviks than competitive globalism. But after Stalin's death, the universalist strand of the ideology was given new life, and Soviet leaders much expanded the resources invested in expanding their roles in the international system.

Ideology, then, in my opinion, was the primary source of the Soviet competitive urge. But once this urge was acted upon, a number of very important reinforcing factors came into play that could have a life of their own, even if the ideology were to be transformed. One such factor is nationalism, which expressed itself in a foreign policy elite that is very status- and prestige-conscious, sensitive to slights, and constantly demanding recognition of the "arrival" of competitive Soviet global power.[9] When denied such recognition, Soviet officials express aggrievement that is not explicable in ideological terms. They consider themselves the Rodney Dangerfields of the old international order, and they want some respect, even as they seek to lead the "new" international order committed to revising the old order.

A second reinforcing factor that can take on a life of its own is geopolitical. Global competition is a game or process that has a strong tendency to acquire a zero-sum quality, at least in the eyes of the main actors. Under such circumstances, there is a strong tendency for each side to assume that its failure to develop leverage will lead the other side instead to acquire that leverage. The game, then, becomes self-sustaining, regardless of the original motivation for entering it.

This combination of the ideological, the nationalistic, and the geopolitical provides strong grounding for Soviet leaders' determination to continue playing the role of competitive global power, even if they remain willing to sacrifice specific goals for the sake of higher priority concerns. For these reasons, the betting man would wager that the Soviets are in the Middle East to stay.

Soviet Postures in Pursuit of Interests

By what means do the Soviets pursue their interests in the Middle East? Like all great powers, the Soviets employ the full range of instruments for advancing and protecting interests: economic assistance, arms transfers, cultural diplomacy, persuasion, arm-twisting, and the like. For purposes of generalization about the conditions under which some means are used rather than others, I find it more useful to think in terms of four alternative postures the Soviets (or any other great power) may assume in seeking to attain their goals: confrontation, competition, collaboration, or avoidance. It is important to bear in mind that none of those postures is generous in intent. States normally pursue their interests, as they define them, as predictable costs they are willing to bear. Some postures (for example, avoidance and collaboration) may seem more generous to the competing great power, but they are surely not intended to be.

Confrontation refers to threats or actions that are based upon use of the military instrument in ways that contain high potential for escalation. Thus, arms transfers per se are not necessarily confrontational, unless they are of a sort and in a context that predictably contain high escalation potential. Competition refers to all efforts to curry influence and gain allies through means, and in a context, that does not contain high potential for escalation, but that is typically at the expense of competing great powers or their clients. Collaboration refers to efforts to coordinate actions with great power competitors in order to expand the mutual interests of the competitors in the region. Thus, collaboration, in contrast to competition, is a posture that does not view the competitive rivalry as a zero-sum game in all respects. Avoidance is a posture of nonengagement in a specific train of events.

Under Stalin, the dominant posture toward the Middle East was one of avoidance. Khrushchev led a switch to a general posture of competition with the West. During the Brezhnev era, and especially after the disastrous war of June 1967, the Soviets switched to a mixed general posture that I have called "collaborative competition."[10] At the same time, they have proved willing at times to escalate the competition into a confrontation, while in other instances they have engaged in avoidance behavior. The question is: Under what conditions do they supplement their general posture with tactics that do not fit the posture?

The failure to distinguish between confrontational and competitive behavior accounts for much misunderstanding, especially in the more politicized literature on Soviet policy in the Middle East. Because the legitimacy of Soviet status as a competitor for influence in the region has never been accepted by U.S. leaders, Soviet competitive behavior has typically been treated as confrontational (that is, provocative), while Soviet collaborative offerings have been written off as disingenuous.[11] Depending upon one's definition of U.S. interests in the region, the approach just mentioned may be a fruitful means of defending U.S. positions, but it does not get us very far in understanding variations over time in Soviet behavior.

When have the Soviets proved willing to confront? During the Brezhnev era, the incidents that clearly meet the definition are threats to intervene during the 1967 war, Soviet assumption of the air defense of Egypt in the "War of Attrition" in 1970, and the Soviet threat to intervene to save the Egyptian Third Army during the October 1973 war.[12] What these cases have in common, and what is also suggested by the diplomatic record, is a Soviet determination to prevent a "strategic defeat" for a client-state. The definition of strategic defeat, to be sure, can vary. In 1967, given the brevity and decisiveness of the Israeli preemption, there was relatively little the Soviets could do to prevent the destruction of the Egyptian and Syrian air forces, or to prevent Israeli seizure of the Sinai, the Golan Heights, and the West Bank. (The fallback position for the Soviets was to prevent Israel from trying to march further toward Damascus or Cairo, with all the implications that would have had for the survival of the governments of those countries.) In 1970, Israeli deep penetration bombing of Egypt followed the destruction of Egyptian air defenses along the Suez Canal. Statements by Israeli officials at the time indicated an intention to bring Nasser to his knees, and thereby to topple his government. Soviet assumption of Egyptian air defenses put an end to deep penetration bombings, and possibly saved Egypt from military prostration.

In 1973 the situation was somewhat different. Egypt and Syria had launched an attack on Israel, which sent Israeli forces reeling during the early stages of the war. After the Israeli counterattack, however, the initial Arab gains were wiped out, and the status quo ante effectively reestablished. At that point, the Soviets were pushing hard for a cease-fire. But the Israelis preferred to push the advantage they had finally gained. They surrounded the Egyptian Third Army in the Sinai, and could have annihilated it, in what would have constituted a major strategic defeat for Sadat. This was the point at which the Soviets threatened to intervene. As things turned out, they did not have to, for Nixon and Kissinger were also eager to avert such a strategic defeat for Egypt.

Threats to intervene qualify as confrontational acts even if they are tempered by extreme caution. We have learned, for example, that the threats of 1967 and 1973 (as well as those of 1956) were made only after the Soviets felt reasonably confident they would not have to act on the threats. The conclusion to be drawn is that the Soviets are not high risk-takers in their Middle East policy, though they are willing to confront. The experience of 1970 supports this interpretation. The Soviets were willing to intervene militarily on a large scale, but in a way that was almost entirely defensive, that did not encourage Egypt to launch a counteroffensive, and that had relatively low potential for further escalation of the situation.

One could make the case that other acts during these years also constituted confrontational behavior and require a different explanation. Before the 1967 war, the Soviets planted rumors in Damascus that contributed to escalation of the situation. During 1970, they encouraged or abetted violation of the summer cease-fire, moving up SAM missiles and creating a virtually impregnable air defense along the Suez Canal. And before the October 1973 war, the Soviets delivered SCUD missiles to Egypt when they sensed that Sadat was likely soon to go to war. Whether these acts qualify as confrontational or as highly competitive is problematic but need not detain us. They clearly straddle the divide between the two categories. Explaining them is another matter. The summer 1970 cease-fire violation may qualify as an effort—not unknown on either side of the Middle East conflict—to consolidate gains in a moment of ambiguity. Soviet action in 1967, in contrast, may have resulted from a Soviet belief that the situation would not get out of hand. Soviet behavior in 1973 appears to have resulted from a realization that Sadat was out of control, that nothing they did would dissuade him from going to war, and that a Soviet gesture of support would both maintain the Soviet image as military patron and deter Israel from retaliating against the Egyptian heartland. Until we know much more about Soviet decision-making in these episodes, we cannot safely generalize from these cases about the conditions under which Soviet confrontational behavior is likely. Yet we can, I think, safely assert the lesson to be drawn from the earlier three cases: that Soviet predisposition to confront is raised dramatically when a client-state is faced with a defeat that threatens the survival of its government, or that puts its capital militarily at risk.[13]

Let us turn now from confrontational to competitive behavior. I have already noted that a general posture of competition in the

Middle East has characterized Soviet policy there since 1955, when Khrushchev led the Soviets out of Stalinist continentalism and breathed new life into the universalist strand of the ideology. But what determines the specific level of competitive assertiveness? More specifically, under what conditions do the Soviets markedly up the competitive ante—through much-expanded arms transfers, the transfer of much more sophisticated weapons systems, or strong encouragement of Arab clients to damage U.S. interests?

The Soviets fashion themselves the military and political patron of several Arab clients in the confrontation with Israel. As such, the Soviets under Brezhnev typically upped the competitive ante whenever the United States increased its support for Israel (for example, after delivery of a shipment of advanced fighter-planes) or whenever the Israelis inflicted a tactical defeat on Soviet clients. Since the 1967 war, this pattern has been rather clear and consistent, though with an occasional lapse dictated by unusual circumstances of the moment (for example, a Soviet effort to persuade a client to moderate its negotiating position).

The Soviets also up the ante when they experience a loss that may not be of Israeli or U.S. doing. Thus, after Sadat expelled Soviet military personnel in July 1972, the Soviets moved quickly to deepen their ties with other clients and to expand ties with nonclients (often, of a more radical stripe). Thus, in these cases we are dealing with a general Soviet tendency to compensate for losses by attempting to solidify existing relationships and develop new ones. Similarly, the Soviets decided only in 1980 to comply with Syrian insistent requests (dating from 1978) to sponsor a massive buildup of Syrian ground forces. The decision to sponsor the buildup, if it was not triggered by Camp David and the Reagan administration's talk of a "strategic relationship" with Israel, may have been part of an effort to pressure Iraq, which had been distancing itself from the USSR.

A fourth condition for increased competitive assertiveness by the Soviets is a perception that the United States, through secret diplomacy or explicit strategy, is seeking to exclude the USSR from the peace settlement process. To the Soviets, such exclusionary diplomacy, as practiced by Nixon, Ford, Carter, and Reagan, represents containment by other means. Correctly, they perceive it to be an effort to mediate the Arab–Israeli conflict through Washington alone, rather than through U.S.–Soviet collaboration, in order to effect a settlement that will both reduce Arab–Israeli tensions and reduce Soviet influence in the region. To Moscow, this represents a very high level of competitive assertiveness on the part of the United States. They do not treat it as cause for confrontation, since the

United States is not seeking to overthrow the regimes of their clients. But they do treat it as zero-sum competition, in which the United States places highest priority on driving a wedge between Moscow and its clients in the region. Hence, the appropriate response, in Soviet eyes, has been to up the ante themselves, usually by expanding arms transfers, the transfer of more threatening weaponry, or deepening support for the more radical and intransigent forces in the region. At each step along the way during the 1970s, one finds analogous Soviet responses to U.S. efforts at exclusion. The crescendo, of course, came in 1979, with the signing of the Camp David accords. Until then, the Soviets had upped the competitive ante without signs of actively seeking to obstruct and disrupt the peace process. Since Camp David, however, both Soviet press commentary and Soviet behavior in the region (for example, deepening ties with the George Habash faction of the PLO; deepening ties with Libya; and diplomatic pressure on Syria) have suggested Moscow may consider it better to have no peace settlement, even of the Soviet-preferred variety, than to have a settlement mediated exclusively by Washington.

Would the Soviets be willing to reduce their level of competitive assertiveness in response to meaningful U.S.–Israeli restraint, or in response to less exclusionary U.S. mediation of the conflict? Perhaps, but we cannot say with confidence, for the hypothesis has never been adequately tested. A close examination of the diplomatic interaction between the superpowers reveals that Moscow and Washington were engaged in a game of approach-avoidance, in which neither side wanted to appear to be pressuring its client more than the other was.[14] Moreover, the continuous U.S. commitment to exclusionary diplomacy meant that U.S. leaders rarely created opportunities to test Soviet intentions.

This leads us into the issue of collaboration. Under what conditions do the Soviets come forth with meaningful collaborative offerings for reducing the level of Arab–Israeli confrontation and restraining the U.S.–Soviet competition in the region? In fact, since December 1968, the Soviet negotiating position regarding a Middle East settlement has been remarkably consistent. With slight variations resulting from changing circumstances on the ground and from the dynamics of the U.S.–Soviet approach-avoidance diplomatic relationship, the Soviet position has been comprised of the following desiderata:

1. U.S.–Soviet comediation of the settlement process, either through collusion behind-the-scenes or through cochairmanship of the Geneva Conference, or through some combination of the two;

2. Israeli withdrawal from territories occupied during the June 1967 war (with the possibility of minor border adjustments remaining as an open question);
3. Establishment of a Palestinian homeland of some sort on the West Bank and Gaza Strip.
4. U.S.–Soviet (and perhaps other great power) collaboration to provide concrete guarantees of the security of all states in the region, including Israel.

Many U.S. politicians, and some U.S. specialists on Soviet policy in the Middle East, write off the Soviet negotiating position as self-evidently disingenuous, and accuse the Soviets of "doing nothing to encourage an Arab–Israeli settlement."[15] These analysts view Soviet collaborative offerings as entirely tactical. In their view, confrontation and competition, with an occasional display of avoidance behavior, comprise the entire repertoire of Soviet behavior patterns in the Middle East. Collaborative offerings are tactical components of a strategy of conflict-perpetuation. The Soviets, it is claimed, have a stake in maintaining a condition of "no war and no peace" in the region, because they perceive such a situation as conducive to maintaining the dependence of their clients on their military patronage.

My own reading of the evidence leads to a different conclusion. It is not that the Soviets do not want a settlement that will defuse the constant threat of war in the region; it is rather that the Soviets have been consistently committed to the realization of a particular kind of settlement, one that is based on the four terms outlined above. Relatedly, it is not that the Soviets are against peace in the region; it is rather that they have absolutely no illusions about the degree of harmony between Arabs and Israelis that a settlement could bring about, regardless of the intentions of individual leaders in Moscow, Washington, Jerusalem, Cairo, or Damascus. Thus, U.S. analysts who denigrate the Soviet collaborative impulse define the alternatives in the region as either conflict or harmony. In contrast, the Soviets (and most Israeli specialists on Soviet policy, I might add) define the alternatives as continuous confrontation versus "armed peace," by which is meant a stand-down, normalization of diplomatic relations, and settlement of the most war-threatening issues.[16]

Once we accept that the Soviets define the only realistic alternatives in these terms, it is easier to believe that they believe their negotiating position to be realistic and just. Yet there are many other reasons to believe this as well. First, some U.S. diplomats claim that the Soviet negotiating position must be disingenuous because it is an obvious nonstarter: they knew we could not live with the terms. In fact, William Rogers, Joseph Sisco, and Cyrus Vance all displayed considerable interest in Soviet negotiating terms and in the Soviet vision of a realistic settlement, while Henry Kissinger for several years cleverly concealed his disinterest in Soviet terms. Thus, this argument for Soviet insincerity is untenable.

A second argument is that the Soviets feign interest in collaboration in order to lull U.S. leaders into believing that a potentially fruitful process is underway (thereby reducing the chances for Soviet–American confrontation) while keeping the pot boiling on the ground. In fact, there is negligible evidence to suggest that the Soviets are self-confident about their ability to walk such a tightrope between competition and confrontation. Put differently, they have not displayed self-confidence about their ability to keep the pot boiling without letting it boil over. They may have believed as much before the June 1967 war, but Israeli military doctrine from 1967 onward made such self-confidence extremely difficult to maintain. For Israeli commitment to a strategy of preemption, coupled with the Israeli practice of counteroffensive and escalation when attacked first (as in the War of Attrition and the 1973 war), meant that the military situation could easily get out of control regardless of the state of diplomatic exchanges between Moscow and Washington. The ascension to power of the Likud in Israel in 1977 served only to reinforce this perception, as did heightened fears that the next war could be nuclearized.

A third argument is that the Soviets perceive perpetuation of the confrontation to be in their interest, for such perpetuation maintains or deepens the dependence on the USSR of her clients in the region. On the face of it, this looks like a compelling argument, for control of the "military option" available to the Arabs has long been the main Soviet asset in its relations with regional clients. Yet this argument is also seriously flawed (though perhaps not conclusively capable of being rejected), for two reasons. First, the Soviet vision of an armed peace does not include a degree of harmony that would end superpower competition for influence in the region. There would remain plenty of opportunities for arms transfers, and for military–political patronage of clients. Second, research by Oded Eran suggests that a reevaluation took place in Moscow after the 1973 war.[17] The burden of this reevaluation was the conclusion that the consolidation of Soviet influence in key Middle East capitals required a lengthy period of stabilization of international relationships in the region, and that perpetuation of the Arab–Israeli confrontation had become a threat to the Soviet ability to maintain reliable allies. Eran's research needs to be updated and expanded, but it strongly suggests that the Soviets have come to believe that the absence of a settlement is working against Soviet interests in the Middle East. Since we take for granted that competing great powers pursue their interests, even when they seek ways to manage their rivalry through collaboration, we should not be searching for altruism in Soviet (or, for that matter, U.S.) collaborative offerings. We should, however, look for signs that the Soviets perceive a settlement on the terms indicated to be in their interest.

How much flexibility is there in the Soviet negotiating position? The basic terms are broad, vague, and, to some extent, open-ended. The Soviet position has vacillated regarding details, such as: (1) the scope of minor border adjustments to accompany Israeli withdrawal; (2) the precise size, international status, and governing authority (the PLO?) of a Palestinian state; (3) the forms to be taken by superpower guarantees of a settlement; and (4) the possible follow-ups to such a settlement (for example a mutual embargo of certain types of arms transfers to the region). These are, of course, important details. Depending on circumstances, they can make the difference between success and failure in negotiations. Yet the failure of the Soviets to specify these details reflects their flexibility, not intransigence: the Soviets have zigzagged over time on these issues, at times indicating willingness to adopt a moderate position, at other times taking the hard line. More importantly, though, the extent of Soviet flexibility on details has almost never been tested. The essence of exclusionary diplomacy was to reject the basic Soviet negotiating position and to go it alone. Hence, Washington and Moscow never developed an ongoing collaborative relationship in Middle East diplomacy through which the limits of Soviet flexibility might have been explored. One thing can be asserted with reasonable confidence, though. The striking continuity of the basic Soviet negotiating terms since December 1968 suggests a depth and breadth of commitment to the contours of that plan which is probably very great. Whatever flexibility might have existed at the margins probably would not have been allowed to compromise the basics—even if a collaborative negotiating process had become regularized.

The Soviet Response to the War in Lebanon

The war in Lebanon during the summer of 1982 provides a recent test of my analysis of the dynamics of Soviet policy in the Middle East. In my opinion, the analysis passes the test, for the Soviet response pattern to the events of June through September 1982 was consistent with previous patterns exhibited in the Brezhnev era.

On 6 June the Israeli Defense Forces launched "Operation Peace for Galilee," a land, sea, and air invasion of Lebanon. At first, the proclaimed goal was to eliminate all terrorist bases capable of hitting northern Israel from southern Lebanon, meaning that Israeli leaders were determined to push twenty-five miles into Lebanon. At the same time, the Israeli Air Force struck at Syrian bases and SAM missile emplacements in the Bekaa Valley of eastern Lebanon. Both operations were striking and immediate successes. The occupation of southern Lebanon took but a few days, while the air battles with Syria produced the most lop-sided victory since the June 1967 war: the entire Syrian SAM defense system in the Bekaa Valley was destroyed, as were eighty-one Syrian jet-fighter, with the loss of only one Israeli plane. By 12 June Israel declared a unilateral cease-fire in the Bekaa Valley.

Not so in western Lebanon, where Israeli ground forces pushed rapidly beyond the twenty-five-mile zone, not stopping until they had laid seige to the capital city of Beirut. There they surrounded West Beirut, entrapping up to ten thousand PLO soldiers, and subjecting that half of the city to days of heavy bombardment by air and sea. Thereafter, both the projected Israeli losses from an effort to occupy West Beirut, and pressure from the United States on Israel not to level the city, led to a tense and extended period of seige. After many weeks of international diplomacy, an agreement was reached that provided for the evacuation of PLO soldiers and their families from West Beirut, and their dispersal among several Arab countries. The evacuation was supervised by an international military force comprised of U.S., French, and Italian soldiers. This did not prevent a massacre of Palestinian refugees in the Sabra and Shatila refugee camps outside Beirut by Lebanese Christian Phalangists, abetted, in turn, by the Israeli authorities' decision not to take precautions.

The Soviet response to Israel's victories in Lebanon was a decidedly passive one.[18] In the early days of the war, various Arab leaders, as well as leading spokesmen for the PLO, appealed urgently to the USSR to get involved to stop the invasion. In short, they appealed for a confrontational Soviet act. Instead, they were treated to a display of Soviet avoidance behavior. Through diplomatic channels, Moscow informed Arab leaders that the Soviet armed forces would not confront Israel. Brezhnev also sent urgent messages to President Reagan, at several stages of the conflict, demanding an end to the Israeli offensive, but those messages were noteworthy for their failure to issue the kinds of ultimatums to which the Soviets had resorted in earlier Arab–Israeli wars.

Thus, the Soviets did nothing to prevent the Israeli victories over both the PLO and Syrian forces. But they did ensure against the contingency they most wanted to avoid: the spread of Israeli–Syrian fighting into Syria proper. In the early days of the war, Moscow warned Washington of the real possibility of Soviet intervention in the event of such spill-over. Perhaps to prepare for this contingency, or perhaps to lend credibility to the warning, the Soviets placed airborne divisions on alert, reinforced the Mediterranean fleet, requested the right to fly over Turkey, and engaged in a moderate resupply of the Syrian armed forces. None of this qualifies as confrontational behavior in the immediate context, however, for these threats and preparations were decoupled from the immediate train of events—the Israeli victory in the Bekaa, the Israeli occupation of Beirut and her threat to liquidate PLO forces therein.

While the Soviets engaged in avoidance behavior with respect to the immediate train of events, their longer-range response during fall to winter of 1982–1983 was to up the competitive ante in response to the tactical defeat experienced by their client, Syria. They rebuilt the Syrian armed forces, supplied command and control technologies for battlefield coordination (previously denied Syria due to fear of losing these advanced technologies to the Israelis), constructed two SAM-5 missile bases (anti-aircraft missiles never before introduced outside the Warsaw Pact), and staffed the command and control as well as missile bases with Soviet military personnel—all of which would sharply increase the costs to the Israelis of a renewal of war with Syria. In addition, to destroy these technologies, the Israelis would have to kill large numbers of Soviet personnel, with all this could imply for escalation of the conflict.

How might we explain the Soviet failure to rescue the PLO and Syria in Lebanon? Numerous explanations could be put forth, and have appeared in journalistic commentary. Let me begin with the explanations I find least persuasive.

1. *Logistical:* this posits that, for the Soviets to have stopped the Israeli juggernaut before it reached Beirut, or to have prevented the Syrian defeat in Bekaa, would have required so rapid and massive a Soviet intervention (fifteen divisions, one analyst has estimated)[19] that the costs would have been prohibitive. While probably true as far as it goes, this explanation ignores the fact that a confrontational response can take the form of a threat to intervene. For the Soviets to have intervened to liberate the Egyptian Third Army in October 1973 would also have required a massive force. But they were at

least willing to threaten to do so. In 1982 they would not even do that.

2. *Medicinal:* Brezhnev's fragile health, according to this explanation, introduced a paralysis into the Soviet foreign policy decision-making process. Failure to confront reflected lack of energy, not lack of will. I find this implausible as well. Brezhnev's health was poor before the invasion of Afghanistan, yet decisive action was taken. Also, Soviet policy toward Western Europe and in the INF negotiations was active and flexible during the first half of 1982, despite the state of Brezhnev's health.

3. *Arab disunity:* this is one of the official Soviet excuses, voiced in response to appeals from Arab leaders for Soviet intervention. As the Soviets put it, if the Arab states were not willing collectively to defend Beirut, why should the Soviets? This too strikes me as implausible. The Soviets gave many indications of being willing to defend Syria proper against spillover, regardless of the state of Arab unity. That they were not willing to do the same for the PLO in Lebanon requires an explanation.[20]

4. *Protect priority goals:* this explanation sees Soviet temporizing as a reflection of the relatively low priority they place on the Middle East in their foreign policy hierarchy of preferences. Above all else, they wanted arms control with the United States (in particular, to forestall the installation of Pershing-2 missiles in Europe), detente with Western Europe, and continued economic relations with Western Europe and the United States (the gas pipeline, subsidized credits, high-technology imports, and grain). Intervention and confrontation in the Middle East could have so polarized East–West relations that these priority goals might well have been sacrificed. This statement of Soviet priorities is probably accurate as far as it goes, but, in my opinion, it was not decisive in Soviet calculations during June 1982. For, in the face of provocation, the Soviets have proven their willingness to confront the United States in the Middle East, even during the heyday of detente. They flooded Egypt with weaponry from fall 1972 to fall 1973, and they threatened to intervene during the October war. To be sure, they made every diplomatic effort to insulate the detente process from the reverberations of these acts. But the fact that they were willing to take the chance of damaging detente indicates that, at a given level of provocation, they are willing to confront to protect their priority interests within the Middle East.

This brings me to the explanation I find most plausible: that the war in Lebanon did not threaten Soviet priority interests within the Middle East. It is important to bear in mind that Soviet willingness to engage in confrontational behavior in that region has been rare. As I argued in the previous section of this chapter, the Soviets' risk-taking propensity has been low, and their willingness to intervene has typically hinged on the need to prevent a strategic defeat for a client-state. The PLO is not a state, and Syrian losses in the Bekaa constituted a tactical, not a strategic defeat. Had the war spilled over into Syria proper, with Israel on the offensive, such a strategic defeat for a client-state would have been imminent. Soviet threats and preparations during summer 1982 indicated a predisposition to intervene to prevent that.

On the basis of past experience during the Brezhnev era, the longer-term Soviet response to the Syrian tactical defeat was also predictable. They upped the competitive ante with the introduction of SAM-5 missiles, advanced command and control, and Soviet personnel. Such escalation of the competition in the face of a loss, and in the absence of genuine U.S.–Soviet collaboration to de-escalate the competition, had been the Soviet modus operandi for at least fifteen years.[21]

The Soviet failure to rescue the PLO reflects both the Soviet attitude toward taking risks for the sake of social movements (after all, they have never sacrificed other goals for the sake of persecuted communist parties in the Arab world, and the PLO is not even communist), and the PLO unwillingness to respond to Soviet demands for a change in Palestinian strategy. Authentic transcripts of discussions between Soviet Politburo-members and PLO leaders (some published in the early 1970s and others captured in Lebanon) reveal consistent Soviet urging that the PLO recognize the State of Israel, abandon international terrorism, and give higher priority to a political over a military strategy for attaining their goal of acquiring a state of its own. Thus, the basic Soviet negotiating position, outlined earlier in this paper, has never been accepted by the PLO. As punishment, the Soviets were not willing to renounce their role as military patron (that is, supplier) of the PLO. But they have also never been willing to go to the mat on their behalf, either: not in Jordan in 1970; not in Lebanon in 1975–1976; and not in Lebanon in 1982.

How are these generalizations likely to be affected by the political successions going on in Moscow since the death of Brezhnev? In other words, does the process of political succession have an important influence on Soviet propensity to confront in defense of priority Middle Eastern interests? I would answer with a qualified "no."

The striking continuity in the basic Soviet negotiating position on an Arab–Israeli settlement, coupled with the consistently low propensity for risk-taking and intervention, suggest to me a rather broad consensus within the Soviet political establishment as to what is important in foreign affairs. That is, there may be a great deal of bargaining, conflict, and disagreement over tactics and costs; but there is probably a high degree of consensus as to basic strategy. If this conclusion is correct, and barring a rash act forced through in a moment of tension by a forceful leader, we would not expect the process of political succession to raise markedly the Soviet propensity to intervene if fighting breaks out again within the borders of Lebanon.

However, the situation on the ground is different from what it was in June 1982, and that situation could create dynamics and ambiguities that could lead to Soviet intervention. With SAM-5s and SS-21s in Syria, a renewal of large-scale fighting between Syrian and Israeli forces (should that come to pass) would be more difficult to confine within the borders of Lebanon. Were Israel to seize the initiative and push into Syria to eliminate the SAM-5s by air or land, both the self-imposed and the external pressure on Moscow to intervene would be immense. At a minimum, I would expect them to make credible threats of intervention, accompanied by a demonstrated willingness to defend Damascus.

This statement, I realize, flies in the face of the claim that, during periods of political succession, Soviet leaders typically turn inward and concentrate on domestic problems. Yet that claim is over-generalized and distorts the historical record. During 1954–1955, Khrushchev led the Soviets out of their continental isolationism into a new era of global activism; indeed, that was one of his foreign policy appeals. And one important feature of that global activism was the Egyptian–Czechoslovakian arms deal of 1955, which was the centerpiece of Soviet reentry into the Middle East as a self-proclaimed global power. Similarly, during 1965–1967, the Soviets devoted considerable resources to building up their Mediterranean fleet, and during the months leading up to the June 1967 war, they were uncharacteristically incautious in fanning the flames of conflict. It is tempting to conclude that the political fluidity of a succession period allows those inclined toward global activism more easily to seize the initiative, but this might be a premature conclusion given the limited sample and data base at our disposal. At a minimum we can declare that the historical evidence does not support the claim that the process of political succession reduces Soviet propensity for risk-taking in the Middle East.

Conclusion

The main Soviet goals in the Middle East are to consolidate and expand Soviet influence with prospective client-states, to acquire strategic assets for use in the ongoing geostrategic competition with the United States, to avoid confrontation with the United States, and to reduce U.S. influence and strategic leverage in the region. However, the Middle East ranks rather low in the overall hierarchy of Soviet foreign policy priorities, exceeded by Soviet concerns as a superpower and continental power. On the other hand, among global power concerns, the Middle East may rank highest in Soviet priorities, which explains why the Soviets have been willing to confront the United States in defense of clients in the Middle East.

The Soviets have employed four distinct tactics in seeking to advance their interests in the Middle East: confrontation, competition, collaboration, and avoidance. Under Brezhnev they were most consistently competitive and collaborative—determined to compete with the United States for influence and allies, but ready to collaborate with the United States to settle the Arab–Israeli conflict. Such a settlement would entail U.S.–Soviet collusion to bring about an armed peace in the region, with Israeli withdrawal from occupied territories, the creation of a Palestinian state, and superpower guarantees of border security for all states in the region, including Israel. The degree of flexibility in the Soviet position, though, has never been fully tested, for U.S. foreign policy has generally been to seek a settlement that would reduce Soviet influence and exclude Soviet co-leadership of the settlement process.

While collaboration and competition have coexisted as consistent features of Soviet policy in the region, Soviet leaders have also engaged in confrontational and avoidance behavior. Typically, they have been willing to confront in order to prevent a strategic defeat of a client-state. Their policies more generally have been cautious, seeking to avoid confrontation with the United States. The most conspicuous examples of avoidance behavior have been in conditions when the PLO was being decimated, and the Soviets did nothing to protect it.

The Soviet reaction to the Israeli invasion of Lebanon has been consistent with these generalizations about Soviet policy under Brezhnev. The Soviets rejected confrontational behavior in defense of the PLO (or Beirut more generally). But they did signal their willingness to confront if Israeli–Syrian hostilities degenerated into a war on Syrian territory with the real prospect of a strategic defeat for the Assad regime. And, after the war was under control, the Soviets upped the competitive ante by rebuilding the Syrian armed forces and introducing a Soviet-manned SAM-5 air defense system into Syria. The process of political succession would not be likely to alter the threshold for Soviet confrontational behavior in the event of a renewal of major conflict between Israel and Syria, and especially if those hostilities spill over into Syrian territory.

Notes

1. On Khrushchev's strategy, see Thomas Wolfe, *Soviet Strategy at the Crossroads* (Cambridge: Harvard University Press, 1965), and Arnold Horelick and Myron Rush, *Strategic Power and Soviet Foreign Policy* (Chicago: University of Chicago Press, 1966).

2. Robert Legvold, "The Nature of Soviet Power," *Foreign Affairs* 56 (October 1977), 49–71.

3. We cannot say with certainty just how confident Soviet leaders feel, or how clearly they define specific trade-offs (hence, my frequent use of conditional phrasing in this section). On the other hand, extensive Western scholarship on the evolution of Soviet perspectives and perceptions suggests a secular decline of optimism in Soviet views of the international system, a rise in uncertainty, ambivalence, and appreciation of constraints, and a major impact of the reality of nuclear weapons on Soviet thinking about the feasibility of fundamentally transforming the existing international system.

4. The concept, geostrategic rivalry, is from Alvin Z. Rubinstein, *Red Star on the Nile: The Soviet-Egyptian Influence Relationship since the June War* (Princeton: Princeton University Press, 1977).

5. Contrast Abraham S. Becker, "The Politics of Confrontation-Avoidance," in Abraham S. Becker, Brent Hansen, and Malcolm Kerr, *The Economics and Politics of the Middle East* (New York: American Elsevier Publishing Company, Inc., 1975), 99–111, with Galia Golan, *Yom Kippur and After* (London: Cambridge University Press, 1977), 1–20.

6. For the term, confrontation-avoidance, see Becker (note 5).

7. For this argument, see Guf Ofer, "Economic Aspects of Soviet Involvement in the Middle East," in Yaacov Ro'i, ed., *The Limits to Power* (London: Croom Helm, 1979), 67–95.

8. Richard Pipes, "Militarism and the Soviet State," *Daedalus* 109 (Fall 1980), 1–12.

9. For the strongest statement of this view, with respect to Soviet Middle East policy, see O.M. Smolansky, "The United States and the Soviet Union in the Middle East," in Grayson Kirk and Nils H. Wessell, eds., *The Soviet Threat: Myths and Realities* (New York: The Academy of Political Science, 1978), 99–109.

10. For documentation of this assertion, along with further discussion of the concept, "collaborative competition," see George W. Breslauer, "Soviet Policy in the Middle East, 1967–1972: Unalterable Antagonism or Collaborative Competition?" in Alexander George, *Managing U.S.–Soviet Rivalry: Problems of Crisis Prevention* (Boulder: Westview Press, 1983), 65–106.

11. For this perspective, see Henry Kissinger, *White House Years* (Boston: Little, Brown, 1979), chapters X, XIV, XV, and XXX.

12. For details of these crises, see Lawrence L. Whetten, *The Canal War: Four-Power Conflict in the Middle East* (Cambridge: The M.I.T. Press, 1974); see also George (note 10), chapters 7, 9.

13. It is more difficult to say whether the Soviets would confront if a client were threatened by strategic defeat at the hands of a local Arab state that was not tied to the United States as directly as is Israel.

14. This statement is bound to be controversial, for many observers seem to believe that the United States has frequently pressured Israel to a significant extent. Yet I have not seen an objective test of the extent of such pressure. Instead, the fact that the Israeli government has loudly protested the delay in delivery of fighter planes when the United States wanted to show displeasure has been taken as the indicator of significant "U.S. pressure." Obviously, the Israeli government has a stake in continuously protecting loudly, even when experience has taught them that the planes will eventually be delivered. A broader examination of U.S. and Soviet real pressure on their clients would probably conclude that neither side has been applying strong pressure during the past fifteen years geared toward behavior modification, partly because the lack of U.S.–Soviet collaboration has led both Moscow and Washington to be very wary of appearing to engage in unilateral pressuring of allies. The single exception may be President Carter's pressure on Menachem Begin at Camp David in 1978.

15. Alvin Z. Rubinstein, "The Soviet Union's Imperial Policy in the Middle East," *Middle East Review* 15 (Fall/Winter 1982–1983), 21, see also 19–24; see also the literature cited in Breslauer (note 10 and note 1).

16. See Breslauer (note 10); also, Ro'i (note 7), passim.

17. Oded Eran, "The Soviet Perception of Influence: The Case of the Middle East, 1973–1976," in Ro'i (note 7), 127–148.

18. My reconstruction of the Soviet response is based on Galia Golan, "The Soviet Union and the Israeli War in Lebanon," *Research Paper No. 46* (Jerusalem: The Hebrew University, Soviet and East European Research Centre, October 1982); also Karen Dawisha, "The U.S.S.R. and the Middle East," *Foreign Affairs* 61 (Winter 1982–1983), 438–452.

19. Amnon Sella, "The Soviet Attitude Towards the War in Lebanon—Mid-1982," *Research Paper No. 47* (Jerusalem: The Hebrew University, Soviet and East European Research Centre, December 1982). Sella makes this estimate on the basis of a careful analysis of the local situation and of Soviet military science. However, he does not argue that the logistical situation was the main, much less the only, reason for Soviet failure to intervene.

20. For this argument, see Robert O. Freedman, "The Soviet Union, Syria, and the Crisis in Lebanon: A Preliminary Analysis," mimeo (Baltimore: Baltimore Hebrew College, 1983).

21. Indeed, more recently, we have witnessed another manifestation of this pattern. In September 1983 intense U.S.–Saudi diplomatic efforts took

place, geared toward restoring a cease-fire among warring factions within Lebanon. Syria was the key outside actor involved in the fighting, and its government's position essentially determined the possibilities for a cease-fire. When the cease-fire was finally negotiated, U.S. diplomats began suddenly to speak publicly about "legitimate Syrian interests in Lebanon," a sign that secret concessions might have been made to Damascus in the process of negotiation. Meanwhile, Moscow looked on, uncertain as to whether the United States was seeking to drive a wedge between Moscow and Damascus. About one week later, the U.S. government announced that the Soviets had upped the competitive ante once again, transferring SS-21 missiles to the Syrians. These are very advanced ground-to-ground missiles.

6
The Soviet Union and the Persian Gulf

Dennis Ross

Much has happened in the Middle East and the Persian Gulf over the last several years.[1] King Hussein's decision not to negotiate the future of the West Bank and the failure of the Israeli–Lebanese agreement on withdrawal are only the latest in a series of events that have shaped the choices and behaviors of local actors and affected the positions of the superpowers in the region. If the Shah's fall and the Soviet invasion of Afghanistan created a sense of imminent danger about the Soviet threat to our vital interests in the Gulf, the Iran–Iraq war, the deterioration of Soviet–Iranian relations, and the conflict in Lebanon, reassured many that indigenous factors in the area would constrain the Soviets and limit the threat they could pose to our regional interests. Because Hussein's decision and the Syrian undoing of the Israeli–Lebanese agreement are seen by many as further proof that local political realities have a way of frustrating superpower objectives—ours as well as theirs—it is unlikely to change this view.

But should we accept this view? Are the factors that constrain the Soviets real and enduring? Are those factors that so concerned us about the Soviet threat two years ago no longer relevant or evident? Are the Soviets demonstrating any less interest or determination in achieving their regional goals? And, are they indicating in any way that they believe that their regional strategy is not working and needs to be redefined or changed?

A basic theme in what follows is that notwithstanding a number of setbacks and related difficulties in the region, the Soviets remain determined to pursue their regional goals and also remain generally satisfied with the strategy they have adopted for achieving these

An earlier version of this chapter was published in the winter 1984 issue of *Political Science Quarterly*.

goals. This does not mean that the Soviets would not like to be doing better, but it does mean that given regional trends, their available options, the asymmetries in U.S. and Soviet stakes in the region, and the risks they are prepared to run, their current strategy continues to make far more sense than any alternative.

The Soviet Position in the Persian Gulf

Clearly, this is a sentiment not shared by some Western observers of Soviet policy in the area. In viewing Soviet passivity in response to events in Lebanon in the summer of 1982, Karen Dawisha drew a very different conclusion and went so far as to suggest that the Soviets might be in "eclipse" in the region because they lack options or opportunities for making gains. In her words:

> Soviet immobilism over Lebanon can be attributed not only to a lack of opportunities provided by the Arab states for greater Soviet participation, it can also be put down to a marked Soviet disinclination to get involved. And this disinclination extends beyond the confines of the Lebanese conflict to encompass a more general malaise in Soviet policy toward the region.[2]

Dr. Dawisha and others identify the underlying causes for Soviet difficulties and limitations in the region as:

> The rise of Islamic fundamentalism and its basic hostility to atheistic communism.
>
> The emergence of oil wealth and the means this provides states like Saudi Arabia to use their wealth to influence and moderate the politics of the Syrians, PLO, etc.
>
> The availability of Europeans as alternative suppliers of sophisticated arms to the Arabs, reducing dependencies on the Soviets for military hardware.
>
> Increasing emphasis on development and modernization among the oil rich, whether moderates or radical, and an understanding that one must look to the West and not the East for necessary technologies and expertise.
>
> The absence of a charismatic leader like Nasser who mobilizes mass support throughout Arab lands, who defines the baselines of an Arab consensus, who puts pro-Western regimes on the

defensive, and whose regional aims converge with at least near-term Soviet interests.[3]

While there is a measure of truth revealed in each of these factors, one needs to view them with some caution. Though there is much inherent hostility to communism in the Middle East–Persian Gulf region, it is the West generally and not the East that is seen "as the culturally disruptive power that challenged or undermined Islam in these societies."[4] Moreover, with a Moslem population that will reach 70 million by the turn of the century, the Soviets may find it easier to gain entry into the Islamic world than we might imagine. As Alexandre Benningsen has noted, the Soviets adopted an "Islamic strategy" in the 1970s, using religious leaders from Central Asia to showcase the reconciliation of Islam and communist development, to initiate exchange with religious authorities from the Moslem world, and to establish ties with the clergy in states like Saudi Arabia where diplomatic relations do not exist. While Afghanistan has dealt this strategy a setback, Soviet Moslems should not be discounted as a potential bridging element to the Middle East–Persian Gulf.[5] Brezhnev's statement at the Twenty-Sixth Party Congress that "the liberation struggle can develop under the banner of Islam" was surely an attempt to highlight the possibilities for reconciliation. (At the same time, it is important to remember that bridges run two ways, and the outside appeal of Islam could yet be a disruptive factor within the Soviet Union—something that is sure to induce Soviet caution in using their Moslems as a bridge.)

Though the oil states have certainly sought to use financial incentives as a way to moderate the behavior of states like Syria, one sees few examples where this has actually altered or significantly influenced radical behaviors on important issues or led them to pursue a course of action they were not prepared to accept anyway. If anything, the influence seems to work in the opposite direction, with the radicals taking the money and extracting promises that bind the oil states more closely to their positions. For example, in Lebanon, it is the Syrians who influenced the Saudis and not the reverse.

While all the local states—with the possible exception of Iran—prefer U.S.–Western technology for development, there is not at this point any indication that those who currently depend on Soviet weaponry truly believe that the Europeans can replace the Soviets as their main suppliers. (Augment their forces, yes; allow them to learn more about Western technologies in order to combat the Israelis, yes; give them greater leverage against the Soviets, yes; but actually replace the Soviets as suppliers, no.) Only the Soviets can supply arms in the quantity and quality and with the kind of speed necessary to meet the needs and satisfy the appetites of the states that depend on the Soviets for arms.

Finally, while Nasser may be gone, two points are worth noting. First, he did not forge consensus in the Arab world, he helped foster, in the words of one observer, an "Arab cold war."[6] Moreover, his mass appeal and his ability to put those leaders identified with the U.S. on the defensive was not sufficient to prevent the Saudis from inviting in a U.S. squadron of F-100s to deter Egyptian forces in Yemen from attacking Saudi territory. Secondly, in Ayatollah Rouhollah Khomeini there is a charismatic leader today in the region, whose appeal carries across borders and who has succeeded in making those in the Gulf defensive about their ties to the West. To the extent that he succeeds in undermining Western-oriented regimes in the Gulf, he will be serving Soviet interests.

This is not to say that many local factors do not impede or inhibit the Soviets; they surely do. It is to say that these factors may not limit the Soviets as much as some may think or wish.

Moreover, before one concludes that the Soviets are in eclipse in the region, that they basically (if unhappily) accept this, and that we can, therefore, relax our own regional security efforts, one needs to consider several other factors and potential regional developments.

Soviet Provision of SAM-5s and Other Equipment

First, the Soviet decision to provide the Syrians SAM-5s (and other advanced air defense equipment) is extremely significant in terms of what it reveals about the Soviet attitudes and their willingness to run risks in the area. The Soviets have never transferred this system outside the Soviet bloc, and, at least for some time to come, the Soviets will have to man the system—and its related air defenses in Syria.[7]

What this suggests is that, much like in Egypt in 1970, the Soviets have basically assumed responsibility for Syrian air defense. As Alvin Rubinstein has pointed out, this did not necessarily translate into great influence over Egyptian policy,[8] but it surely raised Soviet stakes in Egypt then and it has raised Soviet stakes in Syria now.

As such, it clearly has also raised the risks the Soviets are running in Syria. Though the Soviets undoubtedly hope that their presence will deter Israeli military moves against Syria—much as it deterred Israeli deep-penetration raids during the War of Attrition in 1970—they knew when they made the decision that they were facing an

Israeli leadership (particularly given Sharon's proclivities) that was quick to use force against perceived threats.

What made the decision even more risky—and different from the 1970 case—was the fact that the SAM-5s cover a significant amount of airspace over Israel itself. This, alone, made an Israeli preemption likely if a war seemed imminent, particularly because no Israeli military leadership would be likely to feel that it could afford to permit Soviet capabilities and presence in Syria to constrain Israeli military options to the point that Israel was forced to fight a war on terms or ground rules that favored Syria. Thus, the Soviets must have known when they made the decision that they faced a considerable risk of Israeli preemption.

Their need to respond to an Israeli preemption—particularly if it were successful and the Israeli losses were relatively limited—makes the Soviet decision even more notable. Indeed, for reasons relating mostly to the Soviets' sensitivity about their status and image as a superpower and the high costs for any Soviet leadership of being humiliated or appearing weak, the Soviets are likely to feel compelled to respond—perhaps by increasing their ground force presence and operational responsibilities in Syria and providing the Syrians with even more threatening equipment. Again, while this might deter the Israelis and put greater pressure on the U.S. to constrain them, it might also create an escalatory cycle that is difficult to control and that requires the Soviets to up the ante further. Traditionally, the Soviets have been very reluctant to put themselves in this kind of a situation. Yet, this is precisely what they have done in Syria.

If nothing else, this tells us that the Soviets were and are running significant risks, as they measure risks, in Syria. At a minimum this indicates that there is not a "marked Soviet disinclination to get involved" in the region.[9] On the contrary for them to be willing to run such risks, the Soviets must be quite determined to stay very much involved in the region and must regard their stakes in Syria and the area as sufficiently high to warrant their taking these kinds of chances. Why are they so determined to stay involved and why is Syria sufficiently important to them to justify their running these kinds of risks? The answer is twofold. First, the Soviets seem to believe that an essential condition for being regarded as an unquestioned superpower with global influence is to have presence and influence in the Middle East (broadly defined), and to preserve this they seem to be willing to pay quite a lot and to take some bold steps.

Second, the Soviets perceive Syria as the key to their position in the Middle East and the Persian Gulf. So long as Syria opposes U.S.-backed negotiations or agreements, Syria provides the Soviets assured entrée to Arab–Israeli issues—a basis on which to claim that the Soviet Union must be a party to any attempts to resolve the conflict, and their best means for disrupting potential agreements and highlighting the futility of trying to exclude them from any peace-making efforts. Besides ensuring Soviet involvement in Arab–Israeli issues as well as a claim to being an arbiter of the conflict, Syria is also important to the Soviets because it provides important pressure points on and potential access to the Gulf states. Indeed, with a larger number of radical PLO groups increasingly under Syrian control, the Assad regime's ability to put pressure on the Saudis and other Gulf states is likely to grow; continuing Syrian–Iraqi hostility and the extensive Soviet buildup in Syria gives the Iraqis an additional incentive in not drawing too much away from the Soviets; and Syrian–Iranian ties may provide the Soviets a vehicle for influencing Iranian behavior. Finally, Syria is also important to the Soviets for military reasons. Access to Syrian ports and airfields—something that may now be upgraded along earlier Egyptian lines—provides the Soviets important military benefits with regard to operating in the eastern Mediterranean and countering U.S. naval forces. It also offers the Soviets the best means for countering U.S. military presence in the region; in fact, the need in Soviet eyes to demonstrate that the entry of U.S. forces into Lebanon would draw a Soviet response in kind, may be one of the reasons the Soviets have increased their force presence in Syria so much. The Soviets have consistently emphasized since the early 1970s that one of the best indications that the correlation of forces has shifted in socialism's favor is that the United States could not again intervene in Lebanon unilaterally as it did in 1958. Though we introduced forces as part of the Multinational Forces (MNF) and as peacekeepers, the Soviets have persistently referred to our forces in Lebanon (and Sinai as well) as representing a U.S. military bridgehead in the region—and increasing their forces in Syria may, in part, represent a response to this.[10]

In short, Syria is very important to the Soviets' position in the region, and, as a result, they are running risks over it. This tells us that they are not about to accept passively a decline in their regional position.

The "Objective Realities" in the Region Have Not Changed

Notwithstanding the absence of obvious Soviet gains in the region since Afghanistan, those factors that originally triggered wide concern about the area remain:

While the oil market has clearly changed, Western dependency on Gulf oil and the vulnerability to its cut-off remains significant and remains a potential source of real leverage for those hostile to the United States.

Geographic asymmetries that favor the Soviets and mean that they have significant force close to the region are an enduring fact.

Soviet capabilities for intervention continue to improve as their power projection capabilities are upgraded.

Western-oriented regimes in the Gulf remain militarily weak and continue to feel very vulnerable.

The potential for instability and radical change in the area remains strong, and creates possible opportunities for Soviet meddling.

If nothing else, the existence of these objective realities should remind us that there are not a lot of reasons to feel complacent about our security in the Gulf. While we have taken a number of steps to improve our position in the area, new shocks in the region would undoubtedly set off tremors in the West. And, the important point to note here is that new shocks are possible, particularly in Iran.

The Uncertainties of Succession in Iran

No one can predict with any confidence what will happen in Iran when Khomeini passes from the scene. In the words of Eric Rouleau, "the plethora of forces on the political scene, each one obeying its own internal and evolving dynamics, makes it impossible to hazard any valid prognosis for the medium or long term."[11] While the mullahs recognize the problem of succession and have been working to institutionalize their rule, there are tremendous centrifugal forces at work in Iran. Even with Khomeini in power, the vestiges of Kurdish, Azerbaidzhani, Turkoman, Baluch, and other grievances and desires for autonomy have been strongly felt. Without Khomeini's moral authority, ethnic separatism and the struggle for power among contending factions within the Islamic Republican Party—and the remnants of the left—may be difficult to control. (The fact that the Revolutionary Guard may also be split into different factions closely paralleling the divisions within the IRP can only increase the prospect of a serious struggle for power after Khomeini dies.)

Even if this struggle does not devolve into civil war, Iran is likely to be plunged into a period of greater internal turmoil. In such an environment the scope for covert Soviet action and support for particular groups will increase. The more violent the struggle, the more the Soviets are likely to be involved—especially given their interest in anything that happens along their border and their ability to provide "communications, arms, training, and a sanctuary (through a porous frontier)"[12] to the sides they prefer.

Though events may not unfold in this fashion, the scenario is plausible and should not be ignored. At a minimum, this suggests that there are outcomes in the coming Iranian succession which could redound to the Soviets' benefit (particularly, if more radical or pro-Soviet factions emerge) and could, therefore, have a basic effect on the shape of the region.

In light of the SAM-5s in Syria, objective realities in the region and the coming succession in Iran, there is good reason not to jump to the conclusion that the Soviet position is in decline (or the Soviets perceive it to be in decline) in the region. Though there is often a tendency in the West to view events in a "freeze-frame"—what is today must always be—Soviet leaders are most unlikely to share such an outlook. They have, after all, been socialized to take a longer view of history; indeed, a view that emphasizes that history moves forward not in a straight line but rather in zigs and zags, a formulation a Soviet commentator has used to describe the revolutionary situation in Iran today.[13] Even while working hard to prevent (or at least position themselves to cope with) setbacks, such a view makes it possible to live with reverses.

In the Persian Gulf and the Middle East more generally the Soviets have few illusions about their friends and clients. Yet while trying to build their leverage and position within certain states, they tolerate a certain lack of control and even endure setbacks because the area is important to them in their global competition with the United States. What specific goals do the Soviets have in the Persian Gulf? What tools or strategies do they use for achieving these objectives?

Soviet Goals in the Region

Soviet goals in the region reflect a variety of concerns and interests. To begin with, the Soviets see the Persian Gulf area, like any on its periphery, as being a potential launching point for intrigues and threats. Along all their borders or nearby regions, the Soviets favor weak states with regimes that are friendly and responsive to Soviet concerns and needs. In this way, the Soviets can minimize the threats they face and in real terms meet a traditional and abiding Soviet objective: the pushing of threats farther and farther away from the Soviet homeland.

But what does this require? It requires that the only foreign ties or presence permissible in these areas are those sanctioned by the Soviets, and it therefore requires in Soviet eyes ongoing efforts to undermine the ties and erode the presence of hostile powers (especially the United States) in contiguous areas like the Persian Gulf. Largely for defensive reasons, the Soviets strive to impose as a basic objective a kind of limited sovereignty on the states along their periphery.

In the Gulf this impulse has certainly found historical expression in Soviet policies and attitudes toward Iran. In the late nineteenth and early twentieth centuries the Russians protested against internal developments in Iran (for example, building railroads) that might have military utility. Subsequently, Soviet concern about the use of Iranian territory for attacks on the USSR led to the conclusion in 1921 of a treaty that in Articles 5 and 6 gave the Soviets the right to send troops into Iran if a third party militarily intervened there or used Iranian territory as a base for an attack on Soviet territory. The 1921 treaty was used to justify the Soviet seizure of northern Iran in 1941, and, though Iranian governments have renounced the treaty as unfair,[14] the Soviets continue to insist on its validity.[15] While in reality the Soviets have not succeeded in imposing "limited sovereignty" on Iran on the other Gulf states over the last two decades, they probably see the revolutionary situation in Iran as making this goal more achievable in time. Indeed, given the general weakening of the Northern Tier states, the Soviets probably see progress having been made toward this goal and toward the goal of removing barriers to their influence in the Gulf.[16]

The desire to remove or prevent the emergence of possible barriers to the southern expansion of Soviet influence also seems to be a driving impulse in Soviet behavior toward the area. Though it goes beyond the main Soviet defensive concern about the Gulf (which emphasizes the need to minimize potential threats to the Soviet Union and push them farther and farther away), it responds to traditional Soviet fears of Western encirclement. Breaking Western-inspired containment has been seen by the Soviets as critical to their global competition with the United States, and also critical to their achievement of full-fledged and universally recognized superpower status, something for which they are, as indicated above, prepared to pay quite a bit to achieve.

It is within this light that the more offensive side of Soviet goals in the Persian Gulf becomes apparent. Breaking the Northern Tier barrier is important precisely because the Soviets see this as allowing them to establish a presence in the Middle Eastern and Persian Gulf area and from there to project their power internationally. Indeed, because this whole region amounts to being a land-bridge to Africa and the Indian Ocean basin, establishing a secure foothold is critical to the improvement of Soviet strategic power and international position. Hence, even without the oil resources of the area, its proximity and geopolitical centrality were bound to trigger great Soviet interest in establishing meaningful presence and the kind of dominion or arbiter status that the British had once enjoyed in the area—both because of the impact this would have on the perception of Soviet international standing and because being ensconced in this strategic passageway would facilitate Soviet power projection and impede or check that of its adversaries.

From the foregoing, it is clear that the Middle East and Persian Gulf area would be of significant interest to the Soviets even if the Western world was not dependent on the region's oil. The fact that it is, however, increases the Soviets' interest in establishing their presence and leverage within and among the countries of the region. Establishing such leverage and the appearance of being able to affect (or potentially even disrupt) the flow of oil from the area promises the Soviets big payoffs. At the very least, if the Soviets could achieve some leverage over the flow of oil, they could manipulate European and Japanese dependency to erode the cohesion of the Western alliance and also make our allies more responsive to their interests. (If there is any doubt about this, note how the Europeans have failed to support Washington's Middle East policy, including resupply for Israel during the 1973 war, out of fear of jeopardizing their oil supplies.) More overt Soviet control over Persian Gulf oil would, inevitably, have a much more fundamental effect on the U.S. global position and the overall balance of power.

This is not to say that the risks of seeking such control, particularly if done directly are low; they are not. It is to say that the payoffs from Soviet gains or U.S. losses are very high. And the Soviets are not blind to these payoffs. They frequently refer to the strategic significance of the area and the West's dependency on the region's oil, even while they disclaim that they are any threat to it.[17]

Aside from proposing a "zone of peace" and a dismantling of foreign bases, the Soviets have also called for a conference to resolve how access to and the flow of regional oil might be guaranteed[18]—something that would put them in a position of having some say on the flow of oil from the region. This Soviet call, which was punctuated by hints that they too might be a user of Gulf oil, reflected not only the Soviet desire to gain a kind of arbiter status over the flow of Persian Gulf oil, but also the Soviet interest in gaining greater access to it.

Anticipated energy production problems may not make the Soviets a net oil importer, but they do make it difficult for the Soviets to continue to export oil for critical hard currency earnings and also meet the energy needs of their Eastern European allies—needs which are expected to grow by 250 percent by the end of the decade.[19] Given the Soviet need to continue to import technology from the West and the need to avoid the politically worrisome implications of energy-induced economic problems in East Europe, the Soviets may have increasingly stronger incentives in gaining access to Persian Gulf oil at concessionary rates. What this suggests is that the Soviet Union's interests in the Persian Gulf may now be "fueled" not only by the proximity of the area, its geopolitical centrality, and Western dependency on the region's oil, but also by its own, or more likely its allies, increasing oil needs.

What instruments or political–military options do the Soviets have for gaining access to Persian Gulf oil? Indeed, what tools or options do the Soviets have for achieving their near- and longer-term goals in the Persian Gulf: reducing and eventually removing U.S. influence and presence in the region; building and formlizing their own; creating Soviet leverage within the area to breed local responsiveness to Soviet needs and interests (for example, on security and oil); and achieving Soviet arbiter status over even local decisions?

The Soviets have a wide range of options for achieving at least some of these goals gradually and at relatively low risk, assuming they remain content to make progress gradually. The indirect nature of many Soviet options reduces the level of risk to the Soviets by posing threats that are ambiguous, deniable, or simply difficult to respond to. Moreover, in some cases Soviet options appear benign and conventional (for example, gaining access to Persian Gulf energy, by offering economic and technical assistance in return for oil and gas, something they have done with both Iraq and Iran); or, if not benign, at least conventional for the Soviets and not considered illegitimate by many in the West. For example, trading arms for oil is a Soviet option that might not be benign, but might be viewed by many in the West as understandable and, in fact, has been increasingly employed by the Soviets. (This is an option that involves not only radical or erstwhile radical oil states like Libya, Algeria, and Iraq, but also the more conservative regimes in the Gulf that from time to time have paid for Syrian and Iraqi arms purchases with oil.) Similarly, Soviet propaganda targeted on and against Gulf states, is generally taken as a given, even if it is clearly not benign. Soviet propaganda plays on themes designed to put U.S. friends on the defensive:

> The United States, through the RDF, seeks to seize Arab oil or at least, cow the Arabs into surrendering their resources to avaricious capitalist appetites.
>
> Those, especially oil states, in the region who support U.S. military plans or identify in any way with the United States are corrupt quislings eager to sacrifice the natural resources of their country and willing accomplices to neo-colonialist exploitation.
>
> Notwithstanding rhetorical disagreements, the United States supports Israeli expansionism and through Israel builds its own military presence and outposts in the region, seeks to impose a *diktat* on the Arabs, deprives the Arabs of justice and control of their own destiny, and so on.[20]

While we may think such propaganda must have limited effect, and even the Soviets are likely to regard it very cynically, several points need to be remembered. First, such propaganda strikes a responsive chord among many in the area, where defiance of the West responds to basic instincts and a continuing sense of grievance. Second, it is not simply articulated by the Soviets but repeated over and over again and conveyed through and accepted by local front groups and leftist parties giving it some local currency. Third, for regimes that lack a popular base and feel vulnerable, such charges are bound to be a source of real concern and fear, particularly because they play on the political culture and mass psychology of the area. At a minimum, such propaganda raises the costs of association with U.S. plans and initiatives.

Though the effect on regimes that feel weak and vulnerable to such charges should not be discounted, the Soviets clearly have other more direct and significant means for raising the costs of association with the United States and giving local regimes an incentive to be more responsive (or at least sensitive) to Soviet interests. These means are coercive in character and grow out of the Soviet ability to make life difficult for those who are seen as being hostile to their interests. Putting pressure on and making life difficult for regimes that already feel vulnerable can take many forms: providing an umbrella of protection to make it easier for a state like Syria to engage in trouble-making; covertly supporting an increase of terrorism by radical Palestinian groups against moderate regimes in the Gulf; facilitating and supporting the provocative People's Democratic Republic of Yemen (PDRY) behavior along the Saudi or Omani borders (or, if North Yemen again begins to stray toward the United States, against the Yemen Arab Republic); providing major new arms shipments or visibly increasing Soviet proxy presence in the PDRY, Ethiopia or Libya, and others that threaten the Gulf or Red Sea states; or supporting with arms, material, and even advisers secessionist groups in Iraq or Iran.

All of these reflect the leverage the Soviets may have over threats to local states. The more vulnerable the local states feel to threats of subversion, cross-border raids, and more overt state-to-state conflict, the more they may feel driven to avoid offending the Soviets or taking actions the Soviets regard as hostile. That then Crown Prince Fahd states: "We do not compete with the Soviet Union in any way. Nobody can use us as a tool. In the circumstances we cannot but admit that the Soviet Union is a major power and that we want no problems with it,"[21] seems to reflect his appreciation of the high cost of opposing the Soviets. Similarly, the emphasis on nonalignment in the area responds not only to the political heritage of the region and the costs of association with the United States given this history and the Arab–Israeli issue, but also to an understanding that openly being arrayed against the Soviets may prove costly.

This is an understanding most keenly felt by regimes with a general Western orientation that see themselves as being quite vulnerable to neighboring threats and to subversion and insurgencies supported from the outside—a vulnerability that nearly all the Gulf states perceive. But even erstwhile Soviet friends, such as Iraq, are likely to understand the Soviet ability to manipulate threats against them and to limit how far they go in angering the Soviets. Saddam Hussein's reticence "about attacking the Soviets in public,"[22] as well as his observation that a truly non-aligned position requiring restoration of diplomatic ties with the United States was not possible once "the [Iran–Iraq] war broke out," (presumably because this was not the time to do something the Soviets didn't like) may also reflect this.[23]

That the Soviets see the value or payoffs of putting pressure on Western-oriented states that may feel vulnerable was implied very clearly by Gromyko in conversations with Arafat. In the documentation of one such meeting, which was captured by the Israelis in

Lebanon and publicly released, Gromyko observed that Saudi behavior had been "much more positive" than expected in the Baghdad I and II summits, and he attributed this to:

> The atmosphere existing in . . . [both] conferences. The opinion of the Syrians is that there are several weak points in Saudi Arabian policy expressed in the feelings of some members of the Royal Family, who think their defense and support can only come from the Americans.
>
> It seems that the 'Steadfastness Front' states have already gained some experience in handling Saudi Arabia and applying pressure on it.[24]

The Soviets are also quite willing to apply pressure directly and not to be particularly subtle about it. In a recent interview, King Hussein reported that during his visit to Moscow in December 1982, Andropov took him aside and issued a warning on President Reagan's peace initiative: "I shall oppose the Reagan plan, and we will use *all our resources* to oppose it. With due respect, all the weight will be on your shoulders and they aren't broad enough to bear it."[25]

Besides seeing the value of applying pressure (directly or through others) against local states, the Soviets also appear to see the payoffs of reminding local leaders of their ability to manipulate threats against them. The Andropov warning to Hussein is one indicaton of this. The Soviet penchant for making broad, sweeping proposals for the area, which imply an offer of restraint in return for a certain responsiveness to Soviet interests, may be another. Without this responsiveness, the Soviets typically imply that there is "simply no prospect of stability or restraint in the region."[26]

Their offers of "implied restraint" are manifested not only in sweeping proposals like the Portugalov proposal in February 1980 or Brezhnev's offer to link Afghanistan with broad security in the Gulf at the Twenty-Sixth Party Congress in April 1981, but apparently also in bilateral dealings with local states. As William Quandt notes, in regular meetings that occur between Saudi and Soviet diplomats, the Soviets persistently emphasize that they share the Saudi interest in regional stability and that the Saudis and the Soviets have much to talk about of mutual interest in this regard—something "the Saudis see as a not very subtle way of reminding them that South Yemen and other Soviet clients can make life unpleasant and that the Soviets could be helpful if the Saudis were to make some political concessions."[27]

The Soviet aim is to force an accommodation to the realities of their power and, therefore, an accommodation to Soviet interests. How successful have the Soviets been? Here, the answer depends on how one defines success. Shahram Chubin believes that local leaders do, in fact, understand that they must accommodate themselves to the realities created by Soviet power in order to reduce the prospect of Soviet mischief-making in periods of domestic upheaval, counter Soviet criticism and related propaganda and disinformation, and limit Soviet military support (including arms, advisers, and proxies) for regional adversaries.[28]

But has this meant anything in terms of the actual behavior of regional states? The answer is a qualified yes. The Soviet strategy has succeeded in achieving, at least in part, some of the Soviet negative goals including the distancing of Gulf regimes from U.S. policies, the unwillingness to be seen supporting U.S. plans and initiatives, and the more fervent espousal and adoption of nonalignment in international politics. On the other hand, the Soviets have so far not experienced much success in terms of achieving their positive goals, for example, formalizing their own presence and control outside of places like the PDRY, establishing significant influence or leverage over local decisions, or gaining access to oil on concessionary terms. Put another way, while local regimes are increasingly mindful of the costs of embracing the United States, they have not yet seen the need to embrace the Soviets.

Whether the Soviets can use a strategy of intimidation and coercion based largely on their ability to manipulate threats against local regimes to achieve more than limited negative goals, is not clear. But the main point to consider here is that the Soviets may well believe that this strategy has already achieved a lot, particularly because in Soviet eyes it is probably seen as contributing to U.S. losses in a region where U.S. stakes, and the stakes of the Western world, remain greater than theirs.

If nothing else, this should tell us that the relevant criteria to use in evaluating whether the Soviets regard their strategy as satisfactory and successful are Soviet, and not U.S. criteria. In this regard, the Soviets have reason, as Alvin Rubinstein has written, to be generally satisfied with the trends in the region.[29] So long as they are making at least incremental progress and see the prospect of continuing opportunities given regional rivalries, local instability, and local partners whose own aims converge with theirs, the Soviets are likely to remain satisfied with their current strategy of intimidation that poses indirect threats to U.S. interests.

This seems especially true given the absence of available alternatives to the Soviets; a more benign policy offers them few partners since the Soviets have little to offer outside of the military area. It would also require a basic change in the psychology of Soviet leaders who have been socialized to take advantage of opportunities in their global competition with the United States, and local circumstances will continue to breed dissatisfied actors and new opportunities to undermine the United States and its friends in the region. Alternatively, a more directly threatening posture in an area of such vital importance to the United States could well trigger direct U.S. military responses and threaten all-out war between the United States and the USSR. A willingness to run this kind of risk in the Persian Gulf—without a fundamental change of circumstances—would also require a change in the psychology of Soviet leaders who, even if socialized to exploit opportunities, have also been traditionally admonished not to be adventuristic.

In short, what we should expect from the Soviets in the area is more of the same; a strategy of intimidation designed in the near term to make it costly for Gulf states to identify with the United States. The Soviets will surely work to improve their leverage and military presence in the region, with the aim of increasing their ability both to intimidate and narrow the choices available to local actors. In Soviet eyes, their increased presence in and support for the Syrians and growing Syrian leverage in the region—especially in the aftermath of what has been seen in the area as a Syrian victory in Lebanon—work to achieve these ends. More direct threats are unlikely, but shouldn't be ruled out in all circumstances. Elsewhere, I have discussed the circumstances that might trigger more direct Soviet threats and military intervention,[30] and I will not repeat that discussion here, except to say that the most likely Soviet threat of military intervention would be in response to a civil war in Iran. In this circumstance, with instability and turmoil along their border and the possibility that pro-Western forces could prevail, the Soviets might well seize northern Iran. Before discussing how we ought to counter the Soviet strategy of coercion, it is worth making some general points on Soviets risk-taking propensities.

Soviet Risk-taking Propensities

As a general principle, it might be said that the Soviets will continue to avoid putting themselves in a situation that directly invites or inevitably threatens confrontation with the United States. Confrontation and war with the United States are seen in cataclysmic terms. While threats to Soviet core values or the viabililty of the socialist commonwealth have in Soviet eyes always been worth risking confrontation over—if for no other reason than the Soviet system and CPSU rule over it might be jeopardized otherwise—few other Soviet interests have been traditionally put in this category. Since the Soviets have seen confrontation as potentially jeopardizing everything they have achieved and since they believe time and the march of history are on their side, few other interests have seemed important enough to warrant running significant risks of confrontation with the United States.

What is difficult to know or predict at this point is how the changing balance of power over the last decade and an emerging Soviet elite that has not experienced the devastation of World War I, the Civil War, the purges, and World War II will change Soviet definitions of what constitutes a risk. Certainly, the Soviets have frequently told us over the last decade about the changed correlation of forces and the need for the U.S. leadership to face up to the new realities of power.[31] But while the Soviets have been more assertive around the globe, there have been few signs that the Soviets seem genuinely prepared to run much greater or qualitatively new risks in pursuit of potential opportunities.

What we should perhaps expect are not basic changes in risk-taking propensities, except insofar as the Soviets may be less willing to suffer strategic reversals that cast doubt on their superpower status or that reintroduce "threats" along the Soviet border. Their current behavior in Syria may reflect the former and their potential reaction to Iranian contingencies the latter. On the whole, they are likely to continue to take a hard-headed look at a potentially threatening situation and evaluate their overall interests, the balance of the respective stakes of the United States and USSR, the balance of power between the United States and its respective allies in the area, and the military options they have available.[32]

Over the PLO (and for that matter the Syrians) in Lebanon, the Soviets made it quite clear that they were not prepared to run much risk.[33] (Syria itself, as suggested above, is viewed differently.) In addition to their relatively low stakes in Lebanon and their other pressing political interests and preoccupations at the time (particularly in Europe), the fact is that the Soviets saw themselves having few good military options. In this, as well as previous Arab–Israeli cases, the relatively unfavorable military balance in the area, given the U.S.

and allied presence in the Mediterranean and the local Israeli superiority, seem to have given the Soviets pause. Note, for example, that in response to a question on Hungarian television, Vadim Zagladin, a Central Committee member and first deputy chief of the Central Committee's International Department, stated:

> What do you have in mind with this 'permitted or not permitted?' Well, what has happened? There is a war between Israel and one of the Arab countries, aggression against an Arab country. Under these circumstances, what should the Soviet Union do? Should it attack Israel? This is a rather impossible situation.[34]

Impossible one gathers not simply because this could trigger a major confrontation with the United States, but also because the relatively small Soviet forces that could be introduced quickly into the theater would be no match for the Israelis. Presumably, if the Soviets did introduce forces—as they threatened to do in 1973—the purpose would be not to fight the Israelis but rather to signal them not to go farther and to signal the United States of the danger of the situation so that the U.S. would restrain the Israelis. Soviet sensitivity to the military balance and their lack of good military options in the eastern Mediterranean/Arab–Israeli context have been used by the Soviets to explain inaction in both the 1956 and 1967 wars. During the Suez crisis, Zhukov told the visiting president of Syria: "How are we to go to the aid of Egypt? Tell me! Are we supposed to send our armies through Turkey, Iran and then into Syria and Iraq and on into Israel and so eventually attack the British and French forces?"[35] Similarly, when an Arab delegation led by Boumediene visited Moscow after the 1967 war and castigated the Soviets for not intervening to save the Egyptians or Syrians in the war, Brezhnev told him that he and the Arabs must understand that "the communication line between us and you is very long" and to get to you we must "fly through pro–Western airspace."[36] Interestingly, Gromyko also referred in his 1979 meeting with Arafat to the great "physical distance between us" in implying that the Soviets could not do much, even while they sympathized with the PLO's struggle against the Israeli attack in Southern Lebanon.[37]

While all these statements may be self-serving and designed to rationalize why the Soviets could not intervene, it is interesting that they all reflect a strong military logic. Even if useful for explaining Soviet behavior to the Arabs, one suspects that these statements reflected some basic Soviet judgments on whether they could risk intervening in some way. If so, the Soviet military calculus may have an important, though not necessarily predominating, impact on Soviet willingness to intervene in a crisis situation.

The significance of this for the Gulf should not be missed. Indeed, while our stakes are high, the military balance and Soviet military options may look much more favorable in the Gulf than they do in the Middle East, particularly given shorter distances, the relative weakness of the local forces in the area, limited U.S. presence in the immediate vicinity, and the much greater power the Soviets can bring quickly to bear. A favorable military balance will not suddenly induce Soviet adventurism, but could make them feel more able to intimidate the West and also to deter U.S. presence or intervention, at least in a place like Iran.

In the Fertile Crescent area, Soviet military options are not good. Not only are U.S. naval forces superior and nearby, but the Soviets cannot move heavy forces to the area quickly and any forces they could introduce piecemeal would be no match for the Israelis. In this sense, Soviet intervention with conventional forces would be far more for their symbolic effect and the signal it would send to the United States and the Israelis than for their military value in tilting the balance. The only thing that would really alter this situation would be the prepositioning of Soviet ground equipment and aircraft in Syria. Should we see the buildup of Soviet arms in Syria vastly exceed what Syria can man and absorb and also signs that the Soviets are maintaining weapons stocks in depots, then the picture of Soviet military options in the area would look different.

The U.S. Response to Soviet Policy

How should the United States respond to the Soviet strategy which is designed to challenge it with primarily indirect threats, apply pressure within the region directly and through local partners, and take advantage of the image of Soviet power and ability to provide all manner of military support to insurgent groups and other regional clients? There is no simple response to such a strategy. Not only must we use a multiplicity of instruments—military, diplomatic, economic, and intelligence—to counter the Soviets but, in addition, we must employ these instruments with subtlety, at all times recognizing what is possible with the different regimes in the area and what is likely to make them more and not less secure.

It is the sense of vulnerability and weakness that so many local states share that makes our task difficult and that makes a strategy of intimidation potentially effective. We can do much to deter direct external threats by the Soviets or their radical clients against regimes important to the United States; but irredentist claims, disparities in and rivalries for power, the socially disruptive effects of modernization and the related resurgence of fundamentalism, ethnic diversity and loyalty to specific clans or tribes, and the absence of fully legitimate and recognized bases on which to rule, among other things, contribute to the vulnerability of many Gulf states and cannot be easily addressed by the United States. Indeed, many of the Gulf regimes that look to the United States for protection are, nonetheless, fearful of relying too openly on the United States for their own defense, except in extreme circumstances, where the immediate survival of the regime is at stake.

That does not mean that the U.S. should despair or is helpless in countering the Soviet strategy and reassuring local states against Soviet-inspired or supported coercion. Most of the Gulf states do, after all, still look to the United States for protection. It does mean, however, that the United States should do as much as it can in the area of infrastructure development, joint exercises, access to facilities, and so on, with states that feel capable of cooperating with the United States openly; yet it should engage in discreet forms of security cooperation such as joint threat assessment and joint contingency planning with the others. Even while recognizing the political constraints, we need to be opportunistic in trying to expand the scope of our cooperation and to establish precedents for greater American security involvement with the Western-oriented states in the area.

In general, three basic objectives ought to guide the U.S. response to the Soviet strategy:

> Within the limits of what is politically possible, develop our military presence in and around the region and improve our capability for bringing power to bear in the area.
>
> Bolster the capabilities of local states to deter and cope with local threats.
>
> Work with local states to manage the developmental process and to ameliorate regional conflicts, particularly the Arab–Israeli conflict.

The first objective is important basically because the Soviets must not think that the risk of making a military move into the Gulf is low. If the military balance were to shift too much in the Soviet favor, their view of the risks of a military move might change, particularly if they believe it was possible to present the United

States with a military fait accompli and preempt our involvement. By building our regional presence and capability to bring power to bear in a way that rules out any quick or easy military successes for the Soviets, we make any such re-evaluation unlikely. We also remind the Soviets that our stakes remain high in the area, that we mean to defend them, and that the pursuit of a more threatening approach to the area is too risky; thus, further adding to deterrence and militating against a Soviet view that the risks of a military move into the Gulf may not be great.

Besides enhancing deterrence, developing our presence—to the extent that is politically feasible—is important also for countering or offsetting the shadow that Soviet power casts over the area; being able to cast a shadow of our own, perhaps from "over or on the horizon," is essential for offsetting the specter of Soviet coercion and for reassuring our friends against threats manipulated from the outside. It is also important for reassuring our friends against military threats from more powerful regional adversaries, something that could become even more important to Gulf states if there were a clear-cut winner or a resolution of the Iran–Iraq war.

Obviously, being able to reassure local states is the key to countering the Soviet strategy of intimidation and coercion. Building our own presence in politically acceptable ways is one element in providing this reassurance. Another is provided by the second objective: bolstering the capabilities of our regional friends. This provides reassurance by making local states more confident about their own ability to cope with local threats and more confident in us as a reliable security partner. Clearly, bolstering the military capabilities of our local friends cannot be done indiscriminately. It must take account of the absorptive capacities of these states, the actual threats they confront and the weapons that would be most useful in countering them, and the effect that certain kinds of arms transfers are likely to have on the Arab–Israeli and perhaps other balances (for example, Pakistan–Indian), and on the prospects for Arab–Israeli peace.

The last objective of managing the developmental process and ameliorating local conflicts is important for minimizing Soviet opportunities to exert leverage. At one level, working with local states to manage the process of modernization intelligently is difficult, but surely necessary. The grinding poverty in some of the regional states as well as the social dislocation caused by rapid modernization in the other wealthier oil states, both provide fertile breeding grounds for dissatisfaction and turmoil. It is no less important for the United States to focus on developing a strategy for managing these socioeconomic problems, particularly at a time when declining oil revenues will affect both the rich and poor states in the region, than it is for the United States to develop a strategy for coping with the military problems in the area.

At another level, making progress toward an Arab–Israeli peace settlement would be very important; not because the sources of instability and conflict will disappear in the Gulf if there were Arab–Israeli peace, they surely will not; nor because our friends in the Gulf will suddenly embrace us and invite in a U.S. military presence if Palestinian grievances disappear; this won't happen for a number of reasons including fear of fundamentalist reaction to such a posture. But rather because making progress toward Arab–Israeli peace will deny the radicals a "stick" to use against U.S. friends in the Gulf, it will make some of these regimes less defensive about association with the United States, and it will facilitate security cooperation with both the Arabs and Israelis. Thus, while ameliorating the Arab–Israeli conflict will not solve U.S. problems in the Gulf or remove the various Soviet means of leverage, it would make it somewhat easier to respond to these problems and the Soviet strategy.

The Soviet Response to U.S. Policy

In general, U.S. strategy of the last few years has embodied many of the broad principles and objectives outlined above. How have the Soviets responded to this strategy? Obviously they have not liked it. They have waged an increasing propaganda campaign against the buildup of U.S. military forces in the area, suggesting that this constitutes the real threat to the area and juxtaposing it against their sweeping proposals for a zone of peace. They also charge that U.S. arms transfers to the Saudis, Pakistanis, and others represent a threat to peace and serve only imperialist aims, and that Camp David, Egyptian–Israeli peace, the Reagan plan, and the Israeli–Lebanese agreement, reflect a U.S.–Israeli attempt to impose a capitulationist course on the Arabs.[38]

Little in this propaganda is new, though its intensity and the prominence the Soviets give their own proposals on regional peace and security does suggest some increased concern and awareness of the growing importance of the region. But, otherwise, Soviet behavior has not varied a great deal; perhaps, again revealing that the Soviets are generally satisfied with regional trends and also lack viable alternatives to their present course given their regional interests.

How might a change in the character of the U.S. approach affect the Soviets? For example, how might they react to approaches that were either more accommodating or, alternatively, more offensive in putting pressure on Soviet positions and friends in the region? The rationale for the former would be that if we invite the Soviets to be a regional arbiter and meet their security concerns, they will accept this arrangement and support regional stability. For the latter, it would be that if they are going to exercise coercion against our friends and position in the area, we ought to do the same in return, thereby building the Soviet incentive in restraint.

Would the Soviets react in the desired manner to either of these approaches? My guess in general terms is probably not. The accommodating route assumes the Soviets will alter their broad interests in the region, forsake trying to erode and supplant our influence and presence, and be content to have a kind of equal status in the region with the United States that also limits the regional U.S. military capability. While it is quite possible that the Soviets would accept such an arrangement for a time—particularly because it would confer on them the kind of status that they would like to have in the region, support other broad international objectives, and perhaps also reduce the burdens of supporting some of their regional clients—it is difficult to see the Soviets resisting the temptation to take advantage of opportunities to damage our regional position that would be bound to occur sooner or later. Much as we hoped strategic detente would give the Soviets a stake in stability and limit their trouble-making tendencies in the Third World, so too would the accommodating approach bank on the Soviets foresaking opportunities in the Middle East and the Persian Gulf in return for regional detente and a certain regional standing.

One would feel more hopeful about this taking place—and, indeed, about the whole accommodative approach—if one could see a sign of some change in Soviet attitudes toward competition and struggle with the United States. In this regard, until one sees some evidence that the Soviets genuinely understand that they cannot consistently work to undermine U.S. interests and still expect the United States to be responsive and sensitive to their interests, there is not much hope for accommodative approaches working in places like the Persian Gulf.

What better example of the Soviet impulse to seize perceived opportunities in the area—regardless of the costs to potential understandings with the United States—than their behavior during the

Iranian hostage crisis. Aside from generally excusing seizure of the hostages (saying it was "understandable"), the Soviets did all they could to prevent a resolution of the issue by warning of U.S. tricks and an imminent U.S. invasion even during the final delicate negotiations for release of the hostages.[39]

It is worth noting that the most striking evidence of a Soviet change of heart might not even necessarily occur in the region; for example, signs that the Soviets really were focusing attention on solving internal problems and that they would no longer be content to have external success substitute for a lack of internal progress would be very significant, particularly as it would mean that one very strong Soviet impulse for taking advantage of opportunities would disappear. Whether this would translate into a further softening of Soviet attitudes toward the character of competition with the United States is difficult to know but it would be a trend worth encouraging.

The point, in any case, is that there is currently not much reason to believe that a purely accommodative approach would produce the desired Soviet response for any enduring period. This does not mean that accommodation on individual cases should be ruled out. There may be times when accommodation would serve U.S. interests and, in these instances, it ought to be explored. For example, if the Soviets were truly interested in a face-saving way to remove their military presence and get out of Afghanistan, it would be in the U.S. interest to help them do so.

Is the pressure approach likely to be any more successful than the accommodative approach? Again, the answer is probably not. In response to increased pressure on Soviet positions and clients, the Soviets are bound, at least initially, to try to prove to us that such a posture will not deter them, and, in fact, is likely to harm us far more than them because of their greater ability to manipulate threats against our friends. This is not something we should take lightly.

Nevertheless, there may be circumstances where opportunities exist for the United States—or more likely for U.S. regional friends with appropriate support from the United States—to put pressure on trouble-making Soviet clients. From the standpoint of reassuring U.S. friends, making it clear that those who threaten friends of the United States cannot do so with impunity, and raising the costs of trouble-making for the Soviets and those who do their regional bidding, it may be important to do so.

Thus, much like the accommodative approach, there may be cases where the circumstances (in terms of provocation, opportunity, and limited costs to our friends) are right for pursuing a more offensive approach. On the whole, however, the general principles and objectives noted above and the approach they embody makes sense, with both accommodation and pressure being considered on a case-by-case basis.

Conclusion

In closing, it is useful to recapitulate the main points of this chapter:

> While the Soviets have not appeared to make much recent headway in the region, the United States has little reason either to be complacent about its security position or to conclude that the Soviets are a superpower in eclipse in the Gulf. Objective realities haven't changed; opportunities to improve their position (or undermine ours) remain; and their determination to preserve their position is clear.
>
> The Soviets have reason to think that over time their strategic position vis-à-vis the region has improved and that their strategy for eroding the U.S. position in the area has been succeeding. While doing better at achieving negative than positive goals, the Soviet strategy reflects their patience, the risks of threatening the United States too directly, and the options available to them.
>
> On the whole, the Soviets are likely to be satisfied with their strategy and what they have achieved in a region that remains more important to the United States than to them. If nothing else, this tells U.S. policymakers that they should evaluate Soviet success or failure in Soviet and not U.S. terms.
>
> The U.S. approach to countering the Soviet strategy requires sufficient local presence and security assistance to militate against any change in the Soviet assessment of the risk of more direct military moves and to reassure local states against extra-regional and local coercion. In addition, ameliorating local causes of instability and conflict is also important for denying the Soviets opportunities for leverage.

In the end, the United States needs to accept the fact that competition in this area (like competition more generally) will not be resolved overnight. The United States can neither force the Soviets into submission nor accommodate them in ways that end competition between them—though elements of pressure and accommodation make sense in appropriate circumstances. The challenge for the United States in the Gulf and elsewhere is to protect U.S. interests, while avoiding conflict. Something that sounds like a good prescription for any policy.

Notes

1. Though I will generally be discussing the Persian Gulf, one cannot discuss the Gulf in isolation from the Middle East. Indeed, most observers, myself included, consider the Middle East and Persian Gulf to be part of the same region. Countries throughout this area are linked by culture, religion, language, history, and a sense of shared destiny. Aside from these linkages and the linkage created by the Arab–Israeli conflict, there are also other factors that bind the area from North Africa to the Gulf—for example, the surviving monarchies see their future intertwined, as a threat to one portends threats to all.

2. See Karen Dawisha, "The USSR in the Middle East: Superpower in Eclipse?" *Foreign Affairs,* vol. 61, no. 2 (Winter 1982–1983), 446. Reprinted with permission. Copyright Karen Dawisha, 1982.

3. Ibid., 443–444.

4. Shahram Chubin, "Gains for Soviet Policy in the Middle East," *International Security,* vol. 6, no. 4 (Spring 1982), 130.

5. See, Alexandre Benningsen, "USSR & Islam," in Walter Laqueur et al., eds., *The Pattern of Soviet Conduct in the Third World: Review and Preview,* 1982, an unclassified study prepared for the Office of Net Assessment, U.S. Department of Defense, 7–25.

6. Malcolm H. Kerr, *The Arab Cold War: Gamal'Abd al-Nasir and His Rivals, 1958–1970,* 3rd ed. (London: Oxford University Press, 1971), passim.

7. For discussion of the Soviet presence and responsibilities in Syria, the SAM-5 and related deployments to Syria, and Israeli reactions and concerns, see Hirsch Goodman's "The Fuss about the SAM-5s," *Jerusalem Post* (International edition), 9–15 January 1983, 1; William Beecher, "Israel Is Keeping Jets out of Range of Syrian Missiles," *Boston Globe,* 30 April 1983, 3.

8. See, Alvin Z. Rubinstein, *Red Star on the Nile: The Soviet–Egyptian Influence Relationship since the June War* (Princeton: Princeton University Press, 1977), passim.

9. Dawisha, op. cit., 449.

10. Vsevolod Ovchinnikov, "International Review," 1st ed., *Pravda,* 27 March 1983, 4. Under the heading of "Pseudopeacemakers," Ovchinnikov talks about the United States repeating the Sinai scenario in Lebanon and

of using its "role of 'mediator' in the Israeli–Arab conflict to secure another bridgehead for a direct U.S. military presence in the Near East."

11. Eric Rouleau, "Khomeini's Iran," *Foreign Affairs,* vol. 59, no. 1 (Fall 1980), 19.

12. Chubin, op. cit., 143.

13. D. Volskiy, "Iran at the Cross-Roads," *Novoye Vrema,* no. 2, 7 January 1983, 13.

14. The Iranians renounced it in 1959 and then again in October 1979. There was, however, a clause that precluded unilateral abrogation.

15. See, Shahram Chubin, *Soviet Policy toward Iran and the Gulf,* Adelphi Papers no. 157 (London: International Institute for Strategic Studies, 1981), 11.

16. For an interesting discussion of this, see Alvin Rubinstein, *Soviet Policy toward Turkey, Iran, and Afghanistan: The Dynamics of Influence* (New York: Praeger, 1982), vii.

17. For a survey of Soviet statements reflecting this see, Ilya Zemstov, "Regional Stability and Soviet Interests in the Persian Gulf," *Crossroads,* (Winter–Spring 1982).

18. A good article laying out the Soviet "zone of peace concept" in the Gulf, the Indian Ocean, and elsewhere is V.F. Petrovskiy, "Zone of Peace," *SShA: Ekonomika, Politika, Ideologiya,* no. 7 (July 1982) especially 13–16; see also Portugalov's statement reported by *Tass,* 29 January 1980.

19. David Price, "Soviet Relations in the Gulf," in Laqueur et al., eds., *Soviet Conduct in the Third World,* 7.

20. For a number of Soviet articles that repeat these continuing themes, see Vladimir Bogachev, "If It So Seems to the Pentagon," *Tass,* 6 Jan. 1983; Boris Rachkov, "Damage to OPEC by Capitalism," Moscow in Arabic, *FBIS,* 29 December 1982, H-3; Vladimir Peresada, "Billions for the Aggressor," 2nd ed., *Pravda,* 25 December 1982, 8.

21. William B. Quandt, *Saudi Arabia in the 1980s: Foreign Policy, Security and Oil* (Washington: The Brookings Institution, 1981), 70.

22. Dawisha, op. cit., 46.

23. Saddam Hussein interview with Congressman Stephen Solarz, reported by Iraqi news agency, *FBIS* (Middle East and Africa Daily Report) 8 January 1983, E-7.

24. "Protocol of Talks Between PLO and Soviet Delegations in Moscow," 13 November 1979, among documents Israelis released (Jerusalem, June 1982), 16.

25. Reported in Karen Elliott House, "Hussein's Decision: King Had US Pledges on Peace Talks but Met a Maze of Arab Foes," *Wall Street Journal,* 14 April 1983, 1 and 16. Reprinted by permission of *The Wall Street Journal,* copyright Dow Jones and Company, Inc., 1983. All rights reserved.

26. Chubin, op. cit., 132.

27. Quandt, op. cit., 71.

28. Chubin, op. cit., 132.

29. Alvin Rubinstein, "Soviet Policy in the Middle East: Perspectives from Three Capitals," in Robert H. Donaldson, ed., *The Soviet Union and the Third World: Success or Failure* (Boulder: Westview, 1980), 160.

30. See my "Considering Soviet Threats in the Persian Gulf," *International Security,* vol. 6, no. 2 (Fall 1981), 159–180.

31. This has been a persistant theme of almost all articles dealing with international politics since the early 1970s. In the early 1970s at the height of detente, the changed correlation of forces and the U.S. need to face up to it was used to explain why SALT, detente, et cetera were possible. Since the late 1970s, the theme has been that the cold warriors have tried to resist these changes and reimpose a "positions of strength" policy. See, G. Arbatov, "The Foreign Policy of the USA on the Threshold of the 1980's," *SShA: Ekonomika, Politika, Ideologiya* no. 4, Moscow, 1980. For an interesting article that repeats these themes but worries that the United States may not face up to these realities see Alexander Bovin, "Political Observer's Opinion: Impasses at the Crossroads," *Izvestiia,* 20 Januray 1983, 5.

32. See Francis Fukuyama's discussion of some of these elements in "Nuclear Shadow Boxing: Soviet Intervention Threats in the Middle East," *Orbis,* Fall 1981, especially 595–597.

33. Gromyko was quoted by Arab sources as saying that a show of force (that is, flying troops to Syria) in response to a PLO request was "out of the question" and that the Soviet Union would not go beyond its current diplomatic efforts and "would not budge one inch from its present Middle East policy." Quoted in Dawisha, op. cit., 441.

34. Interview with Vadim Zagladin, Budapest Domestic Television, *FBIS,* 17 September 1982.

35. Mohammed Heikal, *Cairo Documents* (London: New English Library, 1972), 142.

36. Abd al-Majid Farid, who was Nasser's personal secretary, recounts this episode in his *Abd Al-Nasir's Secret Papers* (Washington: JPRS 72223, Translations on Near East and North Africa), 14 November 1978.

37. Israeli Captured Documents, op. cit., 17.

38. Again these are common themes. Articles that repeat them include, Oleg Fomin, "International Review: Key to a Settlement," *Sovetskaya Rossiya,* 4 December 1982; V. Vinograadov, "Dangerous Progress," *Krasnaia zvezda,* 14 December 1982, 3; Demchenko, "Under Pressure from Washington: What Lies Behind the Lebanese–Israeli Agreement," 1st ed., *Pravda* 20 May 1983, 4.

39. See, for example, the *Pravda* editorial, 17 January 1981.

7
Soviet Commercial Behavior with Western Industrial Nations

John P. Hardt and Donna L. Gold

Overview

Politics and Commercial Behavior

Despite the overriding role of politics in determining Soviet commercial behavior, most Western projections of Soviet trade seem to be based on the assumptions that market forces predominate. A degree of economic mirroring on the part of the West tends to result in the over- or underestimation of trade prospects. A clarification of the interrelationship of politics and economics in Soviet commercial behavior is essential in order to improve the accuracy of Western forecasts of East–West trade.

The framework and structure of Soviet commercial behavior are governed by politics. Considerations of security, sovereignty, and continuity of the socialist system dominate commercial policy. Decisions are centralized in the political bureaucracy to ensure this dominance. The international division of labor, or comparative advantage, has long been a part of Soviet economic theory. However, its application in terms of East–West trade (that is, pursuing a more general policy of importing goods based on quality and cost regardless of whether those items are produced domestically) has been more recent. Even though the application of this concept has made Soviet commercial behavior more responsive to relative domestic costs and world market conditions, economic factors remain secondary to political ones, and hence the volume, structure, and direction of Soviet trade with the West have all varied in a context that political forces rather than market forces would explain.

In the West, politics are less of a factor in foreign commerce. Although Western political authorities also involve themselves in trade issues on grounds of security, sovereignty, and maintenance of the pluralistic market system, their interventions either to facilitate or to restrict trade are not, as a rule, central to the commercial process. The policymaking and administration of Western foreign trade are primarily in private hands, and domestic and world market factors tend to prevail over political considerations except to some extent in bilateral commercial relations with communist countries.

Because of these differences in the role that politics play in Eastern and Western commercial behavior, many Western policymakers have tended to underrate the weight that the Soviets accord to political factors in determining their commercial policy toward the West. Indeed, Western governmental policy may affect East–West trade more by influencing the political climate than by directly intervening in the actual terms of trade. Political confrontation or cooperation between the post-Brezhnev leadership and the U.S. president may prove to be the major variable in East–West and U.S.–Soviet commercial relations, especially for the near term. Relations between the Soviet leader and other Western heads of state are also important, particularly when economic issues divide Washington and other Western capitals, as they did during the 1982 "pipeline" incident.[1]

Because politics play such a pivotal role in Soviet commercial behavior, they should be given more consideration in Western analyses of Soviet–Western trade. Conventional Western projections of East–West trade (discussed in more detail in this chapter) are generally based on the premises of a stable political climate and variable economic conditions. Just as fluctuations in economic factors (for example, the selling price of oil, domestic growth projections, and the availability and terms of credit) must be taken into account, so too must changes in political relationships be considered. At a minimum, all Western forecasts of Soviet–Western trade should include explanations of both the political and economic premises upon which they are based.

Some Central Observations

The perspective developed in this discussion is based on the study of post-Stalin Soviet assessments of Western governmental, business, and bank predictions of Soviet commercial relations. It is important to note that the USSR and the Eastern European states vary in their commercial behavior. In recent years, differentation among the Soviet Union and its Eastern European allies has become more apparent. In this discussion reference will primarily be made to Eastern commercial behavior as it is correlated with and directed by Soviet behavior. Intrabloc trade is assumed to influence, but not dictate,

Soviet commercial behavior. Given these qualifications, four central observations can be presented.

1. *In Soviet commercial behavior, considerations of national security, sovereignty, and systematic continuity are accorded priority over comparative economic advantage.* Political considerations are the key determinants of the foreign economic behavior of the USSR. Considerations of national security, sovereignty and systemic continuity may inhibit or encourage commercial relations. Conventional economic factors also influence foreign commerce, but their influence is maximized only when political concerns are satisfied and thus minimized. Whereas the separation of trade from politics seems possible in Western countries, the intertwining of political and economic factors is central and inextricable in explaining Soviet behavior.

2. *A range of Soviet and Western scenarios for East–West trade interact and reinforce patterns in each camp.* Soviet behavior interrelates with a wide range of Western policies. For example, a Western policy perceived by the Soviets as discriminatory may reinforce a Soviet policy of economic independence. The same is true of the reverse; that is, a Soviet policy of economic independence from the West may reinforce a Western policy that the Soviets consider discriminatory. Alternatively, a Western policy that involves positive governmental participation may encourage more cooperation with the Soviets. Heightened commercial outreach on the part of the Soviet Union may likewise facilitate a corresponding Western policy.

Western and Eastern policies in other areas—arms control, human rights, regional issues—may also influence East–West commercial relations. Favorable developments in the East–West political relationship, for example, the successful conclusion of a strategic or conventional arms limitation agreement, may have more of an impact on Soviet–Western commercial relations than an easing of credit restrictions because of the primacy of politics in Soviet commercial behavior.

3. *Soviet foreign policies in various regions of the world may appear to conflict with economic imperatives.* Soviet commercial relations with the United States and Western Europe in recent years seem to be more compatible with Soviet political considerations than with the economic requirements of comparative advantage. Likewise, for political reasons, the Soviet leadership appears to have refrained from moving toward regional economic interdependence with Japan and the Pacific powers despite the economic desirability of their cooperation in developing the resources of eastern Siberia.[2]

4. *Usual economic variables affect Soviet–Western commercial relations within the political context of Soviet foreign trade.* Security, sovereignty, and systemic continuity provide the political framework that conditions Soviet trade with the West. Within that framework, the Soviet need for grain, which depends on harvests, and the Soviet need for technologies, which depends upon planned industrial projects, influence import levels. Moreover, earnings from exports of oil, gas, gold, minerals, and arms—the leading sources of hard currency—significantly affect the Soviets' ability to import. The availability of Western credits and the Soviet willingness to use them also shape import plans.

Historical Perspective[3]

In the Stalinist period, trade was based on the need to relieve critical bottlenecks (that is, absolute disadvantages) in the domestic economy. This trade policy was exemplified by the importation of missing components needed to complete planned, priority industrial-projects. Credit was avoided because it was viewed as a negative lever of capitalist influence.[4]

Under Stalin's successors, comparative advantage, or the international division of labor, replaced absolute advantage as the central feature of Soviet commercial policy; short-term major projects gave way to long-term ventures. The watershed in this change was the major automotive deal with the Italian firm, Fiat, in 1966. In that contractual relationship, the Soviets agreed to long-term commitments based on comparative costs and relative technical efficiency. Food, consumer goods, and transport facilities were subsequently added to a broader range of imports based on comparative advantage. Credit was accepted as a normal part of trade. First European and Japanese then U.S. commercial interests encouraged this measured degree of East–West economic interdependence.

The United States and its allies likewise became moderately dependent on the Soviet market. Increased Western imports of Soviet energy, especially oil, added to the growing Western import dependence on the East. As sales of grain, energy equipment, and other capital goods became profitable for sectors of Western economies, a modest degree of sectoral export dependence also became apparent.

Although the Soviet Union not only accepted but sought normalized trade with the West during the Brezhnev years, the USSR never behaved as a Western commercial nation. Economic factors, including the selling price of hard currency items (particularly oil) and the availability and terms of credit, do not adequately explain many of the developments that occurred in Soviet commercial relations with the West over that time period. For example, the grain import policies that made the United States the preferred supplier of Soviet wheat, corn, and soybeans from 1972–1979 were probably more preferential than economic factors dictated. In the case of the reverse policy, followed after the U.S. partial grain embargo in 1979, political factors again were primarily responsible for the swing away from the U.S. market. Likewise, proposed U.S.–Soviet cooperation in natural gas development in 1972–1974 had a political rationale—detente—dominating the relative economic merits. Finally, there was the subsequent shift of Soviet industrial orders from the United States to Western Europe in the wake of the Afghanistan sanctions. Although such changes were required by U.S. export restrictions in the short run, they reflect political as much as economic constraints in the longer term.[5]

Thus, when looking back on Soviet commercial behavior and when attempting to look forward, it is necessary to evaluate Soviet calculations of economic comparative advantage in the hierarchy that places the political considerations of security, sovereignty, and systemic continuity highest in their scale of values.

A Context for Assessing and Projecting Soviet Foreign Economic Behavior

Factors Influencing the Soviets in Commercial Relations with the West

1. *Security of the homeland—the national security interests of the party and government leaders:* the security of the Soviet homeland is of paramount interest to the Soviet leadership. The Soviet decision to shoot down an unarmed commercial jetliner (Korean Air Lines flight 007) on 1 September 1983, was a graphic, if not extreme, example of the dominance of the sanctity of borders and the security of military installations as factors in Soviet foreign policy.

To the extent that foreign commercial relations may be viewed as representing a serious threat to socialist international security, they would be unacceptable to Soviet leaders. Security and sovereignty interests of the Soviet Union in their Asian policy, aggressively interpreted by the Soviets, have overridden their economic imperatives for making the enormous investment need to develop the Soviet Far East and eastern Siberia into productive regions. The completion of the Baikal–Amur Railroad to enhance access to the rich resources of east Siberia, which is intended as an export base for Soviet participation in the expanding Pacific region, is, at least temporarily, a casualty of the security policy. Moreover, the conflict over the Northern Territories and other outstanding issues with Japan are central determinants in an economically counterproductive Soviet Asian policy.[6] Losses in hard currency earnings have apparently not been calculated against the gains in sovereignty and security—security in this case has been presumed to be an absolute not a comparative consideration.[7]

The pervasive secrecy in domestic economic matters that extends to controlling the publication of civilian as well as military data is detailed evidence of an unusual extension of security to economic affairs. Examples of civilian data withheld from the public include figures related to material stocks, new inventions, and the production of critical materials. The direct involvement of foreign engineers, quality controllers or even observers in Soviet enterprises may still be considered by many Soviet leaders as "spies in their midst."

This obsession with sovereignty and security often stops economic interaction at the Soviet border and thereby limits the effectiveness of Western technology within the Soviet economy.[8] The traditional openness of Western societies to institutional, technological, and economic influences from abroad has been severely limited in the Soviet Union. An apparently greater preference for nontrade channels of technological flow (for example, espionage), as well as the ratio of commercial to KGB officers accredited to Soviet missions abroad further reflects a penchant for security and secrecy.

Soviet concern over internal and external threats to security extends beyond the USSR to vital areas such as Eastern Europe. The ambiguous discussions in the West of the so-called Sonnenfeldt Doctrine illustrate Western difficulties in interpreting this security factor in Soviet policy and determining how best to react to it. The withdrawal of Poland, Hungary, or other countries from the Warsaw Pact or Council for Mutual Economic Assistance (CMEA) may be considered non-negotiable based on the raison d'être of these alliances. For example, the Brezhnev Doctrine maintains that Soviet security interests are paramount to those of the USSR's East European allies. This doctrine was used to justify Soviet intervention in Czechoslovakia in 1968 and continues to provide the rationale for current Soviet policy toward East European independence. The use of the Brezhnev Doctrine may not be clear and predictable in all contingencies, but its past applications provide evidence of Soviet preoccupation with the security of the Eastern bloc that it controls.

When Soviet leaders meet with Western officials, arms control and weapons issues are the first item on the Soviet agenda. If mutually beneficial economic relations are seen as a catalyst to progress in security areas, then trade concessions may be made. Whereas potential for successful arms negotiations may directly facilitate Soviet commercial flexibility, economic need does not appear to dictate concessions in arms negotiations. Even in cases of political concern involving economic costs, such as the 1984 Soviet Olympic boycott, security is used as the primary explanation.

2. Sovereignty of the state—those elements of national policy which are deemed to be the preserve of any sovereign state—but seem to be particularly emphasized in the historical view of Soviet leaders: respect within the community of nations and acceptance of the legitimacy of Soviet claims to be a global superpower are important aspects of the Soviet view of sovereignty. Anything that threatens or erodes this superpower position is likely to be opposed. To the extent that this great power role of the USSR is enhanced, acceptance of international norms of behavior may not only be acceptable but desirable. The Soviet Union's acceptance of norms of international behavior is evidenced by its being a party to U.N. conventions, its continued participation in an expanded Helsinki (CSCE) process, and its tolerance of CMEA nations joining international financial institutions (IMF, World Bank, and GATT). As long as Soviet acceptance of such norms heightens their international role as well as the legitimacy of the Eastern bloc in the world community of nations, the Soviets view these international standards as positive rather than negative interventions in the sovereignty of the Eastern bloc.

The Soviets seem more responsive to outside pressures contained in international agreements to which they are a party and in which they are perceived as equal. Acceptance of a modified right to emigrate through the Helsinki process may be viewed in this broader political context. The Soviets' willingness, at least for most of the 1970s, to accept an emigration policy so contrary to their historical and sovereign sensibility should not be attributed solely or primarily to potential access to tariff benefits and Western credits but more to domestic political judgments and a combination of foreign and domestic policy interests.[9]

3. Systemic continuity of the Marxist–Leninist system of government, including the dominant role of the Communist party, the leading role of the USSR in the socialist camp, and the continuation of certain critical economic planning and management institutions: the ideological view that socialism and capitalism are in competition and that one must prevail is still in force. Although the Soviets consider the establishment of socialism and communism to be an historical inevitability, they are inclined to take steps to ensure this outcome. Because party leaders lack traditional Western legitimacy, they are less secure. Any lessening of party influence in determining long-term economic policy as well as in the day-to-day functioning of the economy is viewed by the regime as potentially destabilizing. Indeed, any internal and external forces that encourage the transformation of the economy and one-party system in the direction of a market economy and a pluralistic political system may be perceived as a threat to the fundamental legitimacy of the party.

Western analysts often view changes in Soviet planning and management as necessary reforms toward a market economic system, for example, market socialism. Soviet leaders, however, consider the same requirements as new economic mechanisms (NEMs) within the socialist system. NEMs that modify the traditional Stalinist role of the party in both society and the economy have been permitted, even encouraged, in Eastern Europe and the Soviet Union. The decisions to introduce such changes are based on balanced political economic cost-benefit judgments. Some examples of NEMs include the system of decentralized agricultural management in Hungary and Bulgaria and the decentralized industrial complexes in the German Democratic Republic (GDR).

The degree of systemic flexibility introduced in the Eastern bloc is not predetermined but is a gray area for trial and accommodation. Under certain circumstances, some variant of the Polish government's policy of establishing a dialogue between the government, church, and "freely formed trade unions" may eventually be accepted by Moscow, not only as a temporary expedient but as a viable policy for Poland as well. Moscow may also agree to direct Western investments in Poland, Western management of Polish enterprises, and/or the establishment of other forms of Western multinational involvement in Polish factories (for example, equity ownership, rights to repatriation of profits, and quality control of production) depending on the degree to which such changes are perceived by the Soviet leadership as increasing the stability of the Jaruzelski regime and improving the health of Poland's economy within tolerable limits.

Participation in "buy-back" arrangements and countertrade and acceptance of credit are examples of the Eastern bloc's systemic flexibility. These measures have been introduced to facilitate foreign trade with the West.

4. Comparative advantage or the international division of labor: traditionally, the USSR has been concerned about economic bottleneck relief in planned projects—absolute economic advantage. In recent years, however, timeliness and the superior quality of Western goods have caused the Soviets to consider the benefits of comparative economic advantage. These can be illustrated by the importation by the USSR of: Western feed grain for Soviet livestock; Western automotive, computer, metal working, and energy equipment technology for major Soviet projects; and Western economic techniques for planning and management.

In time, the Soviet economy could independently produce all these goods, although less efficiently and effectively than if Western goods and technologies were used. The priority sectors of food and agriculture, energy, metallurgy, and transportation may be permitted to compete with defense in claims on domestic investment. They may also be allowed to command increased imports from the West.

Factors Limiting Western Commercial Policy toward the East

The political–economic policies of Western governments limit and influence Soviet policy toward Western trade. All Western nations take the official position that the Soviet Union and CMEA are not isolated or discriminated against; economic warfare is not an official policy. However, Western definitions of normal trade vary from country to country and administration to administration.

Politics influence Western commercial behavior through government intervention in the private trading sector. Although this intervention appears to be less pervasive or significant than in the centrally controlled Soviet context, a political–economic act such as an embargo or a large government-supported commercial agreement is as much a political as an economic matter from the Soviet perspective. Thus, a grain embargo or a long-term grain agreement may have a more direct effect on bilateral political relations than on commercial intercourse.

Several factors influence the interplay of Western economics and diplomacy:

1. Security, protection of the homeland (for example, the continental United States and other geographic areas of vital security interest to the states and governments of the various Western na-

tions): for the United States, traditional security concerns are handled through arrangements with NATO countries, Japan, South Korea, and other nations. In economic relations, export controls and other limits on economic intercourse are designed to restrict "trading with the enemy." The Export Administration Act (EAA) of 1979 like its predecessors, the Export Control Act of 1949 and the Export Administration Act of 1969 (amended in 1974 and 1977) establishes the basis of U.S. trade policy with the East. Under the EAA, export licensing to communist countries is regulated in accordance with U.S. national security interests, U.S. foreign policy objectives, and, to a lesser extent, limitation on domestic supplies. The EAA is the means by which the United States puts into practice the recommendations of the multilateral Consultative Group Coordinating Committee (CoCom). CoCom consists of all NATO members except Spain and Iceland, plus Japan.[10]

The relationship between economics and security concerns as it pertains to East–West trade is currently being reviewed in four ongoing alliance studies, which were announced by President Reagan on 13 November 1982, when the remaining sanctions on the sale of energy equipment to the USSR were removed. These four studies focus on:[11]

1. General premises: a general reassessment of objectives and strategies of Western economic relations with the East, especially the Soviet Union; undertaken within the NATO Economic Secretariat, Brussels;
2. Strategic trade: a re-examination of strategic trade controls within CoCom, Paris;
3. Energy: an evaluation of the benefits and costs in energy trade, especially import of Soviet gas and export of Western energy equipment; based at the International Energy Agency, OECD, Paris;
4. Credit: an exploration of possible ways to harmonize credit policy and thereby reduce the prospect of subsidization or provision of preferential credit to the USSR and other communist countries; undertaken by the OECD, Paris.

A fifth study, a general OECD study on East–West economic relations, was added after President Reagan's announcement and paralleled the NATO study.

The topics under consideration in these five studies illustrate the wide scope of economic issues related to security questions: Does Soviet economic health threaten Western security? Does significant technology transfer to the Soviet military flow through industrial processes and industrial exchanges? What compromises "strategic trade?" Discussions surrounding these questions highlight the range of Western views on these sensitive topics. Although alliance views are far from monolithic, there does seem to be a common interest in focusing more on the political-security aspects of Western commercial relations with the East. For example, the up-grading of the NATO Economic Secretariat as a forum for consultations on East–West trade policies illustrates the increasing political-security focus of Western commercial relations with the East. The studies listed above, when completed, will provide greater insight into how the West views the relative importance of security issues as compared to economic concerns in East–West trade.

2. *International norms of behavior—acceptance of limitations in global relations, especially superpower relations throughout the world:* since the bilateral agreement on the "Basic Principles of Relations" was signed at the Nixon–Brezhnev summit of 1972, the Soviet Union and the United States have held differing views of its intended meaning.[12] The Soviets argue that they are a superpower and, therefore, are at least entitled to exercise the same rights as the United States in order to enhance their international influence. Moreover, they maintain that the Nixon–Brezhnev agreement did not establish explicit rules or restraints, although the Soviets point to U.S. involvement in Chile, El Salvador, and Grenada as examples of unacceptable U.S. behavior, and that the agreement did not establish any mechanism for enforcement of "codes of conduct."

The United States, however, interprets the agreement quite differently. From the U.S. point of view, Soviet interventions in Angola, Afghanistan, Central America, and elsewhere were not only unwarranted but contravened these bilateral understandings. As a result of such Soviet actions, the United States has in some instances, notably Afghanistan, withheld economic benefits and instituted economic sanctions against the USSR. Other Western nations, however, have followed U.S. actions only in varying degrees.

3. *Acceptance of Western domination of international economic institutions and the global market:* the Soviets participated in the Bretton Woods Conference but never joined the international economic institutions that were outgrowths of that meeting—the IMF, GATT, and the World Bank. Western countries nonetheless continue to see the stability of the global economic system as substantially aided by, if not dependent upon, the effective operation of those three bodies, and, therefore, find it advisable for Eastern countries to participate in those financial organizations.

4. *Economic profitability from East–West interdependence:* for many of the early postwar years, the volume of East–West trade was below a level of profitability that had significant impact on the economic well-being of major Western industrial and agricultural sectors. Western exports generally served political purposes, for example, West German trade with East Germany—"intra-German trade." Following the oil pipeline sanctions imposed by NATO in 1962, industrial trade with the East began to provide jobs and markets for sectors of West European economies. Likewise, in the 1970s, agricultural trade became important to the economic health of the key agricultural sectors in the United States, Canada, and other grain exporting nations.

In cases where the threshold of domestic economic profitability has been reached, Western countries are usually reluctant to sharply limit trade to meet the diplomatic aims of the state. In countries where important sectors have become, or are perceived, to be dependent on access to the Soviet market for profit, increased employment and production, commercial relations have become an important political force. In 1982, a number of important sectors in OECD countries had crossed the threshold of significant profitability, including the following key sector exports to CMEA (19 to 40 percent of total trade): grain from Canada, Australia, France, and the United States; steel plates from Austria, Italy, and West Germany; and machine tools from France, Italy, West Germany, and Switzerland.[13] The significance of Soviet imports is clear, and in the 1980s the scale of these imports may determine the sector profitability of German pipe producers and U.S. corn and wheat farmers.

Alternative Soviet and Western Scenarios for East–West Trade

Alternative Political Scenarios for Soviet Commercial Behavior[14]

The policy context for Soviet consideration of economic factors in determining commercial behavior may be considered in three different illustrative patterns or scenarios:

1. *An independent or autarkic policy of restricting trade with the West to confining economic exchange to the CMEA bloc:* this policy would be a return toward the Stalinist, independent policy of the past. It would require greater use of Soviet energy and other natural resources within CMEA along with reduced reliance on im-

portant Western technology imports for economic modernization, reduced reliance on grain and other agricultural imports from grain exporting nations, and limited use of Western governmental and commercial credit. An independent policy might be reinforced by limited hard currency earning potentials and restrictions in Western trade policy. This policy would probably coincide with a return to East–West hostility on all fronts, which characterized the cold war period.

2. *A selective modernization policy of trading in limited economic areas with particular Western industrial countries depending on the political environment:* this policy would basically represent a continuation of the strategy practiced during the Brezhnev era. It would favor foreign importation in priority areas such as energy equipment and agriculture and defer in others; it would favor some Western countries (for example, Western Europe) for industrial trade and others (for example, the United States) for major grain imports. The United States might be either a preferred or residual supplier in agricultural and industrial trade depending on U.S. foreign policy and trade legislation. The 1983 U.S.–Soviet Long-Term Grain Agreement assures normal grain trade for 1983–1988, that is, potentially a return of the United States to the pre-Afghanistan position of preferred supplier.

3. *An interdependence policy of trading with a wide variety of goods and technologies with all or most Western industrial nations using all available measures to cope with hard currency needs, including joint ventures and direct investment:* the outer links of this policy would be the adoption of normalized trading practices, that is, practices in line with world market norms and the provisions of "Basket II" of the Helsinki Final Act, at least insofar as a state trading nation could accommodate these practices.

Alternative Scenarios for the Western Industrial Countries

Western political considerations influencing commercial policy with the East may also be discussed in terms of patterns: discriminatory—a return to the restricted trade policy of the past; neutral—a policy that neither promotes preferential terms nor intervenes with embargoes or other restrictions; or competitive—a policy that conforms to the normal commercial practices of most Western countries but, by U.S. standards, appears preferential in the degree of positive governmental intervention.

Western economic relations with the East might tend toward one of the following three courses during the 1980s:

1. *A discriminatory policy of restricting Eastern access to Western technology and credits:* such a policy would be an extension of the sanctions imposed by the Carter and Reagan administrations. Such a policy would be based on the view that communist and Western systems are locked into a basic conflict of values for long-term dominance. In classical economic terms, this policy could be called neo-mercantilist and, in more modern terms, the Soviets and others refer to it as economic warfare.

2. *A neutral policy of governmental nonintervention in East–West trade:* because the forces of supply and demand would determine Soviet access to Western goods and credits, this policy may be considered a market policy. It may also be termed a laissez-faire policy. Although this policy has not been consistently followed to date, it may currently be considered closer to the West German avoidance of direct use of government credits and the U.S. refusal to provide government credits to the East. The agreements in principle contained in the alliance studies described previously seem to be in line with this approach.

3. *A competitive policy under which all Western governments would actively promote East–West trade by offering Eastern countries guaranteed access to supplies and favorable terms for credits:* this policy may also be called the Helsinki option after the Final Act signed there at the conclusion of the Conference on Security and Cooperation in Europe in 1975. It may be identified with the general European policy from 1966 to date and the U.S. policy of economic detente during the Nixon administration.[15]

Prospective East–West Interaction

1. *Effect of extreme scenarios of change—change in the Soviet Union either toward independence or interdependence:* if the West attempted to isolate the USSR by adopting highly discriminatory Eastern trade policies, the Soviets would probably be inclined to focus more on CMEA integration, on the development of domestic projects outlined in their plans, and on internal control mechanisms. This suggests that the first scenario (discriminatory policy) for the West would likely encourage acceptance of the first scenario (independence) by the East, and vice versa. But if the West broadly accepted a competitive policy and tried to draw the USSR into a higher degree of interdependence with the West (the third scenarios in each case), then the Soviets would be more likely to consider, and possibly to

emphasize, cooperative ventures, acceptance of market norms of performance, and direct involvement of Western economic interests in the USSR.

2. *Foreign policy effects of Soviet domestic–foreign economic policy:*[16] how the Soviet leadership views security threats and opportunities over the course of the 1980s could influence which domestic economic strategy it adopts. If new security threats and opportunities are perceived, then the leadership is more likely to opt for a strategy of increased control focusing on defense-related projects. If, however, the leadership feels that the security needs of the USSR have been met and that there are no promising opportunities or threats encouraging the further projection of Soviet military power abroad, then the leadership could turn its attention to the domestic economy and focus on economic modernization.

The adoption of an economic strategy of building up the Soviet military sector may be caused by changes in Asia, especially regarding China; changes in the U.S. nuclear arsenal; or changes in Europe, particularly concerning the Federal Republic of Germany. In the coming decades, extreme developments in Asia, such as the conclusion of a formal military alliance between the United States and the People's Republic of China or the sale of U.S. arms to the PRC, would cause the Soviet leadership to enhance their military posture. Also, the unlikely West German acquisition of nuclear weapons would greatly increase the priority of defense in the view of the Soviet leaders. Soviet opposition to deployment of the Pershing-2s in Europe has attempted to conjure this rather extreme image of enhanced danger to the Soviet homeland. Perceptions of developments in Western weapons policies alone are enough to influence Soviet planning.[17] Opportunities to fill power vacuums in the Middle East, South Africa, or in other strategic areas would also tend to elevate defense priorities.

Although it seems obvious that external factors could cause the Soviet leadership to give increased priority to defense, these factors do not appear capable of having the opposite effect. A perceived lessening of the NATO or China threat would not necessarily lead the Soviet leadership to reduce its military preparations or deployment of weapons or troops.

An absence of foreign threats could, however, permit the leadership to give greater consideration to selective domestic economic priorities. In a neutral foreign policy context, major domestic crises such as an overall economic growth slowdown; severe imbalances in investment or shortages of critical goods (for example, grain, steel, hydrocarbons); deficiencies in labor supply or transport; natural disasters (for example, poor harvests); or financial opportunities or problems (for example, increased oil prices or the nonpayment of East European debt to the West) might become the priority items on the Soviet leadership's agenda.

The two strategies of military augmentation and economic modernization need not be mutually exclusive. A situation could present itself whereby the Soviets could choose to take advantage of a perceived exploitable security opportunity in one area, and concurrently seek economic cooperation in another. Increased military allocations would be accompanied by some degree of economic modernization. An example of such a case would be if the United States and its allies, either in Europe or Japan, lacked agreement on a common policy toward the East and hence the Soviets decide to exploit a perceived security opportunity in Europe or Asia as it cultivated economic cooperation with certain Western nations. Differences in the West on both missile deployment and trade policy with the East have been situations that the Soviets tried to foster and use to their own advantage.

If the Soviets saw it necessary to build up greatly their military and reinstitute the Stalinist system of control, their approach to international relations would probably revert back to a two-camp, anti-imperialist policy. Soviet objectives would likely be to exploit tensions between Western capitalist countries and to deny the West access to needed resources in the developing world. The Soviet Union would largely withdraw from the global economy but would use available trade, credit, and technology flows to divide the West.

The Soviet Union would also be inclined to accelerate its policy of sowing disunity in Asia. In addition to continuing their military buildup in Kamchatka, the Sea of Okhotsk, the Kuriles, and the Soviet Maritime Provinces, the Soviets might intensify their efforts to encircle China. A militarily strong Vietnamese ally in Southeast Asia, a Soviet-controlled Afghanistan in Southwest Asia, and a revived, close Soviet–North Korean strategic relationship in Northeast Asia might accomplish this task sufficiently to cause serious Chinese security concerns.

If the Soviet leadership were instead to decide to give priority to selective domestic modernization, a decision made possible by positive correlation with security, sovereignty, and systemic continuity concerns, the USSR would likely increase its participation in the world economic community, possibly seeking membership in international organizations such as GATT, the World Bank, and the IMF. The Soviet Union might possibly side with northern countries on North–South issues, for example, trade and commodity agreements (though not necessarily rejecting military assistance in certain targets of opportunity in the Third World), and might begin to behave in line with some mutually acceptable codes of international conduct. In addition, Soviet dealings with Western Europe might more closely conform with those envisaged by the Helsinki Final Act in the areas of military, commercial, political, and social relations. Such interaction could result in a reduction of military buildups and a further easing of international tensions.

Economic interdependence with the West could greatly enhance the performance of the Soviet economy. U.S. technology, management expertise, and possibly large long-term credit facilities could be particularly important to the development of Soviet agriculture and energy development. If cooperative ventures with the United States were to increase the technological level of Soviet agriculture and energy to approximate that of the United States, then the productive capability of those two sectors of the Soviet economy would be greatly improved. The critical margin in food and energy availability might spell the difference between deficiency and sufficiency in Soviet economic performance in those critical areas.

Because the USSR can obtain industrial technology from other countries, that is, Western Europe and Japan, on favorable credit terms and often in exchange for raw materials and energy products, the Soviets do not have to be overly concerned with unilateral U.S. industrial export restrictions. Although agricultural exports provide the United States with some more unique leverage, long-term grain agreements insulate this commercial exchange from political interventions, for example, embargoes.

A domestic economic strategy of modernization fostering economic interdependence and cooperation and a reduced emphasis on defense appear to hold considerably more benefits for the Soviet Union. A time of diminished international tension would encourage an expanded economic relationship between the East and West. The benefits of Western trade and civilian technology could provide both the impetus and resources for domestic modernization.

Some, however, do not see an improved East–West relationship as favoring this scenario. Rather, in their view, such a situation would only give the Soviets more of a chance to build up their military. They see economic modernization as only benefiting the military sector. Among those making such arguments is Secretary of Defense Casper Weinberger. He has repeatedly stressed that U.S. trade, especially in technology serves to foster the advancement of the Soviet military and hence forces the United States to spend more on its own defense effort to counter Soviet achievements. At a conference at the Georgetown Center for Strategic and International Studies in the fall of 1982, Secretary Weinberger made the following remark about the trading of oil and gas technology and equipment: "[I]t is hard to see how trade of this kind that has had such an obvious military advantage . . . can do anything but increase the danger to all of us."

Should the Soviet leadership decide to make the necessary policy and administrative changes internally that would allow for an economic strategy of domestic modernization, the Soviets may possibly avoid a time of troubles and enter a period of economic renaissance.

Alternative Soviet Balance of Payments Projections

Conventional Western Projections of Soviet Commercial Behavior

Conventional Soviet–Western balance of payments projections are based on estimates of hard currency export earnings and estimates of the availability and use of Western credit. These estimates are likely to be accurate only if the political context remains constant. Changes in political factors favoring or discouraging commercial relations are likely to make the projections too low or too high.

Recent projections of Soviet and East European trade by Daniel Bond and Lawrence Klein derive a range of outcomes for the period from 1982 to 1988 (see table 7–1).[18] This range of trade estimates is responsive to the following international variables: real Gross Domestic Product (GDP), growth in the OECD countries, the strength of the dollar relative to other major Western currencies, international interest rates, world nonfuel import prices, and world fuel import prices.

Bond and Klein's projected "steady improvement" in Soviet trade turnover for the 1980s—up to two-thirds increase in the next six years—is based on relatively optimistic estimates of Soviet hard currency export income from oil, gas and other exports as compared to the assessments of Gregory Grossman,[19] Hedja Kravalis,[20] and Richard Portes.[21] Moreover, according to Grossman, Kravalis, and Portes, Soviet earnings from the sale of gold and other nontrade income would not offset the trade imbalance implied by a steady improvement in Soviet imports. Therefore, the deficit in trade would require Western credit and an increase in their hard currency debt.

Most Western specialists do not consider the Soviet ability to

Table 7–1
Soviet Hard Currency Trade Projections with the West 1982–1988
(Billions of dollars)[a]

	1982	*1988*		
		Baseline	*Optimistic*	*Pessimistic*
Soviets				
Imports	26.0	43.5	45.5	44.5
Exports	26.2	39.9	42.1	39.1
Balance	.2	−3.6	−3.4	−5.4

Source: Daniel Bond and Lawrence Klein, "The Global Environment and Its Impact on the Soviet and East European Economies," paper presented at the Workshop on East–West European Economic Interaction, Moscow, 20–22 September 1983. Reprinted with permission.

[a]Three scenarios have been examined: a baseline, an optimistic scenario, and a pessimistic scenario. Their features can be summarized as follows:

> The baseline scenario assumes a moderate recovery in the Western economies beginning in 1983, with (GDP) Gross Domestic Product growth rates in the OECD countries averaging less than 2 percent over the forecast period 1983–1988. There is a steady decline in the dollar over most of the period, a drop in increase rates in 1983–1984 with only modest increase rates thereafter, gradually rising fuel trade policies following a drop in 1983–1984, and fairly strong increases in nonfuel trade prices. This baseline projection of world economic conditions was prepared in late 1982 and would not, in mid-1983, be considered the most likely outlook, particularly for the period 1983–1984. We are mainly concerned with comparisons between other scenarios and the baseline case. The comparisons are insensitive to small changes in the baseline. Domestic economic growth rates are projected to average 2.1 percent per year for Eastern Europe as a whole and 2.6 percent for the Soviet Union.
>
> The optimistic scenario assumes a somewhat stronger recovery in the Western economies relative to the baseline, even lower interest rates, and more rapid increases in nonfuel prices. Other world variables correspond to the baseline assumptions. Domestic economic growth rates are assumed to be slightly higher than in the baseline.
>
> The pessimistic scenario assumes a somewhat weaker recovery in the Western economies relative to the baseline, a stronger dollar over the period 1983–1985, significantly higher interest rates, and lower fuel trade prices—especially over the next three years. Domestic economic growth rates are assumed to be lower than in the baseline.

finance the deficit implied by the Bond—Klein projections to be a serious constraint. While Allen Lenz sees credit terms and supplies as major problems for CMEA-Six trade with the West throughout the decade, he views the Soviet Union as an exception.[22] With low debt service ratios and a strong resource base, Lenz estimates that the Soviet Union could expand its debt sufficiently to cover annual imbalances of \$3–\$6 billion for some time without serious payment problems. As the Soviet Union chose to reduce their net deficit to about $10 billion in 1982 by reducing imports and stepping up oil sales, the Soviet constraint on borrowing seems more relevant than Western banking restraints on lending.[23]

Again, the key differences between the Bond–Klein forecast of steady improvement and the other assessments mentioned are especially attributable to differences in projected oil and gas income and credit. Projections of OECD growth and the U.S. interest rates, of course, influence the evaluations of likely trends in energy prices and credit terms. If oil exports declined, prices fell, and gas sales did not offset the decrease in hard currency income from oil exports, then overall exports and imports might be expected to fall, if the Soviets were not able or willing to finance projected trade deficits. If Western official and commercial credit windows were closed, then economic projections for 1982–1988 would range from about the current turnover level to markedly lower levels of trade, that is, below those estimated by Bond and Klein.

Implicit in oil export earnings is not only the assumed OPEC price, but also the relationship between oil exports and domestic supply. Recent developments have challenged the premise that domestic and CMEA needs would have priority and oil exports to hard currency countries might be a residual. Actually, Soviet discussions appear to include the possibility that from time to time energy exports related to financing import needs will come first, leaving domestic and CMEA energy recipients as residual claimants. It may even be suggested that oil exports rise according to the need to earn hard currency, for example, in 1982 when as much as 80 percent of the Soviet hard currency earnings came from energy sales, and they substantially cut back their net debt.

Soviet Commercial Behavior in the Context of Soviet Policy

Soviet–Western trade patterns, as described above, that range from "no change" to "steady improvement" are only likely to develop if the political context of Soviet commercial policy remains unchanged. While it is always possible that the political context for Soviet commercial relations with the West may remain reasonably constant throughout the 1980s, this is not likely. What is more likely is that there will be shifts—possibly major shifts—in the international political environment, as well as in the Soviet domestic political environment. Such shifts would invalidate the conventional Western forecasts of Soviet–Western trade, for those outcomes would then turn out to be either not high enough or not low enough. If the forecasts turn out to be not high enough, that would mean a trade-stimulating environment existed, that is, a combination of a Soviet policy of increased interdependence and a Western consensus on a competitive policy. If instead the forecasts turn out to be not low enough, that would mean that a trade-restricting environment existed, that is, a combination of a Soviet policy of independence and a Western consensus on a discriminatory commercial policy.

Trade Stimulating Environment. Trade stimulation involves either a greater ability on the part of the Soviets to earn more hard currency to pay for imports or increased Western flexibility to allow for increased economic cooperation to enhance trade and/or defer Soviet payments. A number of methods could facilitate this environment, including payment for imports, nontrade income and credit and capital flows.

Payment for Imports. Conventional sales of hydrocarbons on the world market for hard currency have been insufficient to finance Soviet imports of grain, technology, et cetera. Countertrade (exports tied to imports), buy-back arrangements, and other forms of barter have consequently become increasingly important, particularly in East–West European trade. Countertrade was a central agenda item at the Madrid talks on Basket Two of the Helsinki Agreement; however, no change in policy resulted from that meeting. It is possible that countertrade may eventually become equally important to conventional trade in the financing of Soviet imports.

Buy-back arrangements or compensation agreements have long been favored by Soviet trade officials. The "gas for pipe" deal discussed between the United States and USSR in the early 1970s was the prototype to be extended to arrangements of "steel for metallurgical equipment," "autos and trucks for equipment," and other similar arrangements. In 1975–1976, there were discussions concerning Soviet production of spark plugs manufactured in plants built by the Bendix Corporation (a U.S. company) and marketed through the international supply system of Bendix. In the early negotiations for steel-making technology, the Germans were understandably reluctant to accept Soviet steel for German metallurgical equipment. In the future, however, gasified coal from the Soviet Kansk–Achinsk deposits may be accepted for German equipment and pipe.[24] There have also been reports of Soviet interest in exchanging Moskvitch auto production for Western equipment and technology, for example, a buy-back Renault version of a Moskvitch.[25]

Critical to the success or failure of buy-back arrangements have been and will continue to be the political cycles of East–West relations. The Pepsi Cola for Stolichnaya Vodka exchange seems to have been one of the few deals that has withstood the ups and downs of the 1970s and 1980s without interruption or cancellation. Prior to the Soviet invasion of Afghanistan in 1979, the U.S. and the USSR discussed industrial cooperation in developing up to twenty-nine major projects, including the petroleum development of the Caspian and Sakhalin offshore deposits, electric steel production, and aluminum facilities. Joint development in metallurgy, trucks, and energy was envisaged in conjunction with the Baikal–Amur regional development in the mid-1970s, which was to include the development of both the railroad to the Pacific and the resources of the region. The development of Yakutia natural gas reserves was the centerpiece of the project. The United States, Japan, and the Soviet Union all cooperated in the exploration of gas deposits. After concluding that the resources were commercially exploitable, the project was shelved—in part a casualty of deterioration in political relations.

Since the Afghanistan sanctions, the Soviet Union has expressed interest in a new combine production complex and has looked to International Harvester as the logical Western partner to provide the production capability for a replacement for the standard Soviet combine. As part of the Brezhnev "Food Program," this deal was reaffirmed by the Andropov regime at the U.S.–USSR Trade and Economic Council meeting in November 1982. The following year, a U.S.–USSR agricultural exhibit was held in Moscow.[26] Only with a favorable change in Soviet–Western (especially U.S.–Soviet) relations are such trade-stimulating activities likely to produce their expected results.

Commercial cooperation between the East and West could be facilitated by improving Soviet access to Western markets. This could be accomplished by: the reduction of tariffs (that is, the granting of most-favored-nation status by the United States); the lowering of quotas in the Common Market; and the moderation of Western laws on dumping, countervailing duties, and market disruption. U.S. restrictions in the fur trade—the "Seven Deadly Skins" ruling—might also be removed or reduced along with other institutional restraints that limit Soviet access to U.S. domestic markets, including those that restrict Soviet sales of hydrofoils and the assemblage of autos in the United States.

Nontrade Income. Tourism is currently a major hard currency earner and prospective increases may be considered substantial. Continued

Soviet control over the foreign travel of its citizens suggests that tourist income is likely to remain unbalanced. The flow of Western tourists to the Soviet Union, however, has been particularly sensitive to the political environment as evidenced in the post-Afghanistan and post-KAL periods. Expanded tourism relates to airline and water transport rights, as well as to tourist facilities. Had the Moscow Olympics not been boycotted, the income generated would have been substantial.

Merchant marine income from third country trade (that is, cross trade) was expanding in the 1970s, approaching 10 percent of Soviet balance of hard currency payments. For a time, the possibility of the Soviet Union joining the Atlantic and Far Eastern Maritime Conventions was discussed, meaning higher maritime income and stable access to world commerce for the Soviets.

Credit and Capital Flows. Credit worthiness results from both an economic and a political judgment. Official credit facilities in loans and guarantees not only expand the supply of loanable funds but improve the terms. Western commercial banks tend to "follow the flag" of their governments in and out of the Soviet market.

Direct investment and joint ventures are possible in CMEA countries, as well as in other communist nations. Investment laws in Yugoslavia, Romania, and Hungary indicate varying patterns. The conclusion of joint venture arrangements emulating the PRC's foreign trade zones suggest even wider flexibility. Although direct investment, equity ownership, and foreign participation within the Soviet system are the most advanced forms of foreign economic cooperation, such types of foreign involvement continue to be seriously discussed. The potential for further acceptance of foreign economic cooperation by the CMEA countries and other countries (that is, the PRC) has been demonstrated.

Tripartite cooperation has also been established between the CMEA, the developed West and developing countries. The modest developments, heralded in the 1970s, have been muted in the 1980s due in the main to the hardening of political relations and the recession.[27]

Trade Restricting Environment. Trade restrictions involve either a reduction in the ability of the Soviet Union to earn more hard currency to pay for imports or an increase in Western restrictions of credit or capital flows to the USSR. Methods of trade facilitation may not only be limited but reversed.

Payments for Imports. Exports of materials—oil and gas—may be restricted to give priority to domestic needs and those of the CMEA. The "national treasure" motive for keeping "black" and "blue gold" (that is, oil and gas) for domestic use only still has its high level supporters within the Soviet leadership.

All flexible mechanisms for furthering trade such as cooperative agreements and industrial cooperation bring with them foreign interventions, dependency, and vulnerability. To some Soviet officials, foreign experts will always be considered spies, whether in business suits or uniforms. Moreover, these officials see few absolute advantages to Western trade: feed grain—corn and soy concentrates—are more effective for animal husbandry but may be dispensed with, albeit at lower levels of efficiency; Western imports may facilitate technological change but destabilize the traditional system of planning and management. East European sources of machinery and consumer goods are considered more secure and promote CMEA integration as well.

Western Credit and Capital Flows. In 1976, Soviet "bankers" seemed to override "planners" in reducing Western debt servicing costs and credit-related vulnerability. The political rationale for the conservative Soviet credit policy was probably to avoid Western political leverage, even the requirements of Western conditionality. The conditions that usually accompany Western credit, even if rescheduling is not directly involved, include the sharing of information and the relinquishing of some control over the domestic Soviet economy. Avoidance of such security and political costs was probably considered a political gain.

Enhanced Western Restriction. Soviet–Western commercial relations would no doubt be chilled if CoCom licensing criteria were expanded to take account of indirect as well as direct strategic flows and if foreign policy criteria were freely applied in trade and credit considerations. Specific U.S. actions to limit either imports of goods produced by "forced labor" or specific products, such as nickel and ferro silicon, would likewise have a political and economic trade-restricting effect.[28]

Conclusion: Politics over Economics in Soviet Commercial Behavior

The interaction of Soviet and Western policy from the Stalinist 1950s to the succession period of the 1980s is a general trend toward more interdependence and trade facilitation correlating with distinct political cycles in Soviet–American relations. This process provides the framework for Soviet commercial behavior. Most Western projections of Soviet–Western trade implicitly accept an assumption of stability in this political pattern. This assumption, however, runs counter to recent historical experience and seems especially inappropriate for the future. East–West and U.S.–Soviet political relations are more likely to fluctuate and less likely to be constant in the decade ahead. If this is the case, most conventional economic trade projections for the USSR are likely to be either too low or too high. Good political relations will facilitate more trade and poor relations less trade than those conventional economic forecasts would suggest. Therefore, political as well as economic assumptions should be made explicit in forecasts of Soviet foreign trade.

Furthermore, Soviet commercial relations with the various developed regions of the world—North America, Japan, and Western Europe—are determined more by political factors than by comparative advantage. Success or failure in arms control negotiations, regional problems, human rights, and overall political relations contribute to an environment of trade stimulation or trade restriction in the regional as well as global context. There may be variants that promote commercial relations in some regions and dampen trade prospects in others.

The 1980s and 1990s appear likely to be different from the decade 1974–1984. If the current political environment continues, there will probably be a sharp compartmentalization of Soviet trade: agricultural trade for the United States and industrial trade for the other OECD countries. Besides East–West tensions, there are West–West tensions that must be relieved in order to prevent this bifurcation of Soviet trade. U.S. and European trade policy with the East remain at variance. The United States continues to favor agricultural exports and to restrict nonmilitary industrial trade. Meanwhile, most European trade with the East is in the industrial area. By implementing an Eastern trade policy based on consensus, the West can counteract this tendency toward a division of Western trade with the East.[29] If there is a divergence in alliance policy, there may also be a divergence in the East–West trade environment: an environment of trade restriction with the United States and an environment of trade facilitation with the Eurasian countries. From the Soviet side, even if there is not a major divergence in alliance policy, the USSR might differentiate trade policy in order to divide the allies.

Notes

1. U.S. Congress, Senate, Committee on Foreign Relations, *Economic Relations with the Soviet Union*, Hearings, 97th Congress, 2nd session,

1982; U.S. Congress, Joint Economic Committee, *East–West Trade: Prospects to 1985* (Washington: U.S. Government Printing Office, 1982); U.S. Congress, Joint Economic Committee, *East–West Commercial Policy: A Congressional Dialogue with the Reagan Administration* (Washington: U.S. Government Printing Office, 1982).

2. See the chapter by Hiroshi Kumura on "Soviet Policy toward Japan" in this volume.

3. John P. Hardt and George D. Holliday, *U.S.–Soviet Commercial Relations: The Interplay of Economics, Technology Transfer, and Diplomacy,* report prepared for the U.S. Congress, House, Committee on Foreign Affairs (Washington: U.S. Government Printing Office, June 1973).

4. Stalin's policy was reinforced by Western economic isolation of the Soviet Union; see John P. Hardt and Kate S. Tomlinson, "Soviet Economic Policies in Western Europe," in Herbert Ellison, ed., *Soviet Policy Towards Western Europe* (Seattle: University of Washington Press, 1983), 159–208.

5. U.S. Congress, Senate, Committee on Foreign Relations, *Western Investment in Communist Economies: A Selected Survey on Economic Interdependence* (Washington: U.S. Government Printing Office, August 1974) and U.S. Congress, House, Committee on Foreign Affairs, *An Assessment of the Afghanistan Sanctions for Trade and Diplomacy in the 1980's* (Washington: U.S. Government Printing Office, 1981).

6. *Washington Post,* 10 September 1983, 1 and 12.

7. Allen S. Whiting, "Siberian Development and East Asia: The Strategic Dimension," in Robert G. Jenson, Theodore Shabad, and Arthur W. Wright, eds., *Soviet Natural Resources in the World Economy* (Chicago: University of Chicago Press, 1983), 232–247.

8. George Holliday, "Western Technology Transfer to the Soviet Union: Problems of Assimilation and Impact on Soviet Imports," in U.S. Congress, Joint Economic Committee, *Soviet Economy in the 1980's: Problems and Prospects,* vol. I (Washington: U.S. Government Printing Office, 1982), 514–530.

9. Yaacov R'oi, "The Soviet Jewish Anomaly," *The Jerusalem Quarterly* (Winter 1979); William Korey, "Human Rights and the Helsinki Accords," *Headline Series,* 264 (New York: Foreign Policy Association, 1983).

10. For more information on CoCom see: John P. Hardt and Kate S. Tomlinson, "The Potential Role of Western Policy toward Eastern Europe in East–West Trade," in Abraham Becker, ed., *Economic Relations with the USSR* (Lexington: Lexington Books, 1983), 111–127.

11. John P. Hardt, "Alternative Scenarios for the Atlantic Alliance," *Berichte des Bundesinstituts für Ostwissenschaftliche und Internationale Studien,* 39, 1983.

12. Alexander L. George, "The Basic Principles Agreement of 1972: Origins and Expectations," in Alexander L. George, ed., *Managing U.S.–Soviet Rivalry: Problems of Crisis Prevention* (Boulder: Westview Press, 1983), 107–118.

13. Selected OECD sources.

14. U.S. Congress, Senate, Committee on Foreign Relations, *The Premises of East–West Commercial Relations* (Washington: U.S. Government Printing Office, December 1982).

15. Hardt, "Alternative Scenarios for the Atlantic Alliance."

16. This section is based on an article by John P. Hardt and Kate S. Tomlinson entitled "Economic Factors in Soviet Foreign Policy" in *Soviet Foreign Policy in the 1980s,* Roger E. Kanet, ed. (New York: Praeger, 1982), 37–57.

17. If the CIA calculation of a modest 2 percent annual rise in defense costs from 1976 to 1981 with a leveling of military procurement is correct, this would suggest that the Brezhnev leadership acted neither on the basis of an enhanced threat nor on the basis of an opportunity to upgrade the military priority. See U.S. Congress, Joint Economic Committee, *Allocation of Resources in the Soviet Union and China, 1983,* Hearings, 20 September 1983 (Washington: U.S. Government Printing Office, 1983).

18. Daniel Bond and Lawrence Klein, "The Global Environment and Its Impact on the Soviet and East European Economies," paper presented at the Workshop on East–West European Economic Interaction, Moscow, 20–22 September 1983.

19. Gregory Grossman and Ronald L. Solberg, *The Soviet Union's Hard-Currency Balance of Payments and Creditworthiness in 1985* (Santa Monica: The Rand Corporation, 1983).

20. Hedja Kravalis, "U.S.S.R.: An Assessment of U.S. and Western Trade Potential with the Soviet Union Through 1985," in *East–West Trade: The Prospects to 1985.*

21. Richard Portes, "Deficits and Detente: Report of an International Conference on the Balance of Trade in the Comecon Countries," The Twentieth Century Fund, 1983.

22. Allen Lenz, "Controlling International Debt: Implications for East–West Trade," paper written for the Workshop on East–West European Interaction, Moscow, 20–22 September 1983.

23. Joan Parpart Zoeter, "U.S.S.R.: Hard Currency Trade and Payments" in *Soviet Economy in the 1980's: Problems and Prospects,* vol. II, 479–506.

24. John Taliague, "Soviet Still Seeks Bonn Energy Deal," *New York Times,* 17 April 1983.

25. Anthony Robinson, "Journey's End for Moskvitch," and "Britain Likely to Boost Exports to Russia," *Financial Times,* 26 April and 24 May 1983, respectively.

26. Serge Schmemann, "U.S. Agricultural Show Opens in Moscow Park," *New York Times,* 18 October 1983. Personal discussions of one of the authors with Soviet economic and trade officials in April–May 1983 indicated that an increment of $2 billion in Soviet imports of agricultural technology was possible in an improved political environment.

27. Patrick Gutman, "Tripartite Industrial Cooperation and East Europe," in U.S. Congress, Joint Economic Committee, *East European Eco-*

nomic Assessment, vol. II (Washington: U.S. Government Printing Office, 1981), 823–871.

28. Kenneth B. Noble, "Treasury Uneasy on Soviet Trade Issue," *New York Times,* 9 November 1983. After numerous exchanges between members of Congress, particularly Senator Armstrong, and various Executive agencies, a comprehensive study of "forced labor" in trade was initiated by the International Trade Commission.

29. Hardt, "Alternative Scenarios for the Atlantic Alliance."

8
Soviet Policy on Nuclear Weapons and Arms Control

Lawrence T. Caldwell

Soviet policy on nuclear weapons and arms control collided fiercely with the policies of the Reagan administration on those same issues in November and December of 1983. The resulting crisis went beyond the jockeying for position that is customary in negotiations between the superpowers. Both Washington and Moscow seemed to pull back for a period early in 1984, to shift gears, to look for new ground on which to meet—as if both leaderships realized that this crisis carried risks that potentially went beyond what they had experienced before and beyond what the stakes in the current disagreement could reasonably be argued to merit. This crisis speaks volumes about Soviet national security and foreign policy midway through the 1980s.

The Unravelling of INF and START

The pace of events prior to the first NATO deployments in the fall of 1983, of ground-launched cruise missiles (GLCMs) in Britain and Italy, and of Pershing-2 intermediate range ballistic missiles in West Germany suggested the high drama of a major international crisis. Throughout early 1983 both sides had maneuvered for position—making marginal adjustments of their positions in the Geneva talks over intermediate nuclear forces (INF). In August and September, each took final-hour initiatives.[1] But neither side thought an agreement was at hand.

Moscow then turned up the heat. Central Committee official Leonid Zamyatin threatened explicitly in Hamburg on 12 October, what had previously been implicit—that the Soviets would walk out of the negotiations once NATO deployments began.[2] Twelve days later the Soviets formally threatened that they would retaliate by deploying new missiles in East Germany and Czechoslovakia.[3] A last minute, highly charged debate in Bundestag on 22 November ended in a vote to go forward with deployments of Pershing-2s on German soil. The Soviets had made powerful efforts to influence the voting of the German parliament; a threatening article by Defense Minister Dmitrii Ustinov appeared in *Pravda* and the German government announced it had received but declined to reveal the contents of a letter from Andropov to the German Chancellor Helmut Kohl.[4]

The day following the West German vote the first components of NATO Pershing-2s arrived in Germany and the Soviets walked out of the INF negotiations in Geneva.[5]

In Britain, missile components for the GLCMs had been arriving throughout the fall, and Defense Minister Michael Heseltine had announced to Parliament on 14 November that the first cruise missiles had arrived at Greenham Common that same day.[6] The Italian defense ministry announced on 27 November that the first cruise missile components had arrived at Sigonella, but did not say precisely when.[7] NATO had deployed the missiles as it had threatened since 1979 if no INF agreement had been achieved by late 1983.

Moscow retaliated. It announced that "further participation [in the INF talks] was impossible."[8] It cancelled its March 1982 unilateral pledge not to deploy any additional SS-20s. It declared that it had accelerated preparations for deployment of new missiles in East Germany and Czechoslovakia. And, it said that "corresponding Soviet systems will be deployed" near the United States. On 5 December, Marshal Nikolai Ogarkov, chief of the General Staff, warned that the Strategic Arms Reduction Talks (START) might also be broken off, and three days later when they adjourned for the Christmas break the Soviets declined to set a date for the next round of those negotiations.[9] On 15 December, the Warsaw Pact similarly refused to set a date for resumption of the Mutual and Balanced Force Reduction talks (MBFR) when they recessed in Vienna.[10] The whole fabric of nuclear arms control negotiation had unravelled.

This was the imbroglio out of which U.S. and Soviet leaders attempted to extricate themselves in the months following December 1983. President Reagan made what the administration billed as a major conciliatory speech on the eve of the Conference on Disarmament in Europe (CDE) that convened 17 January in Stockholm.[11] Reagan identified three problem areas: the use of force in solving international disputes, the reduction of arms stockpiles, the need to establish "a better working relationship" with the Soviet Union. The president argued that "1984 finds the United States in the strongest position in years to establish a constructive and realistic working relationship with the Soviet Union." On the basis of "realism, strength and dialogue" he contended that the superpowers could "deal with our differences peacefully through negotiations."

This U.S. initiative was met by a very chilly Soviet response in the form of an interview given by ailing General Secretary Andropov to *Pravda* and published on 25 January.[12] Andropov said that the "President's speech does not contain a single new idea, any new proposals either on the question of limiting nuclear arms in Europe or on other questions." He interpreted the 17 January speech as rhetoric designed to "dispel the concern of peoples" over Washington's nuclear policy, and he demanded "practical deeds" from the United States, including "a return to the situation that existed before the commencement of the deployment of Pershing-2 and cruise missiles in Europe." Although Andropov was gravely ill and would die within a month, his interview underlined the Kremlin leadership's deep suspicion of the administration's purposes. It was the very basis of the Reagan speech that was at issue between the two superpowers. Reagan saw his administration's military buildup as the sine qua non of a new dialogue. Andropov saw the military buildup as the end of U.S. policy and all talk of dialogue as simple public relations hoopla designed to mitigate administration difficulties with segments of European and U.S. public opinion.

This first round in the effort to diffuse tensions was complicated by a bureaucratic struggle in Washington. President Reagan was under pressure to publicly charge the Soviets with violating past arms control agreements.[13] Soviet sensitivities to these charges that kept surfacing in the U.S. press were revealed in late January when they counterattacked with an aide memoire that detailed Soviet complaints about the U.S. "fulfillment of the legal and political commitments it has assumed" in the field of arms limitation.[14]

More importantly, General Secretary Andropov died on 9 February, and was succeeded by Konstantin Chernenko. While there was some evidence of struggle over the Chernenko succession, including evidence that the struggle was related to national security policy, the new general secretary moved quickly to consolidate his position.[15] His initial foreign policy statements seemed to hold out hope for an improvement in U.S.–Soviet relations. Vice President Bush attended the funeral in Moscow and returned with cautious optimism after his meeting with Chernenko.[16] Then, Chernenko made a major speech on 2 March in which he argued that "detente had struck deep roots" and called for a "drastic change in Soviet–American relations and in the international situation as a whole."[17]

Nonetheless, the new Soviet leader began to harden his position within a very few weeks.

The Reagan administration proposed a new treaty on chemical weapons and offered a new proposal for reduction in combat troops in the MBFR talks during April.[18] It made another conciliatory statement following the May meeting of NATO foreign ministers in Washington, and President Reagan made what again the administration billed as another major attempt to improve relations in a speech to the Irish Parliament on 4 June.[19] In each case, Moscow responded with the same line it had taken the preceding January, indeed the line that had evolved during 1981–83: that the Reagan administration was not a reliable negotiating partner, that its profession of commitment to improved relations lacked substance and hid its deeper purpose of achieving military superiority, and that the professed shift in U.S. policy was related to an effort to refurbish Reagan's image as a peacemaker prior to the 1984 presidential election.

Washington switched tactics. President Reagan called for "quiet diplomacy" and suggested that a summit so arranged might be a good idea.[20] By the end of June, the Soviets agreed to private talks over chemical weapons and progress was made in upgrading the "hot line" link between the capitals. Moreover, the Soviets proposed talks over space-based weapons and seemed to be caught off guard when the United States accepted the offer. Despite these low-level signs of warming, Moscow steadfastly refused to discuss the issues abandoned in Geneva. The dramatic unravelling of INF, START, and MBFR and the inability of the Reagan administration to splice them back together were rooted partly in the issues of the talks themselves. But the imbroglio in U.S.–Soviet nuclear arms control policy, of course, also reflected a larger distrust between Moscow and Washington.

The Nuclear Issues

U.S. and Soviet policy toward nuclear weapons has always been entangled in the broader issues of international politics. The initial strategic arms limitation talks (SALT I) were born out of Soviet adjustments in foreign policy following the invasion of Czechoslovakia in 1968, the West German elections that made Willy Brandt chancellor in the fall of 1969, and the U.S. election that made Richard Nixon president and brought Henry Kissinger to the center of power. The SALT I agreements very nearly died with the U.S. mining of

North Vietnamese harbors and the crisis that action precipitated in the Soviet Politburo during May of 1972. The complex strategic arms agreements that it took Washington and Moscow seven years to complete between 1972 and the Vienna Summit in June 1979 stalled in the intricate politics of the U.S. Senate during the summer and fall of that year; then ratification was abandoned by the Carter administration following the Soviet invasion of Afghanistan in December. Thus, it is not surprising that the technical issues of negotiations are often dwarfed by higher politics.

Nonetheless, the positions staked out by the Soviet Union and United States in arms negotiations suggest their objectives for nuclear weapon policy. The combined picture of Soviet negotiating tactics in START and INF since 1981, even the picture contained in the public record, provides invaluable insights into Moscow's policy.

Intermediate Nuclear Forces (INF)

In the U.S. arms control and national security communities, where disagreement is the norm, the perception is widely shared that the Soviet SS-20 program represented a destabilizing and aggressive step in the arms race. Subsequently, Soviet spokesmen tried to persuade Western publics that the SS-20 was simply a modernization of missile systems that had long been part of the "Euro-strategic force balance" and that NATO and Warsaw Pact nuclear capabilities in the European theater remained in rough balance at about 1,000 weapons systems on each side. Such a contention so stretched the truth and required such egregious and self-serving accounting that very few informed observers of any political persuasion in the West accepted the Soviet contention. It was Chancellor Helmut Schmidt of West Germany, on other issues regarded by Moscow as a "realistic" politician, who first drew attention to the SS-20 problem in an address to the International Institute for Strategic Studies in 1977.[21] And, the broad perception within NATO that the Soviets had taken a destabilizing step up the arms-race spiral helped to forge the consensus in NATO that led to the "dual track" policy late in 1979.[22] This NATO policy called for negotiations with the Soviet Union on intermediate nuclear forces, but if no satisfactory agreement could be reached prior to 1983, NATO would go forward along the separate track of deploying 108 Pershing-2 and 464 ground-launched cruise missiles (GLCMs) as a counterweight to the Soviet SS-20 buildup.

The negotiations were slow in getting started. They were complicated by the sharp deterioration of U.S.–Soviet relations following the invasion of Afghanistan and the Carter administration's announcement of retaliatory measures in late 1979 and early 1980. The efforts to get talks started became ensnared in the U.S. elections and in a new crisis brewing in Poland.

It was late 1981 before the negotiating track was laid, and two years had been lost off the clock toward deployments. Since the implicit threat of NATO deployments was supposed to provide the Soviets with incentives to negotiate, the shorter time might have been thought to have increased the pressure. President Reagan made the essence of his administration's policy public in a speech to the National Press Club on 18 November.[23] His proposal was the famous "zero option": the United States is prepared to cancel its deployment of Pershing-2 and ground-launched cruise missiles if the Soviets will dismantle their SS-20, SS-4 and SS-5 missiles. Two aspects of the President's speech probably drew careful attention in Moscow and produced violent attacks from low-level Soviet spokesmen. Reagan had presented a view of Soviet nuclear superiority in the European theater that the Soviets rejected utterly. He had also gone public with the U.S. position before negotiations had begun. This led Soviet observers to conclude that the administration regarded the INF negotiations as having at least a very high content of public relations.

Four days later, in Bonn, Soviet President Brezhnev gave the official Soviet response to zero option, what he called "genuine zero option."[24] He refuted President Reagan's presentation of the balance of forces in Europe by saying that the "present ratio between the medium-range nuclear means of the two sides is . . . one to one" and the United States wishes "to change it to about two to one favoring NATO." He called for a moratorium on "new systems in Europe," in exchange for which the Soviets would "discontinue further deployment of its SS-20s" and "unilaterally reduce a part of our medium-range nuclear weapons in the European part of the U.S.S.R."

The U.S. position was incorporated into a formal treaty proposal submitted at the negotiations on 2 February 1982, and Brezhnev made a more detailed set of Soviet proposals in the following day:

> a bilateral freeze would be in effect during the Geneva talks;
>
> British and French missiles would be counted toward the U.S. total;
>
> each side would make "equal cuts"—starting from roughly 1,000 each, they would cut to 600, then 300 intermediate systems;
>
> each side would decide which of its own systems would be destroyed.[25]

This latter provision contained the key to early Soviet efforts in the INF talks. Brezhnev's Bonn speech had proposed a moratorium on introduction of "new systems," which seemed to imply no new NATO systems while the Soviets could retain their SS-20s. The idea was unacceptable to Washington. It would give the Soviets a modern missile and leave NATO with no corresponding U.S. system. But his proposals had also carefully retained for Moscow the choice that all reductions could come from the older SS-4s and SS-5s. Moreover, even if the Soviets proposed overall reductions in numbers of systems, they could, arguably, reduce SS-4s and SS-5s by a number greater than their planned deployment of additional SS-20s. Since the SS-20s carried three warheads, total Soviet warheads would actually grow while NATO would be left without any of what Washington regarded as "offsetting" systems—the Pershing-2s and GLCMs. The February proposal retained that option—to destroy older systems while keeping the SS-20s. And, in early 1982 all Soviet promises to freeze new deployments of SS-20s were linked to a corresponding NATO commitment not to deploy Pershing-2 and GLCMs and were limited to the "European part of the U.S.S.R.," leaving Moscow the option of continuing SS-20 deployments in Asia.

Brezhnev made a dramatic speech to the Soviet Trade Union Congress on 16 March 1982 that retained the same framework but carried the policy several steps further.[26] He announced a unilateral moratorium on "deployment of medium-range nuclear armaments in the European part of the U.S.S.R." The Soviet freeze was not dependent, as his proposal had been the preceding November, on a mutual moratorium. He also announced that the Soviets would reduce "a certain number of its medium-range missiles on its own initiative," providing that there were no "new aggravation of the international situation." These unilateral moves were accompanied by a threat. Should the United States and NATO go forward with its deployments, Brezhnev threatened, "this would compel us to take retaliatory steps that would put the other side, including the United States itself, its own territory, in an analogous position."

The Trade Union speech represented Soviet policy during the remaining months of Brezhnev's life. Moscow still retained the option of continuing deployments opposite China and Japan, and the press in the West continued to report additional SS-20s in the Soviet Far East. It did promise a freeze on SS-20s in the European part of the USSR without requiring a formal bilateral moratorium. And, it promised reduction of missiles, which of course, could be made from older SS-4 and SS-5 systems.

President Reagan responded by saying that the Soviets were still seeking to legitimize their superiority and that the U.S. was still committed to achieving equal, verifiable reductions.[27]

By the early spring of 1982, both sides had been locked into mutually incompatible positions. Two things happened in the summer to embellish this picture but did not alter it fundamentally. First, the Soviets announced another unilateral initiative—a pledge by Foreign Minister Gromyko at the United Nations not to be the first to use nuclear weapons.[28] And, the two INF ambassadors in Geneva—Paul Nitze from the United States and Yuli Kvitsinsky from the Soviet Union—took their now famous "walk in the woods." The public record of this intriguing effort to break out of the positions into which the two sides had become locked is surprisingly detailed. Strobe Talbott of *Time* magazine has provided a detailed account of these negotiations and has possibly served as a conduit for some officials in the U.S. government to get their positions on record.[29] This proposal would have cut through the U.S. insistence on "global limits" and Soviet determination to avoid restrictions on deployments in Asia. It would have combined U.S. determination to get some deployments with Soviet insistence that there be no new U.S. or NATO missiles. It would have limited each side to seventy five launchers in Europe: the Soviets would have had 225 warheads aboard seventy-five SS-20 launchers and the United States would have had 300 warheads aboard seventy-five GLCM launchers, each of which carries four single-warhead missiles. The Nitze–Kvitsinsky "deal" fell apart. It was not accepted by President Reagan, and the Soviets rejected it when the two ambassadors reconvened in Geneva on 29 September.[30]

Brezhnev died in November and was succeeded by Yuriy Andropov as general secretary. Andropov quickly took a series of initiatives in Soviet policy, including a new Soviet proposal for INF on 21 December.[31] This time the Soviets would "retain in Europe only as many missiles as are kept there by Britain and France. . . . this means that the Soviet Union would reduce hundreds of missiles, including dozens of . . . the SS-20."

Throughout 1983 each side jockeyed for position, trying to seem flexible in public but without advancing any new positions. INF had become a test of wills. The administration was determined to demonstrate that Moscow could not prevent deployment of NATO missiles. And, the Soviet Union now went public with a threat that, according to Talbott, it had made privately in the negotiations a year earlier, it would walk out of the negotiations once deployments actually began.[32] There was some additional effort just before the crisis of November, but it came to nothing. Each side seemed for a while to suggest a new solution: 140 missiles on each side. But by now Moscow's suspicions of the Reagan administration probably precluded any agreement, and Andropov had not been seen in public since mid-August, suggesting that national security policy probably rested in the hands of Foreign Minister Gromyko and Defense Minister Ustinov, both of whom were now identified with a very hard line on U.S.–Soviet relations.

START

It was not accidental that the Strategic Arms Reduction Talks (START) did not get under way until more than six months after INF. The Soviets had taken the "principled position" that the SALT II agreements of 1979 represented a solemn commitment by both sides, should be ratified by the U.S. Senate, and in the absence of formal ratification should be honored in spirit and in letter. Indeed, the identification of President Reagan with political opposition to the SALT II accords provided one of the most important components of fundamental Soviet suspicion of his administration's intentions in the military competition between the superpowers.

Against this background of skepticism, President Reagan outlined the basic approach of his administration to strategic arms negotiations in a commencement address at Eureka College in Illinois on 9 May 1982.[33] He envisioned a two-stage process. In the first stage each side would reduce from approximately 7,500 warheads on strategic missiles to about 5,000. This one-third reduction would meet the president's criterion of "real reductions," as opposed to codifying the existing strategic balance, a criticism he had made of the SALT process. In a second stage, the two sides would negotiate "equal ceilings" on "throw weight." That proposal addressed another criticism that conservatives had made of SALT II—that it had left the Soviets with too many of their largest missiles (the SS-18s and SS-19s) whose rocket power enabled them to lift very large payloads. Opponents of SALT II had charged that the Soviets possessed a substantial advantage in the yield of warheads on these missiles and that they could conceivably also add multiple independently targetable re-entry vehicles (MIRVs) beyond the limits established by SALT II. It was central to the conservative critique of SALT II that the Soviet throw weight advantage constituted a loophole through which the Soviets could "break out" of the constraints imposed by those agreements.

Thus, the equal throw weight ceiling proposed by Reagan for START demonstrated to his conservative political supporters his administration's commitment to close that loophole and also signalled to Moscow their "toughness" on equal limits for both sides. Equal throw weight, it was argued, would reduce U.S. dependence on Soviet good faith in compliance with the warhead limits. If each side had approximately equal throw weight the physical limits of yield and warhead ratios to rocket thrust would constrain Soviet opportunities for breaking out of the arms control regime between the powers.

It was subsequently made public that the president had sent Brezhnev a letter on 7 May outlining his ideas and calling for talks to begin in June. The Soviet leader responded within two weeks, and President Reagan announced in his Memorial Day speech that talks were set to begin at the end of the next month in Geneva.[34] Ambassadors Edward L. Rowny on the U.S. side and Viktor P. Karpov on the Soviet side opened the negotiations on 29 June.

Once the talks were underway, more details of the U.S. position became public.[35] The proposed agreement would have limited each side to 850 ballistic missiles with no more than 5,000 warheads. Of those, not more than 2,500 warheads would be allowed on land-based missiles (ICBMs). Bombers would be limited to levels in place at the time of the agreement, and the Soviets would have separate subceilings on their largest missiles. These "collateral constraints" called for reductions in the Soviet SS-18 force (308 with ten MIRVs each in 1982), SS-17s (150 with four MIRVs each) and SS-19 (330 with up to six MIRVs each) to a combined subceiling of 210, of which only 110 could be SS-18s.

The Soviet proposal called for a total of 1,800 missiles and bombers.[36] There could be no more than 1,200 multiple warheads on land-based and sea-based intercontinental missiles (ICBMs and SLBMs) plus bombers carrying air-launched cruise missiles (ALCMs), of which no more than 1,080 could be mounted on ballistic missiles (ICBMs and SLBMs) and only 680 could be carried on ICBMs. These cuts were to be accomplished by 1990. Soviet public discussions, including the statement made by Ambassador Karpov when he first arrived in Geneva, called for qualitative as well as quantitative limits, presumably referring in part to the incipient deployments of U.S. cruise missiles.[37]

These remained the basic positions of the two sides, although Washington made a great deal of effort in June 1983 to project the image of greater flexibility, and Ambassador Rowny did take back to Geneva a modification of the U.S. position that had been hammered out in the National Security Council.[38] The ceiling contained in the new proposal was apparently raised from 850 missiles to around

1,200. That modification reflected complicated politics over the basing mode for the MX missile. President Reagan had appointed the Commission on Strategic Forces (commonly referred to as the Scowcroft Commission, after its chairman, former National Security adviser General Brent Scowcroft), and it recommended that the United States move away from MIRVs toward single warhead missiles. That change in U.S. forces would, presumably, require the higher missile ceiling in START.

But, more importantly for the U.S.–Soviet strategic relationship, President Reagan announced in March 1983 that the administration would undertake intense research on technology that would make it possible to "intercept and destroy strategic ballistic missiles before they reach our own soil or that of our allies."[39] This strategic defense initiative (SDI) was predictably attacked by Soviet propaganda organs, but came increasingly to dominate Soviet thinking about its military relationship with the United States during the year that followed.

In the fall of 1983, the Reagan administration put still another proposal before the Soviets in START. This incorporated ideas first advanced by Senators Williams S. Cohen and Sam Nunn—the so-called "build-down" technique.[40] Comprehensive details of these proposals have not surfaced in public, but the basic idea is to require that each side remove two land-based missile warheads for each new one deployed, and three sea-based ballistic missile warheads for each two new ones deployed. The goal was to get at least 5 percent reductions each year as each side reduced its arsenals of warheads toward the 5,000 limit originally proposed by the United States.

The Soviets attacked the build-down idea in public, but by the time of its introduction in October 1983, the crisis over INF dominated the strategic relationship. During the first half of 1984, the Reagan administration tried various ploys to lure the Soviets back into serious discussions of INF and START, but made no headway. There was considerable talk about joining the two sets of issues in one comprehensive negotiation, but the Soviets continued to reject a return to the INF negotiations as long as U.S. missiles were deployed in NATO.[41] Indeed, Moscow seemed to have backed itself into a corner—by refusing to negotiate yet insisting that the danger of war had risen perceptably. When they proposed discussions of space weapons on 29 June 1984, the Reagan administration sensed an opening.[42] It accepted the initiative, but counter-proposed that the new talks include outstanding issues over INF and START. The Soviets were surprised by the acceptance, but rejected the U.S. precondition that issues other than space-based defenses be included.[43]

The Pattern of Soviet Policy

Soviet negotiating positions in INF and START throughout 1981–1983 fall into a pattern that suggests the outlines of a nuclear weapons policy.

First, statements by Kremlin leaders make it clear that they take great pride in their achievement of superpower status and what they regard as a rough nuclear parity with the United States. They occasionally suggest that this achievement has required economic sacrifices of their generation, but sacrifices in which they take pride not unlike those they articulate concerning World War II. Therefore, the basis of U.S. policy in the Reagan administration makes no sense in their terms. The notion that they would scrap the SS-20 in INF or large numbers of SS-17s, SS-18s, and SS-19s in START cuts directly against this pride. Their own proposals—the 1,800 limit in START and the negotiating positions by which they have sought to retain their most capable and modern system (the SS-20) in INF—suggest the degree to which they want to protect the results of the economic sacrifice.

In both sets of negotiations they have taken conservative positions. They have attempted to preserve the current balance and have regarded U.S. attempts to restructure the balance as evidence that the Reagan administration lacks serious intentions for arms control. Soviet leaders say their conservatism on these matters is a product of their belief that theater and strategic forces are roughly balanced at the beginning of the 1980s. Of course it is the Reagan administration's belief that the Soviets have serious advantages in the current balance that underlies its own efforts to restructure—especially its proposals to reduce the numbers of SS-18s to 110 and all MIRVed ICBMs to 210. It is this fundamentally different view of the current balance that creates the distrust between Moscow and Washington, and has prevented progress in the negotiations. Soviet refusal to yield its advantages constitutes evidence to many in the Reagan administration that it intends to have superiority in nuclear weapons.

The Soviet position in the INF talks changed appreciably. Even if one regards the unilateral moratorium on SS-20 deployments undertaken by Brezhnev in March 1982 and the unilateral pledge not to be the first to use nuclear weapons in June 1982 as plays for the uninformed public, the Soviet proposal in February and the Andropov offer in December of that year both would have required some reductions in the SS-20 force as well as scrapping all of the SS-4s and SS-5s. Moscow was willing to pay a price to avoid NATO's Pershing-2s and GLCMs. Those proposals, of course, would have left the Soviets with substantial numbers of the SS-20 and NATO without comparable systems, but that willingness to accept reductions in their most modern theater nuclear missile system probably also suggests a real worry in Moscow. They probably believe that the Pershing-2s, in particular, would complicate military operations in wartime and possibly also worry that NATO's INF increases the risk to Soviet command and control systems in a way that reduces Moscow's confidence in times of intense crisis.

Finally, Soviet concern with President Reagan's Strategic Defense Initiative and willingness to propose negotiations on those issues even at a time when they are rigidly maintaining their boycott of START and INF probably suggests the worry that the United States has real advantages in the technologies likely to be developed in this new form of military competition. The Kremlin leadership certainly knows that its own economy will be strained throughout this decade at least, and its traditional sense of inferiority in technological innovation has undoubtedly been heightened by its perception that the Reagan administration has set out to steer the military competition into channels that would put the Soviet economy at serious disadvantage. Thus, the prospect of competition in space-based military systems constitutes a powerful incentive to Soviet leaders, one that may cut across the policy put in place with the walkout in Geneva.

The Political Context

These deductions from the record of Soviet behavior in INF and START do not tell the whole story. Rather, Soviet negotiating patterns in 1981–1983 reflect a larger political struggle over national security policy that depended at its core on Soviet judgments about the purposes of the Reagan administration. As in all cases involving matters of Soviet military decision-making, we have very imperfect evidence about this larger picture. But its contours can be discerned, and its importance to understanding Soviet behavior is so great that it requires careful, if painstaking, analysis.

Some elements in Soviet perceptions of the United States are troubling. In Moscow, too, uncertainty and disagreement have appeared concerning the nature of the challenge laid down by the Reagan administration. There has also been hesitation about the appropriate Soviet response.

The most dramatic Soviet statements regarding the Reagan administration claim that the danger of war has escalated since 1981.

If Americans were to read them literally, the mood in Moscow was clearly alarming. The resolution issued by the Central Committee Plenum in June 1983 accused the United States of "hatching crazy plans for world domination [and] pushing mankind to the brink of a nuclear catastrophe." Konstantin Chernenko had used identical language on the danger of war in his speech to that Plenum.[44] Chief of the Soviet General Staff Nikolai Ogarkov had been asserting during 1981–1983 that international politics contains strong parallels to the 1930s, an allusion with powerful symbolism among the Soviet people who continue to hold World War II as the most important experience shaping their modern national identity.[45]

It is both a symptom and a cause of the deterioration in U.S.–Soviet relations that this verbal inflation about the danger of war has been so little noted in the United States. There has been a general tendency to dismiss such language as rhetoric, either by those who have a low regard for all verbal communications emanating from Moscow or by those who see the escalation of rhetoric in Soviet pronouncements as the natural consequence of the polemical high ground seized by Washington.

There are good reasons for regarding Soviet statements on this issue as more than propaganda, and the process by which Soviet leaders have come to make such charges in public tells us a good deal about their perceptions of the Reagan administration. Soviet assessments of the administration's policies and explanations for the deterioration of relations varied considerably during its first two years. They did not suggest a campaign coordinated by the Central Committee's International Information Department or the Foreign Ministry. On the contrary, this diversity of opinion suggested a dynamic political issue. That near uniformity has appeared in Soviet discussions since late 1983 both suggests the gravity with which the Kremlin views the current crisis and underlines the hesitation and differences of opinion of the earlier period.

The issues contained in Soviet discussion relations with the United States are varied. For example, both in the scholarly press and in speeches by the political leadership during 1981–1983, Soviets seemed to be wrestling with significant issues: when did detente go wrong—with the election of President Reagan, with the imposition of sanctions following the invasion of Afghanistan, with the ascendency of National Security Advisor Zbigniew Brzezinski, or with a "systemic turn to the right" in U.S. politics, usually dated from the OPEC embargo and retreat from Vietnam in 1973–1975?[46] Does the Reagan administration seek to achieve a form of military superiority which will have essentially political purposes or does it actually seek to reduce public resistance to the very idea of war, including by nuclear means? Do U.S. actions require a change in Soviet policy toward a more confrontational tact or is the policy of differentiating relations among capitalist states and maintaining selective cooperation with the United States adequate to deal with the newly confrontational U.S. policy? Can the United States upset the military balance with its proposed defense programs or is that balance relatively stable given Soviet determination to make marginal adjustments in its own programs?

Soviet discussion of these issues sometimes had the appearance of political debate. For example, Marshal Ogarkov took the lead in warning that U.S. policy was in effect pushing the world toward "the brink of war," beginning with an article in the party journal *Kommunist* in July 1981.[47] He continued to push that extreme interpretation throughout 1981 and 1982. He seemed to be calling for a variety of responsive measures—mobilization of economic resources in peacetime to be prepared for the outbreak of war, changes in the command structure which would facilitate Soviet capacity to wage war especially in the early stages of nuclear hostilities, new measures to reinforce the traditional theme of the Soviet military for "readiness," and during Brezhnev's final two years Ogarkov was noticeably restrained in his public adulation for the General Secretary and for the foreign and security policies identified with his leadership.

Other political and military leaders have used different formulas on most of these issues. For example, during Brezhnev's last years Defense Minister Dmitrii Ustinov invariably described the intentions of the U.S. administration's defense program as intending to achieve "military superiority," and accused Washington of preparing for war, or of preparing for a global nuclear war, but he did not until 1983 describe the international situation as being on the brink of nuclear war.[48]

Chernenko's references to detente in his 2 March 1984 speech also carried the intriguing possibility of debate within the leadership. No Politburo members had made such references since before Brezhnev's death in 1982. The Politburo leadership was slow to make charges of mental instability in their adversaries, but such personal attacks began to appear with increasing frequency during 1983 in parallel with more alarmist references to the danger of war. Defense Minister Ustinov, after two years of carefully avoiding the more extreme language of some other military leaders on the risks of war wrote in *Pravda* on 9 May 1983, that "certain hotheads" in the United States and Europe by their "insane actions have brought the world to the brink of a universal nuclear catastrophe."[49] The only other such reference by a Politburo member came in a Brezhnev speech to an unusual gathering of military leaders just before his death, when he had argued that Washington was "threatening to push the world into the flames of a nuclear war."[50] Of course, attacks on U.S. defense policy and the alleged increase in the risk of war are consistent with Brezhnev's report to the Twenty-Sixth Party Congress in 1981. But charges like those of Ustinov and Chernenko are the product of a steady escalation of what Politburo members have been willing to say on this issue.

What was the meaning of these Soviet perceptions about the risk of war? First, the diversity of the issues carried in Soviet discussion of superpower relations, nuances in positions taken by various participants in the public discussion of those issues and the alteration of positions across time by some members of the top leadership all point toward the existence of real political discussion in the Kremlin.

Second, if the Soviet leadership, or some portion of it, really does believe not just that U.S. policy threatens to push the world into nuclear war, which, after all, is not so very different from various U.S. descriptions of the potential consequences of Soviet military policy, but that the actual state of affairs has gotten to the brink, it is obviously a matter of grave concern. This vision of the relationship is close to the one by Ambassador George Kennan in 1983—"a march toward war—this and nothing else."[51]

Serious men in Moscow may have confronted that stark possibility. They understand that these extreme descriptions of the present moment imply radical steps in their own policy. If relations have gotten to such a fix, strong logic must drive toward the kind of economic mobilization Ogarkov called for, toward even greater resources for the Soviet defense budget, toward stockpiling resources and relocating industries, and toward forms of command and control consistent with doctrine. So extreme are the implications of this perception that—to the degree that it is genuine and widely shared—it simply must dictate radical policy responses.

Nonetheless, the moment is not right for such responses by the Soviet Union. Economic growth has slowed. While the successions of Andropov and Chernenko to the number one position have appeared to be among the smoothest on record, changes in leadership of the Kremlin are notoriously unstable. Historically they have also implied a preoccupation with domestic affairs. If we can judge by the activities of the post-Brezhnev leadership thus far, their own priorities will be to restore a sense of movement in the economy, to promote progress in exploiting science and technology for the promotion of economic growth, and to overcome a general sense of inertia and loss of direction which developed among the urban, industrial, and political elite during the final years of the Brezhnev leadership.

How do these essentially domestic priorities fit with the claim that U.S.–Soviet relations have reached the brink of war? While they do not preclude radical Soviet responses to the perception of threat, they are not fundamentally compatible with increased hostility. The dilemma posed by an acknowledged increase in the danger of war and a preference for concentrating policy efforts on domestic economic and political issues has been resolved within the Soviet leadership by the argument that whatever the intentions of the Reagan administration, its possibilities are less than its ambitions. Washington is constrained by objective political and economic factors.

In the Soviet view, two of the most persuasive of these constraints are at stake in the START-INF imbroglio. First, above all, there is Soviet power. If Moscow takes the danger of war seriously, this is not the time to tinker with the essence of that power—Soviet strategic nuclear forces. Thus, the Kremlin's perceptions of U.S. defense policy and the consequent increase in the danger of war reinforce its suspicion of the deep cuts for Soviet strategic forces contained in U.S. START proposals and of U.S. insistence on protecting Pershing-2 and GLCM deployments in INF. The Soviet view of the Reagan administration's overall defense policy makes it nearly impossible for it to accept, or for that matter to take seriously, its arms control proposals.

The second principal constraint engaged by their boycott of the START and INF talks is popular opposition in the West. The Soviets have taken a long-term gamble that resistance will build in the United States and Western Europe to the policies of the Reagan administration, that this resistance will constrain its policy options and that, eventually, opponents of the Reagan policy will form the basis of popular movements that will oust the conservatives from power in Washington, Bonn, and London. The gamble is risky, of course, because the Soviets have no illusions that such a fundamental change in politics is likely in the near term. And, to the degree that they believe that the danger of war has actually increased, of course, they must maintain at least minimum levels of cooperation with President Reagan, Prime Minister Thatcher, and Chancellor Kohl. The walk-out in Geneva and the refusal to get drawn into substitute negotiations during the first half of 1984 fit this strategy of keeping the heat on popular resistance. But Washington is also gambling that this strategy will not survive Reagan's re-election.

That may be. The invitation to negotiate space-based defenses may be the Kremlin's hedge against a second Reagan administration. But, it would be foolish to expect Soviet capitulation on the issues of INF and START. Not just because they are tough bargainers; rather, because they see their positions as preserving the two basic constraints against their adversary's defense and foreign policies. Because they take a far blacker view of those policies than supporters of the administration credit, they will also hold far more tenaciously to their own positions on nuclear arms. The future is bleak for strategic and theater arms control agreements.

Notes

1. A representative and early example of the Soviet effort came in a statement Yuriy Andropov made to a group of visiting Senators that announced the Soviets were prepared to reduce "a considerable number" of its SS-20s. *Pravda,* 18 August 1983, 1.

2. *Los Angeles Times,* 13 October 1983, 1.

3. Threats had been made repeatedly in the weeks before the Bundestag vote. See, for example, the communiqué following Gromyko's visit to East Germany, *Pravda,* 19 October 1983, 3. *Pravda* carried the announcement that "preparatory work is underway" on 25 October 1983, 2; also, *New York Times,* 25 October 1983, 1.

4. *Pravda,* 19 November 1983, 4 and *New York Times,* 21 November 1983, 6.

5. *New York Times,* 24 November 1983, 1.

6. *New York Times,* 15 November 1983, 1.

7. *New York Times,* 28 November 1983, 1.

8. *Pravda* and *Izvestiia* carried a brief announcement on 24 November 1983, 4 that ". . . the U.S.S.R. delegation announced it is discontinuing the current round of talks without setting any date for their resumption"; see also, *New York Times,* 26 November 1983.

9. Ogarkov's implied threat came at a press conference held jointly with party official L.M. Zamyatin and First Deputy Minister of Foreign Affairs G.M. Korniyenko on December 5, *Pravda,* 6 December 1983, 4; see also *New York Times,* 6 December 1983, 1.

10. *New York Times,* 16 December 1983, 1.

11. *New York Times,* 17 January 1984, 8.

12. *Pravda,* 25 January 1984, 1.

13. See, for example, articles in *New York Times,* 14 January 1984, 1 and *U.S. News and World Report,* 16 April 1984, 53.

14. *Izvestia,* 30 January 1984, 4.

15. For an interesting discussion of this succession, see Marc D. Zlotnik's article "Chernenko Succeeds" in *Problems of Communism,* March-April 1984. Additional evidence of controversy may be found in the contrast

between Chernenko's 2 March speech, which can be found in *Pravda,* 3 March 1984, with its positive reference to detente, and the more negative position to which he retreated subsequently.

16. See Vice President Bush's statement in Moscow on 14 February, *New York Times,* 15 February 1984, 4.

17. *Pravda,* 3 March 1984, 1–2.

18. See reports in the *Washington Post,* 5 April 1984, 1 and 19 April 1984, 1 and the *Washington Times,* 20 April 1984, 6.

19. *New York Times,* 5 June 1984, 4.

20. *New York Times,* 15 June, 1984, 12.

21. Schmidt, Helmut, "1977 Alastair Buchan Memorial Lecture", *Survival,* January-February 1978.

22. Communiqué issued at a special meeting of NATO Foreign and Defense Ministers, 12 December 1979.

23. *Washington Post,* 19 November 1981, 14.

24. *Pravda,* 24 November 1981, 1.

25. His first discussion came in a 3 February meeting with the representatives of the Socialist International, *Pravda,* 4 February 1982, 1. But *Pravda* released many more details in an article on 10 February 1982, 4.

26. *Pravda,* 17 March 1982, 1–2.

27. *New York Times,* 17 March 1982.

28. The no-first-use pledge came in a letter from Brezhnev published by *Pravda* and *Izvestiia* on 16 June 1982, 1. Gromyko's speech was printed the next day; also in *New York Times,* 16 June 1982, 1.

29. Strobe Talbott, "Behind Closed Doors," *Time,* 5 December 1983, 18.

30. Ibid, p. 32.

31. His proposal came in a speech on the occasion of the Sixtieth Anniversary of the USSR, *Pravda,* 22 December 1982, 1–2.

32. Strobe Talbott, "Behind Closed Doors," *op. cit. 22.*

33. *New York Times,* 10 May 1984, 1.

34. *New York Times,* 1 June 1984, 1.

35. Leslie Gelb for the *New York Times,* 29 June, 1982, 1.

36. Details of the Soviet position can be found in articles in the *New York Times* on 31 July 1982, 1 and 14 July 1983, 1.

37. As reported on Soviet domestic radio on 27 June 1982, reported in *Foreign Broadcast Information Service, Daily Report: Soviet Union,* 28 June 1982, AA1.

38. *New York Times,* 9 June 1983, 1.

39. *New York Times,* 24 March 1983, 20.

40. *New York Times,* 4 October 1984, 1.

41. See, for example, Chernenko's "interview" in *Pravda,* 14 June 1984, 1.

42. *New York Times,* 30 June 1984, 1.

43. See the Soviet government statement carried by *Pravda* on 1 July 1984, 1; also *New York Times,* 2 July 1984, 4.

44. Chernenko's speech was reported in *Pravda,* 15 June 1983; the communiqué was carried in *Pravda,* 16 June 1983.

45. The key documents are an article that appeared in *Kommunist,* No. 10, July 1981, 80–91; his short book published in February, 1982, *Vsegda V Gotovnostii K Zashchite Otechestva (Always in Readiness to Defend the Fatherland),* Moscow, 1982; his V.E. Day article in *Izvestiia,* 9 May 1982.

46. A representative sample can be found in a conference report carried by two issues of the Soviet journal *SSLA: Economika Politika Ideologiya,* No. 5, May 1982, 119–127, No. 6, June 1982, 118–127; an article by A. Bovin in *Izvestiia,* 4 July 1982; V. Falin's article in *Znamya,* No. 4, April 1982, 190–202 and Leonid Zamyatin's article in *Literaturnaia Gazeta,* 30 June 1982, 14.

47. *Kommunist,* No. 10, July 1981, 80–91.

48. A representative sample is found in Ustinov's article in *Pravda,* 25 July 1981; his address on the occasion of the 1981 revolution celebration, *Pravda,* 7 November 1981; Ustinov's own book published in February 1982, *Sluzhem Rodine, Delu Kommunizma* (Moscow 1982) and his V.E. Day article in *Pravda,* 9 May 1982.

49. *Pravda,* 9 May 1983.

50. *Pravda,* 28 October 1982.

51. This reference is contained in a speech by Ambassador George Kennan to the American Committee of East–West Accord in Washington, D.C., in May 1983.

9
Conclusion

Dan Caldwell

Ever since the founding of the United States, its people have been alternately fascinated, angered, and confused about Russian society and politics.[1] The establishment in 1917 of a new government in Russia which many Americans (particularly Woodrow Wilson) perceived as hostile to U.S. interests further complicated the task of understanding the Russians and developing an effective approach for dealing with the USSR.

Just as people of the United States have a difficult time fathoming Soviet society and politics, Soviets also have substantial difficulty understanding U.S. society and politics. The closed nature of the Soviet political system makes it hard for Americans to find answers to their questions, while those Soviets who have access to U.S. newspapers and periodicals and who are able to travel to the United States are overwhelmed with information. In Joseph Nye's words, Soviet intentions ". . . may be a 'black box' to us, but we may confuse them with our 'white noise.' "[2]

The contributors to this book have sought to open the lid of the Soviet "black box," even if only slightly, in order to contribute to the understanding of what factors motivate Soviet international behavior in particular regions and functional issue areas. Only through an understanding and appreciation of these factors can Americans formulate an effective U.S. policy for dealing with the USSR.

In this concluding chapter, I will: (1) summarize the factors that motivate Soviet foreign policy described by the contributors to this book; (2) indicate how these factors influence the Soviets' assessment of their foreign policy priorities; (3) raise several important sets of questions concerning Soviet international behavior; and (4) present some prescriptions for U.S. policy stemming from the analyses contained in this book. I should add that while I have tried to summarize

---

I would like to thank Mark Garrison for his comments and suggestions on this chapter.

the various perspectives represented by the contributors to this volume, the views contained in this chapter are mine and may or may not be shared by the other contributors.

Factors Motivating Soviet International Behavior

Herbert Simon has noted: "A complex decision is like a great river, drawing from its many tributaries the innumerable component premises of which it is constituted."[3] Foreign policymaking concerns complex decisions and therefore, to use Simon's analogy, "many tributaries." Political scientists, however, have focused most often on the two principal tributaries leading to a decision: domestic (or internal) and international (or external) factors.

This dichotomous (and somewhat arbitrary) characterization has led to the creation of substantial bodies of literature concerning both domestic[4] and international[5] determinants of Soviet foreign policy. It is, of course, impossible to determine definitively which set of factors has greater influence on the making and substance of Soviet policy; however, most analysts believe that domestic factors such as geography, climate, history, domestic politics, and political culture are more important than international factors. To the extent one can draw a clear distinction between internal and external factors (and increasingly many foreign policy analysts doubt that this can be done), this book focuses primarily on external influences. However, given the importance and, in some cases, the close relationship between some external and internal factors, I will briefly discuss some of the more prominent domestic factors.

Domestic Sources

Most authors of Russian and Soviet history books begin by commenting on two physical attributes: the harsh climate of Russia and its tremendous size. One need not develop a Russian analogue of Frederick Jackson Turner's "frontier thesis" to accept the fact that the climate and geography of Russia have had an important influence on Soviet foreign policy. Of course, the difficulty comes in trying to establish how, in what ways, and to what extent such basic factors have influenced Russian and Soviet international behavior.

Another undeniable influence is history. For example, the fact that Russia and the Soviet Union have been invaded numerable times from both the East and the West has undoubtedly contributed to the distrust and fear that Soviets have of foreigners, and many Western observers have commented on Soviet "paranoia." However, given the history of Russia and the Soviet Union, this paranoia may be justified. (I am reminded of the aphorism: "Even paranoids have some real enemies.") In World War II, which the Soviets call the Great Patriotic War, twenty million Soviets lost their lives, fifty times the number of Americans killed (400,000). It is no wonder that the Soviets attempt to keep alive the memory of such a catastrophic national experience. It is this historical memory of World Wars I and II that undoubtedly affects Soviet attitudes toward the Federal Republic of Germany, which are cautious and wary and sometimes even hostile.

Another domestic source of Russian and Soviet foreign policy is political culture which Lucian Pye has defined as "the set of attitudes, beliefs, and sentiments which give order and meaning to a political process and which provide the underlying assumptions and rules that govern behavior in the political system."[6] Thus political culture is "the product of both the collective history of a political system and the life histories of the members of that system."[7] Elements of Soviet political culture include Great Russian nationalism, Russian peasant village culture, and Marxist–Leninist ideology.

Confronted by a hostile climate characterized by extreme temperatures, Russian peasants were able to subsist, but rarely prospered, by farming. Often Russian peasants would harvest no more than three kernels of grain for each kernel they planted. In such a harsh environment, there was no room for risk, and Russian peasants sought to minimize all risks in order to survive.[8] Numerous scholars have pointed out that Soviet leaders have sought to minimize risks in their conduct of foreign policy, and it is likely that this characteristic stems at least in part from the Russian peasant past.

Great Russian nationalism is a second component of contemporary Soviet political culture notwithstanding the fact that only about half of the present population of the USSR is Russian in ethnic origin. In times of crisis, Soviet leaders have often depended upon the patriotic feelings of Soviet citizens to carry them through the crisis. This was clearly Stalin's strategy during World War II in his references to "Mother Russia" and the loosening of restrictions against the Russian Orthodox church, which is an institution of Russian nationalism as well as religion. According to one prominent Sovietologist, ". . . the interaction of the dimensions of Soviet nationalism—Russian in substance, Soviet in form—constitutes a crucially important explanatory factor in Soviet international behavior."[9]

Marxist–Leninism provides the official ideology of the Soviet state and the basis for both regime and policy legitimation. Despite the fact that Marxism–Leninism was the most internationalist of nineteenth century ideologies, it has merged with Russian nationalism and the resulting synthesis is Soviet communism.[10] At one time, scholars portrayed ideology as the key to understanding Soviet politics and foreign policy. However, today most scholars believe that while ideology to some extent influences Soviet foreign policymaking, it does not play the most important role. As Hiroshi Kimura notes in chapter 4, while ideology played an important role in the early years of the USSR, Soviet leaders over time have become more pragmatic and less ideological in their approach to international relations. Numerous examples of Soviet pragmatism could be cited. Perhaps one of the more graphic instances of this orientation occurred in May 1972 when President Nixon visited Moscow and signed the SALT I agreements only days after he had ordered the bombing of Hanoi and Haiphong and the mining of North Vietnamese seaports. In this attack, a Soviet supply ship was accidentally bombed and a Soviet seaman was killed.[11] The Soviets protested mildly, but the Moscow summit meeting proceeded as scheduled. If confronted with a choice of pursuing their own national interests and being ideologically inconsistent or remaining ideologically consistent and sacrificing Soviet interests, Soviet leaders have most often chosen the first alternative.

Domestic policies in the Soviet Union is another very important domestic influence on Soviet international behavior. Given the degree of centralization in the Soviet government, the orientation to foreign policy of the top Soviet leaders is extremely important, as the various foreign policies pursued by different Soviet leaders illustrates. Stalin followed a policy of autarky; Khrushchev opened relations with the West in the late 1950s and early 1960s; and Brezhnev implemented detente with the United States. It is clear, as the contributors of this book point out, that the post-Brezhnev leadership will have a substantial impact on Soviet international behavior; however, as of mid-1984, it is unclear how the succession transition will work out (that is, who will succeed Chernenko) and in what foreign policy directions the new leadership will go.[12] We will return to the succession question later in this chapter.

Domestic factors clearly have a very significant influence on Soviet international behavior. What about international factors?

International Influences on Soviet Foreign Policy

In this section, I will discuss international (or external) factors that influence Soviet behavior and given these factors, the relative importance of various regions and issue areas to the Soviets. In doing this, I have drawn on the findings of the previous chapters.

Seweryn Bialer has suggested that Soviet leaders appear to have two basic types of foreign policy priorities: absolute and relative.[13] Absolute priorities are at the highest level of importance and "can be considered the minimal, irreducible requirements of Soviet foreign policymaking."[14] According to Bialer, there are two absolute priorities: the security of the homeland and the protection of the Soviet empire. The studies in this book confirm Bialer's observation; each of the contributors refers to the paramount Soviet concerns as the protection of the homeland and close allies.

Like any dichotomous typologies, Bialer's is somewhat arbitrary. There is one factor that a number of contributors in this volume cite as very important to the Soviets: the desire to be recognized throughout the world as one of the world's two superpowers. This factor seems to be growing in importance and is also a very salient factor in U.S.–Soviet relations. As Richard Pipes has noted: "One of the highest priorities of the Soviet Union in dealing with the United States has been to gain recognition as an equal . . . and hence a country with a legitimate claim to have its say in the solution of all international problems. . . ."[15]

Bialer describes the relative priorities as those "that carry variable weights in Soviet foreign policymaking and whose importance as determinants of Soviet international behavior changes sometimes very quickly and perceptibly."[16] Included in this category are enhancing Soviet political influence in the international system and economic development by importing technology and grain and obtaining credit from the West. A third relative priority suggested by the studies in this book is ideology. Often analysts mention ideology, as George Breslauer notes in chapter 5, "if only then to write off its importance." Several of the case studies in this volume, however, suggest that under certain conditions ideology remains a significant source of Soviet international behavior.

According to the reformulated Bialer typology, there are three absolute Soviet foreign policy priorities: protection of the homeland, maintaining the security of the Soviet empire, and recognition (particularly by the United States) of the USSR as a superpower. In addition, there are three relative priorities: the extension of Soviet political influence throughout the world, economic development of the USSR, and promotion of Marxist–Leninist ideology. How are these priorities reflected in Soviet international behavior?

If one accepts the typology described above, then it is clear that the United States is of the uppermost concern to Soviet leaders because the United States presents an actual or potential threat to each of the six Soviet priorities. As Lawrence Caldwell points out in chapter 8, the U.S. nuclear arsenal is capable of destroying the USSR many times over. In addition, the United States has rhetorically incited unrest in Eastern Europe and called for "rolling back" communism there; and most recently, President Reagan has questioned both the legitimacy of the Soviet regime and the place of the Soviet Union in the international system. Soviet leaders have taken these attacks very seriously because they thought that the United States had, during the period of detente, recognized for once and for all the domestic legitimacy and the superpower status of their country.[17]

The United States also poses a substantial threat to the relative priorities of Soviet foreign policymaking. As the world's other superpower, the United States alone has the military capability to challenge the extension of Soviet political influence throughout the world. Indeed, this very goal—the containment of communism—has been the preeminent objective of U.S. foreign policy since 1947.[18] In economic terms, the Soviet Union, as John Hardt and Donna Gold note in chapter 7, depends heavily on the United States for agricultural imports and on other Western countries for technological imports. Lastly, the United States, as the world's leading capitalist power, presents an ideological challenge to the USSR. Thus, the United States is the number one foreign policy concern of Soviet leaders. As Nikita Khrushchev graphically put it: "The case of international tension is like a cabbage. If you tear off the leaves one by one you come to the heart. And the heart of this matter is relations between the Soviet Union and the United States."[19]

In chapter 2, Sarah Terry points out that the Soviet Union considers the security of Eastern Europe second only to the protection of the Soviet homeland. In a very real sense, the security of the USSR is dependent on the security of Eastern Europe since it constitutes a buffer between Western Europe and the Soviet Union. The creation of this buffer was not the idea of the communists; indeed, this was a long-held objective of the Russian tsars. Eastern Europe now constitutes the major part of the Soviet empire, and no full-fledged member of this commonwealth since Albania has been allowed to secede, as Hungary, Czechoslovakia, and Poland have all discovered.

Terry notes that a U.S. policy of actively encouraging and supporting opposition elements within one or more Eastern European countries in order to destabilize an existing regime would call forth a militantly hard-line Soviet response because Soviet leaders place such a high priority on Eastern Europe. At the other end of the spectrum, a U.S. policy of disengagement and disinterest in East

Europe would, according to Terry, have little impact on Soviet behavior in the area, again because the Soviets place such a high priority on the region. A policy of mixing negative sanctions and positive incentives is most likely to enable the United States to exert some influence over Eastern European events without triggering hostile Soviet actions. The "consequences of options" approach, particularly as employed by Sarah Terry in her study of East Europe, helps to explain Soviet priorities in the area and possible intended, and just as importantly, unintended, results of different U.S. policies.

If protection of the homeland—what B. Thomas Trout refers to as "independently guaranteed security"—is the preeminent priority of Soviet leaders, then they must be concerned about the People's Republic of China, as clearly they are. I have already referred in chapter 1 to the nuclear and conventional military threat to the Soviet homeland that the PRC poses for the USSR. Given the paramount importance that the Soviets place on protection of their homeland, a U.S. policy of providing the Chinese with military equipment would greatly heighten Soviet fears and anxieties. While such a policy could have some short-term benefits for the United States and NATO (for example, the possible redeployment of some Soviet divisions now stationed in Eastern Europe to the Soviet Far East), the long-term consequences of the U.S. arming the PRC are negative, and not just in terms of U.S.–Soviet relations. It was not so long ago that Chinese and U.S. soldiers fought in Korea. Imagine how much better the Chinese could have done in the Korean War with U.S. weapons.

As Trout points out, Soviet policy toward China, however, is not simply the result of the rational calculation of costs and benefits; rather Soviet fear of and hostility toward the Chinese appears to result, at least in part, from underlying racial fears. Numerous Western observers have noted the existence of this factor. Kimura notes the possible influence of racial fears in determining Soviet policy toward Japan in chapter 4. It is, of course, impossible to determine just how important this factor is in affecting Soviet international behavior. The fact that racial attitudes do play a role, however, is an important reminder that foreign policymakers are not simply the political equivalent of the hypothetical "rational decision-makers" of economics and that nonrational factors can play a significant role in influencing the making and substance of foreign policy in the Soviet Union as well as in other countries.

As the contributors to this book note, the importance of ideology in determining Soviet foreign policy has declined since the founding of the new Soviet government in 1917. Pragmatic calculation has replaced revolutionary élan. In the case of China, however, ideological factors do appear to play a role. Soviet leaders want to be considered as the rightful heirs of Marx and Lenin and deeply resent Chinese charges that they are revisionists.

In addition to these threats, China poses a challenge to the Soviet relative priority of extending Soviet political influence throughout the world. For instance, in Southeast Asia, China and the Soviet Union back opposing sides in the Vietnamese–Kampuchean conflict; and in South Asia China supports Pakistan, the USSR India. And this competition for political influence is not limited to Asia; the Soviets and the Chinese have also competed with each other in Africa (for example, Tanzania).

Perhaps the most important potential trading partner for both the PRC and USSR is Japan. Yet, as Kimura has shown, Soviet policy toward Japan does not make sense. It seems that the Soviets could resolve the most important obstacle to expanding trade by returning the Northern Territories to Japan;[20] however, the Soviets refuse to do so and thereby defy "rational" explanations of Soviet foreign policymaking in this case. Perhaps part of the reason for Soviet intransigence is related to Soviet racist attitudes towards Asians, including Japanese, or perhaps even a lingering resentment of the Japanese defeat of Russia at Port Arthur in 1904. (Lest this reference be dismissed as arcane or irrelevant, it should be noted that Admiral Sergei Gorshkov, the commander-in-chief of the Soviet Navy, has focused a great deal of attention in his writings on the Russo–Japanese War in drawing lessons for the modern Soviet Navy.)[21]

Recalling the absolute priority the Soviets place on protecting their homeland, there is a plausible explanation for Soviet policy toward Japan. Traditionally, Russian and Soviet leaders have viewed the USSR as a continental power and the defense of the homeland was the responsibility of the army. However, as the Soviet Union began to emerge as a superpower in the 1960s, it built up its navy. In addition, the USSR began deploying nuclear weapons on its submarines in the early 1960s.

The Soviet Union's principal naval bases are along the Murmansk fjord, Kronstadt, Sebastopol in the Black Sea, and Vladivostok and Petropavlovsk in the Far East. If one looks at a map, the problem that bedevils Soviet naval planners is readily apparent: submarines and ships going to and from these ports with the single exception of Petropavlovsk must pass through "choke points" controlled by countries friendly to the United States. If the Soviets were to return the Northern Territories to the Japanese, the islands could become Japanese or U.S.–Japanese anti-submarine warfare (ASW) bases thereby increasing the vulnerability of Soviet ships and submarines going to or from Vladivostok. So for security reasons alone, Soviet leaders may have decided to forego substantial economic benefits (for example, Japanese assistance in developing Siberian resources) for strictly national security reasons.

Kimura asserts that Soviet policy toward Japan is simply a reflection of Soviet policy toward the United States. Part of the reason for this is what Kimura refers to as the Soviet obsession with military strength and the failure to recognize the increasing salience of economic power. Japan now has the second largest gross national product in the world, qualifying it as an economic superpower. Despite this fact, the Soviets continue to treat Japan as simply a "junior partner" of the United States. As the economic situation worsens in the USSR, predicted by almost all Western analysts of the Soviet economy, this attitude could perhaps change. But at present, as Kimura notes, there are few signs of change in the Soviet approach to Japan.

As previously noted, Soviet leaders place a high (but relative and not absolute) priority on extending Soviet political influence throughout the world, primarily in the developing countries of Asia, Africa, Latin America, and the Middle East. Of these Third World regions, as George Breslauer notes, the Soviets have given the highest priority in recent years to the Middle East. In their policies toward this region, Breslauer notes that the Soviets have employed four different tactics to advance their interests: confrontation, competition, collaboration, and avoidance.

Soviet interests in the Middle East and the Persian Gulf region in the future will be increasingly influenced by two factors: the Soviets' concern over their superpower status and economics. As previously noted, Soviet leaders are very concerned that other countries, particularly the United States, recognize the USSR as a superpower and accord it appropriate involvement in regions and issues in which Soviet leaders consider their country's interests at stake. By the early 1970s, the Middle East was such a region. In 1972, Anwar Sadat expelled Soviet forces from Egypt. Following the stalemated Arab–Israeli war of 1973, an international conference which included the USSR was convened at Geneva to negotiate a long-term peace settlement for the Middle East. But the Geneva negotiations were quickly eclipsed by Henry Kissinger's "shuttle diplomacy" and later by the Carter administration's efforts which culminated in the Camp David agreement. The Soviets felt that they had been closed out of the Middle East by the United States and that this was a violation of the spirit if not the letter of the Basic Principles agreement of

1972.[22] While the Soviets favored a joint U.S.–Soviet approach to negotiating peace in the Middle East, the United States pursued a unilateral approach. In the second volume of his memoirs, Henry Kissinger noted: "Our strategy sought to reduce the Soviet role in the Middle East because our respective interests in the area (and our different diplomatic styles) could not be reconciled. . . ."[23] Soviet efforts in the Middle East from 1973 to 1983 suggest that they were trying to reestablish their influence in the area and that they considered this effort justified by their position as one of the world's two superpowers.

A second motivation for Soviet policy in the Middle East and the Persian Gulf region is economic. Since the 1973 Arab–Israeli war, world energy prices have increased dramatically. It is estimated that from 1973 to 1980 the USSR provided its Eastern European allies subsidies of nearly $60 billion to pay for energy supplies.[24] If Soviet and Eastern European oil production decreases, as some have predicted, Soviet interest in the oil-rich Gulf could shift from "denial" to "acquisition," to use Breslauer's terms. According to Ross, it is clear that the Soviets are hardly "on the eclipse" in the region and that their interest in it remains high for both political and economic reasons.

Some Uncertainties

Despite the attention that scholars, U.S. government agencies, and private research institutes have devoted to the analysis of Soviet international behavior, some very important questions remain unanswered. In this section, I would like to address four of the most significant issues that the contributors to this book have raised: the objectives of Soviet foreign policy, the Soviet propensity to take risks in pursuit of foreign policy objectives, the future economic development of the USSR, and the succession question.

From 1917 and throughout the cold war, many in the West believed that the Soviet Union was a revolutionary state and that its leaders would not be satisfied until they had achieved world domination. This was clearly the view of John Foster Dulles as well as many others; however, it is not a widely held view today. Rather, most analysts of Soviet foreign policy believe that the Soviet Union is a country that has relatively recently achieved its status as a great power and that it is, like great powers before it, attempting to maximize its influence in the world at minimum cost. This is not to say that the Soviet Union is like every other great power, for there clearly are some distinctive characteristics of Soviet international behavior. It is to say, however, that it is more accurate to think of Soviet foreign policy objectives in the traditional terms of statecraft rather than as driven by a relentless desire for world domination.

If Soviet leaders have been attempting to take over the world, they have done so in an extremely careful, and not revolutionary, manner. As Richard Pipes has pointed out, Soviet leaders are "mindful of the Russian proverb: 'If you don't know the ford, don't step into the river,' [and] they do not plunge into contests blindly; they rarely gamble, unless they feel the odds are overwhelmingly in their favor."[25] Partially as a result of Russian political culture, Soviet policymakers have "a highly developed aversion to risk and an intense preoccupation with economic and political security as they understand them."[26] I have described elsewhere how Soviet leaders particularly sought to avoid direct confrontations with the United States throughout the cold war and detente periods.[27] In the three most serious U.S.–Soviet crises of the cold war—over Berlin in 1948 and 1961 and Cuba in 1962—Soviet leaders sought to limit their risks.[28]

The evidence of the analyses in this book supports the view of Soviets as risk averters. At the same time, the evidence indicates that the Soviet Union is a pragmatic, opportunistic power and that it will seek to expand its influence in situations of low risk that promise some gain for the USSR. This conclusion conforms with other recent studies of Soviet international behavior.[29]

Lenin is cited as having said: "The very deepest roots of both the internal and foreign policy of our state are shaped by economic interests."[30] Apparently things have not changed a great deal since these words were written. In the conclusion to an ambitious and careful recent study of the future of the Soviet system, Robert Byrnes has written: "The most visible determinant of Soviet policy in the 1980s and the most complicated, far-reaching, and difficult policy decisions are the consequences of the slowing rate of economic growth and unprecedented conditions of resource stringency."[31]

The prevalence of economic factors in the cases analyzed in this book is striking. The authors of almost all of the chapters in this book mention economics as playing a role in influencing Soviet policy. However, the economic factor, as described in the case of Japan, is still secondary to the absolute foreign policy priority of security as Hardt and Gold point out. If the pessimistic forecasts of Western economists for the Soviet economy hold, it is possible that Soviet leaders will be forced to place greater emphasis on economic development goals and to somewhat de-emphasize security concerns. That development, however, is less likely than an alternative scenario: in the face of mounting economic crisis, Soviet leaders could point to real or fabricated "mounting international tensions" and call for the Soviet people, to use the Russian idiom, "to loosen their belts," that is, gain weight by eating more bread and potatoes and less meat.

An important uncertainty concerning the future direction and substance of Soviet foreign policy is the succession question. In the context of Soviet international behavior, there are at least five succession questions and not simply the Soviet succession as is usually discussed. Analysts of Soviet policy must consider the possible effects of leadership changes in the United States, Eastern Europe, the People's Republic of China and Iran, as well as the USSR.

Seweryn Bialer has pointed out that in the sense of a change at the elite stratum of the Soviet government, there has been only one true succession in the USSR, and that occurred during the late 1930s.[32] According to Bialer, the Soviet Union is only now involved in its second succession. Following Leonid Brezhnev's death and the accession to power of Yuriy Andropov, most analysts of Soviet politics predicted that the Andropov period would be a transition period. This prediction has now been repeated for the Chernenko regime. It is very likely that the Politburo has placed a hold on any new foreign policy initiatives until Chernenko's successors—the new generation of Soviet leaders—take over. Only then will we begin to be able to determine the likely future course of Soviet foreign policy.

But the Soviet succession will not occur in a vacuum, because, as Sarah Terry points out, four of the communist party leaders in Eastern Europe are seventy years of age or older: Zhivkov in Bulgaria, Kadar in Hungary, Husak in Czechoslovakia, and Honecker in the GDR. With the exception of Hungary, there has been little effort to bring in a new generation of leaders to key decision-making positions. In Poland and Romania, the leaders are somewhat younger but are vulnerable to a rapid turnover because of political and economic troubles in the two countries.

Given the regional and global interests of the Soviets, they will be concerned about political succession in three other states. Deng Xiaoping is now seventy-five years old and, though some attempt has been made to place younger officials in positions of responsibility, members of the old guard are still in the most important positions. Given the closed nature of Chinese society, it is very difficult to know what stance toward the USSR the new generation of Chinese leaders will adopt. The last U.S. president to serve a full two terms in office was Dwight Eisenhower. For various reasons (for example, shifts of public opinion, assassination, and so on), U.S.

politics are very volatile and clearly affect U.S. policy toward the USSR. Lastly, the succession in Iran following the death of the Ayatollah Khomeini could affect the Soviet calculation of costs, risks, and opportunities in that country.

What normally is referred to as "the" succession crisis of the Soviet Union should be considered as multiple, "overlapping succession struggles" (to use Terry's term) that could have substantial influence on Soviet international behavior.

In analyzing the Soviet policy on nuclear weapons and arms control, Lawrence Caldwell notes that the Soviet policy is motivated by several factors, all of which are related to Soviet concerns about security. In their nuclear weapons programs, the USSR is presently attempting, according to Caldwell, to offset what they perceive as U.S. technological superiority. In short, the Soviets are trying to undercut U.S. weapons modernization programs. The Soviet Union has made a tremendous investment in developing, building, and deploying nuclear weapons during the past quarter century. Soviet leaders believe that this cost was justified because, more than any other single factor, Soviet nuclear weapons qualified the USSR as an equal to the United States. However, Soviet leaders believe that the current U.S. programs are designed to give the United States superiority over the USSR, and they are very concerned about this possibility.

Implications for U.S. Policy

By predicting likely Soviet responses to a wide range of U.S. policies, the contributors to this volume have described the principal factors that motivate Soviet international behavior, which, broadly speaking, include four sets of factors: the decision-making process, fears, goals, and limitations. In describing these clusters, I will address both the domestic and international component of each.

The process by which decisions are made in the USSR undoubtedly affects Soviet international behavior. The fundamental premise of Kremlinology is that predictions about Soviet domestic politics and foreign policy can be made if we know who wields power. In a time of succession, it is particularly difficult to tell how power is distributed among the small group that makes Soviet policy. This is because the various factions sort themselves out during the succession period. Over time coalitions among individuals and organizations are built and a consensus emerges. The foreign policy priorities of the leadership group in the USSR have a great impact on Soviet international behavior, but those priorities are often difficult to discern, particularly during succession periods.

The chapters in this book have demonstrated that Soviets are motivated by fears. Having suffered innumerable invasions over centuries, Soviets fear their neighbors, particularly Germany and China. In addition, they fear the United States because of its power, technological prowess, and out of a concern for its intentions. Soviet leaders may not take their own rhetoric seriously anymore, but they certainly pay attention to U.S. leaders' attacks. As Lawrence Caldwell notes, the Soviets are now fearful that the United States is attempting to regain a position of strategic superiority.

Russian political culture and Soviet politics are oriented to what is perceived as the good of the community, rather than the good of the individual. As a result, Soviets distrust any who challenge the state. That is why dissidents have little support within the USSR. The Soviets fear and resent any intervention into what they consider to be domestic matters. For example, Soviet leaders deeply resented the Jackson–Vanik Amendment which linked the granting of most-favored-nation status to the USSR to Soviet emigration practices.

The Soviet fear of foreign intervention into domestic matters and the fear of domestic turmoil is extended to members of the "socialist commonwealth." When Soviet leaders believe that a breakdown of domestic order is near, they will intervene, as they have done in different ways in Hungary, Czechoslovakia, Poland, and Afghanistan.

The goals of the Soviet leadership for foreign policy constitute a third set of factors that influence Soviet international behavior. As noted earlier in this chapter, Soviets want to see the USSR accepted by the world as a superpower and by the United States as an equal. And the USSR has, as Lawrence Caldwell notes, spent a tremendous amount in order to achieve this status. The other paramount goals are to defend the homeland and the Soviet empire. But providing for the absolute defense of these areas in the nuclear era is impossible, and yet Soviet (and for that matter most U.S.) leaders persist in thinking about security in traditional prenuclear terms.

Soviet secondary or relative goals include the extension of Soviet influence throughout the world, economic development, and support for the values of Marxism–Leninism.

Soviet goals are not pursued in a vacuum; rather, there are a number of limiting factors that constrain the USSR. The Soviet economy with its many glaring weaknesses is a principal constraint. Another is the countervailing political and military power of other countries, particularly the United States and its allies. These, then, are the main internal and external factors that affect Soviet international behavior—the decision-making process, fears, goals and limitations. How can the United States affect these factors?

The first point to note is that the USSR is too big, too wrapped up in its own problem, and too much a captive of its history to be effectively manipulated from outside. Influencing Soviet behavior is not simply a case of behavior modification, although some aspects of the U.S. policy of detente under Nixon and Kissinger seemed to assume that dealing with the USSR was simply a matter of coming up with the right mix of rewards and punishments.

Even though the Soviet Union by and large determines its own international behavior, there are things that the United States can do to protect its interests against Soviet encroachment and to encourage the USSR along paths less threatening to the outside world. For example, U.S. military power must be clearly sufficient to allay any Soviet misapprehension about easy conquests, but it should not be so threatening as to cause the Soviets to divert even more resources into defense or, worse yet, to attempt military pre-emption before the United States regains superiority over the USSR.

Actual attempts by the Soviet Union to expand its power by military force, as in Afghanistan, must be met with an effective response. The United States can support the buildup of local forces friendly to the United States, as Dennis Ross advocates for the Persian Gulf region, to deter Soviet aggression. If the Soviets intervene into an area, the United States in many cases can support local resistance. If that is not possible, then the United States can rely on political and economic sanctions, preferably in concert with U.S. allies.

It is best for the United States to have a realistic view of U.S.–Soviet relations in the Third World; competition and conflict between them are inevitable given the fact that both countries attempt to maintain and, where possible at an acceptable cost, expand their influence. To portray all conflict in the Third World in East–West terms is a mistake; rather the United States should search for local and regional solutions before creating an East–West confrontation.

Leaders of the United States must be clear about U.S. objectives and priorities in the world. At the most basic level, Americans want to defend their homeland and their allies. And they want to preserve the American way of life, which includes economic well-being. Americans need to decide if there are other vital interests beyond these. Should the United States risk war to defend access to Persian Gulf oil? Americans must make this decision and make sure that the Soviets understand U.S. priorities and objectives.

Along with firmness, the United States must demonstrate a willingness to negotiate on issues, such as nuclear arms control, of common interest to the United States and USSR. Any U.S. proposals should, obviously, be in the United States interest but they must not be unilaterally so as the zero option INF and Reagan START proposals clearly were. There must be some hope by both sides of an agreement or negotiations will be meaningless. If there is a perception by one or both sides that one is out to do the other side in, negotiations cannot succeed.

Nor can a U.S. policy that counts on a radical change in the USSR succeed. If U.S. leaders want to wait until communism has been thrown into the "dustbin of history" until they negotiate with the Soviets, then we have a long and dangerous wait ahead of us.

Andrei Sakharov has said that there is no issue of greater importance at the present time than the control of nuclear weapons. An elementary knowledge of the number and types of weapons in the arsenals of the United States and USSR makes this clear. There are essentially two choices for the United States on this issue: to build up our nuclear arsenal in hopes of gaining peace through strength or to attempt to negotiate a cap to the competition in nuclear arms while competing in areas that do not threaten the future of civilization. The major findings of this volume point to the advisability of the latter option and the dangerous futility, given the sources of Soviet international behavior, of the former. If the United States and USSR are successful in avoiding nuclear war, the long-term prospects for U.S. foreign policy are bright.

Notes

1. John Lewis Gaddis, *Russia, the Soviet Union and the United States: An Interpretive History* (New York: John Wiley, 1978).

2. Joseph J. Nye, Jr., "Can America Manage Its Soviet Policy?" in Joseph J. Nye, Jr., ed., *The Making of America's Soviet Policy* (New Haven: Yale University Press, 1984), 332.

3. Herbert A. Simon, *Administrative Behavior: A Study of Decision-Making Processes in Administrative Organization* (New York: The Free Press, 1947).

4. See, for example, Seweryn Bialer, ed., *The Domestic Context of Soviet Foreign Policy* (Boulder: Westview Press, 1981); Alexander Dallin, "Soviet Foreign Policy and Domestic Politics: A Framework for Analysis," *Journal of International Affairs*, vol. 23, no. 2 (Winter 1969), 250–265; and Morton Schwartz, *The Foreign Policy of the USSR: Domestic Factors* (Encino, Calif.: Dickenson Publishing Company, 1975).

5. The literature focusing on external influences on Soviet foreign policy is much more extensive than that focusing on domestic factors. See Eric P. Hoffmann and Frederic J. Fleron, Jr., eds., *The Conduct of Soviet*

Foreign Policy (Chicago: Aldine–Atherton, 1971); Alvin Z. Rubinstein, *Soviet Foreign Policy since World War II: Imperial and Global* (Cambridge: Winthrop Publishers, 1981); and Adam B. Ulam, *Expansion and Coexistence: Soviet Foreign Policy 1917–73,* 2nd ed. (New York: Praeger, 1974).

6. Lucian W. Pye, "Political Culture," in *International Encyclopedia of the Social Sciences,* (New York: The Free Press, 1969).

7. Ibid.

8. Richard Pipes, *Russian under the Old Regime* (New York: Charles Scribners, 1974), 8.

9. Seweryn Bialer, "Soviet Foreign Policy: Sources, Perceptions, Trends," in Bialer, ed., *The Domestic Context of Soviet Foreign Policy,* 429.

10. Adam Ulam, "Russian Nationalism," in Bialer, ed., *The Domestic Context of Soviet Foreign Policy,* 3.

11. Richard Nixon, *RN: The Memoirs of Richard Nixon* (New York: Grosset and Dunlap, 1978), 607.

12. Seweryn Bialer, *Stalin's Successors: Leadership, Stability, and Change in the Soviet Union* (New York: Cambridge University Press, 1980); Jerry F. Hough, *Soviet Leadership in Transition* (Washington: The Brookings Institution, 1980).

13. Bialer, "Soviet Foreign Policy: Sources, Perceptions, Trends," in Bialer, ed., *The Domestic Context of Soviet Foreign Policy,* 432.

14. Ibid.

15. Richard Pipes, *U.S.–Soviet Relations in the Era of Détente* (Boulder: Westview Press, 1981), 81.

16. Bialer, "Soviet Foreign Policy: Sources, Perceptions, Trends," in Bialer, ed., *The Domestic Context of Soviet Foreign Policy,* 432.

17. Lawrence T. Caldwell and Robert Legvold, "Reagan Through Soviet Eyes," *Foreign Policy,* no. 52 (Fall 1983): 3–21.

18. John Lewis Gaddis, *Strategies of Containment: A Critical Appraisal of Postwar American National Security Policy* (New York: Oxford University Press, 1982).

19. *New York Times,* 11 May 1959, 3.

20. Fuji Kamiya, "The Northern Territories: 130 Years of Japanese Talks with Czarist Russia and the Soviet Union," in Donald S. Zagoria, ed., *Soviet Policy in East Asia* (New Haven: Yale University Press, 1982), 121–152.

21. Admiral Sergei G. Gorshkov, *Red Star Rising at Sea* (Annapolis: Naval Institute Press, 1978).

22. Alexander L. George, "The Basic Principles Agreement of 1972," in Alexander L. George, ed., *Managing U.S.–Soviet Rivalry: Problems of Crisis Prevention* (Boulder: Westview Press, 1983), 115.

23. Henry A. Kissinger, *Years of Upheaval* (Boston: Little, Brown, 1982), 943.

24. Michael Marrese and Jan Vanous, *Implicit Subsidies and Non-Market Benefits in Soviet Trade with Eastern Europe* (Berkeley: Institute of International Studies, 1983).

25. Pipes, *U.S.–Soviet Relations,* 26.

26. John M. Joyce, "The Old Russian Legacy," *Foreign Policy,* no. 55 (Summer 1984): 132–153.

27. Dan Caldwell, *American–Soviet Relations: From 1947 to the Nixon–Kissinger Grand Design* (Westport: Greenwood Press, 1981).

28. On the Berlin cases, see Hannes Adomeit, *Soviet Risk-Taking and Crisis Behavior: A Theoretical and Empirical Analysis* (London: George Allen and Unwin, 1982).

29. See, for example, Zagoria, *Soviet Policy in East Asia.*

30. Quoted by Signey I. Ploss, "Studying the Domestic Determinants of Soviet Foreign Policy," in Hoffman and Fleron, *The Conduct of Soviet Foreign Policy,* 78–79.

31. Robert F. Byrnes, "Critical Choices in the 1980s," in Robert F. Byrnes, ed., *After Brezhnev: Sources of Soviet Conduct in the 1980s* (Bloomington: Indiana University Press, 1983), 428.

32. Bialer, *Stalin's Successors: Leadership, Stability, and Change in the Soviet Union,* 68.

Bibliography

This bibliography is designed to assist anyone who would like to do further research on the topics analyzed in this book. In addition, there are three sections concerning regions not addressed in this book. Some of the more readily available Soviet resources are listed; however, those focusing their research on Soviet policy will need to supplement the listings in this bibliography with additional Soviet sources.

This bibliography is divided into the following ten topical sections: (1) Soviet foreign policy; (2) U.S.–Soviet relations; and Soviet policy toward (3) Europe; (4) Asia; (5) the Middle East and Persian Gulf; (6) economics and trade; (7) military policy and arms control; (8) South Asia; (9) Africa; and (10) Latin America.

Soviet Foreign Policy

Adomeit, Hannes, *Soviet Risk Taking and Crisis Behaviour, from Confrontation to Coexistence.* Adelphi Paper no. 101. London: International Institute for Strategic Studies, 1973.

———. *Soviet Risk-Taking and Crisis Behavior: A Theoretical and Empirical Analysis.* London: George Allen and Unwin, 1982.

———. "Capitalist Contradictions and Soviet Policy" *Problems of Communism,* vol. 33, no. 3 (May–June 1984): 1–18.

Aspaturian, Vernon V. *Process and Power in Soviet Foreign Policy.* Boston: Little, Brown, 1971.

Bertram, Christoph, ed. *Prospects of Soviet Power in the 1980s.* London: Archon Books, 1980.

Bialer, Seweryn. *Stalin's Successors: Leadership, Stability and Change in the Soviet Union.* New York: Cambridge University Press, 1980.

———. "The Harsh Decade: Soviet Politics in the 1980s." *Foreign Affairs,* vol. 59, no. 5 (Summer 1981): 999–1020.

———. "The Soviet Union and the West in the 1980s: Detente, Containment or Confrontation?" *Orbis,* vol. 27, no. 1 (Spring 1983): 35–58.

———, ed. *The Domestic Context of Soviet Foreign Policy.* Boulder: Westview Press, 1981.

Bjorkman, Thomas N. and Zamostny, Thomas J. "Soviet Politics and Strategy toward the West: Three Cases." *World Politics,* vol. 36, no. 2 (January 1984): 189–214.

Brown, Archie and Kaser, Michael, eds. *Soviet Policy for the 1980s.* Bloomington: Indiana University Press, 1983.

Buchanan, Thompson R. "The Real Russia." *Foreign Policy,* no. 47 (Summer 1982): 26–45.

Byrnes, Robert F., ed. *After Brezhnev: Sources of Soviet Conduct in the 1980's.* Bloomington: Indiana University Press, 1983.

Dallin, Alexander. "Soviet Foreign Policy and Domestic Politics: A Framework for Analysis." *Journal of International Affairs,* vol. 23, no. 2 (Winter 1969): 250–265.

Donaldson, Robert H. *The Soviet Union and the Third World: Success or Failure.* Boulder: Westview Press, 1980.

Duncan, Raymond W., ed. *Soviet Policy in Developing Countries.* Waltham: Ginn–Blaisdell, 1970.

———, ed. *Soviet Policy in the Third World.* New York: Pergamon Press, 1980.

Dunn, Keith A. "Mysteries About the Soviet Union." *Orbis,* vol. 26, no. 2 (Summer 1982): 361–380.

Edmonds, Robin. *Soviet Foreign Policy 1962–1973: The Paradox of Soviet Power.* London: Oxford University Press, 1975.

Ermarth, Fritz. "The Soviet Union in the Third World: Purpose in Search of Power." *Annals of the American Academy of Political and Social Sciences,* November 1969.

Feuchtwanger, E.J. and Nailor, Peter, eds. *The Soviet Union and the Third World.* New York: St. Martin's Press, 1981.

Gelman, Harry. *The Brezhnev Politburo and the Decline of Detente.* Ithaca: Cornell University Press, 1984.

Gray, Colin and Strode, Rebecca. "The Imperial Dimension of Soviet Military Power." *Problems of Communism,* vol. 30 (November–December 1981): 1–15.

Haselkorn, Avigdor. *The Evolution of Soviet Security Strategy: 1965–1975.* New York: Crane, Russak, 1978.

Hoffman, Erik P. and Fleron, Frederic Jr., eds. *The Conduct of Soviet Foreign Policy,* 2nd ed. Chicago: Aldine–Atherton, 1977.

Horelick, Arnold L. "The Cuban Missile Crisis: An Analysis of Soviet Calculations and Behavior." *World Politics,* vol. 16, no. 3 (April 1964): 363–389.

———, and Myron Rush. *Strategic Power and Soviet Foreign Policy.* Chicago: University of Chicago Press, 1966.

Horelick, Arnold L., Johnson, A. Ross, and Steinbruner, John D. *The Study of Soviet Foreign Policy: Decision-Theory-Related Approaches.* Sage Professional Papers in International Studies, no. 02-039. Beverly Hills and London: Sage Publications, 1975.

Hosmer, Stephen T. and Wolfe, Thomas. *Soviet Policy and Practice toward Third World Conflicts.* Lexington: Lexington Books, 1983.

Hough, Jerry. "The Evolution of the Soviet World View." *World Politics,* vol. 32, no. 4 (July 1980): 509–530.

Joshua, Wynfred and Gibert, Stephen P. *Arms for the Third World: Soviet Military Aid Diplomacy.* Baltimore: Johns Hopkins University Press, 1969.

Kanet, Roger E., ed. *The Soviet Union and Developing Nations.* Baltimore: Johns Hopkins University Press, 1974.

———, ed. *Soviet Foreign Policy and East–West Relations.* New York: Pergamon Press, 1982.

Kaplan, Stephen S. *Diplomacy of Power: Soviet Armed Forces as a Political Instrument.* Washington: The Brookings Institution, 1981.

Katz, Mark N. *The Third World in Soviet Military Thought.* Baltimore: Johns Hopkins University Press, 1982.

Kennan, George. "The Sources of Soviet Conduct." *Foreign Affairs,* vol. 25, no. 4 (July 1947): 566–582.

———. *Russia and the West under Lenin and Stalin.* Boston: Little, Brown, 1960.

———. *On Dealing with the Communist World.* New York: Harper and Row, 1964.

Khrushchev Remembers. Translated and edited by Talbott, Strobe. Boston: Little, Brown, 1970.

Khrushchev Remembers: The Last Testament. Translated and edited by Talbott, Strobe. Boston: Little, Brown, 1974.

Kirk, Grayson and Wessell, Nils H., eds. *The Soviet Threat: Myths and Realities.* New York: The Academy of Political Science, 1978.

Kobysh, Vitalii. "There is an Exit from the Impasse." *Literaturnaia Gazeta,* no. 51 (22 December 1982).

Laqueur, Walter, ed. *The Pattern of Soviet Conduct in the Third World.* New York: Praeger, 1983.

Legvold, Robert. "The Nature of Soviet Power." *Foreign Affairs,* vol. 56, no. 1 (Fall 1977): 49–71.

———. "The Super Rivals: Conflict in the Third World." *Foreign Affairs,* vol. 57, no. 4 (Spring 1979): 755–778.

Luttwak, Edward. *The Grand Strategy of the Soviet Union.* New York: St. Martin's Press, 1983.

McCauley, Martin, ed. *The Soviet Union after Brezhnev.* New York: Holmes and Meier, 1984.

Ober, Robert F. "Power and Position in the Kremlin." *Orbis,* vol. 26, no. 4 (Winter 1983): 849–868.

Pipes, Richard. "Soviet Global Strategy." *Commentary* (April 1980).

Ponomarev, B., Gromyko, A., and Khnostov, V., eds. *History of Soviet Foreign Policy, 1945–1970.* English edition. Moscow: Progress Publishers, 1979.

Ra'anan, Uri. "Moscow and the Third World." *Problems of Communism* (January–February 1965).

Rubinstein, Alvin. *The Foreign Policy of the Soviet Union.* New York: Random House, 1960.

———. *Soviet Foreign Policy since World War II: Imperial and Global.* Cambridge: Winthrop Publishers, 1981.

———. "Superpower Rivalry in the Third World." *Orbis,* vol. 27, no. 1 (Spring 1983): 28–34.

Rush, Myron. "Guns over Growth in Soviet Policy." *International Security,* vol. 7, no. 3 (Winter 1982–1983): 167–179.

Schwartz, Morton. "The USSR and Leftist Regimes in Less Developed Countries." *Survey,* vol. 19 (Spring 1973).

———. *The Foreign Policy of the USSR: Domestic Factors.* Encino: Dickenson Publication Co., 1975.

Shulman, Marshall. *Stalin's Foreign Policy Reappraised.* Cambridge: Harvard University Press, 1964.

Simes, Dimitri K. *Detente and Conflict: Soviet Foreign Policy 1972–1977.* Washington Papers, vol. 5, no. 44. Beverly Hills and London: Sage Publications, 1977.

———. "Detente—Russian Style." *Foreign Policy,* no. 32 (Fall 1978): 47–62.

———. "The Death of Detente?" *International Security,* vol. 5, no. 1 (Summer 1980): 3–25.

———. "Disciplining Soviet Power." *Foreign Policy,* no. 43 (Summer 1981): 33–52.

———. "The New Soviet Challenge." *Foreign Policy,* no. 55 (Summer 1984): 113–131.

Strode, Dan L. and Strode, Rebbecca V., "Diplomacy and Defense in Soviet National Security Policy." *International Security,* vol. 8, no. 2 (Fall 1983): 91–116.

Strong, John W., ed. *The Soviet Union Under Brezhnev and Kosygin.* New York: Van Nostrand Reinhold Company, 1971.

Taubman, William. *Stalin's American Policy: From Entente to Detente to Cold War.* New York: Norton, 1982.

Triska, John F. and Finley, David D., *Soviet Foreign Policy.* New York: Macmillan, 1968.

Ulam, Adam. *Expansion and Coexistence: Soviet Foreign Policy, 1917–1973,* 2nd ed. New York: Praeger, 1974.

———. *Dangerous Relations: The Soviet Union in World Politics.* New York: Oxford University Press, 1983.

U.S. Congress. Congressional Research Service. Library of Congress. *The Soviet Union and the Third World: A Watershed in Great Power Policy?* Report to the Committee on International Relations, U.S. House of Representatives, 8 May 1977.

———. *Soviet Policy and United States Reponses in the Third World.* Washington: U.S. Government Printing Office (March 1981).

Valenta, Jiri. "Soviet Use of Surprise and Deception." *Survival,* vol. 24, no. 2 (March–April 1982): 50–60.

Wolfe, Thomas. *Soviet Strategy at the Crossroads.* Cambridge: Harvard University Press, 1964.

Yanov, Alexander. *Detente after Brezhnev: The Domestic Roots of Soviet Foreign Policy.* Policy Papers in International Affairs. Berkeley: Institute of International Studies, 1977.

Zagoria, Donald S. "Into the Breach: New Soviet Alliances in the Third World." *Foreign Affairs,* vol. 57, no. 4 (Spring 1979): 733–754.

Zimmerman, William. *Soviet Perspectives on International Relations.* Princeton: Princeton University Press, 1969.

U.S.–Soviet Relations

Arbatov, Georgiy. *The War of Ideas in Contemporary International Relations.* Moscow: Progress Publications, 1973.

——— and Oltmans, William. *The Soviet Viewpoint.* New York: Dodd, Mead and Company, 1981.

Barnet, Richard J. *The Giants: Russia and America.* New York: Simon and Schuster, 1977.

Bialer, Seweryn and Afferica, Jean, "Reagan and Russia." *Foreign Affairs,* vol. 61, no. 2 (Winter 1982–83): 249–271.

Brement, Marshall. *Organizaing Ourselves to Deal with the Soviets.* P-6123. Santa Monica: The Rand Corporation, 1978.

Brzezinski, Zbigniew. *Power and Principle: Memoirs of the National Security Advisor, 1977–1981.* New York: Farrar, Straus, Giroux, 1983.

Caldwell, Dan. *American–Soviet Relations: From 1947 to the Nixon–Kissinger Grand Design.* Westport: Greenwood Press, 1981.

Caldwell, Lawrence T. and Diebold, William, Jr. *Soviet–American Relations in the 1980s: Superpower Politics and East–West Trade.* New York: McGraw–Hill, 1981.

——— and Legvold. "Reagan Through Soviet Eyes." *Foreign Policy,* no. 52 (Fall 1983): 3–21.

Dallin, Alexander and Lapidus, Gail W. "Reagan and the Russians: United States Policy toward the Soviet Union and Eastern Europe." In Oye, Kenneth A., Lieber, Robert J., and Rothchild, Donald, eds. *Eagle Defiant: United States Foreign Policy in the 1980s.* Boston: Little, Brown, 1983, 191–236.

Draper, Theodore. "Détente." *Commentary,* vol. 57 (June 1974): 25–47.

———. "Appeasement and Détente." *Commentary,* vol. 59 (February 1976): 27–38.

Gaddis, John Lewis. *The United States and the Origins of the Cold War, 1941–1947.* New York: Columbia University Press, 1972.

———. *Russia, the Soviet Union and the United States: An Interpretative History.* New York: John Wiley, 1978.

———. *Strategies of Containment: A Critical Appraisal of Postwar American National Security Policy.* New York: Oxford University Press, 1982.

———. "The Rise, Fall and Future of Detente." *Foreign Affairs*, vol. 62, no. 2 (Winter 1983–84): 354–377.

George, Alexander L., ed. *Managing U.S.–Soviet Rivalry: Problems of Crisis Prevention.* Boulder: Westview Press, 1983.

——— and Smoke, Richard. *Deterrence in American Foreign Policy: Theory and Practice.* New York: Columbia University Press, 1974.

Gibert, Stephen P. *Soviet Images of America.* New York: Crane, Russak, 1977.

Haig, Alexander M., Jr. *Caveat: Realism, Reagan, and Foreign Policy.* New York: Macmillan, 1984.

Halle, Louis J. *The Cold War as History.* New York: Harper and Row, 1967.

Hyland, William G. *Soviet–American Relations: A New Cold War?* R-2763-FF/RC. Santa Monica: The Rand Corporation, May 1981.

———. "Clash with the Soviet Union." *Foreign Policy*, no. 49 (Winter 1983–83): 3–19.

Kegley, Charles and McGowan, Pat, eds. *Foreign Policy USA/USSR.* Beverly Hills and London: Sage Publications, 1982.

Kennan, George F. *The Cloud of Danger: Current Realities of American Foreign Policy.* Boston: Little, Brown, 1977.

———. *The Nuclear Delusion: Soviet–American Relations in the Atomic Age.* New York: Pantheon Books, 1982.

Kissinger, Henry A. *White House Years.* Boston: Little, Brown, 1979.

———. *Years of Upheaval.* Boston: Little, Brown, 1982.

———. "How to Deal with Moscow." *Newsweek* (November 29, 1982), 30–32, 37.

Lafeber, Walter. *America, Russia and the Cold War, 1945–1971,* 2nd ed. New York: John Wiley, 1972.

Laqueur, Walter. "Reagan and the Russians." *Commentary*, vol. 73, no. 1 (January 1982): 19–26.

———. "U.S.–Soviet Relations." *Foreign Affairs: America and the World 1983*, vol. 62, no. 3 (1984): 561–586.

Melanson, Richard, ed. *Neither Cold War nor Detente: Soviet–American Relations in the 1980s.* Charlottesville: University of Virginia Press, 1982.

Mil'shtein, M.A. "At a Dangerous Crossroads." *SShA: Ekonomika, Politika, Idelologiya*, no. 10, October 1978. Reprinted by U.S. Joint Publications Research Service 7238.

Nixon, Richard M. *RN: The Memoirs of Richard Nixon.* New York: Grosset and Dunlap, 1978.

———. *The Real War.* New York: Warner Books, 1980.

———. *Real Peace.* Boston: Little, Brown, 1983.

Nye, Joseph S., Jr., ed. *The Making of America's Soviet Policy.* New Haven: Yale University Press, 1984.

———. "Can America Manage Its Soviet Policy?" *Foreign Affairs, vol. 62, no. 4 (Spring 1984): 857–878.*

Paterson, Thomas G. *Soviet–American Confrontation: Postwar Recon-*

struction and the Origins of the Cold War. Baltimore: Johns Hopkins University Press, 1973.

Pipes, Richard. *U.S.–Soviet Relations in the Era of Détente.* Boulder: Westview Press, 1981.

Podhoretz, Norman. *The Present Danger.* New York: Simon and Schuster, 1980.

Schwartz, Morton. *Soviet Perceptions of the United States.* Berkeley: University of California Press, 1978.

Shulman, Marshall D. "On Learning to Live with Authoritarian Regimes." *Foreign Affairs,* vol. 55, no. 2 (January 1977): 325–328.

———. "Toward a Western Philosophy of Coexistence." *Foreign Affairs,* vol. 52, no. 1 (October 1973): 35–58.

———. *Beyond the Cold War.* New Haven: Yale University Press, 1966.

Sivachev, Nikolai and Yakoliev, Nikolai N. *Russia and the United States: U.S.–Soviet Relations from the Soviet Point of View.* Chicago: University of Chicago Press, 1979.

Ulam, Adam B. *The Rivals: America and Russia since World War II.* New York: Viking, 1971.

———. "How to Restrain the Soviets." *Commentary,* vol. 70, no. 6 (December 1980).

U.S. Congress. Senate. Committee on Foreign Relations. *Perceptions: Relations Between the United States and the Soviet Union.* Washington: U.S. Government Printing Office, 1979.

Vance, Cyrus. *Hard Choices: Critical Years in American Foreign Policy.* New York: Simon and Schuster, 1983.

Welch, William. *American Images of Soviet Foreign Policy.* New Haven: Yale University Press, 1970.

Yergin, Daniel. *Shattered Peace: Origins of the Cold War and the National Security State.* Boston: Houghton Mifflin, 1977.

Soviet Policy toward Europe

Adomeit, Hannes. "Soviet Perceptions of West European Integration: Ideological Distortion of Realistic Assessment?" *Millenium: Journal of International Studies* (Spring 1979): 1–24.

Albright, David E. "On Eastern Europe: Security Implications for the USSR." *Parameters,* vol. 14, no. 2 (Summer 1984): 24–36.

Brown, J.F. "Detente and Soviet Policy in Eastern Europe." *Survey,* vol. 20, nos. 2–3 (Spring–Summer 1974): 46–58.

———. *Relations Between the Soviet Union and Its East European Allies: A Survey Report.* R-1742-PR. Santa Monica: The Rand Corporation, 1975.

Brzezinski, Zbigniew, *The Soviet Bloc: Unity and Conflict.* Cambridge: Harvard University Press, 1967.

Dawisha, Karen and Hanson, Philip, eds. *Soviet–East European Dilemmas: Coercion, Competition and Consent.* New York: Holmes & Meier, 1981.

Douglass, Joseph D. *Soviet Military Strategy in Europe.* New York: Pergamon, 1980.

Ellison, Herbert, ed. *Soviet Policy toward Western Europe: Implications for the Atlantic Alliance.* Seattle: University of Washington Press, 1983.

German, Robert R. "Norway and the Bear: Soviet Coercive Diplomacy and Norwegian Security Policy." *International Security,* vol. 7, no. 2 (Fall 1982): 55–82.

Hakovirta, Harto. "The Soviet Union and the Varieties of Neutrality in Western Europe." *World Politics,* vol. 35, no. 4 (July 1983): 563–585.

Holloway, David and Sharp, Jane M.O., eds. *The Warsaw Pact: Alliance in Transition?* Ithaca: Cornell University Press, 1984.

Hutchings, Robert L. *Soviet–East European Relations: Consolidation and Conflict, 1968–1980.* Madison: University of Wisconsin Press, 1983.

Jones, Christopher D. *Soviet Influence in Eastern Europe: Political Autonomy and the Warsaw Pact.* New York: Praeger, 1981.

Korborski, Andrzej. "Eastern Europe as an Internal Determinent of Soviet Foreign Policy." In Bialer, Seweryn, ed. *The Domestic Context of Soviet Foreign Policy.* Boulder: Westview Press, 1981, 313–334.

Legvold, Robert, "The Soviet Union and West European Communism." In Tokes, Rudolf L., ed. *Eurocommunism and Detente.* New York: New York University Press, 1978.

May, Ernest R. "Soviet Policy and 'The German Problem.'" *Naval War College Review,* vol. 36, no. 5 (September–October 1983): 18–36.

Moreton, Edwina. "The Soviet Union and Poland's Struggle for Self-Control." *International Security,* vol. 7, no. 1 (Summer 1982): 86–104.

——— and Segal, Gerald, eds. *Soviety Strategy toward Western Europe.* Boston: George Allen and Unwin, 1984.

Pipes, Richard, ed. *Soviet Strategy in Europe.* New York: Crane, Russak, 1976.

Pridham, Kenneth. "The Soviet View of Current Disagreements between the United States and Western Europe." *International Affairs,* London (Winter 1982–83): 17–31.

Stent, Angela. *From Embargo to Ostpolitik: The Political Economy of West German–Soviet Relations 1955–1980.* New York: Cambridge University Press, 1981.

Terry, Sarah Meiklejohn, ed. *Soviet Policy in Eastern Europe.* New Haven: Yale University Press, 1984.

Valenta, Jiri. "The Explosive Soviet Periphery." *Foreign Policy,* no. 51 (Summer 1983): 84–100.

———. "Soviet Options in Poland." *Survival,* vol. 23, no. 2 (March–April 1981): 50–59.

Vanous, Jan. "East European Economic Slowdown," *Problems of Communism,* vol. 31, no. 4 (July–August 1982): 1–19.

Vincent, R.J. *Military Power and Political Influence: The Soviet Union and*

Western Europe. Adelphi Paper no. 119. London: International Institute for Strategic Studies, 1975.
Volgyes, Ivan. "Eastern Europe After Succession." *Orbis,* vol. 27, no. 1 (Spring 1983): 20–27.
Wettig, Gerhard. *Community and Conflict in the Socialist Camp: The Soviet Union, East Germany and the German Problem 1965–1972.* New York: St. Martin's, 1975.
Wolfe, Thomas. *Soviet Power and Europe, 1945–1970.* Baltimore: Johns Hopkins University Press, 1970.

Soviet Policy toward Asia

Dibb, Paul. "Soviet Capabilities, Interests and Strategies in East Asia in the 1980's." *Survival,* vol. 24, no. 4 (July–August 1982): 155–162.
Ellison, Herbert J., ed. *The Sino–Soviet Conflict: A Global Perspective.* Seattle: University of Washington Press, 1982.
Garthoff, Raymond L., ed. *Sino–Soviet Military Relations.* New York: Praeger, 1966.
Gelman, Harry. "Outlook for Sino–Soviet Relations." *Problems of Communism* (September–December 1979).
———. *The Soviet Far East Buildup and Soviet Risk-taking against China.* R-2942-AF. Santa Monica: The Rand Corporation, 1982.
———. "Soviet Policy toward China." *Survey,* vol. 27 (Autumn–Winter 1983): 165–174.
Griffith, William E. *The Sino–Soviet Rift.* Cambridge: MIT Press, 1964.
———. "Sino–Soviet Rapprochement." *Problems of Communism,* vol. 32, no. 2 (March–April 1983): 20–29.
Hensel, Howard M. "Asian Collective Security: The Soviet View." *Orbis* (Winter 1976).
Horelick, Arnold. "The Soviet Union's Asian Collective Security Proposal: A Club in Search of Members." *Pacific Affairs* (Spring 1974).
Hyland, William G. "The Sino–Soviet Conflict: A Search for New Security Strategies." *Strategic Review,* vol. 7, no. 4 (Fall 1979).
———. "The Sino–Soviet Conflict: A Search for New Security Strategies." In Richard H. Solomon, ed. *Asian Security in the 1980's: Problems and Policies for a Time of Transition.* Cambridge: Oelgeschlager, Gunn and Hain, 1980.
Johnson, Chalmers. "Japan, the USSR, and Northeast Asia." *Problems of Communism,* vol. 32, no. 1 (January–February 1983).
Jukes, Geoffrey. *The Soviet Union in Asia.* Berkeley: University of California Press, 1973.
Kataoka, Tetsuya. "Japan's Northern Threat." *Problems of Communism,* vol. 33 (March–April 1984): 1–16.
Kim, Joungwon Alexander. "Soviet Policy in North Korea." *World Politics,* vol. 22, no. 2 (January 1970): 237–254.

Kimura, Hiroshi. "Japan–Soviet Relations: Framework, Development, Prospects." *Asian Survey,* vol. 20 (July 1980).

———. "The Soviet Proposal on Confidence-Building Measures and the Japanese Response." *Journal of International Affairs,* vol. 37, no. 1 (Summer 1983): 81–104.

Levine, Stephen I. "The Soviet Perspective." In John Bryan Starr, ed. *The Future of U.S.–China Relations.* New York: New York University Press, 1981.

Lieberthal, Kenneth G. *Sino–Soviet Conflict in the 1970's: Its Evolution and Implication for the Strategic Triangle.* R-2342-NA. Santa Monica: The Rand Corporation, 1978.

Mathieson, R.S. *Japan's Role in Soviet Economic Growth.* New York: Praeger, 1979.

Pollack, Jonathan D. *The Sino–Soviet Rivalry and Chinese Security Debate.* R-2907-AF. Santa Monica: The Rand Corporation, 1982.

Segal, Gerald, ed. *The Soviet Union in East Asia.* London: Heinemann, 1983.

Solomon, Richard, ed. *The China Factor: Sino–Soviet Relations and the Global Scene.* Englewood Cliffs: Prentice–Hall, 1981.

Stephan, John J. *The Kuril Islands: Russo–Japanese Frontier in the Pacific.* Oxford: Clarendon Press, 1974.

———. "The Kuril Islands: Japan versus Russia." *Pacific Community,* vol. 7 (April 1976).

———. "Soviet Approaches to Japan: Images Behind the Policies." *Asian Perspective,* vol. 6, no. 2 (Fall–Winter 1982).

Stuart, Douglas T. and Tow, William T., eds. *China, the Soviet Union, and the West: Strategic and Political Dimensions in the 1980s.* Boulder: Westview Press, 1982.

Swearingen, Roger. *The Soviet Union and Postwar Japan: Escalating Challenge and Response.* Stanford: Hoover Institution Press, 1978.

Westwood, James T. "Japan and Soviet Power in the Pacific." *Strategic Review,* vol. 11, no. 4 (Fall 1983): 27–35.

Whiting, Allen S. *Siberian Development and East Asia: Threat or Promise?* Stanford: Stanford University Press, 1981.

Zagoria, Donald S. *The Sino–Soviet Conflict 1956–1961.* Princeton: Princeton University Press, 1962.

———. *Vietnam Triangle: Moscow, Peking, Hanoi.* New York: Pegasus, 1967.

———. "Korea's Future: Moscow's Perspective." *Asian Survey,* vol. 17, no. 11 (November 1977): 1103–1112.

———, ed. *Soviet Policy in East Asia.* New Haven: Yale University Press, 1982.

———. "The Moscow–Beijing Detente." *Foreign Affairs,* vol. 16, no. 4 (Spring 1983): 853–873.

Soviet Policy in the Middle East and Persian Gulf

Benningsen, Alexandre. "Soviet Muslims and the World of Islam." *Problems of Communism* (March–April 1980).

Breslauer, George W. "Soviet Policy in the Middle East, 1967–1972: Unalterable Antagonism or Collaborative Competition?" In Alexander L. George, ed. *Managing U.S.–Soviet Rivalry: Problems of Crisis Prevention.* Boulder: Westview Press, 1983, 65–106.

Chubin, Shahram. *Soviet Policy towards Iran and the Gulf.* Adelphi paper no. 157. London: International Institute for Strategic Studies, 1980.

———. "Gains for Soviet Policy in the Middle East." *International Security,* vol. 6, no. 4 (Spring 1982): 122–152.

———. "The Soviet Union and Iran." *Foreign Affairs,* vol. 16, no. 4 (Spring 1983): 921–949.

Confino, Michael and Shamir, Shimon, eds. *The U.S.S.R. and the Middle East.* Jerusalem: Israel University Press, 1973.

Dawisha, Adeed and Dawisha, Karen. *The Soviet Union in the Middle East.* London: Heinemann, 1982.

Dawisha, Karen. *Soviet Foreign Policy towards Egypt.* London: Macmillan, 1979.

———. "The U.S.S.R. in the Middle East: Superpower in Eclipse?" *Foreign Affairs,* vol. 61, no. 2 (Winter 1982–83): 438–452.

Freedman, Robert O. *Soviet Policy towards the Middle East Since 1970,* 2nd ed. New York: Praeger, 1978.

Fukuyama, Francis. "A New Soviet Strategy." *Commentary* (October 1979).

———. *New Directions for Soviet Middle East Policy in the 1980s: Implications for the Atlantic Alliance.* P-6443. Santa Monica: The Rand Corporation, February 1980.

———. *The Soviet Union and Iraq Since 1968.* N-1529-AF. Santa Monica: The Rand Corporation, July 1980.

Glassman, Jon. *Arms for Arabs: The Soviet Union and War in the Middle East.* Baltimore: Johns Hopkins University Press, 1975.

Golan, Galia. *Yom Kippur and After: The Soviet Union and the Middle East Crisis.* New York: Cambridge University Press, 1977.

———. *The Soviet Union and the Israeli War in Lebanon.* Research Paper no. 46. The Soviet and East European Research Centre, Hebrew University of Jerusalem, October 1982.

Heikal, Mohamed. *The Cairo Documents.* New York: Doubleday, 1973.

———. *The Road to Ramadan.* New York: Quadrangle/New York Times Book Co., 1975.

———. *The Sphinx and the Commissar: The Rise and Fall of Soviet Influence in the Middle East.* New York: Harper & Row, 1978.

Herzog, Chaim. *The War of Atonement.* Boston: Little, Brown, 1975.

Kass, Ilana. *Soviet Involvement in the Middle East: Policy Formulation, 1966–1978.* Boulder: Westview Press, 1978.

McNaugher, Thomas L. "Balancing Soviet Power in the Persian Gulf." *The Brookings Review* (Summer 1983): 20–24.

O'Ballance, Edgar. *The War in Yemen.* Hamden: Archon Books, 1971.

Pajak, Roger F. "Soviet Arms and Egypt." *Survival* (July–August 1975).

———. "Arms and Oil: The Soviet–Libyan Arms Supply Relationship." *Middle East Review* (Winter 1980–1981).

Price, David Lynn. "Moscow and the Persian Gulf." *Problems of Communism* (March–April, 1979).

Quandt, William B. *Soviet Policy in the October 1973 War.* R-1864-ISA. Santa Monica: The Rand Corporation, May 1976.

———. *Decade of Decisions: American Policy Toward the Arab–Israeli Conflict, 1967–1976.* Berkeley: University of California Press, 1977.

Ramazani, R.K. "Security in the Persian Gulf." *Foreign Affairs,* vol. 57, no. 4 (Spring 1979): 820–835.

Roberts, Cynthia A. "Soviet Arms-Transfer Policy and the Decision to Upgrade Syrian Air Defenses." *Survival,* vol. 25, no. 4 (July–August 1983): 154–164.

Ro'i, Yaacov, ed. *The Limits to Power: Soviet Policy in the Middle East.* New York: St. Martin's Press, 1979.

Ross, Dennis. "Considering Soviet Threats to the Persian Gulf." *International Security,* vol. 6, no. 2 (Fall, 1981: 159–180.

Rubinstein, Alvin, Z. *Red Star on the Nile: The Soviet–Egyptian Influence Relationship since the June War.* Princeton: Princeton University Press, 1977.

———. "The Soviet Union and the Arabian Peninsula." *World Today* (November 1979): 443–451.

———. *Soviet Policy toward Turkey, Iran, and Afghanistan: The Dynamics of Influence.* New York: Praeger, 1982.

———. "The Soviet Union's Imperial Policy in the Middle East." *The Middle East Review* (Fall–Winter 1982–1983).

Sadat, Anwar. *In Search of Identity: An Autobiography.* New York: Harper and Row, 1977.

Sella, Annon. *The Soviet Attitude towards the War in Lebanon—Mid-1982.* Research Paper no. 47. The Soviet and East European Research Centre, Hebrew University of Jerusalem, December 1982.

———. *Soviet Political and Military Conduct in the Middle East.* New York: St. Martin's Press, 1981.

Von Hollen, Christopher. "Don't Engulf the Gulf." *Foreign Affairs,* vol. 59, no. 5 (Summer 1981): 1064–1078.

Whitten, Lawrence L. *The Canal War: Four Power Conflict in the Middle East.* Cambridge: MIT Press, 1974.

Soviet Economic Behavior

Becker, Abraham, ed. *Economic Relations with the USSR.* Lexington: Lexington Books, 1983.

Bergson, Abram. "Soviet Economic Slowdown and the 1981–1985 Plan." *Problems of Communism,* vol. 30, no. 3 (May–June 1983): 24–36.

Bertsch, Gary, "U.S.–Soviet Trade: The Question of Leverage." *Survey,* vol. 25 (Spring, 1980: 66–80.

Bialer, Seweryn. "The Politics of Stringency in the USSR." *Problems of Communism,* vol. 29 (May–June 1980): 19–33.

Birman, Igor. "The Financial Crisis in the USSR." *Soviet Studies,* vol. 32 (January 1980).

Campbell, Robert W. *The Economics of Soviet Oil and Gas.* Baltimore: Johns Hopkins University Press, 1968.

———. *Soviet Technology Imports: The Gas Pipeline Case.* Discussion Paper no. 91. Santa Monica: The California Seminar on International Security and Foreign Policy, February 1981.

de Pauw, John Whylen. *Soviet–American Trade.* New York: Praeger, 1979.

Evanson, Robert K. and Lutz, James M. "Soviet Economic Responses to Crises in Eastern Europe." *Orbis,* vol. 27, no. 1 (Spring 1983): 59–82.

Fewtrell, David. *The Soviet Economic Crisis: Proposals for the Military and the Consumer.* Adelphi Paper no. 186. London: International Institute for Strategic Studies, 1983.

Finley, David D. "Detente and Soviet–American Trade." *Studies in Comparative Communism,* vol. 8 (Spring–Summer 1975): 66–97.

Friesen, Connie M. *The Political Economy of East–West Trade.* New York: Praeger, 1976.

Gardner, H. Stephen. *Soviet International Economic Relations: Recent Trends in Policy and Performance.* Discussion Paper no. 90. Santa Monica: The California Seminar on International Security and Foreign Policy, February 1981.

Goldman, Marshall I. *Soviet Foreign Aid.* New York: Praeger, 1967.

———. *Detente and Dollars: Doing Business with the Soviets.* New York: Basic Books, 1975.

———. *The Enigma of Soviet Petroleum: Half Empty or Half Full?* Boston: George Allen and Unwin, 1980.

———. *The U.S.S.R. in Crisis: The Failure of an Economic System.* New York: Norton, 1983.

Grossman, Gregory. "An Economy at Middle Age." *Problems of Communism,* vol. 25, no. 2 (March–April, 1976).

Grossman, Gregory and Solberg, Ronald L. *The Soviet Union's Hard Currency Balance of Payments and Creditworthiness in 1985.* Santa Monica: The Rand Corporation, April 1983.

Hanson, Philip. "Soviet Imports of Western Technology." *Problems of Communism*, vol. 27, no. 6 (November–December 1978): 20–30.

———. "Economic Constraints on Soviet Policies in the 1980s." *International Affairs* (London), vol. 57, no. 1 (Winter 1980–1981).

———. *Trade and Technology in Soviet–Western Relations.* New York: Columbia University Press, 1981.

Hardt, John P. and Gold, Donna L. "Andropov's Economic Future." *Orbis*, vol. 27, no. 1 (Spring 1983): 11–19.

Holzman, Franklyn D. *International Trade Under Communism: Politics and Economics.* New York: Basic Books, 1976.

———. *The Soviet Economy: Past, Present and Future.* New York: Foreign Policy Association, 1982.

——— and Legvold, Robert. "The Economics and Politics of East–West Relations." *International Organization*, vol. 29 (Winter 1975): 275–320.

Hoffmann, Erik P. and Laird, Robin F. *The Politics of Economic Modernization in the Soviet Union.* Ithaca: Cornell University Press, 1982.

Jensen, Robert G., Shabad, Theodore, and Wright, Arthur W. *Soviet National Resources in the World Economy.* Chicago: University of Chicago Press, 1983.

Lambeth, Benjamin and Lewis, Kevin N., "Economic Targeting in Nuclear War: U.S. and Soviet Approaches." *Orbis*, vol. 27, no. 1 (Spring 1983).

Marrese, Michael and Vanous, Jan. *Implicit Subsidies and Non-Market Benefits in Soviet Trade with Eastern Europe.* Berkeley: Institute of International Studies, University of California, 1983.

Miller, James R. "The Prospects for Soviet Agriculture." *Problems of Communism*, vol. 26, no. 3 (May–June 1977).

Nagorski, Zygmunt, Jr. *The Psychology of East–West Trade: Illusions and Opportunities.* New York: Mason and Lipscomb, 1974.

Nove, Alec. *The Soviet Economic System.* London: George Allen and Unwin, 1980.

Pisar, Samuel. *Coexistence and Commerce.* New York: McGraw–Hill, 1970.

Roosa, Robert V. et al. *East–West Trade at a Crossroads: Economic Relations with the Soviet Union and Eastern Europe.* New York: New York University Press, 1982.

Sutton, Anthony. *Western Technology and Soviet Economic Developments.* Vols. 1–3. Stanford: Stanford University Press, 1968–1973.

U.S. Congress. House of Representatives. Committee on Foreign Affairs, Subcommittee on Natural Security Policy and Scientific Developments. *Soviet Commercial Relations: The Interplay of Economics, Technology Transfer, and Diplomacy.* Washington: U.S. Government Printing Office.

U.S. Congress. Joint Economic Committee. *Soviet Economy in a New Perspective.* Washington: U.S. Government Printing Office, 1976.

———. *Soviet Economy in a Time of Change.* Washington: U.S. Government Printing Office, 1979.

———. *East–West Commercial Policy: A Congressional Dialogue with the*

Reagan Administration. Washington: U.S. Government Printing Office, 16 February 1982.

———. *East–West Trade: Prospects to 1985.* Washington: U.S. Government Printing Office, 18 August 1982.

———. *Soviet Economy in the 1980s: Problems and Prospects.* Vols. 1 and 2. Washington: U.S. Government Printing Office, 31 December 1982.

———. *The Political Economy of the Soviet Union.* Hearings. 98th Congress, 1st Session, 1983.

U.S. Congress. Senate. Committee on Foreign Relations. *Western Investment in Communist Economies: A Selected Survey on Economic Interdependence.* Washington: U.S. Government Printing Office, August 1974.

———. *The Premises of East–West Commercial Relations.* Washington: U.S. Government Printing Office, December 1982.

Valkenier, Elizabeth Kridl. "The USSR, the Third World and the Global Economy." *Problems of Communism* (July–August 1979).

———. *The Soviet Union and the Third World: An Economic Bind.* New York: Praeger, 1983.

Wädekin, Karl–Eugen. "Soviet Agriculture's Dependence on the West." *Foreign Affairs,* vol. 60, no. 4 (Spring 1982): 882–903.

Wilczynski, Josef. *The Economics and Politics of East–West Trade.* New York: Praeger, 1969.

Zaleski, Eugene and Weinert, Helgard. *Technology Transfer Between East and West.* Paris: Organization for Economic Cooperation and Development, 1980.

Soviet Military and Arms Control Policy

Alexander, Arthur Y. *Decision-Making in Soviet Weapons Procurement.* Adelphi Papers, nos. 147–148. London: International Institute for Strategic Studies (Winter 1978–1979).

Arbatov, A. " The Strategy of Nuclear Madness." *Kommunist* 6 (1981).

Arnett, Robert L. "Soviet Attitudes toward Nuclear War: Do They Really Think They Can Win?" *The Journal of Strategic Studies* (September 1979): 172–191.

Berman, Robert and Baker, John C. *Soviet Strategic Forces: Requirements and Responses.* Washington: The Brookings Institution, 1982.

Bloomfield, Lincoln P., Clemens Jr., Walter C., and Griffiths, Franklyn. *Khrushchev and the Arms Race: Soviet Interest in Arms Control and Disarmament, 1954–1964.* Cambridge: MIT Press, 1966.

Bogdanov, Radomir and Semeiki, Lev. "Soviet Military Might: A Soviet View." *Fortune* (26 February 1979), 46–52.

Caldwell, Lawrence T. *Soviet Attitudes toward SALT.* Adelphi Paper, no. 75. London: International Institute for Strategic Studies, February 1971.

———. *Soviet Security Interests in Europe and MFR.* Discussion Paper no.

72. Santa Monica: The California Seminar on International Security and Foreign Policy, April 1976.
Cohen, Stuart A. "SALT Verification: The Evolution of Soviet Views and Their Meaning for the Future." *Orbis*, vol. 24 (Fall 1980): 657–684.
Dallin, Alexander. *The Soviet Union, Arms Control and Disarmament.* New York: School of International Affairs, Columbia University, 1969.
Douglass, Joseph D. and Hoeber, Amoretta M. *Soviet Strategy for Nuclear War.* Stanford: Hoover Institution Press, 1979.
Erickson, John. *Soviet Military Power.* London: Royal Institute, 1971.
———. "The Soviet View of Deterrence: A General Survey." *Survival*, vol. 24, no. 6 (November–December 1982): 242–251.
Ermath, Fritz. "Contrasts in American and Soviet Strategic Thought." *International Security*, vol. 3, no. 2 (Fall 1978): 138–155.
Gallagher, Matthew and Spielmann, Karl. *Soviet Decision-Making for Defense: A Critique of U.S. Perspectives on the Arms Race.* New York: Praeger, 1975.
Garthoff, Raymond. *Soviet Strategy in the Nuclear Age.* New York: Praeger, 1958.
———. *Soviet Military Policy.* New York: Praeger, 1966.
———. "SALT and the Soviet Military." *Problems of Communism* (January–February 1974).
———. "Negotiating with the Russians: Some Lessons from SALT." *International Security*, vol. 1, no. 4 (Spring 1977): 3–24.
———. "Mutual Deterrence and Strategic Arms Limitation in Soviet Policy." *International Security*, vol. 3, no. 1 (Summer 1978): 112–147.
———. "SALT I: An Evaluation." *World Politics*, vol. 31, no. 1 (October 1978): 1–25.
German, Robert K. "Nuclear-Free Zones: Norwegian Interest, Soviet Encouragement." *Orbis*, vol. 26, no. 2 (Summer 1982): 451–476.
Gorshkov, Admiral Sergei. *The Sea Power of the State.* Elmsford: Pergamon, 1979.
Gray, Colin. *The Soviet–American Arms Race.* Lexington: Lexington Books, 1976.
Hedlin, Myron. "Moscow's Line on Arms Control." *Problems of Communism*, vol. 33, no. 3 (May–June 1984): 19–36.
Holloway, David. *The Soviet Union and the Arms Race.* New Haven: Yale University Press, 1983.
Hyland, William G. "Soviet Theater Forces and Arms Control Policy." *Survival*, vol. 23, no. 5 (September–October 1981), 194–199.
Jackson, William D. "The Soviets and Strategic Arms: Toward an Evaluation of the Record." *Political Science Quarterly*, vol. 94, no. 2 (Summer 1979): 243–262.
———. "Soviet Images of the U.S. as Nuclear Adversary, 1969–1979." *World Politics*, vol. 33, no. 4 (July 1981): 614–638.
Kolkowicz, Roman, Gallagher, Matthew P., and Lambeth, Benjamin S. *The Soviet Union and Arms Control: A Superpower Dilemma.* Baltimore: Johns Hopkins University Press, 1970.
Leebaert, Derek. *Soviet Military Thinking.* London: George Allen and Unwin, 1980.

Legvold, Robert. "Strategic 'Doctrine' and SALT: Soviet and American Views." *Survival,* vol. 21 (January–February 1979): 8–13.

Lockwood, Jonathan Samuel. *The Soviet View of U.S. Strategic Doctrine.* New Brunswick: Transaction Books, 1983.

McCGwire, Michael, ed. *Soviet Naval Developments: Capability and Context.* New York: Praeger, 1973.

McConnell, James M., and Dismukes, Bradford. "Soviet Diplomacy of Force in the Third World." *Problems of Communism* (January–February 1979).

Meyer, Stephen M. "Soviet Military Programmes and the 'New High Ground.' " *Survival,* vol. 25, no. 5 (September–October 1983): 204–215.

———. *Soviet Theatre Nuclear Forces: Part I: Development of Doctrine and Objectives; Part II: Capabilities and Implications.* Adelphi Papers nos. 187 and 188. London: International Institute for Strategic Studies, 1983–1984.

Mil'stein, M.A. and Semejko, L.S. "Problems of the Inadmissability of Nuclear Conflict." *International Studies Quarterly,* vol. 20, no. 1 (March 1976).

———. " 'R&D' through Soviet Eyes." *Bulletin of the Atomic Scientists.* (February 1977): 33–38.

Newhouse, John. *Cold Dawn: The Story of SALT.* New York: Holt, Rinehart and Winston, 1973.

Nogee, Joseph. "Soviet Nuclear Proliferation Policy." *Orbis,* vol. 34 (Winter 1981): 751–769.

Ogarkov, N. "Military Science and the Defense of the Socialist Fatherland." *Kommunist* 7 (May 1975). Reprinted in U.S. Joint Publications Research Document 71451.

Ra'anan, Uri. *The USSR Arms the Third World.* Cambridge: MIT Press, 1969.

Ross, Dennis, "Rethinking Soviet Strategic Policy: Inputs and Implications." *The Journal of Strategic Studies,* vol. 1, no. 1 (May 1978): 3–30.

Smith, Gerald. *Doubletalk: The Story of the First Strategic Arms Limitation Talks.* Garden City: Doubleday, 1980.

Snyder, Jack L. *The Soviet Strategic Culture: Implications for Limited Nuclear Options.* R-2154-AF. Santa Monica: The Rand Corporation, September 1977.

Snyder, Jed C. "European Security, East–West Policy, and the INF Debate." *Orbis,* vol. 27, no. 4 (Winter 1984): 913–970.

Sokolovskiy, Marshal V.D., ed. *Soviet Military Strategy,* 3rd edition. Translated, annotated and edited by Scott, Harriet F. New York: Crane, Russak, 1975.

Sonnenfeldt, Helmut and Hyland, William G. *Soviet Perspectives on Security.* Adelphi Paper no. 150. London: International Institute for Strategic Studies, 1979.

Spielman, Karl F. *Analyzing Soviet Strategic Arms Decisions.* Boulder: Westview Press, 1978.

Talbott, Strobe. *Endgame: The Inside Story of Salt II.* New York: Harper and Row, 1979.

Trofimenko, Henry. "The 'Theology' of Strategy." *Orbis.* (Fall 1977).

———. "Political Realism and the Realistic Deterrence Strategy." In *Nu-*

clear Strategy and National Security Points of View. Robert J. Pranger and Roger L. Labrie, eds. Washington: American Enterprise Institute, 1977, 38–53.
———. "Changing Attitudes toward Deterrence." ACIS Working Paper 25. Los Angeles: Center for International and Strategic Affairs, UCLA, July 1980.
———. "Counterforce: Illusion of a Panacea." *International Security,* vol. 5, no. 4 (Spring 1981): 28–48.
Wessell, Nils H. "Arms Control and 'Active Measures'." *Orbis,* vol. 27, no. 1 (Spring 1983): 5–10.
Wit, Joel. "Soviet Cruise Missiles." *Survival,* vol. 25, no. 6 (November–December 1983): 249–260.
Wolfe, Thomas W. "Military Power and Soviet Policy." In Griffith, William E., ed. *The Soviet Empire: Expansion and Detente.* Lexington: Lexington Books, 1976.
———. *The SALT Experience.* Cambridge, Mass.: Ballinger, 1979.
Zheleznov, R. "Monitoring Arms Limitation Measures." *International Affairs,* vol. 7, Moscow, (1982): 75–84.

Soviet Policy toward South Asia

Bradsher, Henry S. *Afghanistan and the Soviet Union.* Durham: Duke University Press, 1983.
Budhraj, Vijay. "Major Dimensions of Indo–Soviet Relations." *India Quarterly* (January–March 1975).
Collins, Joseph J. "Afghanistan: The Empire Strikes Out." *Parameters,* vol. 12 (Spring 1982): 32–41.
———. "The Soviet–Afghan War: The First Four Years." *Parameters,* vol. 14, no. 2 (Summer 1984): 49–62.
de Riencourt, Amaury. "India and Pakistan in the Shadow of Afghanistan." *Foreign Affairs,* vol. 61, no. 2 (Winter 1982–1983): 416–437.
Donaldson, Robert H. *Soviet Policy toward India: Ideology and Strategy.* Cambridge: Harvard University Press, 1974.
———. *The Soviet–Indian Agreement: Quest for Influence.* Denver: Graduate School of International Studies, University of Denver, 1979.
Fukuyama, Francis. *The Future of the Soviet Role in Afghanistan: A Trip Report.* N-1579-RC. Santa Monica: The Rand Corporation, September 1980.
———. *The Security of Pakistan: A Trip Report.* N-1584-RC. Santa Monica: The Rand Corporation, September 1980.
Hammond, Thomas T. *Red Flag over Afghanistan: The Communist Coup, the Soviet Invasion, and the Consequences.* Boulder: Westview Press, 1984.
Harrison, Selig S. "Dateline Afghanistan: Exit through Finland?" *Foreign Policy,* no. 41 (Winter 1980–1981): 163–187.

———. *In Afghanistan's Shadow: Baluch Nationalism and Soviet Temptations.* Washington: Carnegie Endowment for International Peace, 1981.

———. "A Breakthrough in Afghanistan?" *Foreign Policy,* no. 51 (Summer 1983): 3–26.

Hart, Douglas M. "Low Intensity Conflict in Afghanistan: the Soviet View." *Survival,* vol. 24, no. 2 (March–April 1982): 61–68.

Horn, Robert C. *Soviet–Indian Relations.* New York: Praeger, 1983.

———. "The Soviet Union and Sino–Indian Relations." *Orbis,* vol. 26, no. 4 (Winter 1983): 889–906.

Litwak, Robert, Chubin, Shahram, and George, Timothy, eds. *India and the Great Powers.* London: Gower, 1984.

Malhuret, Claude. "Report from Afghanistan." *Foreign Affairs,* vol. 62, no. 2 (Winter 1983–1984): 426–435.

Monks, Alfred L. *The Soviet Intervention in Afghanistan, 1979–1980.* Washington: American Enterprise Institute, 1981.

Newell, Nancy Peabody and Newell, Richard S. *The Struggle for Afghanistan.* Ithaca: Cornell University Press, 1981.

Rose, Leo E. "The Superpowers in South Asia: A Geostrategic Analysis." *Orbis,* vol. 22 (Summer 1978).

Rubinstein, Alvin Z. "Afghanistan: Embraced by the Bear." *Orbis,* vol. 26, no. 1 (Spring 1982): 135–154.

Thomas, Raju C.C. "Prospects for Indo–U.S. Security Ties." *Orbis,* vol. 27, no. 2 (Summer 1983): 371–392.

U.S. Congress. House. Committee on Foreign Affairs. *An Assessment of the Afghanistan Sanctions for Trade and Diplomacy in the 1980s.* Washington: U.S. Government Printing Office, 1981.

U.S. Department of State. "Soviet Dilemmas in Afghanistan." Special Report no. 72. Washington: U.S. Government Printing Office, June 1980.

———. "Afghanistan: Three Years of Occupation." Special Report no. 106. Washington: U.S. Government Printing Office, December 1982.

———. "Afghanistan: Four Years of Occupation." Special Report no. 112. Washington: U.S. Government Printing Office, December 1983.

Valenta, Jiri. "The Soviet Invasion of Afghanistan: The Difficulty of Knowing Where to Stop." *Orbis* (Summer 1980).

———. "From Prague to Kabul." *International Security,* vol. 5, no. 2 (Fall 1980): 114–141.

Wimbush, S. Enders, and Alexiev, Alex. *Soviet Central Asian Soldiers in Afghanistan.* N-1634-NA. Santa Monica: The Rand Corporation, January 1981.

Wolpert, Stanley. *Roots of Confrontation in South Asia: Afghanistan, Pakistan, India, and the Superpowers.* New York: Oxford University Press, 1982.

Soviet Policy toward Africa

Albright, David E. "The USSR and Africa: Soviet Policy." *Problems of Communism.* (January–February 1978).

———, ed. *Communism in Africa.* Bloomington: Indiana University Press, 1980.

———. *The USSR and Sub-Saharan Africa in the 1980s.* The Washington Papers 101. New York: Praeger, 1983.

Bienen, Henry. "Soviet Political Relations with Africa." *International Security,* vol. 6, no. 4 (Spring 1982): 153–173.

Cohn, Helen Destosses. *Soviet Policy Toward Black Africa: The Focus on National Integration.* New York: Praeger, 1972.

Croan, Melvin. "A New Afrika Korps?" *Washington Quarterly* (Winter 1980).

David, Steven. "Realignment in the Horn: The Soviet Advantage." *International Security,* vol. 4, no. 2 (Fall 1979): 69–90.

Durch, William I. "The Cuban Military in Africa and the Middle East: From Algeria to Angola." *Studies in Comparative Communism,* vol. 9, nos. 1–2 (Spring–Summer 1978): 34–74.

Gavtilov, N.I. and Starushenko, G.B., eds. *Africa: Problems of Socialist Orientation.* Moscow: Nauka, 1976.

Griffith, William E. *Soviet Power and Policies in the Third World: The Case of Africa.* Adelphi Paper no. 152. London: International Institute for Strategic Studies, 1979.

Gromyko, Anatoly. "The Imperialist Threat to Africa." *International Affairs,* Moscow (July 1981).

———. "Soviet Foreign Policy and Africa." *Asia and Africa Today* (January–February 1982).

Henze, Paul B. "Communism and Ethiopia." *Problems of Communism,* vol. 30, no. 3 (May–June 1981).

Klinghoffer, Arthur J. *The Angolan War: A Study in Soviet Foreign Policy in the Third World.* Boulder: Westview Press, 1980.

Legvold, Robert. *Soviet Policy in West Africa.* Cambridge: Harvard University Press, 1970.

———. "The Soviet Union's Strategic Stake in Africa." In Jennifer Seymour Whitaker, ed. *Africa and the United States: Vital Interests.* New York: New York University Press, 1978.

Lilley, Robert J. "Constraints on Superpower Intervention in Sub-Saharan Africa." *Parameters,* vol. 12, no. 3 (September 1982): 63–75.

Napper, Larry C. "The African Terrain and U.S.–Soviet Conflict in Angola and Rhodesia: Some Implications for Crisis Prevention," and "The Ogaden War: Some Implications." In Alexander L. George, ed. *Managing U.S.–Soviet Rivalry: Problems of Crisis Prevention.* Boulder: Westview Press, 1983, 155–186 and 225–254.

Nielsen, Waldemar A. *The Great Powers and Africa.* New York: Praeger, 1969.

Papp, Daniel S. "The Soviet Union and Cuba in Ethiopia." *Current History* (March 1979).

Ogunbadegjo, Oye. "Soviet Policies in Africa." *African Affairs,* vol. 79, no. 316 (1980).

Ottaway, Marina S. *Soviet and American Influence in the Horn of Africa.* New York: Praeger.

Remmek, Richard B. "Soviet Military Interests in Africa." *Orbis,* vol. 28, no. 1 (Spring 1984): 83–102.

Roschin, G. "Africa Battling for Economic Liberation."*International Affairs.* Moscow (March 1981): 107–117.

Rothenberg, Morris. *The USSR and Africa: New Dimensions of Soviet Global Power.* Coral Gables, Florida: Institute for Advanced International Studies, 1980.

Simes, Dimitri K. "Imperial Globalism in the Making: Soviet Involvement in the Horn of Africa." *Washington Review of Strategic and International Studies.* Special Supplement (May 1978).

Sherman, Richard F. "Marxism on the Horn of Africa." *Problems of Communism* (September–October 1980).

Tarabrin, Y. "Problems of Africa in the 1980s." *International Affairs.* Moscow (June 1981): 47–57.

Valenta, Jiri. "The Soviet–Cuban Intervention in Angola." *Studies in Comparative Communism* (Spring–Summer 1978).

Vanneman, Peter, and James, Martin. "The Soviet Intervention in Angola: Intentions and Implications." *Strategic Review* (Summer 1976).

———. "Soviet Thrust into the Horn of Africa: The Next Targets." *Strategic Review* (Spring 1978).

———. "Shaping Soviet African Policy." *Africa Insight,* vol. 10, no. 1 (1980).

Wilson, Edward T. *Russia and Black Africa Before World War II.* New York: Holmes and Meier, 1974.

Soviet Policy toward Latin America

Blasier, Cole. *The Hovering Giant: U.S. Responses to Revolutionary Change in Latin America.* Pittsburg: University of Pittsburg Press, 1976.

———. *The Giant's Rival: The USSR and Latin America.* Pittsburg: University of Pittsburg Press, 1983.

Burks, David. *Soviet Policy for Castro's Cuba.* Columbus: Ohio State University Press, 1964.

Dinerstein, Herbert S. "Soviet Policy in Latin America." *American Political Science Review* (March 1967).

———. *The Making of a Missile Crisis, October 1962.* Baltimore: Johns Hopkins University Press, 1976.

Duncan, Raymond. "Caribbean Leftism." *Problems of Communism* (May–June 1978).

Erisman, Michael, ed. *The Caribbean Challenge: U.S. Policy in a Volatile Region.* Boulder: Westview Press, 1984.

——— and John D. Martz, eds. *Colossus Challenged: The Struggle for Caribbean Influence.* Boulder, Westview Press, 1982.

Goldhamer, Herbert. *The Foreign Powers in Latin America.* Princeton: Princeton University Press, 1972.

Gonzalez, Edward. "Castro's Revolution: Cuban Communist Appeals and the Soviet Response." *World Politics,* vol. 21, no. 1 (October 1968): 39–68.

Gottemoeller, Rose E. *The Potential for Conflict between Soviet and Cuban*

Policies in the Third World. P-6668. Santa Monica: The Rand Corporation, August 1981.

Gouré, Leon and Rothenberg, Morris. *Soviet Penetration of Latin America.* Coral Gables, Florida: Institute for Advanced International Studies, University of Miami, 1975.

Jackson, D. Bruce. *Castro, the Kremlin, and Communism in Latin America.* Baltimore: Johns Hopkins University Press, 1969.

Katz, Mark N. "The Soviet–Cuban Connection." *International Security,* vol. 8, no. 1 (Summer 1983): 88–112.

Kirkpatrick, Jeane. "United States Security and Latin America." *Commentary,* vol. 71, no. 1 (January 1981).

Leiken, Robert S. "Eastern Winds in Latin America." *Foreign Policy,* no. 42 (Spring 1981): 94–113.

———. *Soviet Strategy in Latin America.* The Washington Papers, vol. 10, no. 93. New York: Praeger, 1982.

LeoGrande, William M. "The Revolution in Nicaragua: Another Cuba?" *Foreign Affairs,* vol. 58, no. 1 (Fall 1979): 28–50.

———. "Cuban–Soviet Relations and Cuban Policy in Africa." *Cuban Studies,* vol. 10, no. 1 (January 1980).

———. "Cuba Policy Recycled." *Foreign Policy,* no. 46 (Spring 1982): 105–119.

———. "A Splendid Little War: Drawing the Line in El Salvador." *International Security,* vol. 6, no. 1 (Summer 1981): 27–52.

Lévesque, Jacques: *The USSR and the Cuban Revolution.* New York: Praeger, 1978.

Levine, Barry B., ed. *The New Cuban Presence in the Caribbean.* Boulder: Westview Press, 1983.

Lowenthal, Abraham F. "Change the Agenda." *Foreign Policy,* no. 52 (Fall 1982): 64–77.

Luers, William H. "The Soviets and Latin America: A Three Decade U.S. Policy Tangle." *The Washington Quarterly,* vol. 7, no. 1 (Winter 1984): 3–32.

Mastny, Vojtech. "The Soviet Union and the Falklands War." *Naval War College Review,* vol. 36, no. 3 (May–June 1983): 46–55.

Mishin, S. "Latin America: Two Trends of Development." *International Affairs,* Moscow (June 1976): 54–61.

Oswald, Gregory J. and Strover, Anthony S., eds. *The Soviet Union and Latin America.* New York: Praeger, 1970.

Pastor, Robert. "Cuba and the Soviet Union: Does Cuba Act Alone?" In Levine, Barry B., ed. *The New Cuban Presence in the Caribbean.* Boulder: Westview Press, 1982.

Ransom, Harry H. *The Communist Tide in Latin America.* Austin: University of Texas Press, 1972.

Ratliff, William E. *Castroism and Communism in Latin America, 1959–1976: The Varieties of Marxist–Leninist Experience.* Washington: American Enterprise Institute, 1976.

Rothenberg, Morris. *Current Cuban–Soviet Relationships: The Challenge to U.S. Policy.* Coral Cables: Center for Advanced International Studies, University of Miami, 1974.

———. "Latin America in Soviet Eyes." *Problems of Communism,* vol. 32, no. 5 (September–October 1982): 1–18.

Sanchez, Nestor D. "The Communist Threat." *Foreign Policy,* no. 52 (Fall 1983): 43–50.

Sizonenko, Alexander. "USSR–Latin American Countries: Results and Perspectives on Inter-State Relations." *America Latina,* Moscow, nos. 1–2 (1981).

Smith, Wayne S. "Soviet Policy and Ideological Formulations for Latin America." *Orbis* (Winter 1972).

———. "Dateline Havana: Myopic Diplomacy." *Foreign Policy* no. 48 (Fall 1982): 157–174.

Suárez, Andrés. *Cuba, Castroism and Communism, 1956–1966.* Translated by Carmichael, Joel and Halperin, Ernst. Cambridge: MIT Press, 1967.

Theberge, James D. *The Soviet Presence in Latin America.* New York: Crane, Russak, 1974.

Tsokhas, Kosmas. "The Political Economy of Cuban Dependence on the Soviet Union." *Theory and Society,* vol. 9 (March 1980).

U.S. Department of State. *Communist Interference in El Salvador.* Special Report no. 80. Washington: U.S. Government Printing Office, 23 February 1981.

Valenta, Jiri. "The USSR, Cuba, and the Crisis in Central America." *Orbis,* vol. 25, no. 3 (Fall 1981): 715–746.

———. "Soviet Strategy in the Caribbean Basin." *The Proceedings of the U.S. Naval Institute,* May 1982.

———. "Soviet Policy and the Crisis in the Caribbean." In Erisman, H. Michael, and Martz, John, eds. *Colossus Challenged: The Caribbean Struggle for Independence.* Boulder: Westview Press, 1982.

Varas, Angusto. "Ideology and Politics in Latin American–USSR Relations." *Survival,* vol. 26, no. 3 (May–June 1984): 114–121.

Vasileyev, V. "The US's 'New Approach' to Latin America." *International Affairs,* Moscow, vol. 6 (June 1971).

Wiarda, Howard J., ed. *Rift and Revolution: The Central American Imbroglio.* Washington: American Enterprise Institute, 1984.

Index

About the Contributors

George W. Breslauer is an associate professor of political science at the University of California, Berkeley, and chair of the Executive Committee of the Berkeley–Stanford Program on Soviet International Behavior. He is the author of *Khrushchev and Brezhnev as Leaders: Building Authority in Soviet Politics* and coauthor of *Political Terror in Communist Systems* and *Soviet Politics and Society.*

Lawrence T. Caldwell is a professor of political science at Occidental College in Los Angeles, California. He has been a research associate at the International Institute for Strategic Studies, a visiting professor at the National War College and at UCLA, and scholar-in-residence at the Central Intelligence Agency. He is the author of *Soviet and American Relations: One Half Decade of Detente* and *Soviet–American Relations in the 1980s.*

Donna L. Gold is a senior research assistant in Soviet economics at the Congressional Research Service. She received her B.A. from Tufts University and M.A. from Harvard University.

John P. Hardt is the associate director for senior specialists and is a senior specialist in Soviet economics at the Congressional Research Service. He is also adjunct professor in economics at both George Washington and Georgetown Universities.

Hiroshi Kimura is a professor of political science at the Slavic Research Center, Hokkaido University, Sapporo, Japan. During the 1982–1983 academic year, he was a visiting fellow at the Center for International Security and Arms Control at Stanford University. He is the author of numerous articles on Japanese–Soviet relations.

Dennis Ross is the executive director of the Berkeley–Stanford Program on Soviet International Behavior. Until recently he was the deputy director of the Office at Net Assessment in the Department of Defense, and prior to that he served on the Policy Planning Staff in the Department of State. He has published articles in many journals including *International Security, Political Science Quarterly,* and *World Politics.*

Sarah Meiklejohn Terry is an associate professor of political science at Tufts University and a fellow of the Russian Research Center at Harvard University. She is the author of *Poland's Place in Europe: General Sikorski and the Origin of the Oder–Neisse Line, 1939–1943,* which was awarded the American Historical Association's George Louis Beer Prize in European international history since 1895, and the editor of *Soviet Policy in Eastern Europe.*

B. Thomas Trout is an associate professor of political science at the University of New Hampshire. He is chairman of the Consortium for International Studies Education and the coeditor of *National Security Affairs: Theoretical Perspectives and Contemporary Issues* and *Understanding Global Issues: A Framework for Analysis.*

About the Editor

Dan Caldwell is an associate professor of political science at Pepperdine University, Malibu, California. At the time he edited this book, he was associate director of the Center for Foreign Policy Development at Brown University. He is the author of *American–Soviet Relations: From 1947 to the Nixon–Kisssinger Grand Design*, and the editor of *Henry Kissinger: His Personality and Policies.*